Christoph Lymbersky

Market Entry Strategies

Text, Cases and Readings in Market Entry Management

1st International Edition

MANAGEMENT
LABORATORY
PRESS

Market Entry Strategies:
Text, Cases and Readings in Market Entry Management
International Edition 2008

Registered with:
Copyclaim: #10000464, #10000465, #10000466, #10000467, #10000468, #10000469, #10000470
U.S. Copyright Clearance Center (CCC)
ISBN-Agentur für die Bundesrepublik Deutschland in der MVB Marketing- und Verlagsservice des Buchhandels GmbH

Bibliografische Information der Deutschen Nationalbibliothek
Die Deutsche Nationalbibliothek verzeichnet diese Publikation in der Deutschen Nationalbibliografie; detaillierte bibliografische Daten sind im Internet über http://dnb.d-nb.de abrufbar.

Interior Design: © Management Laboratory Press

When ordering this title, use ISBN: 978-3-9812162-9-5 (Softcover)
ISBN: 978-3-9812162-0-2 (Hardcover)

Printed in Hamburg, Germany

www.Management-Laboratory.com

To my parents Edeltraud and Peter Lymbersky:

Without you, this book and so much more would have never been possible.

German:

Für meine Eltern Edeltraud und Peter Lymbersky:

Ohne Euch wäre dieses Buch und so vieles mehr nie möglich gewesen.

Market Entry Strategies

About the Author

Christoph Lymbersky has lived, worked and done research in Germany, France, Australia and the United States. He holds a Master of Accounting as well as a MBA from Bond University in Australia and is a member of the Turnaround Management Association, Sydney and the Strategic Management Society, Chicago.

He has worked for international companies such as IBM and Wal-Mart, has founded and co-founded different companies like COMODEX Internet, the IT – Management Group and B2B Network. Working with clients, managers and CEOs from all around the world led him to focus his research on international management and intercultural differences. Christoph Lymbersky is now the head of the Management Laboratory and consultant to different start-up companies.

Market Entry Strategies

Introduction

This book is designed for students studying international business, but also for professionals working in companies facing market entry decisions.

The first chapter will introduce the concept of an international strategy by focusing on global efficiencies, the components of an international strategy and the development of an international strategy. An emphasis is put on market analysis, competitive positioning and common pitfalls of multinational companies.

The second chapter discusses different entry modes and forms of foreign direct investments. Franchising, licensing, joint ventures, the Greenfield strategy as well as mergers & acquisitions are explained in detail with their advantages and disadvantages. The accompanying case studies for each entry method illustrate common problems outlined in the text.

The third Chapter introduces the reader to the influence of culture on international market entries. Geert Hofstede's, Edward T. Hall's as well as Fons Trompenaars's theories about cultural differences get explained with interesting examples. Managers will find important advice in this chapter on what to take care of, how to prepare for and to avoid cultural clashes.

Each market entry strategy has its impacts on the corporate culture of a company, on its people and on the environment. It is this book's aim to prepare its reader for the interesting strategic decisions that a multinational company faces.

Please visit our website for further information, readings, more case studies and advice. The Management Laboratory will gladly help you in your studies or professional decisions. We in turn are very thankful for any feedback about this book. You are very welcome to write us under:

bookreview@management-laboratory.com

http://www.management-laboratory.com

Hamburg, January 2008

Market Entry Strategies

Acknowledgements

Nobody writes and publishes a book completely by himself. I consider myself very lucky that I have received so much ongoing advice, patience and motivation through my friends who have never asked for anything in return and have always lent me a helping hand.

Marion continuously supported me with inspiring ideas, by keeping me healthy, by turning off the light when it was time to and for listening to me in endless conversations.

Gabor consulted me with things that I needed help with and was always there for a good conversation, regardless if early in the morning or late at night. He has always been the most reliable friend of mine.

Viktor helped me even when he did not have the time to, spent sleepless nights advising me on what I needed most and inspired me to go further than intended.

Market Entry Strategies

Contents

Market Entry Strategies

Structure of this Book

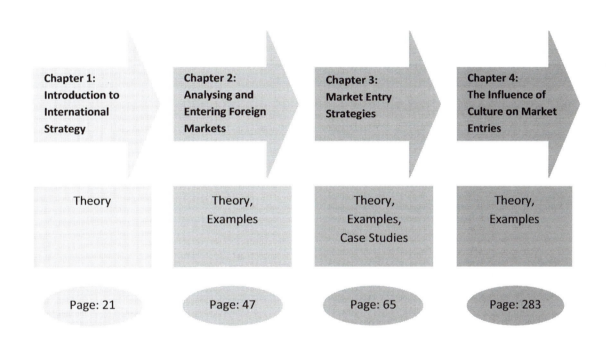

Market Entry Strategies

| Chapter 1: Introduction to International Strategy | Chapter 2: Analysing and Entering Foreign Markets | Chapter 3: Market Entry Strategies | Chapter 4: The Influence of Culture on Market Entries |

| Theory | Theory, Examples | Theory, Examples, Case Studies | Theory, Examples |

| Page: 21 | Page: 47 | Page: 65 | Page: 283 |

Country Profiles Page: 329

Market Entry Strategies

Chapter 1

Introduction to International Strategy

Market Entry Strategies

Chapter 1

Introduction to International Strategy

What is an International Strategy?

Effective international strategic management enables a company to compete successfully in foreign markets and is a comprehensive framework for achieving a firm's fundamental goals [1]. Developing a strategy for a single market is usually an adoption from a strategy developed to compete in multiple countries. Just as strategy, international strategy is an ongoing and comprehensive process that needs to be updated constantly. In a lot of companies as well as in the literature, the development of an international strategy is also called strategic planning. In most businesses strategic planning is the responsibility of the senior managers and upper level executives. Bigger multinational companies sometimes even have special staff departments that assist senior managers with the planning and development process of international strategies. These staff departments are usually involved in a lot of research to aid decision makers in finding the best possible location for a new factory, the right country for a product launch or the right partner for the distribution network.

An international strategy must answer the following six questions:

1. How and where will the company produce the products or services?
2. What products or services does the company want to sell?
3. Where does the company want to sell the products or services?
4. How and where will the company get the necessary resources for the production process?
5. How does the company want to compete with its competitors?
6. What are the key success factors for that company and for that product or service?

Developing a multinational strategy is far more difficult than developing a strategy for only one country because if the entity is only operating in a single country it only needs to deal with one government, one legal system, one currency and with one accounting system. Moreover, it does not have to handle differences in culture or language. Developing a multinational strategy, however, involves dealing with multiple governments, currencies and cultures. The following table exemplifies some of the differences between a company that operates in a single country like Germany and one that operates in multiple countries.

Table 1 Differences Between Single Country Operations and International Operations

Factor	Single Country (Germany)	Multinational Operations
Language	German	Different countries require different languages
Culture	Relatively homogenous	Diverse between and within countries
Labour	Skilled and well trained Labour available	Special training and redesign of production methods might be required
Labour relations	Collective bargaining	Layoff of workers might be easy or, in contrast, impossible; workers might seek change through political process
Economy	Relatively uniform	Wide variation among counties and within countries possible
Politics	Stable and relatively unimportant	Often volatile and of decisive importance
Governmental interference	Minimal and reasonably predictable	Often extensive and subject to rapid change
Financing	Well developed financial markets with different sources available	Capital flows are in some countries subject to government control and are sometimes poorly developed

Factor	Single Country (Germany)	Multinational Operations
Market Research	Data are easy to collect	Data are sometimes difficult and expensive to collect
Money	Euro used throughout Europe	Changes of currency possible, problems can arise because of exchange rates and government policies
Advertising	Only few restrictions, many media available	Media might be limited, many restrictions possible, low literacy rates rule out print media in some countries
Transportation	Quick and effective	Often inadequate, can be dangerous or slow in some countries
Contracts	Backed up by legal system, binding once signed	Might be voided and renegotiated if one party becomes dissatisfied
Control	Always a problem, but centralized control will work	A worse problem; must walk a tightrope between over-centralising and losing control through too much de-centralizing

To master these complexities, it is necessary to implement the international strategy among the company's business units around the world. However, the complexities usually get seen as acceptable tradeoffs compared to the opportunities that come with an internationally operating company and networks. An international business can take advantage of the following three different competitive advantages; global efficiencies, international flexibility and worldwide learning. These advantages are not available to firms that operate in only one market.

Global Efficiencies of International Companies

An international operating company can improve its efficiency in many different ways. Three of them are location efficiencies, economies of scale and economies of scope.

Location Efficiencies

Location efficiencies can be achieved by locating the production or the research and development department in countries and areas where labour is cheap or where a very skilled workforce is available. In this way, the firm can produce its products at a lower price or a higher quality, lower its distribution costs and/or improve its customer service. Many companies, like for example Volkswagen, have parts of their cars produced in China to take advantage of its lower labour costs. These costs are a lot lower in Asian countries than in Volkswagen's home market Germany. And India's supply of skilled and hard working programmers is certainly a reason why IBM has a lot of their programming done in that country.

Economies of Scale

Economies of scale can generally be achieved by manufacturing a product with one machine in a higher volume. The part of the fix costs, which is a part of the total costs, gets smaller with every additional unit produced. Theoretically, a company with two plants producing the same parts or products in two different countries has therefore twice the fix costs of a company that produces the same parts or products in one plant. Daimler, for example, produces its M Class SUV in Alabama and then delivers it to the whole world. This is still cheaper for Daimler than building factories in every major market to serve the local customers.

Economies of Scope

Economies of Scope can be achieved by boarding a company's product lines in each of the countries it enters to lower their production costs and to enhance their bottom lines. For example, if a company enters a new market with only one product, the distribution and marketing costs for this one product might be comparably high. The costs per unit might be lower when the company starts pushing more products into the market, since the distribution channels and marketing efforts can be shared.

International Flexibility

Multinational businesses are faced with changes in demand, economies, political systems, but also with changing laws and many more factors that affect the operation of international companies. Domestic companies only need to focus on one market but do not have the advantage of being able to respond to changes in one country by changing production or processes in another. International firms can exploit this advantage. For example, the chicken processor Tyson Foods has benefited from the increased demand by health-conscious U.S. customers for chicken breasts. In producing more chicken breasts, Tyson also produced more chicken legs and thighs, which are considered less desirable by U.S. consumers. Tyson capitalized on this surplus by targeting the Russian market, where dark meat is preferred over light, and the Chinese market, where chicken feet are considered a tasty delicacy. [1]

Worldwide Learning

By operating in different markets, adjusting business processes and marketing products to different customers a company can also learn a great deal. What a company learns in one country can be used to improve processes in another. For example, if a company faces striking in one country, it has the opportunity to learn about how to deal with a strike. This knowledge can be used to deal with a strike in another country and to end it quicker and more efficiently. Another example of worldwide learning are "emerging opportunities".

General Electric has introduced a system of 12 management councils. The members of these councils are senior executives from different units that meet on a regular basis. Each member of this council needs to present an idea to the council that the other members can use in their own units as well. In this way improvements and ideas get spread quickly within the whole company.

Information Technology & Global Strategies

In this part, we only want to briefly introduce some important improvements that can be achieved with the right IT structure and software.

Information technology has become a crucial part in the development and execution of an internationally operating company. Worldwide connected IT Systems

27

and sophisticated software makes it possible to track single product parts around the world. This is especially useful to avoid shortages of a product or part in one location by ordering parts from another location where there are still enough parts on hand. It also makes it easier to spot trends and to plan ahead to meet them. But IT is also useful in the administration of global human resources, communication and marketing.

Possible Problems in Multinational Companies

However, it is difficult to make use of all three factors mentioned above at the same time. Global efficiencies can be easily achieved by centralising control and responsibility in one location, but it might then be difficult to adjust to local needs and demands.

For example BMW's production and R&D units are located in Germany. In Germany, cup holders are not very important since drivers are not supposed to drink while driving. In fact, on a German autobahn without speed limit, this can be a dangerous thing to do. The research and development department thus only includes one or two cup holders in their car design (if any at all). In the USA, however, cup holders are certainly a criterion for families that want to buy a new car. You can imagine that there are a lot of conflicts between the American sales and marketing units and the German R&D department that from this issue. To overcome the problem, international firms can give more power to local managers and departments to adjust parts of the production, marketing or policies to the needs and wants of customers in each market.

Another problem that can arise if too much power gets centralized in one unit and one area is that global learning might be minimal. If the lessons that can be drawn out of differences in different environments and cultures are constantly ignored, managers might get frustrated. By decentralizing too much power and giving local units more responsibility, problems might come up more than once. This could lead to redundancy. Therefore, a company that wants to support global learning needs to have the right communication channels in place and needs to have an organizational structure that encourages knowledge transfer between its local units and the headquarter. Furthermore, managers need to be encouraged to take advantage of opportunities for global learning. A lot of companies nowadays offer trainee programs to graduates and managers that lead them around the world. The Bayer AG in Germany for example offers highly skilled young managers an International Management Trainee Program where the trainee goes through different job positions in sales, marketing and controlling over the duration of three years in a foreign country. [2]

Strategic Exploration

To find the right balance between global efficiencies, worldwide learning and multinational flexibility companies typically adopt one of the following four strategies.

Figure 1 Trade-off between Global Efficiency and Flexibility

Home Replication Strategy

Some companies directly transfer their main competitive advantages from their home market to a foreign market. This strategy is called home replication strategy. In short, the strategy aims to replicate the home market advantages that a company has in the foreign market that it wants to enter. German car makers for example use the home replication strategy when they try to sell their cars in other countries. German cars are built for safety at high speeds on the German autobahns, since parts of them do not have a speed limit.

However, most other countries do have a speed limit. But BMW, Mercedes Benz and Audi sell their cars all over the world with the image that it is possible to travel very fast and safe with them. Consumers all over the world buy these cars knowing that they could drive 240km/h if it were allowed.

Another example is Toy's R Us, which developed its marketing, distribution and procurement for the U.S. market and believes that this strategy works in all counties where it operates in.

The home replication strategy is often adopted when the need for flexibility and the need for global integration is very low.

Multidomestic Strategy

A company that operates with relatively free subsidiaries in each country is utilising the multidomestic strategy. The multidomestic strategy gives the subsidiaries the freedom to focus on the wants and needs of the customers of the market they operate in. The parent entity gives a lot of power and authority to the top level management within the countries. This means that the subsidiaries can customise their marketing campaigns, products and other operational techniques. This approach is very effective when cultural differences are big. The downside is that economies of scale are very low due to the customisation of distribution, production and marketing. It is also more expensive to coordinate the different subsidiaries than when using a home replication strategy or a global strategy (see below).

The multidomestic strategy is often used when the company needs to adapt to a lot of conditions in each country and when the pressure for global efficiencies is not very high. Examples are companies that are marketing driven like Unilever and Kraft. Their customers need to be targeted with special campaigns in each market and also want fresh food that did not get shipped around the world for weeks.

Global Strategy

The global strategy is almost the opposite of the multidomestic strategy. The global strategy sees the world as one market with a fundamentally homogenous customer worldwide. Its goal is the production of standardised products and services to achieve a very high level of economies of scale. One headquarter usually directs the marketing and production for the world market. The company's power and decision making is thus centralised. It focuses on standardised marketing campaigns and goods as well as on a standardised distribution system. Sony for example designs their products like TV sets, stereos and gaming consoles for the global market. They only need to adapt cheap parts like power supplies and fuses to local markets. For companies that follow a global strategy it is often easy to have their products produced in countries where the production costs are very low.

In this way the global strategy is very similar to the home replication strategy since it operates similarly in every country it enters. The difference is that a firm using the home replication strategy believes that its way of doing business in the home market works all over the world. A company that uses the global strategy, however, develops one strategy for the whole world.

Transnational Strategy

The fourth approach is the transnational strategy. This strategy tries to combine the advantages of the global strategy with the advantages of the multidomestic strategy. A company that uses the transnational strategy tries to achieve the benefit of economies of scale but does not centralise all its decision making and power in one headquarter. It has special units in order to balance between the two goals of flexibility and efficiency. This means that some functions like research and development and parts of the production process can be centralised in certain parts of the world. Other units like the marketing and human resources department might be decentralised to be able to adapt to the local environment and culture. However, it is often expensive to coordinate between the different subsidiaries.

IKEA for example relies on standardisation in order to offer their products at very competitive prices. Customers all over the world buy the same sofas, beds and cupboards. However the marketing needs to be adapted to the local culture. In Sweden, Ikea's home country, it is normal to change furniture a couple of times during the lifetime. In America, however, people change their dining room table only 1.5 times in their life. [3] Thus, IKEA needed a marketing campaign that was tailored to the U.S. Customer and that made customers change their habits. If IKEA had followed the multidomestic strategy, they would have probably changed the dining room tables to high quality products that last for centuries.

Components of an International Strategy

An international strategy has four basic components:

Figure 2 International Strategy Components

Distinctive Competence[1]

A distinctive competence could be anything that a company is doing exceptionally well or better than its competitors. This could be a very well organised distribution network, extremely low production prices, very high quality or a well known and respected brand name. A distinctive competence is seen as necessary to compete outside the home market because a company will face difficulties in competing with local companies that often know the market very well and already have established distribution, production and marketing channels. BMW's brand image of manufacturing high quality luxury cars helps the company to compete with local firms when they enter foreign markets. A company's international strategy usually tries to take advantage of this distinctive competence. The Bosch GmbH in Germany for example was the first company that developed Anti Lock Brakes (ABS) for cars. Since they were the first and have a lot of patents on different systems that are necessary to produce the ABS System they have a competitive competence that makes it hard for other firms to match Bosch. Even today, Bosch has over 50% market share [4] in the ABS market.

---

[1] Dunning calls distinctive competence ownership advantage.

Resource Deployment

Resource deployment answers the question of how resources will be deployed once the market is chosen. A company that wants to open up a subsidiary in another country might choose to only invest a certain percentage in it and get investors to pay for the rest. This is for example the case with Disneyland Paris. A couple of years after its opening, Disneyland Paris came into financial difficulties. Disney, the parent entity, could have solved their financial difficulties without any problems but then might not have had enough money for other ventures or acquisitions.

Scope of Operations

The scope of operations defines where the company wants to go. This can be a geographical region or a certain market like the high quality market or the low cost market. But the scope is tied to the distinctive competence, since resources might not be available in all countries. In other cases the distribution costs are too high to still exploit the advantages of a certain distinctive competence. Therefore, the scope of operations will be focused on where the company is able to exploit its competitive advantages. Texas Instruments for example focuses on digital signal processors that can convert analog signals into digital signals. These chips can be found in mobile phones, stereo systems or modems of all kind. [5] Intel focuses on microprocessors that power most personal computers today. [6]

Synergy

The goal of synergy is to get to the state where the sum of a company's parts is bigger than the parts by itself. British Airways for example sells and gives away merchandising product on their flights. These merchandising products are designed to get people to their internet site to check out new foreign countries and products in their online store. These again are supposed to get the customer to book the next flight with British Airways.

Developing an International Strategy

The development of an international strategy generally consists of two parts: strategy formulation and strategy implementation. In strategy formulation, the company will set goals and work out a strategic plan that will lead the company to reach these goals. In the case of a market entry the formulation part consists of a plan that says what countries or markets to enter and how to enter it. This could for example be through subsidiaries or franchises. We will discuss this topic later on.

Strategy implementation is about developing the necessary tactics to achieve the formulated goals. For example, if British Airways decides to fly to Hong Kong, then this can be a decision made during strategy formulation. But with what kind of airplanes to fly there, what price to charge and how many times a week the connection should be offered would be a decision of strategy implementation. Strategic implementation is usually achieved via the organisation's design, the work of its employees, its control systems and processes. While every strategic planning process is in many ways unique, there is nevertheless a set of general steps that managers usually follow as they set about developing their strategies. [1]

Mission Statement

The mission statement of a company has the purpose of clarifying the company's direction, its values and its purpose. It is also a tool to communicate with share- and stakeholders about the strategic direction of the company. Some mission statements also specify the company's philosophy, desired public image, targeted customer and technologies. The intent of the Mission Statement should be the first consideration for any employee who is evaluating a strategic decision. The statement can range from a very simple to a very complex set of ideas. [7] A simple mission statement would for example be Disney's [8]: "To make people happy." or Merck's: "To preserve and improve human life."

These are 'one-liners', but each is supported by a set of values that set the performance standards and direct the implementation of the mission. For example, Merck, a company that produces pharmaceutical products and provides insurance for pharmacy benefits, publicly states the following values: [9]

- Corporate social responsibility
- Unequivocal excellence in all aspects of the company
- Science-based innovation
- Honesty & integrity
- Profit, but profit from work that benefits humanity

Walt Disney, an entertainment business states their values as follows: [8]

- No cynicism
- Nurturing and promulgation of "wholesome American values"
- Creativity, dreams and imagination
- Fanatical attention to consistency and detail
- Preservation and control of the Disney "magic" [7]

However, a company that operates in different markets might have different mission statements as well. But a company with different mission statements must still ensure that they are compatible with each other. Otherwise it would create the image that different subsidiaries are working against each other.

Environmental Scanning and the SWOT Analysis

A SWOT Analysis summarises the key issues from the business environment and the strategic capabilities of an organisation that are most likely to impact on strategy development. SWOT stands for Strengths, Weaknesses, Opportunities and Threats. The aim of a SWAT Analysis is to identify the degree to which the strength and weaknesses are relevant to and capable of dealing with the changes taking place in the business environment.

Strengths

The strength of a company can be its skilled labour, resources or other advantages that it has over its competitors. But it could also be a well-known brand name, a big cash pool or a big market share. Audi's strengths, for example, are a very skilled workforce, its reputation and very good engineers.

Weaknesses

Weaknesses are shortcomings of skills or resources or other factors that are not beneficial to the firm's business. Weaknesses could be a lack of skilled labour, high production costs, a weak distribution channel or inexperienced managers.

Opportunities

An opportunity for a company would be a market that no competitor entered so far, or the possibility to take over another company that expands or complements its production, services or product range.

In 1999 Vodafone took advantage of the opportunity to take over Mannesmann D2 in Germany, a leading German mobile phone service provider that threatened to enter Vodafone's home market England. Vodafone took advantage of their financial strength: They had enough money to make Mannesmann's stockholders exchange their stocks at a premium. We will discuss this case in more detail in the Mergers and Acquisitions Section.

Threats

Threats to a company could be a shrinking market, aggressive competition, or an instable political system. Federal Express for example faces the threat of a growing international competition from DHL and TNT, but it is also faced with the problem that more and more people use the internet to communicate via instant messengers or email.

The SWOT Analysis is a very important tool for managers to develop the right strategy for entering a market or to evaluate their current position. For the sake of an example, the following table shows the strengths, weaknesses, opportunities and threats to Nintendo.

As can be easily seen, Nintendo has an advantageous ratio of strengths to weaknesses. The analysis was done before the launch of the Wii console in 2006. At that time, Nintendo had experienced ten years of declining sales although it had a lot more strengths than weaknesses. By developing a product based on its strengths, Nintendo could regain an edge over Sony and Microsoft.

Strengths (internal):
- Strong and old brand name
- Strong customer community (fans)
- Very popular "classic" games like Super Mario Brothers and the Legend of Zelda
- Experience in the home console and portable console market
- Niche developer
- Reliable and long-lasting contacts to programmers and developers
- Experienced Research and Development team
- Innovative ideas like e.g. the motion detection sensor integrated into the Wii console
- Headquarters in Japan and America to be closer to the customer
- Market leader in the portable consoles market
- Profitable in a low price segment

Weaknesses (internal):
- Not reaching the customers that they want to reach (yet).
- Console design was not adapted to international market
- Smaller marketing and communication budget then Microsoft and Sony
- Smaller research budget than competitors (Microsoft and Sony)
- Decreasing customer base
- No clear positioning
- Not "trendy"
- Old console designs have not been very good

Opportunities (external):
- Growing potentially feminine customer market
- Potential market from ages 25+
- Potential market in ages 13-
- Comparing to the competition focus on interactive gaming experience
- New attraction to classic games that Nintendo has been famous for
- The portable console market is still growing
- Mass market of first time players

Threats (external):
- Microsoft and Sony buying out famous programmers
- Competitors could try to take over Nintendo
- Microsoft following plans to enter the portable console market
- New market entry
- Losing more market share
- Decreasing sales because of better quality PC games
- Decreasing sales because of software piracy

Following the SWOT Analysis we can now develop the TOWS Matrix which builds up on the strategic position that is outlined in the SWOT Analysis.

The TOWS Matrix

Following the SWOT Analysis, we want to outline different possibilities of how to take advantage of the strengths and opportunities to overcome the weaknesses and threats that Nintendo was facing at that time. Each box of the TOWS (Threats, Opportunities, Weaknesses and Strengths) Matrix is used to identify options that address a different combination of internal and external factors. The TOWS Matrix helps to generate strategic options and should also address their suitability. [10 p. 347]

The upper left corner of the TOWS Matrix describes how to generate options that use the strengths of the company to take advantage of possible opportunities. The upper right corner describes how possible opportunities can be used to overcome given weaknesses. The lower left corner describes how to generate options that take advantage of given strengths to avoid threats to the company or the product. The lower right corner describes how to come up with options that minimise the weaknesses of the firm or product to avoid possible threats.

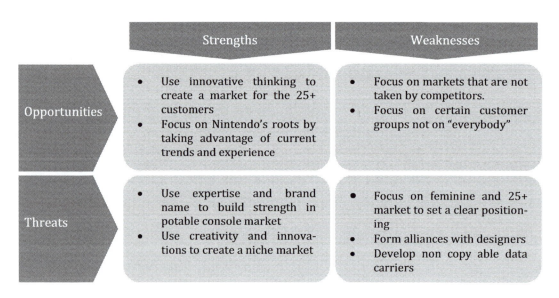

	Strengths	Weaknesses
Opportunities	• Use innovative thinking to create a market for the 25+ customers • Focus on Nintendo's roots by taking advantage of current trends and experience	• Focus on markets that are not taken by competitors. • Focus on certain customer groups not on "everybody"
Threats	• Use expertise and brand name to build strength in potable console market • Use creativity and innovations to create a niche market	• Focus on feminine and 25+ market to set a clear positioning • Form alliances with designers • Develop non copy able data carriers

Figure 3 TOWS Matrix

The TOWS matrix is useful to create strategic options but it also makes it easier to check if these options are suitable.

Strategic Goals

If we look at the SWOT analysis and Mission Statement parts of this book, it becomes clear that planning an international strategy is largely about setting strategic goals. Strategic goals the important objectives that a company wants to achieve. Strategic goals should have the characteristic of being timed, feasible and measurable. The goals should give answers to the questions "when" something is supposed to be accomplished, "how" it is supposed to be accomplished and "how much" of it. Furthermore, the employees that are supposed to reach the goals should be able to reach them. There is no sense in setting goals when the management knows that they cannot be reached. Sure, it can be seen as a motivation to do everything possible to reach them, but impossible goals can also lead to frustration, discouragement and fraud.

An example of a strategic goal could be the number of customers that a theme park wants to attract within a certain time span.

Tactics

After a TOWS Matrix has been created and strategic goals are set the next step is to develop tactics. Tactics usually involve the middle management and focus on the implementation of strategic goals. Before JP Morgan Chase & Co purchased the Bank One Corporation in 2004, both companies had their own tactics. However, when the two companies merged, middle managers in both companies were challenged with the task to integrate Bank One's strategic goals into JP Morgan's tactics. This is particularly important for logistic questions, human resources, information systems and accounting procedures. Both companies' tactics had to be integrated into one way of doing business.

Control Framework

Last but not least, a control framework needs to be developed in order to keep the company in line with the strategic goals set out in the strategy. If a theme park for example wants to have 10 million visitors within a year, but it looks like it is only going to have 8 million visitors, then a control framework would tell them that the original goal will most likely not be reached. The firm could then in turn increase its advertising campaigns to still reach the 10 million visitors within that year. Regular feedback regarding the status to reach the goals is very important to take action when a certain process is not on course.

Levels of International Strategy

There are three different levels of international strategy that Multinational Companies develop within their firm. The three levels are corporate strategy, business strategy and functional strategy.

Corporate Strategy

Each company defines the domain of business that it is operating in for itself. Sony for example competes in the international consumer electronics and entertainment market while Pioneer is only in the audio and video market. These companies are operating in different domains because they have different strengths and weaknesses as well as opportunities and threats. There are three forms of corporate strategy that a firm can operate in: the single business strategy, the related diversification strategy and the unrelated diversification strategy. These are now explained in detail.

The Single Business Strategy

A company that has adopted the single business strategy produces all its revenue with only one product or service. They rely on a single line of business. The advantage of this strategy is that the company has only one line of business they need to focus on. That means that they do not need to share their expertise and resources. They also do not need to monitor more than one market that is relevant to them and have a smaller number of competitors, compared to a company that operates in different markets at once. However, there are a number of disadvantages as well. Since they solely depend on one product or service they are very dependent on changes in the political, social or economic environment. For example, a company that is only producing TV screens might find itself out of business when flat screen displays become more common. The risk therefore is that a company with a single business strategy might not be able to adapt quickly enough to the right trend. However, companies that are successfully operating with this strategy are for example the Airline Emirates and McDonalds.

Related Diversification

A company adopting this strategy finds itself operating in different lines of business with different products or services, which are often related. This is the most common corporate strategy and allows a company to adjust between its lines of business in order to be most competitive in a business that is important at that time. This could for example be a company that offers different products and one or more of them are not generating enough revenue to compete. This company might chose to compensate the losses with gains from other products to stay in that market. This could be beneficial if the firm wants to keep up an image or if it wants to endure in a price war with a competitor. Often the relationship between the different lines of business is defined in the company's mission statement.

A company that is successfully using the related diversification strategy is Accor. The French company operates luxury hotel chains like Novotel and Sofitel, budget hotel chains such as Ibis and is also in the car rental and package tour business. Accor is even operating a theme park close to Paris that is based on the cartoon character Asterix. By operating in all these lines of business, Accor can promote its rental cars in its hotels and get people to sleep in the hotels when they want to visit the theme park.

Related diversification has some significant advantages over the single business strategy. Since it does not only depend on one business, it is less vulnerable to the threat of competition or to changes in the environment. Accor can for example compensate its losses in the theme park business with gains from the hotel chain operations. Also, it is very difficult to compete with Accor since it has a lot channels to promote their products.

An even better example for the related diversification strategy is the Disney Corporation with its theme parks, TV Channels, movie industry and merchandising products. Disney can promote their merchandising products and new movies while people are waiting in line for the rides at the theme parks, or promote the theme parks in its TV Channels.

Another advantage of related diversification for a company can be economies of scale. Since the businesses are related, they will often need the same resources.

Bulk buying makes it possible for these companies to get the resources at very competitive prices and probably cheaper than a competitor who buys a lot less.

It can be easier for a company using the related diversification strategy to enter a new market because it can profit from its experience in its home markets. Pirelli for example, a producer of automobile tires is now also successfully producing rubber fiber optic cables. The experience and expertise gained in the rubber tires market was definitely helpful.

However, there is also a disadvantage. Related diversification can be expensive to coordinate, but it is most likely still cheaper than coordinating an unrelated business. Moreover, since all products or services are related to the same industry, they might still be affected somehow by changes or threats to the whole industry. For Accor for example a downturn development in the tourism industry due to raised oil prices might threaten the whole company at once.

Unrelated Diversification

The third strategy that multinational companies can utilize is the unrelated diversification strategy. Firms that use this strategy are also called conglomerates. In this case a company operates in different industries at the same time. The probably best known example is General Electric (GE). GE operates a television network (NBC), an investment bank, a medical technology company and produces aircraft engines. Another example is Daimler. The German car manufacturer builds cars, trucks, engines, operates a bank and is involved in an information technology company as well as in an aerospace company (EADS). These businesses are totally unrelated and it is therefore hard to find synergies within the different businesses. Companies that are very diverse in their operations are also hard to manage for the holding since they need to have core knowledge of all forms of businesses to make the right decisions for all companies. Apart from that, the competitive advantages gained in one business line can be hard to transfer to other businesses in other industries. This is also the reason why this form of a company is not very common anymore.

On the other hand, conglomerates have some advantages as well. The first one is that it is usually easier for the holding company or the parent entity to raise capital for its subsidiaries. It can then choose how to distribute that money. The second advantage is that the overall riskiness is a lot less for a conglomerate than for a company that operates in only one industry. If one industry is declining or under pressure because of political reasons, for example, then the other subsidiaries in other industries can cover the losses.

Business Strategy

Business strategy deals with the subsidiaries that operate within a company (unlike corporate strategy which focuses on the overall organization). The question that business strategy tries to answer is how the company should compete in the market that it wants to enter. The business strategy helps the subsidiaries or small business units (SBU's) to improve their competitive advantage. Some companies develop a business strategy for each one of their business units while other firms use the same strategy for all their SBU's, but companies usually use the same strategy in all markets that the SBU is present in.

There are three forms of business strategy that we will discuss in this chapter: the diversification strategy, the cost leadership strategy and the focus strategy.

Diversification Strategy

The most common business strategy is the diversification strategy with which the firm tries to differentiate itself from other companies. This is usually done by establishing an image that the small business unit's products are of a very high quality or that they are very special in another way like design or status that is associated with the product. Once an SBU establishes these images, justified or not, they can charge higher prices for their products.

Other companies like Sears in the U.S., Tchibo (the non food business part) or Medion in Germany use the value factor to differentiate themselves from their competitors. In Germany, non coffee products offered at Tchibo are perceived as being of a good quality for a reasonable price. Medion produces electronics with the latest technology, high functionality, modern design, and excellent quality at a low price. [11]

Cost Leadership

As the name suggests, a company using this strategy focuses on very low prices for its products or services. The result is usually that the unit profitability is very low. But it is also part of this strategy to sell big quantities of that product or service. This is why the overall profitability can be quite significant. The company usually tries to compete with its competitors by having the lowest prices in the market. The German grocery stores Aldi and Lidl are very famous for their cost leadership. Their average per unit profit margin on the food articles is as low as 0,5 per cent, but they operate thousands of stores all over the world to be close to their customers and to achieve high volumes in sales. Also the French company BIG Pen Company, which has produced over 100 billion ball pens over the last 60 years, produces these pens as cheap as possible and sells them at very low prices. Other firms that operate using the cost leadership strategy are Hyundai (automobiles industry), Fuji (film) and the LG Group (consumer electronics).

Focus Strategy

A business unit or company that utilises the focus strategy focuses their products or services on the needs and wants of a specific customer group or a specific geographic area. Factors that determine this focus might be the taste in fashion that a group of customers has, its ethnicity, or even the purchasing power associated with the group. Mattel's Barbie dolls for example are targeted at girls between the ages of 4 and 6. Prada targets its fashion at men and women above the age of 45 with a very high income and that want to wear clothes or accessories that are seen rarely on the street. However, this approach is very sensitive to changes and threats in that market. It is important for companies or SBU's operating with a focus strategy to create very high entry barriers to their market.

Functional Strategies

A Functional strategy deals with the question of how functions like finance, human resources, R&D, marketing and operations will be managed. This topic will only be briefly introduced in this book, since there is a lot of literature focusing on each of the topics. The marketing strategy deals with the question how the customer is supposed to be made aware of the product in terms of advertising, pricing, distribution and so on.

International financial strategy sets the guidelines for how the firm's capital structure is supposed to look like, discusses how risks can be reduced, debt policies and foreign exchange holdings. Usually a multinational company has one financial strategy in place that goes for the whole company as well as its subsidiaries.

A Research and Development strategy deals with the direction the company's investments in new products and new technologies are supposed to go in.

HR strategies set guidelines for the company in terms of how people get recruited, trained and how employees will be evaluated.

Finally an operational strategy deals with issues such as the location of plants, technologies available and how the products and services offered will be created.

Market Entry Strategies

Chapter 2

Strategies for Analysing and Entering Foreign Markets

Market Entry Strategies

Chapter 2

Strategies for Analysing and Entering Foreign Markets

Foreign Market Analysis

Firms often try to achieve their goals to increase their revenues, profits and market share by entering into a foreign market or by introducing new products in markets where they are already present. In this book we will focus on necessary steps to expand into a foreign market. To enter a market, a firm must evaluate the market potential, the costs and benefits as well as the associated risks.

Market Potential

The first step should always be to evaluate how big the potential of the market that a firm wants to enter actually is. Publications like "The World Factbook" or the "Commodity Trade Statistics" provide information about a country's public infrastructure, its population, its per capita GDP and its GDP. You can find a list of countries mentioned in this book with this information at the end of the book. These data need to be collected to get a quick overview over a foreign market and to make a decision about a possible market entry. If the company is for example producing high quality products at premium prices, then it probably does not make much sense to enter a market with a very low per capita GDP. Moreover, if for example a company that produces tires is thinking about entering a new market, it needs to collect information about gasoline prices and which percentage of the population owns a car. Are there many company cars like in Germany or are cars often privately leased as in the U.S.? This is important to find out who is actually paying for new tyres. Furthermore, it would be important to find out how long cars are driven, who the manufacturers are to get the cars fitted with their tyres right before the customer buys the car and so on.

The future is also very important to consider in assessing a foreign market's potential. If we take China for example, a country in which only 2 per cent of the population owns a car, it currently might not be that interesting to invest heavily into car factories and distribution networks for an automotive company. However, it is prognosticated that in the year 2020, 20 per cent of the population will be able to own a car. This is an extreme increase within the next couple of years and might justify the decision to make big investments in the near future.

Levels of Competition

Before entering a foreign market, a company needs to know their competitors in that market very well. Questions to answer would be:

- How many competitors are there?
- How big are the competitors (financially, manpower, product range, etc)?
- How are the competitor's market shares?
- What are their pricing and distribution strategies?
- What are their strengths, what are their weaknesses?

These factors then need to be compared to the own competitive position in order to draw conclusions for an own entry strategy. Most big companies are constantly observing different markets in order to react quickly to changes that make it lucrative to expand into that market. Especially markets that are quickly developing and that are undergoing an industrial or regulatory changes are possible targets for many companies. The telecommunication, gas and water industries are good examples of industries that are currently changing. In many countries these industries are or were governmentally owned and operated. Many countries like Germany and France are now more and more liberating these markets, which makes it possible for foreign competitors to enter and to compete in that market.

Legal and Political Environment

Another important aspect to consider before entering a new market is a country's trade policies as well as its legal and political environment. Some countries have a high import tax while some have a low one, depending on what the country perceives as beneficial for them. The U.S. for example has had a very high import tax on steel, which made it almost impossible for other steel companies to export their products to the U.S. and sell them there at a competitive price. The U.S. also has a regulation that restricts foreign countries from acquiring shares in certain U.S. industries. The Deutsche Post for example tried to buy shares in a U.S. freight airline and even though they would actually be allowed to buy up to 25 per cent by U.S. law, they did not get a share. The reason for this could be that the U.S. see some industries as vital for their economy and do not want to see them in foreign hands. This makes a market entry for a company like the Deutsche Post very hard in the USA. [12] Other countries require that foreign companies work in a joint-venture with local companies if they want to sell their products in their country. Some countries have advertising restrictions on certain products. In most western countries it is forbidden to advertise cigarettes on TV. Some governments extend this prohibition to billboards and radio spots.

Sociocultural Influences

Some countries like the U.S. or Japan are very focused on technology in electronic products, which means that they put a great emphasis on new and more features. The In contrast, the Danish electronics manufacturer Bang & Olufsen traditionally focuses on the design of their products. Bang & Olufsen failed to realise this sociocultural difference when they entered the U.S. market with their stylish but low in functionality products. A good way to overcome sociocultural conflicts is to hire local managers who know the market and their customers. Different countries have usually different attitudes towards work and authority. We will discuss this in more detail in the Chapter 4.

A company that tries to apply strategies and products from their home market to new markets without adoption will most likely fail at some point.

Evaluating Costs, Benefits and Risks

Every company must carefully evaluate the costs, benefits and risks related to a new market entry before it performs the entry.

Costs

There are two types of costs associated with a market entry. The first one is direct costs. Direct costs are all costs that occur while planning the market entry, setting up the business, leasing or buying costs, labour costs as well as shipping costs.

This means that direct costs are the costs directly and indirectly related to setting up operations in the new market.

But a company also encounters opportunity costs. These are costs that arise from not being able to invest the money that is necessary for the expansion into other profitable opportunities. If Comodex Internet wanted to expand its operations into Russia by investing EUR 5 million into server hardware, translation of manuals, setting up support offices and hiring staff, then Comodex's managers would not be able to invest that money into other projects. These are opportunity costs.

> Infos on COMODEX Internet:
>
> COMODEX Internet is a German Internet Service Provider offering Webhosting, Server, Intranet Solutions and Groupware to its international clients.

Benefits

There can be numerous reasons for entering a foreign market but every company will evaluate the benefits to be greater than the costs, otherwise they would not go on with that expansion. Common reasons are lower production costs, if labour or parts are cheaper, increased sales and customer base, higher profits and economies of scale. Another reason might be the presence in a market for future benefits, even though if it means to generate losses for a couple of years. If the company expects to have great benefits in the future, it might be reasonable to accept temporary losses.

Risks

A company entering a new market faces a lot of risks. These can be exchange rate changes if the other market has a different currency, but it can also be increased costs because of an increased operating complexity or the risk that the market potential was incorrectly evaluated or that the company chose the wrong entry strategy. Of course there are also risks that might affect the whole market that the company is entering due to changes in government policies, war or terrorism. It is crucial for a company to evaluate all kinds of risk and to analyse all factors that can influence a successful market entry.

When a company wants to go international they need to evaluate different markets before a proper entry strategy can be developed. The different aspects of an expansion decision are very diverse and differ from sector to sector. However, we want to introduce some important points that typically need to be considered.

Market Selection

Selecting the right market is probably the first major decision that a company has to make in formulating a market entry strategy. If it chooses the wrong market, even the best company will face problems that it might not recover from. First, a selection of countries has to be made in order to penetrate their markets now or later. To do so the company should take a look at all available markets. A lot of companies make the mistake of only looking at a few markets to enter and might not see better opportunities that they are not thinking of. A pre-set mind and out-of-the-box thinking can reveal markets that might be a better choice than the most obvious one. Some companies first export to the closest market.

A German company might export to France because it is Europe's second biggest market. However, the cultural differences between the two markets might involve higher costs than entering the culturally more simular American market even though the distance is bigger and logistic costs would be higher. In selecting the right market a company should especially examine the attractiveness of the market, market barriers and the culture. Since culture is very complex and important for a multinational company, we will discuss this topic later on in this book and dedicate a whole chapter to the differences between different cultures.

Market Attractiveness

Market attractiveness is usually put side by side with the combination of its economic potential. In fact, market attractiveness is attractiveness by the volume of the market, the market's potential to grow, the competition, the stability of the market and by entry barriers (which we will discuss below). But there are also company-internal factors that influence the attractiveness of a market. Company goals, the company philosophy, as well as available resources influence how attractive a market is to the individual company. If, for example, the top management in an Italian company is Hungarian, it might be beneficial to enter the Hungarian market over the Spanish one if nobody speaks Spanish and nobody knows the culture well. A market that is attractive to one company within a sector might therefore not be attractive to another company from the same sector. Some companies primarily evaluate a market based on its size. This can be a fatal entry decision, if it does not have the resources and competencies to be successful in that market.

Market Barriers

Market entry barriers are disadvantages which a company that wants to enter a new market has compared to companies that are already present in the targeted market. These barriers can be natural barriers or they can be established by other competitors.

Companies that are already present in a market have a variety of advantages. Due to their existing presence they already have an established customer base and a certain image which another company from a foreign market needs to build first. But there are also political barriers like import tax, import bans and handicaps to trade. The following examples are typical market entry barriers:

Economies of Scale:

Economies of scale are usually known as an advantage for a company that wants to go global. They are certainly a main driver for globalisation, but you should bear in mind that it can also be an entry barrier. Economies of scale are particularly important in production industries. A local competitor that is producing a lot more of a certain product might have an advantage over a company that wants to enter that market with a lower production volume. An already set up distribution network of a local competitor can be an entry barrier as well because the local company might be able to distribute a lot more products for a cheaper price.

Capital Requirements:

The cost of capital required to enter a new market depends on the technology and scale. Setting up an internet company is less cost intense then setting up a mining factory, a power plant or a chemicals laboratory in the foreign country. However, capital requirements can also be an opportunity for other companies that have a lower cost of capital to enter a foreign market.

Supply and Distribution Channels:

In some industries it is common that distribution channels are under direct control of the manufacturers. In this way they can offer their products cheaper since they do not need to run a distribution network that is highly profitable. It just needs to break even in order to function. This makes it hard for another company to enter the same market without building up an own distribution network as well to compete with such a low cost structure. In the last couple of years, some companies have built direct relationships with their customers and do not need to go through wholesalers or other suppliers to sell their products. Well known examples are Amazon and Dell.

Customer or Supplier Loyalty:

It can be very difficult for a company to enter a market where the customers are loyal to one brand. The customers' awareness and perception of that product would need to be changed, which is likely to involve intense marketing expenses. In the manufacturing industries and also in some service industries, where it is necessary to go through suppliers, it might be difficult to get the suppliers to cooperate. Often the already existing companies in the market have a very strong influence on the suppliers and might even exercise control over them in order to keep the new company out of the market. But there are also manufactures that are under strong influence of some suppliers or retailers. This usually depends on the availability of suppliers and manufacturers.

Experience:

Early entrants into an industry gain experience sooner than others. This gives them an advantage in terms of cost and/or customer/supplier loyalty. Of course, this experience will be less valuable when product life cycles are shortening and may be of no value at all when a major discontinuity occurs. The opening up of the public services sector in many countries to competitive forces is a good example of how the accumulated experience of negotiating with the providers of funds was rapidly eroded by a lack of experience in customer care. [10 p. 81]

Expected retaliation: If an organisation that considers entering an industry believes that the retaliation of an existing firm will be so great as to prevent entry, or see that entry would be too costly, this is also a barrier. [10 p. 81] Entering the automobile industry by manufacturing a new series of cars would not be very wise unless a careful strategy is devised to compete with Mercedes-Benz, General Motors, Toyota and others.

Legislation or Government Action:

Almost all governments regulate their markets to some extent. Even countries with a free market economy usually have some legal restrictions on competition, restraints through tax or patent protection. These restrictions can have the purpose of protecting the local customers from potentially harmful products or protecting the local economy from dumping prices and outside competition. If governments remove these protections, some companies face the full force of the free market by hard competition. In many European countries this was the case between 1980 and 2000, when many former public services and governmentally owned companies faced deregulation. Some companies were privatised and some had to be reorganised in order to keep up with competition.

Differentiation:

A company can build an entry barrier by differentiating its products from the competitors' products. The watch manufacturer Swatch created its own market of fashion accessory watches in the 1990's by offering watches in a new design like no competitor before. Differentiation can also be achieved through a higher perceived value. Again, differentiation can also be used to overcome other entry barriers, that is it can be developed to a competitive advantage.

Targeted Market Selection

To make a decision which market to enter range of available markets can be either grouped into smaller groups or it can be filtered according to certain criteria. The grouping technique is a method that is divided into two steps. In the first step, all markets are divided into groups of similar characteristics. The second step is to choose the countries or the country that best fits the criteria that the company wants the market. The filter technique is a process by which all available markets get filtered bi several steps through the criteria that the company wants the market to fulfil. Every filter step restricts the group of possible results. The result is a group of countries that fits the company's criteria and that are possible targets for a market entry strategy. Both techniques ensure that the company examines all possible markets and does not leave one out that would have been overseen by a pre-selection. However, it makes sense to combine both techniques to reduce the possible number of countries by some KO criteria and then grouping them together. It is important to do very careful research on the countries beforehand. The market potential needs to be big and stable enough in order for initial investments to amortise themselves.

The Importance of Basis Strategies

The selection of possible markets to enter does not only depend on external factors. It also depends on the orientation of the company itself. This orientation has significant influence on a company's international operations. There are four different orientations that a company can be classified under:

Ethnocentric Orientation

We can find this type of strategy in companies that are very homeland orientated. Managers of such companies believe that their home strategy will work everywhere in the world. To their minds, their way is the only right way to do business. If these companies operate internationally, then just to supply the home market with resources. They focus heavily on the home market and their international activities only exist to improve their competitiveness. Subsidiaries outside the home country are managed centrally from the home country. The organisation is very stiff and does not leave much room for local adjustments. Higher management positions are filled with employees from the home country. Local employees do not have much influence on the business in terms of management power. This type of strategy seems to be a bit old fashioned but can be very useful for companies that produce products that are associated with a certain country. An example is French Champagne or Italian wine. Some export companies have been applying this strategy successfully in other countries.

Polycentric Orientation

A company with a polycentric organisational structure is well aware of the differences in consumer preferences. They adapt their products and sometimes even try to build up a local image. Nestle is a company that owns nearly 8000 brands [13] all around the world. Some brands like Rossiya and Savionov are local and run by local management. Marketing activities are also planned and executed by the local subsidiaries. A company utilising this orientation needs to take care that the local companies do not develop the desire to be independent and to stop supporting the mother company.

Geocentric Orientation

Geocentric orientated companies provide their products or services to the world market. Their subsidiaries are all parts of a globally operating network. Some are specialised, some are more generally oriented. These companies serve cross-cultural target groups like European children or Asian women. Employees get usually recruited on a global level by their skills regardless of where they are from. The company's strategy is designed to compete with global competitors. The strategic planning is usually centrally coordinated, but the application and interpretation are left to the country divisions.

Regiocentric Orientation

Regiocentric orientated companies group different countries together that show similar characteristics. These characteristics can be the language, a regional aspect or a similarity in customer behaviour. These companies usually have separate headquarters for each region. Their strategy is therefore oriented to fit best to the regional markets. IBM is a company that groups their market to groups such as "Central", "Eastern" and "Western" Europe. Accenture groups the German speaking countries to the group "ASG" – Austria, Switzerland and Germany. [14]

Timing of the Market Entry

After selecting a possible market or a group of markets to enter it is important to choose the right timing. Finding the right timing is called cross-cultural timing strategy. Due to rapidly changing market conditions in terms of technological development, political change and competitive threats, finding the right time to enter a market can be a difficult decision. A cross-cultural timing strategy answers the question whether a company should enter different markets simultaneously or successively. The following three paragraphs will introduce the waterfall strategy, the sprinkler strategy and the wave strategy.

Waterfall Strategy

The waterfall strategy means to enter markets one by one. Each market gets penetrated individually and one at a time. The first market entry is usually into a country where the company sees its best chances to succeed – typically a country that is similar to the home market. Once a secure position in the market has been established, the company enters the next market. This minimises the chance of failure because of a wrong choice that has been made in all markets. The company can also learn from its market entry and improve on its strategy in the following entries.

Benefits of the Waterfall Strategy

- The company can learn from their mistakes.
- The risk of failing in more than one country at the same time is eliminated because products will only be offered to the next market once the prior entry has been a success.
- The waterfall strategy leads to an extension of the product life cycle.
- Resources do not need to be supplied to all countries at once.

Disadvantages of the Waterfall Strategy

- A competitor can use the time a market entry following takes to enter another market.
- Competitors are able to prepare and build up entry barriers if they assume that the company will enter their market as well.

- Good or bad experiences can be misinterpreted which could lead to wrong conclusions about other markets.

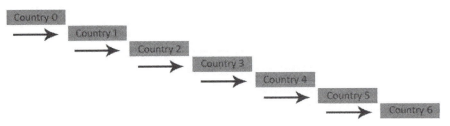

Figure 4 Waterfall Strategy

Sprinkler Strategy

According to the sprinkler strategy a company enters all suitable markets at the same time. Especially geocentrically orientated companies are often using this approach. All available resources such as employees and capital get distributed to all countries to enter the new markets as quickly as possible and to develop a secure market position. Important clients need to be targeted, key suppliers, distributors and multipliers need to be addressed at once in order to enter the market as fast as possible. This market entry approach is as far as possible standardised, which distinguishes it from the waterfall strategy. The sprinkler strategy is also advantageous for companies that produce products with a short life cycle since they do not have the time to enter each market step by step. However, the sprinkler strategy is usually not feasible for small and medium sized companies because of its high demand of skilled management and financial resources.

Benefits of the Sprinkler Strategy

- The early market entry in all suitable markets at the same time contributes to higher market entry barriers for competitors that want to follow.
- Since cash-flows can be generated in more than one market at the same time the amortisation time for fixed costs such as research and development might be quicker.
- The entry risk is shared between all markets.

Disadvantages of the Sprinkler Strategy

- Very capital-intense.
- Mistakes get made in all markets at the same time. Therefore, careful research and planning is very important for the success of the whole company.
- Major false decisions might ruin the whole company.

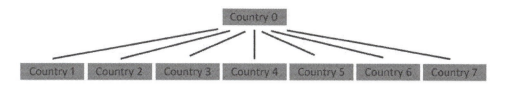

Figure 5 Sprinkler Strategy

Wave Strategy[2]

In the real world, we often find a mixed timing to enter a foreign market. This strategy is called the wave strategy. If the resources are available, this strategy allows a company to enter a group of similar key markets at the same time and then enter more heterogeneous markets in subsequent waves. Markets that get grouped into the first wave are markets that are similar to the home market with little variations. Here the successful concept of the home market can be replicated more easily and differences can be explored. The experience out of these market entries should influence the strategic planning process of the second wave. Once a secure stream of cash-flow can be generated from the first wave, the second wave can be launched. The second wave consists of a group of markets that are different from the home market. If one or more market entry of this second wave fail, the cash-flows from the home country and first wave should be able to make up for the loss. A third wave can be launched once the secure cash-flows from the second wave can be expected. The third wave then consists of countries that are very different from the home country or that are difficult to enter because of high competition or government restrictions.

After a successful entry of all desired markets, exact documentation of all problems should be produced in order to avoid pitfalls and to transfer the experience gained to future management generations.

---

[2] First described by Christoph Lymbersky and the Management Laboratory

Benefits of the Wave Strategy

- The risk of failure is minimised by entering similar markets first.
- Economies of scale can be explored step by step.
- Entries get financed out of existing cash-flows.
- The learning effects are the highest.

Disadvantage of the Wave Strategy

- Capital resources to finance the first wave need to originate from the home market.

Figure 6 Wave Strategy

Market Entry Strategies

Chapter 3

Market Entry Strategies

Market Entry Strategies

Chapter 3:

Market Entry Strategies

Choosing a Mode of Entry

When entering a foreign market, a company can chose between three different decision factors: It can produce its products in its home country and export them as soon as they are completed (home country production) or invest in the other market by buying or building production facilities. The third possibility is building up a branch if the company is in the service industry (host country production, Foreign Direct Investment) or by having local companies perform the production and services for them (licensing, franchising or manufacturing under contract). We will now take a closer look at when Foreign Direct Investments (FDI) occur.

Foreign Direct Investments

Foreign Direct Investment means acquiring foreign assets for the purpose of controlling them. FDI may take many forms, including purchase of existing assets in a foreign country, new investment in property, plant and equipment, and participation in a joint venture with a local partner. [1 p. 164] In his "electric theory", John Dunning says that for a Foreign Direct Investment to make sense, three conditions must be met:

Ownership Advantage

This is a tangible or intangible asset which is also a competitive advantage that another competitor does not have. For example, the company name Coca Cola is an intangible asset which helps Coca Cola to compete in foreign markets. A firm that wants to enter a foreign market usually has the disadvantage that a local firm in the foreign country will know its market in terms of customers and cultural and political factors better. This is called the liability of foreignness. The company therefore needs an ownership advantage over that local company. We will see later on in this chapter that the type of ownership advantage is very important for choosing the appropriate entry mode.

Location Advantage

A foreign direct investment only makes sense if the business that the company wants to generate in the foreign market is more lucrative than doing it in its home country. A common reason is lower labour costs, available resources or local know how. Companies are usually constantly monitoring different markets to react quickly if a new location for their production becomes attractive. "BMW chose Leipzig in the east of Germany as the site for their new production plant in July 2001 for a variety of reasons, including: the economic location of the site (in the geographical centre of Germany between the A9 and A14 autobahns), the availability of specialist personnel, the ability to use existing logistics and suppliers and a good infrastructure for transport and supply. The facility, which required an investment by BMW of €1.3 billion, was also able to benefit from EU European Commission regional grant assistance of €360 million." [15] BMW Chief Executive Helmut Panke pointed out that the company's decision to invest in Leipzig was based on winning unprecedented labour flexibility from German unions. [16] However, if the host country production might have been more attractive then BMW would probably have moved their factory to another country. The current trend is that across much of Western Europe, carmakers and their suppliers are slashing thousands of jobs and transferring production to low-cost Eastern European countries. [16]

Internationalisation Advantage

It must be more beneficial for the company to engage in a foreign business activity than by contracting with a local company. This could for example be the case when the required knowledge is not available in its home country or when the reputation of the company would be at stake when working with a local company. Also, the transaction costs for control, enforcement of contracts and negotiation with contractors are very important in making the decision about the entry mode. If the transaction costs are very high, the firm is more likely to engage in joint-ventures or a Foreign Direct Investment. One of Toyota's important ownership advantages is its very efficient production techniques. This advantage cannot be easily replicated by another company, therefore the transaction costs would be very high. Toyota therefore preferably engages in Foreign Direct Investments and joint-ventures over franchises. If transaction costs are low, the firm will tend to use franchising, manufacturing under contract or licensing as an entry mode. Companies like Merck or the German pharmaceutical firm Bayer prefer to sell their drugs under licensing agreements. Licensing is also favoured by companies with "small pockets" since it is an inexpensive way to expand into foreign markets. Companies with "big pockets" might prefer foreign direct investments since this creates the opportunity to engage in projects with high profit potential and gives them more control over the production and distribution of their products.

To summarise, the decision about which entry mode to adopt is often a trade-off between different advantages and restraints. The following table outlines some of these tradeoffs.

According to a survey from 2004 of 500 global senior executives to explore the corporate expectations for FDI of the Economist Intelligence Unit, China is viewed as the top emerging market for FDI. A U.S. $ 80 billion FDI is forecasted to flow into China in the year 2008. The relative strengths and weaknesses of the potential FDI destination countries and regions are reported in [17 p. 112] the following table:

Tabelle 1 FDI Destination Countries And Regions

	China	Euro area	Japan	Russia	USA	India	New EU entrant	Brazil
New consumer market	49	9	2	5	7	9	15	4
Low cost labor	50	2	0	3	1	29	12	3
New partnership possibilities	20	22	5	5	14	12	14	3
New corporate market	23	22	3	5	17	7	15	4
Access to highly skilled labor force	6	22	7	3	14	30	10	2
New opportunities in outsourcing	16	9	1	3	7	46	12	4
Acquisition opportunities	15	20	2	5	13	8	22	9
Research and development activity	11	20	5	4	22	24	6	3
Great efficiencies in supply chain	17	26	6	2	22	10	9	3

Source: World Investment Prospects: The revivals of globalization (page 11), Economist Intelligence Unit 2004

Exporting to Foreign Markets

When a company sends goods or services to another country with the purpose of selling the goods or to use the services there, this process is called exporting. Exporting is probably the simplest and most common way to expand into a foreign market. Exporting has a lot of advantages that other market entry modes do not have:

1. The firm does not need a lot of capital to export into another country, since it does not need to set up additional staff in the targeted market, it does not need to form subsidiaries and the start-up costs are usually limited to the necessary market research, advertising and the cost that a local distributor wants for distributing the goods to where they will be sold. Some companies not sell their products through a local distributor and set up their own distribution network and distribution centres. This approach can be a bit cheaper since the distributor is not earning his share but the company will still have costs for operating its own network and distribution centres. What approach to take is to be decided on the basis of a case by case decision. However, to go through a local distributor is usually the more flexible way, since a contract with a distributor can be formed and cancelled quicker than setting up and changing a distribution network. Therefore, an own distribution network only makes sense if the company already knows that it will stay in the market for a long time and that it will not change its distribution strategy very often. A company that enters a market for the first time might try to work with a local distributor first, which leads us to the second advantage:

2. Exporting allows a company to enter a market slowly. It can enter the market with one or a few products in selected areas first, adapt its products or services to the local needs and expand the market entry as it becomes appropriate. Tchibo established a Hungary office in Budapest in 1991. Since then, its coffee has been distributed nationwide through a network of retail partners. The takeover of Eduscho in 1997 raised Tchibo to the market-leading position in this country. Today, with coffee blends tailored to na-

tional tastes, Tchibo has a presence throughout the roasted, instant and specialty coffee markets. In 2000, Tchibo began expanding into Romania and South-Eastern Europe from Hungary. [18] Now that the market entry through a local distribution system was successful, Tchibo will enter the market with its own shops to sell coffee and non-food articles like household electronics and clothes labels under its own brand TCM.

The points that motivate a company to enter a foreign market can be described as being proactive and as being reactive.

A proactive motivation would be when a company's research suggests that entering a foreign market would be very beneficial. For example, if the target customer in the home country is very similar to the target customer in the foreign market or if the company wants to lower its average Research and Development costs per unit by exploiting economies of scale. If Ford only sold its cars in the U.S., its per Unit R&D costs would be a lot higher than they are now because Ford is selling its cars to customers around the world.

A reactive motivation would be if the company is somehow forced to enter a new market. This could for example be because the sales in the local market are declining and the company needs to expand its customer base in order to keep its revenue up or if production facilities are not running at their optimal capacities.

Forms of Exporting

There are three main forms of exporting. These are intra-corporate transfers as well as direct and indirect methods of exporting. We will introduce these forms in the following paragraphs.

Indirect Exporting

When a company A sells its products to another local company B and B in turn sells its products to a company in another market then company A is indirectly exporting its goods. This is very common in the computer industry where for example the American company Intel sells their computer processors to another American company, Dell, which assembles computers and then sells them in countries all around the world. The same goes for many car manufactures. Bosch, a German car parts producer, produces its anti-lock brake systems in Germany and sells them to BMW, which build their cars in Germany as well but sell them all around the world.

This method has the disadvantage that the company indirectly exporting does not learn from exporting to another market. Furthermore, there are many other opportunities that the company does not get in touch with such as customer feedback and the optimal exploration of profit margins.

Direct Exporting

Direct Exporting means that the entity directly sells its products or services to the end-user or a distributor in a foreign country. By directly exporting its products, the company gains valuable information about the wants and needs of the customer in terms of feedback. It can also learn a lot about operating internationally and may use this know-how to enter other markets more efficiently. A company selling different sorts of candy might select direct exporting as their exporting method to monitor the likes and dislikes of the customers in the foreign market. Often the taste is different and the candy producer might have to adopt its flavours to local preferences. Direct exporting might be the first step before a direct foreign investment like opening up an own factory to produce the products needed. In this way, the company already knows exactly how the product is supposed to look like and does not need to adopt its production facilities later on.

Intra-Corporate Transfers

An intra-corporate transfer occurs when a firm in one country sells its products or services to a subsidiary in another country. This is very common for companies that produce their products internationally. Airbus for example produces its Airplanes in Hamburg, Germany and Toulouse, France. Almost complete A320 airplanes are moved from Toulouse to Hamburg to get their last finishing. This is done to use productive facilities, the expertise and cost structures of both countries. [19]

Shell ships its oil from its storage facilities in Kuwait to its subsidiaries in Spain to sell it to the local customers. In Kuwait, the transfer is recorded as an export and in Spain it is recorded as an import.

Additional Considerations

Besides choosing the right entry mode, there are some other issues that a company that wants to expand internationally needs to consider. The following paragraphs outline the four most important factors: government policies, marketing concerns and distribution issues.

Government Policies

Most countries have tariffs and special taxes on goods that get imported. The reasons might vary from the government wanting to control the quantity of the import of certain goods and services to simply seeking an opportunity to make money. Simultaneously, a company might encourage their local companies to export by funding special financing programs and through the local chambers of commerce, which provide information about and contacts to various industries as well as countries all over the world.

Marketing Concerns

Often goods or services have a certain image to them that cannot be replicated in another country. For example, Cuban cigars would probably not be perceived as being as good if they would be produced in the U.S.. Even though the tobacco could be exported and then be rolled into cigars in the U.S., which probably would not significantly affect the quality of the cigars. The same goes for German cars. If Mercedes-Benz decided to produce all of its cars in India, Mercedes-Benz's image would probably suffer from this decision.

Producers of goods that undergo a continued change or development need to monitor their markets very closely to ensure that they keep meeting their customers' needs. The length of the supply line between the home and foreign market might make the communication with foreign customers difficult. The entity therefore needs to pay attention to keep up a good level of customer service for all customers that they serve.

Distribution Issues

The distribution though a local company in a foreign market might be a good alternative for a small company that does not have much expertise in distributing their products or services into a foreign market. The selection of a distributor is very crucial to the company that wants to export. They might have to choose between a big distributor that distributes products for other companies as well and a small distributor that distributes only the company's products. However, every distributor wants to earn money as well, which means that the distributor will add a profit margin to the costs that it occurs. You need to know that the distributor will almost certainly try to maximise its profits as well and might therefore try to raise the product's price. It is also possible that the distributor might not market the products or services in a way that maximises the profits for the producer. If it markets the products or services in a wrong way, the producer's reputation might get damaged. Different optimal sales volumes and break even points are often the reason for these problems. The importance of choosing a distributor with the same goals cannot be overestimated.

A company that is very experienced with distribution might choose to enter a foreign market by setting up their own distribution network. The initial costs that this strategy comes with can quickly be offset by additional revenues that the company makes by distributing its product without a middleman. What is more, the company can enjoy the advantage of being in control over the whole distribution process and can adjust every aspect of it to its own needs.

Export Intermediaries

In the following paragraphs we want to introduce three kinds of Export Intermediaries that help businesses with their exports. Export Intermediaries usually offer specialised services like transportation and documentation.

Export Management Company

A company that decides to export its products to a foreign country can do this by hiring an Export Management Company which acts as if it were the company's export department. These EMCs are usually small companies that have expertise in the foreign countries' legal, financial, tax and logistic systems. The EMC establishes the marketing presence in the export market, soliciting orders from foreign customers in the name of the exporter. Invoicing is done in the name of the producer, and the EMC helps the producer with all the details of the export transaction. The exporter bears the risk of non-payment and may be asked to extend credit to the export customer. "Agent" EMCs are paid a commission on export sales. The EMC may suggest an export price, but the principal has final say on price and even on whether to accept the order. [20] Most EMCs also provide consulting services on how to reach potential customers. Some EMCs buy the products from the company that wants to export them and then sell them in the foreign country for a higher price. Others charge the exporter for their services by simply invoicing them. An EMC can be found through industry trade and commodity associations, trade publications or the respective department of commerce. Distributing products through an EMC has the following advantages:

- Export sales come quicker. EMCs already have a network of foreign agents and distributors.
- The product, if compatible, will have a built-in distribution system. If a company were to build their own export business, it would take much longer to get to the point of selling. [20]
- The initial investment will be small compared to other entry modes
- An EMC has the necessary time and expertise to distribute the product to the right places. The exporter can focus on his core business while the EMC exports the products.
- EMCs are usually very professional. The exporter can learn from the EMC and later perform the export itself.

Webb Pomerene Association

The Webb Pomerene Association is a group of U.S. companies within the same industry that coordinates the export activities for its members. The coordination includes market research about the customers and the market that a member wants to enter, contract negotiations such as with freight forwarders and wholesalers, but the association also engages in promotional activities and freight organisation. It might also buy the goods from its members in order to sell them in the foreign country on behalf of the member. The members are mainly concentrated in raw materials and vary from small companies to large firms. These associations have partial exemption from U.S. anti-trust laws, but the associations may not engage in import, domestic or third country trade, or combine to export services. [21]

International Trading Company

An international trading company (ITC) is involved in importing and exporting, which is its major distinction from an EMC. International trading companies provide a wide range of services to its members. Transportation, distribution, market research, customs documentation, financing, marketing and economic intelligence information are only a few of them. Most International Trading Companies operate worldwide and have offices and agents in a lot of different countries. A very famous ITC is the Japanese sogo shosha. They monitor economic conditions in almost every country in the world to provide its members with information and opportunities that arise. Two of its famous members are the Mitsubishi Corporation and Mitsui & Company. [22 p. 113ff] The sogo shosha also offers access to financing from the keiretsu's lead bank.

Other Intermediaries

Some companies have specialised in a variety of services that can be helpful for companies that want to export their goods to a foreign country.

Freight Forwarders are specialised in transporting the goods to the foreign country. They handle customs and obtain permits that are necessary for the transportation.

Export and Import brokers find buyers for companies that want to sell products and find sellers for companies that want to buy products in a foreign country.

Manufacturer's Agents act as agents for the exporter and usually get compensated on a commission basis.

This is just a list of three common specialists. There are a lot more for pretty much every service needed. The chamber of commerce can help in finding the contractor that fits the exporting company's needs.

Advantages of Exporting

Exporting has two main advantages:

- Substantial costs that are associated with for example the Greenfield strategy or FDI are not necessary since the products get manufactured in the home country.
- The company can learn slowly about the new market, their customers and distribution systems in the host country.
- Economies of scale can be achieved for the home country production facilities.
- Easily adjustable to the needs and amount of exports.

Disadvantages of Exporting

However, exporting also has some disadvantages:

- When production in the host country is cheaper, producing at home is not very cost-effective. Many companies produce their products in low labour cost countries and then export their products from there.
- High transport costs might raise the product price.
- Import tax or other tariffs of the host country can make the export uneconomical.
- If the marketing gets done over a local agent, the agent might also serve competitors which would probably decrease the quality of the marketing efforts. To avoid this problem, the company could set up wholly owned subsidiaries in the host country. These subsidiaries would handle the marketing and sales in that country. In this way, tight control over the marketing efforts and sales could be exercised and the cost advantages of producing in one location only could be explored.

International Licensing

Licensing is from a contractual point of view closely related to franchising and is a common form of expansion projects in technology-intense industries. However, licensing also occurs in the food, publishing and sports industry.

By licensing the licensor grants permission to use intellectual property rights, such as trademarks, patents, or technology, under defined conditions to the licensee in return for a fee. [23] By licensing its intellectual property, the company granting the license can take advantage of foreign production without actually investing anything into the production and without managerial responsibilities.

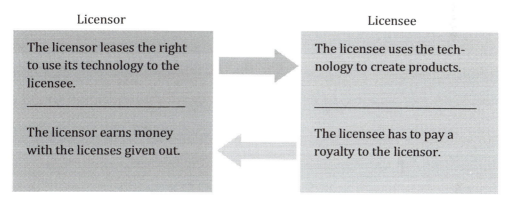

Figure 7 Licensor – Licensee Relationship

Pretty much every licensing agreement is unique; it has to be, because every intellectual property is unique and will be used by the licensee for a unique purpose. The boundaries of the licensing agreement are rules concerning what the licensee is allowed to do and what not. Heineken for example who sells Pepsi Cola in the Netherlands for PepsiCo cannot sell or produce a similar product. A general licensing agreement is a very detailed contract that addresses the following topics:

Compensation

In a licensing agreement the compensation that the licensee receives is called a royalty. The royalty is usually 3 to 5 per cent of the sales, but it can also be a flat fee or a fixed amount per unit sold. Sometimes a licensing agreement even includes a minimum royalty that the licensee has to pay. This minimum royalty shall make sure that the licensee actually tries to sell the products or services instead of just signing the agreement and not selling anything to keep the licensor from entering the market.

Generally, the licensor wants the compensation to be as high as possible; the licensee in turn wants it to be as low as possible. Both companies need to pay attention that their respective contractor will stay motivated to perform the licensing agreements. The licensor needs to pay attention that the compensation is exiting its opportunity costs that it would have, if it entered the market with another strategy.

Sometimes it is necessary to establish production facilities, run marketing campaigns and distribution networks in the host country. The expenses are often covered by the licensee but compensated by a long term licensing agreement.

Establishing Rights, Privileges and Constraints

The licensing agreement also specifies the rights and privileges the licensee has as well as what the constraints are. This is necessary so that the licensee does not take any action that would damage the licensor's reputation, sell information to other companies or underreport the sales volume. Therefore, the license agreement points out how and what kind of records the licensee needs to provide and keep as well as quality standards, how to resolve a dispute and that information about the product or service itself cannot be given to anybody else besides both parties of the agreement.

When does Licensing make sense?

There are a number of internal and external factors that lead a company to utilise a licensing strategy to enter a foreign market. One and probably the most common reason is the lack of knowledge of the market. But there are also other reasons such as insufficient capital for other market entry strategies or not enough managerial resources.

Licensing is also a good way to test a market first and to employ another strategy later on.

It is important that the technology that gets licensed out to another company is not the licensor's core business and to make sure that the licensing partner does not become a competitor in the future.

Some host countries have import restrictions or they impose limits on the royalty fees. Sometimes they do not even allow FDIs in their country. In Spain, France and Ireland, the government needs to approve licensing agreements to become valid.

Another important aspect to consider is how strong the intellectual property legislations in the foreign country are. In some interesting cases, however, companies entered into a licensing agreement with companies where intellectual property was not enforced by government agencies but by the licensee once he became the licensed distributor of a product.

Sometimes a reason to prefer licensing over a merger or an acquisition is that the market is too small to enter by making a Foreign Direct Investment, that is a big investment is not justifiable compared to the returns that the company expects.

The book is written for managers and companies that want to expand their business, therefore our point of view is mainly from the licensor's business. But we also want to mention some main advantages for a licensee because a company also has to view its licensing contract through the eyes of its partner. A licensee does not need to do their own research and development of products, they can just rely on a market-proven product, a product that can be acquired with less risk involved, that is cheaper and faster than a product that the licensee would develop himself.

A trademark remains the licensor's property in eternity, but licenses almost always have a finite end date. Some countries have laws that set a minimum or maximum lifetime for licensing agreement. Some countries even limit the amount of payments that are allowed to go outward of a country in return for a license.

As with franchising, the licensor needs to take care that the licensee keeps certain quality standards and does not ruin the licensor's reputation. Therefore, the licensor needs a control instance that checks upon the licensees in regular intervals. This control team also needs to take care that the licensee maximises the profits for the licensor. Starbucks for example has a team of experts visiting each store once a month to advise and control the locations.

Duration of the Agreement

The duration is a hard term to negotiate because the licensor might see licensing as a short term strategy to enter into a market without big investments and with small risk. The licensee however will usually try to make this agreement a long term venture. In most cases the licensee needs to establish production facilities and cover marketing expenses and the costs of establishing a distribution network. Since the licensee wants to amortise its investments, he will usually seek a long-term contract. For example, the company that has built and is running Disneyland in Tokyo needed to make enormous investments in order to get the place up and running. This company entered into a 100 year license agreement with the Walt Disney Corporation. Usually license agreements are much shorter, though.

Costs of Licensing

Licensing imposes three main expenses that occur to the licensor:

The licensor needs to protect his trademarks, products or patents. Thus, they need to be registered and they need to be enforced in a court of law if the licensee or a competitor breaches them. These costs are called Protection Costs. The costs for searching suitable licensees, testing of products and equipment, as well as training are called Establishment Costs. Sometimes the products need to be modified to suit a certain market. Some managers think that licensing is only a onetime expense and once the agreement is signed they can rely on their royalty fees and sit back. Usually, this is not the case. Maintenance costs occur for auditing, continued market research and enforcement of intellectual property. Finally, it is also important to remember the opportunity costs that a company has if it decides to employ a licensing strategy compared to exporting for example.

Advantages of International Licensing

Given that the company that wants to export by licensing its products to a foreign company explores its market opportunities and capacities of its licenses. Licensing is a relatively low financial risk way to enter a foreign market.

In countries where a firm is not allowed to enter directly by FDI or Mergers & Acquisitions, licensing can be used to still enter the market and getting around entry barriers.

This form of entering a foreign market also allows the licensor to study the sales potential that its products and services have in another country without risking too many managerial or financial resources. Sony for example allows other firms to produce games for its Sony Play Station. The companies producing the games buy a license for each game and can in turn be sure that the game runs on the Sony Play Station and will even be promoted by Sony.

Disadvantages of International Licensing

Licensing limits the licensor and the licensee to not engage in any activities that could create competition for the other party. The licensee for example is typically not allowed to produce and sell products that are similar to the product that he is selling under license. The licensor in turn is usually not allowed to enter the licensee's market with a similar product either.

By licensing a product to another company, the licensor shares technology, patents and/or trademarks with the licensee. Many licensors are therefore concerned that the licensee might use these resources after the license agreement is over and that they are giving away secrets that are crucial for the licensor's success. Many companies for example have problems with Chinese and Indian companies that learn how to produce a certain product and then produce it on their own, without having a license to do so. A way to reduce this risk would be signing a cross-licensing agreement with the partner company. By cross-licensing, one company reveals some valuable intangible assets to the partner but receives also valuable know-how from the partner in addition to royalty payments. Another way to reduce this risk would be to form a joint venture and to license the tangible assets to the joint venture. In this way, all participating partners have an interest of succeeding. Xerox and Fuji did so to reduce the risk of the partners using the know-how of the other company for their own advantage.

Since the licensor does not have tight control over marketing, strategy and the manufacturing process it cannot gain the benefits of an experience curve and cannot learn about the host economies as it would by manufacturing and selling the products itself to host country customers.

A license is unlikely to allow a multinational firm to use its profits (beyond those due in the form of royalty payments) to support a different licensee operating in another country. [24 p. 489]

Case Study: Calvin Klein, Inc. v. Warnaco Group, Inc.[3]

On May 30, 2000, Calvin Klein Trademark Trust and Calvin Klein, Inc. (CKI) filed suit against Warnaco Group, Inc. and Linda Wachner, its CEO, for breaching its jeanswear licensing and distribution contract and, in so doing, diluting the equity of CKI's brand. (See Exhibit 12 for excerpts from Calvin Klein jeanswear licensing agreement and Exhibit 13 for financial terms of the jeanswear license.) CKI charged Warnaco with a total of 18 counts, including trademark infringement, trademark dilution, and intentional misrepresentation. As stated in the filing: Plaintiffs bring this action to protect the integrity of the "Calvin Klein," "CK/Calvin Klein," "CK/Calvin Klein Jeans" and "CK" trademarks. . . . The marks reflect the creative vision of Mr. Calvin Klein, and are among the most respected and well-known designer brands in the world. . . . [Warnaco] has embarked on a program of discounting and mass-marketing of products bearing the Marks, with the intention of maximizing short-term cash flow regardless of the long-term damage to the Marks, CKI, CKI's licensees, and the public that values the Marks as a quality designer brand. . . . [Warnaco has] infringed and diluted the Marks by producing large volumes of goods for sale to unauthorized and inappropriate distribution channels,[4] and by producing goods that were not approved by CKI and not consistent with CKI's design and quality standards. [25]

The suit went on to specify several operational practices at Warnaco that negatively affected the brand, including unauthorized adaptations of designs, failure to follow designer guidelines, and use of cheaper materials in production. Regarding reparations, CKI sought first and foremost an injunction that would prevent Warnaco from taking additional orders for, or distributing cK Calvin Klein Jeans merchandise to, Costco, BJ's, Sam's Club, or "any other channels of distribution that are

---

3 Professor Susan Fournier and Research Associate Jessica Boer prepared this case. This case was developed from published sources. HBS cases are developed solely as the basis for class discussion. Cases are not intended to serve as endorsements, sources of primary data, or illustrations of effective or ineffective management. Copyright © 2002 President and Fellows of Harvard College. To order copies or request permission to reproduce materials, call 1-800-545-7685, write Harvard Business School Publishing, Boston, MA 02163, or go to http://www.hbsp.harvard.edu. No part of this publication may be reproduced, stored in a retrieval system, used in a spreadsheet, or transmitted in any form or by any means—electronic, mechanical, photocopying, recording, or otherwise—without the permission of Harvard Business School. SUSAN FOURNIER JESSICA BOER
4 In its filing, CKI cited the Costco, BJ's, and Sam's Club warehouse clubs as inappropriate channels that were offered firstquality
and "special-cut" goods by Warnaco.

inconsistent with the prestige, value, and reputation of the Marks and which have not been specifically approved by CKI." [25 p. 59] CKI further requested that goods already distributed to such stores be recalled. Additionally, CKI asked the court to terminate Warnaco's license and award CKI unspecified monetary damages as compensation for lost equity in the brand.

Caught off guard by this surprising news, Warnaco immediately issued a statement questioning the motives behind CKI's filing: "The complaint . . . is a desperate attempt by Calvin Klein to cover up and distract focus from the highly deteriorated business state of CKI. Throwing stones at Warnaco is not the answer to CKI's problems, Calvin Klein's failed sale of CKI, or the positions Calvin Klein or CKI are in today." [26] On June 26, 2000, Warnaco countered with its own suit, denying the major allegation of trademark dilution and justifying its distribution of jeanswear through warehouse clubs as an acceptable business practice that fell within the scope of the license agreement. The countersuit claimed that CKI had, in fact, breached the jeanswear license and thereby eroded the brand through practices including missed design deadlines, submission of substandard designs for manufacture, "unreasonable objection to high-quality, commercially attractive design[s]" submitted by Warnaco, Calvin Klein's abdication of design responsibilities, and the abandonment of responsibility to produce effective, nonoffensive, and responsible advertising. [27 p. 56] In its filing, Warnaco also took issue with CKI's portrayal of the licensee as a self-interested party, noting that the firm had invested "substantial effort and resources over many years in developing and protecting the marks": [25 p. 2] "Warnaco is as much an owner of the Calvin Klein trademarks as is CKI. Warnaco has at least an equal interest in preserving their integrity and reputation. These counterclaims are brought to preserve Warnaco's rights as co-owner of the Calvin Klein trademarks and to protect Warnaco from the destructive and self-interested conduct of Mr. Klein." [27 p. 31]

The counterclaim also charged that Klein had defamed and libeled Warnaco through statements made on the *Larry King Live* show (see Exhibit 14) and sought reparations of $200 million for orders allegedly lost in response. Warnaco maintained that this behavior, along with CKI's suit, were intended to help Klein regain control of his trademarks in order to attract a buyer for CKI. News pundits immediately became fascinated with this colorful case starring two of the most provocative personalities in the world of fashion and their superstar lawyers.[5] Analysts

---

[5] David Boies (lead counsel for CKI, noted for his winning antitrust case against Microsoft and Supreme Court support of Al

heralded the lawsuits as precedent setting, noting that this was the first time a licensed manufacturer/distributor had been charged with brand equity dilution or a designer held accountable for ineffective brand advertising. Industry observers remarked that this high-profile legal battle would "rewrite the rules of fashion licensing and distribution" [26 p. 1] and bring into the limelight the tensions faced by every brand steward attempting to balance revenue growth with preservation of the equity of the brand.

Information from the Lawsuit Archives

Distribution Practices and Fashion Retailing

Fashion apparel was distributed through five primary channels: department stores, mass discounters, specialty stores, off-price retailers, and warehouse clubs. Each channel offered a variant combination of the four basic positioning vehicles of retailing: product assortment depth/breadth, price (quality), convenience, and service. Consumers shopped based on their perceptions of and trade-offs among these four attributes, [28 p. 496] though research suggested that assortment and service were particularly important in the fashion world. [29 pp. 29-38] A high degree of cross-shopping across outlets was observed in the apparel category, blurring consumer segmentation along channel lines.[6] Dramatic evolution in fashion distribution patterns across channels had been underway since the late 1980s (see Exhibit 1 Total Apparel by Channel, 1992–1999 for total apparel by channel), reflecting broader trends in consumer behavior as well as the forces of competition and economics at hand.

Gore's case for the presidency) was pitted against Brendan Sullivan (lead counsel for Warnaco, who stood up for Iran-Contra
figure Oliver North).
[6] A large percentage of department store shoppers (77%) also patronized specialty stores, 70% mass merchandisers, 54%
discount stores, and 20% warehouse stores; warehouse clubs shared 85% of their customers with specialty stores, 82% with
department stores, and 82% with discount stores.

Exhibit 1 Total Apparel by Channel, 1992–1999

Channel	1992	1999
Department Stores[a]	23.5%	18.7%
Specialty Stores	18.5%	22.0%
Chain Stores[b]	15.4%	15.9%
Mass-Market Discounters[c]	20.0%	20.1%
Other[d]	22.6%	23.3%

Source: NPD Group data.

[a]Includes Saks Fifth Avenue, Lord & Taylor, Macy's, and others.

[b]Includes Sears, J.C. Penney's, Kohl's, and others.

[c]Includes Wal-Mart, Kmart, Target, and others.

[d]Includes off-price stores, factory outlets, direct mail purchases, Internet purchases, warehouse clubs, and others.

Historically dominating retail apparel sales (and, in turn, being dominated by them), the department store was a large-scale retail format that carried limited-distribution, high-quality, branded merchandise in various departments housed conveniently under one store roof.

Department stores provided superior product displays, ambiance, broad assortment, and excellence in customer service: a value proposition that commanded a premium price. While department stores traded largely on the cachet of the brands they sold, they stood proudly as the innovators in fashion retailing in the 1950s and 1960s. Through innovations such as "window displays, in-store fashion shows, gourmet food halls, in-store services such as hair salons, fixed-price policies, proprietary credit, and free deliveries," [30 p. 4] department stores became sought-after anchors for the rapidly growing suburban malls that defined the retail landscape into the 1980s.

In the late 1980s and early 1990s, however, a wave of bankruptcies and consolidations plagued the retail industry and began a market share decline that would continue throughout the 1990s. Experts attributed department store share loss to merchandise sameness, declining service in the wake of cost-saving initiatives, confusing store layouts, and frequent discounting, which led to a lack of price credibility and a loss of cachet. [31 pp. 3-4] To regain lost ground, stores created specially merchandised branded boutiques, so-called shop-in-shops, that featured the apparel of a single designer, such as Ralph Lauren. Branded concept shops were immediately successful, generating impressive sales and profits, boosting store traffic, and serving broadly as a source of competitive advantage for department stores, particularly vis-à-vis specialty outlets. [32] Concept shops also helped heighten brand awareness for fashion labels nationwide while offering superior control over shop design and merchandising, such that by the early 1990s, the major lifestyle labels had opened thousands of shops between them with plans to roll out many more. [32 p. 6] For example, cK Calvin Klein Jeans had about 400 shop-in-shops in department stores in 1997 and planned to open another 650 to 700 shops in 1998. [33 p. 12]

The proliferation of shop-in-shops brought with it new threats, however, as Bud Konheim, CEO of Nicole Miller, explained: "The enemy is saturation. Sameness breeds discounts. It will all come to a screeching halt. There's a trend to a lack of inventiveness, a homogenization out there, that breeds predictability and boredom."[7] To reduce their concentration on shop-in-shops, department stores moved toward own-label merchandise that built the retailer's own brand (e.g., Federated's I.N.C.). While this alleviated some concerns, critics maintained that by the end of the 1990s, "The basic concept of the department store (was) under fire." [34 p. 1] According to Marvin Traub, former chairman of Bloomingdale's: "Key suppliers are fundamentally concerned with the difficulty of maintaining or growing their businesses with department stores." [35 p. 10] This concern was especially true of midtier department stores such as Macy's and Dillard's, which were being squeezed by discounters such as Target on the low end and by specialty shops and luxury department stores on the high end. [36 p. 10]

Growth in the mass-discounter channel was particularly noteworthy as it came largely at the expense of department stores. National discounters such as Wal-Mart, Kmart, and Target had emerged as strong players in the apparel space with claims for well-known brands at cheaper prices (c.f., Target's slogan of "Expect More, Pay Less"). Similar to department stores, many discounters played on the cachet of branded merchandise, sometimes creating their own brands and at other times gaining exclusive distribution of nationally known brand labels. Target recruited designer Mossimo, for example, to create a clothing and accessories line for the store, while Kmart built an inhouse apparel brand with actress/model Jaclyn Smith to differentiate itself. By 2001, 85% of consumers shopped at discount stores, and 70% reported that they obtained apparel at these stores. [37 p. 1]

---

[7] Apparel comprised 58% of total department store sales in 1999

Apparel sales at specialty chains (e.g., The Gap, Ann Taylor, Abercrombie & Fitch) also skyrocketed in the late 1990s, further encroaching on department stores' turf. Because of their smaller scale, specialty stores were able to deliver trend-right merchandise for a targeted segment of customers. The specialty chain was particularly popular with teen customers, who found large-scale department stores undifferentiated, unresponsive, unwieldy, and too impersonal for their tastes. [36 p. 10]

Two clearance mechanisms for department and specialty stores maintained their presence in the apparel landscape over time. Off-price retailers, such as T.J. Maxx and Loehmann's, and manufacturer's factory outlet stores sold brand-name merchandise at lower prices, as enabled through limited investments in sales associates, real estate, inventory, lighting, or displays. Off-price retailers typically acquired out-of-season branded fashions and split lines (i.e., leftover lines without a full representation of sizes) while factory outlets (some company-owned) sold one brand's excess inventory at discounted prices.

One other significant development in retailing whose impact on apparel thus far had been small was the warehouse club. Started in 1976, club stores grew rapidly during the 1980s and 1990s   see Exhibit 2 Warehouse Club Sales, 1995–1999).

By 1993, the two largest players, Costco and Wal-Mart's Sam's Club, posed a significant threat to supermarkets and general merchandisers with offerings of high-quality, low-priced, branded products. Clubs offered customers savings of 20% on grocery items, which constituted about 63% of total club sales, and savings of 40% to 50% on "hardlines" such as electronics, automotive, and furniture (20% of net sales) and "softlines" including apparel, domestics, jewelry, housewares, and books (12% of net sales). [38 p. 37] In 1999, apparel sales through warehouse stores were approaching $2 billion, or about 1% of the total apparel market, and roughly 4% of club sales. [39]

Exhibit 2 Warehouse Club Sales, 1995–1999

Company	1995	1996	1997	1998	1999
Costco Wholesale[a]	$17.91B	$19.57B	$21.87B	$24.27B	$27.46B
Sam's Club[b]	19.07B	19.79B	20.67B	22.88B	24.80B
BJ's Wholesale Club	2.53B	2.92B	3.23B	3.55B	4.21B
TOTAL	$39.51B	$42.28B	$45.77B	$50.70B	$56.47B

Source: Adapted by casewriters from SEC filings available at Hoovers Online <http://www.hoovers.com>, 2002.

[a] Costco acquired Price Co. in 1993.

[b] A division of Wal-Mart. Wal-Mart, owner of Sam's Club, acquired Pace stores from Kmart in 1993.

Costs at club stores were kept low through operational procedures that minimized labor, real estate, and advertising expenditures. Stores were spare and services minimal: "There are no dressing rooms, service personnel, nice carpets, or attractive furnishings. Floors are concrete—easier to clean— and everywhere are pallets of television sets, dishwashing detergent, disposable diapers and canned goods." [40 p. 1] Clubs also limited the number of SKUs they carried in their 2½ football fields of floor space, stocking 4,000 SKUS compared with 30,000 in a typical supermarket and 50,000 in a discounter. This focused buying strategy further enabled lower prices through empowered supplier negotiations.

Clubs also commanded lower expenditures from manufacturers, including markdown allowances, special fixtures, and co-op advertising budgets, which department stores required for their operation. Despite their spare existence, warehouse clubs had developed a bit of a cachet. Consumers loved the thrill of the "hunt" in club stores and were entertained by the hit-and-miss nature of finding luxury bargains. Brands such as DKNY, Liz Claiborne, Kenneth Cole, Tommy Hilfiger, Ralph Lauren Chaps, Ralph Lauren Polo, Chanel, Cartier, and Rolex, for example, were among those noted on the Web inventory page for Costco in 2000. [41 pp. 16-17] A "Pandora's box effect" was said to operate wherein consumers came to clubs for routine stock-up items but were wooed by the serendipitous discovery of unpredictable treasures: [42 p. 4] "One quarter of all products sold at club stores are known as 'in and out' items that are introduced for one or two months and then removed." [42 p. 4] Detractors charged that club stores traded largely on gray market and counterfeit goods, a claim that the stores vehemently denied. [40] Still, in 1994, Trek Bicycles sued Costco for allegedly diverting 1,500 bikes intended for distribution in India to their U.S. club stores, where they were sold at prices $220 below authorized dealer invoice. According to Trek's attorney: "Damage to Trek's reputa-tion from having the bikes sold without Trek being able to control the quality of assembly and service was incalculable." [40]

Club shopper demographics were in line with the perceived cachet of the outlet. Clubs wooed small-business owners, who comprised about two-thirds of their cus-tomer base, by providing the staples required in business operations, but club shoppers overall were wealthier and better educated than average Americans. Demographic profiles were similar to those for department store customers, in fact, and 82% of warehouse club apparel customers cross-shopped at department stores for their clothing. [43 pp. 269–274] (See Exhibit 3 for customer profiles of selected stores.)

Exhibit 3 Customer Profiles of Selected Stores

	Total Adults	**Costco**	**Bloomingdale's**	**Dillard's**
Graduated high school	33.3%	25.7%	24.0%	29.3%
Graduated college	22.5%	32.0%	42.2%	28.8%
Post-graduate	7.4%	11.0%	17.1%	10.6%
Professional occupation	10.4%	14.0%	22.0%	13.8%
Executive/Admin/Mgr	9.9%	14.3%	13.9%	11.6%
Clerical/Sales/Tech	18.9%	21.4%	22.1%	21.7%
HH income $75,000+	24.2%	39.4%	49.1%	28.1%
HH income $50-$75,000	20.7%	24.8%	18.4%	23.6%
HH income $30-$50,000	23.0%	20.1%	14.0%	24.5%
Age 18-34	32.5%	29.1%	37.7%	32.0%
Age 35-54	39.9%	46.3%	41.3%	43.4%
Age 55+	27.7%	24.5%	21.1%	24.1%
Male	48.0%	46.0%	35.8%	40.5%
Female	52.0%	54.0%	64.2%	59.5%

Source: Adapted by casewriters from Expert Report of Robert C. Blattberg submitted to Williams & Connolly with regard to 00 CIV 4052 filed in the U.S. District Court, S.D.N.Y., Exhibits 2 and 3.

Continued evolution in distribution patterns further complicated the fashion apparel management game. Analysts talked of a trend toward "brand migration" in which premium brands moved from traditional channels of distribution to the mass and discount channels experiencing growth. [44 pp. 13-21] Some manufacturers created sub-brands for the different channels, as with the lower-priced Chaps sub-brand licensed by Ralph Lauren for mainstream markets. Others allowed their ex-isting brands to migrate naturally to the mass chains, as was the case for Jordache and Catalina, now exclusively distributed through Wal-Mart. [45 p. 86] Brand migra-tion was regarded favorably by a host of industry analysts who saw the trend as a natural progression of continued evolution in consumer taste levels, increased price sensitivity among purchasers, and an increased social acceptance of the mass channel. [44] Some regarded migration as an imperative: "If a company does not join the discount store parade, they'll be left behind with an ever-shrinking distribution channel," claimed one analyst. [37 p. 1]

Others, however, cautioned against the risks associated with bringing premium brands into the mainstream and the backlash among department store retailers that was sure to result. [46 pp. 105–122] While the solutions were uncertain, all agreed that distribution strategies were critical in the fashion game.

Channel partner selection decisions were paramount since store image, atmosphere, product display, and price/quality profiles served as extrinsic cues directly influencing brand image perceptions for social identity products. [47] [48 pp. 283–294] Choices regarding distribution intensity were crucial as well, since research had shown that intensive versus selective distribution could make or break a luxury brand. [49 pp. 34-41] It was an increasingly difficult balancing act for fashion apparel managers charged with achieving growth goals while managing channel conflicts and protecting the equities of their brands.

Jeanswear Category Background

Jeans were introduced in 1853 by Levi Strauss, who decided he could make money selling durable pants reinforced with rivets to gold miners facing difficult living conditions on the new frontier. Lee and Wrangler were introduced in the early 1900s and positioned similarly in terms of the tough, American West image that Levi's originated. [50 p. 619] As mass-marketing systems evolved, jeans were distributed primarily through the Army/Navy stores that best captured this functional heritage.

Sparked by Marlon Brando's starring role in *The Wild One* (1953) and James Dean in *East of Eden* (1954), jeans evolved from utilitarian clothing items to symbols of youthful rebellion. By the time of the counterculture era of the 1970s, jeans served as the icon of the anti-establishment, "an endorsement of working-class values and proletarian politics." [51 p. 30] The look on college campuses was unisex and "basic" (i.e., five-pocket styling): a casual, comfortable design that captured the relaxed social standards of the times. Newcomers Landlubber, Viceroy, UFO, Gap, and Dickies joined the popular Levi's brand, whose 501 model became part of the permanent collection of the Smithsonian.

In 1977, the meaning of jeans evolved once again, this time through the vision of designer Gloria

Vanderbilt, who introduced a line of tight-fitting, sexy jeans for women that migrated the category from basics to fashion and pushed jeans from the $20 mark to prices upwards of $50 per pair. Calvin Klein quickly jumped on board the trend as did designers Sasson, Jordache, Guess, and Sergio Valente, spurring unprecedented category growth worldwide and market conditions wherein supply consistently fell short of demand. [51 p. 30] Basic brands like Levi's suffered greatly during the designer-led fashion cycle, as department stores discounted the brands and distribution was expanded to chain stores in attempts to maintain market share. [51 p. 30]

The early 1990s saw jeans return once again to a basics cycle, where they languished as casual wear for several years. A third growth spurt in the category was initiated in 1995, as fashion silhouettes (flares, bootcut, and carpenter styles) with innovative fabrics and washes became popular, especially with teens. "Status casual" jeans brands in the $40-plus price segment further energized the industry, and high-end $100-plus jeans for the extremely fashion- and quality-conscious were born. Notable brand entries included Polo Jeans (1996), Tommy Jeans (Tommy Hilfiger's juniors' line, in 1998), [52 p. 8] DKNY jeans licensed by Liz Claiborne (1998), and Mudd, Diesel, and LEI. Jeans sales growth outpaced that of the apparel market, growing at almost 8% a year in 1997 and 1998 [53 p. 19] to over $11 billion. [54] Growth activity was beneficial not only to specialty shops carrying trendy labels but to department stores selling status casual jeans in shop-in-shops, where women's jeans sales posted 20% gains in 1997 due to the launch of new brands. [55 p. 11] One trade newspaper noted that "Better-priced brands became a welcome relief to department stores struggling with boring basics, and retailers pursued the business relentlessly, clearing out huge floor space for the brands' monumental shops." [56 p. 1]

By 1999, cK Calvin Klein had a 27% market share in women's and juniors' department store jeanswear, while Lee had a 19% share, Tommy 17%, Polo 16%, and Levi's 6%. [53] Jeanswear sales growth tapered once again in 1999 (to 1%, lower than total apparel market growth of 4%) as the market became saturated with status casual brands. [53] According to one apparel consultant: "They aren't really status brands, and they haven't been for a while. They have totally clogged the pipeline. These brands are no longer presenting a unique product." [56] One buyer at Jacobson's rationalized cutbacks in floor space allotments for Polo and Tommy Hilfiger jeans: "Status brands have gotten greedy. They are selling to mass merchants, and we are not going to play that game. Anybody who doesn't control what happens is going to suffer." [56] Retail channels on both ends of the price continuum picked up jeans volume lost by department stores (see Exhibit 4).

Exhibit 4 Jeans Sales by Channel, 1999

Channel	Total Jeans		$40+ Jeans	
	1997	2000	1997	2000
Department Stores	20.6%	18.9%	33.3%	35.0%
Specialty Stores	24.9%	29.7%	30.2%	38.5%
Chain Stores	25.1%	19.5%	24.7%	10.2%
Discounters	16.1%	17.3%	3.4%	0.6%
Off-price Stores/Factory Outlets	8.0%	7.4%	2.5%	3.2%
Other[a]	5.3%	7.2%	5.9%	12.5%

Source: NPD Group data.

[a]Includes direct mail purchases, Internet purchases, sales through warehouse clubs, and others.

Specialty store jeans sales thrived as new $100-plus jeans brands promising better fashion and fit took hold, [57 p. 1] while discounters gained share from teens looking for a particular style or silhouette in lieu of the prestige of a popular brand name. [58 p. 2] Department store status brands became "stuck between ultraexpensive, designer-priced logo looks from Fendi and Gucci, and mass brands like Old Navy and Target, which have been quicker than the megabrands to respond to key trends." [56]

Licensing Practices in the Designer Marketplace

The designer licensing movement took off in the 1970s as a low-risk way for fashion designers to grow their brands without the aid of outside financing or the dilution of the core fashion creation capabilities of their businesses. Fashion designers commonly sought borrowed capabilities in the manufacture and distribution of fragrances and cosmetics, swimwear, footwear, intimate apparel, shoes, belts, handbags, eyewear, and watches, all of which effectively extended the reach of designer labels. License activity in housewares, paints, furniture, bicycles, and even cigarettes was pursued as some designers sought status as true lifestyle brands. At the extreme, Gucci was at one time branded in 22,000 product lines (including disposable lighters and dog food), while Pierre Cardin held 800 product licenses generating $1.5 billion (roughly 90% of sales), a strategy that "may have sacrificed his credibility but made him one of the richest men in France." [59 p. 1]

Licensing activity grew as more and more designer brands went public and were pressured for increased growth and profits on an international scale, often obtained through development of socalled diffusion lines that made the designer accessible to the middle market. [60 pp. 919–937] By 2000, licensing was a staple in the fashion business. In 2000, Jones Apparel Group derived 75% of its $4.2 billion of revenue from licensing brands such as Polo Jeans, Lauren by Ralph Lauren, Nine West, and Evan Picone. [61 p. 12] Liz Claiborne Inc. got almost half of its $3.1 billion in 2000 revenue from licensing brands such as DKNY Jeans, Kenneth Cole, and Laundry by Shelli Segal. [61] Notable licensees that emerged on the fashion landscape included Warnaco Group and VF Corp. for intimates, Estee Lauder for fragrances and cosmetics, and Luxottica and Safilo for eyewear. In a typical licensing deal, designers received a percentage of wholesale sales volume, typically ranging from 5% to as much as 20%, from the licensee in exchange for brand access rights. In one recent deal, Donna Karan got an up-front fee of $30 million plus 7% royalty fees for her DKNY jeanswear license. [62 p. 1] The licensor provided the designs for manufacture as well as the creative strategy and marketing support for the brand. The degree of control granted by the designer to the licensee varied significantly. Martha Stewart's housewares license with Kmart was particularly restrictive, granting MSLO exclusive control over "label descriptions, text on packaging, store displays and advertising text . . . product design, advertising and point-of-sale displays." [63 p. 1] Designers and licensees typically worked in close partnership finalizing designs and sending samples back and forth for approval until a joint sign-off was obtained on the season's product line. The licensee determined the quantities to be sold, sourced materials for manufacture, oversaw production either in-house or through contract workers, and facilitated distribution. Time horizons for licensing deals varied dramatically, ranging from several years to multiple decades. Country terms also varied, with common practice dictating separate licenses for different geographic regions.

By the late 1990s, many fashion designers were reassessing licensing as a brand-building and revenue-generating tool. Christian Dior planned to reduce its 300 licenses to "a handful," and Valentino aimed to decrease the percentage of its revenue derived from licensing from 60% to less than 10% in three years. [64 p. 9] Gucci's CEO, Domenico De Sole, who sought to cancel most of the company's licensed products, commented: "If you are really committed to resurrecting a brand for the long term, you do need to have control over distribution. So licensing doesn't work." [59] As Patrizio Bertelli, president of Prada, noted: "Companies based only on royalties cannot be floated because the financial markets know that they cannot control their assets." [64] Designer Bill Blass found just this complication when he tried to sell his company in 1999 and could not find a buyer. [59] Echoingthis sentiment, when Tommy Hilfiger bought his Tommy Jeans licensee (Pepe Jeans) in 1998, Wall Street applauded the move, sending his stock price soaring by 18% in one day. [65 p. 3] Still, licensing advocates remained, and the practice continued. Vera Wang, a high-end wedding dress designer who launched licenses in 2000 for a crystal line, a fragrance, shoes, and eyewear, commented: "I know I am not able to fund everything in-house. I don't have that sort of infrastructure nor the financial ability. Licensing is a way for my business to make money." [66 p. 6] According to Rose-Marie Bravo, the Burberry's CEO credited with revitalizing the British brand: "You can do licenses with integrity." [64]

Background on the Parties to the Lawsuit

Calvin Klein, Inc. and Mr. Calvin Klein

Calvin Klein, described as "a pioneer of the wholesome, all-American look," [67] was one of the world's most lauded fashion designers and the name behind the legendary brand. Born in 1942 and raised in the Bronx, Klein showed an early interest in fashion, attending New York's High School of Art and Design and The Fashion Institute of Technology before joining design teams at several Seventh Avenue fashion houses. In 1968, armed with a $10,000 investment from his childhood friend Barry Schwartz, Klein struck out on his own with Calvin Klein, Inc. (CKI). Klein's initial line of coats and suits was an immediate success. He recalled: "Mildred Custin, the buyer at Bonwit Teller, put us in business. When I wheeled that rack up, she saw the quality and . . . paid me more than I was asking." [68 p. 4]

By 1970, Schwartz, now an equal partner in CKI, pushed the company's expansion into sportswear. Within five years, the Calvin Klein style was so influential that it was referred to as "a definitive picture of the American look" by *Vogue* magazine. [69] A three-time winner of the prestigious Coty American Fashion Critics' Award, Klein was voted into its hall of fame in 1975.

In 1977, on the heels of Gloria Vanderbilt's designer jeans innovation, Klein brought his company into a new phase by introducing his own jeanswear line. [70 p. 224] "[Jeans were] our first business that could reach a lot of people," reminisced Klein. "I love jeans. They're American. They're not expensive. They're fun to design. Jeans redefined this company, and in a large sense defined who we are to this day." [70] Klein's foray in the jeans world was immortalized in a 1980 ad campaign featuring a provocative 15-year-old Brooke Shields revealing, "Nothing comes between me and my Calvins." In 1983, Klein and Schwartz learned that Carl Rosen, the CEO of Puritan Fashions, their jeanswear licensee, was dying of cancer. [71 p. 1] Concerned about the future of their jeans business, Klein and Schwartz purchased Puritan Fashions for $65.8 million, thus entering the manufacturing game. [72 p. 60]

Innovative line extensions that redefined entire product categories fueled the next phase of growth at CKI. Following his introduction of men's underwear in 1982, Klein put his name on a women's underwear line styled like men's briefs. The line was an instant hit, racking up an estimated $70 million in sales the first year. [73 p. 18] Fragrance line extensions followed with Obsession, launched in 1985 for women and the following year for men. This product marked the first successful use of a master brand in the highly gendered fragrance category, a strategy that was quickly copied by competitors. [74 p. 1] Over the years, three more successful fragrance brands were added—Eternity, Escape, and cK One—bringing Klein to a category leadership position. Klein's edgy ad campaigns, created in-house with legendary fashion photographers Herb Ritts and Bruce Weber, were often noted as a key element behind his branding success. Interestingly, the campaigns that propelled the Calvin Klein brand into stardom were both the most criticized *and* the most celebrated images of the 20th century. [75 p. 4] Of particular note was a 1995 campaign for cK Jeanswear. One emblematic television ad in the series showed young, scantily clad models in a darkened, dingy room having conversations with an older male photographer off screen, as if in "auditions for a low-budget porn movie." [76 p. 22] Designated "kiddie porn" and adding the term "heroin chic" to the public lexicon, [76 p. 22] the campaign sparked an FBI investigation and caused President Bill Clinton to speak out against Klein personally: "It's wrong to manipulate these children, to use them for commercial benefit." [75] While many consumers decried the advertising as "racy" and "exploitative" and objected to its use of "anorexic/emaciated models," [77 p. 12] some felt otherwise.

Members of the cK target audience felt that the ads "looked cool," "promoted equality for genders and races," and conveyed Calvin Klein as "taboo-breaking and norm questioning": perceptions that were "relevant themes for young adults." [78 pp. 363–365] Others saw the campaign as synergistic with the scandalous persona of Calvin Klein himself, whose notorious activities included alleged business dealings with the mob and drug culture dabblings at New York's famed Studio 54. [79 pp. 86–91] In any event, Klein withdrew the ad campaign under pressure from key retailers such as Dayton Hudson, [72] though he maintained its artistic value: "Years from now I believe someone may look at all the commercials I've done and view them as a vignette of the times, a reflection of what people were thinking." [80 p. 61] The heroin chic ads were later displayed in the Whitney Museum of American Art in New York and heralded as an "icon of 1990s advertising that has been copied, emulated, and parodied." [81 pp. 36–51]

CKI fell on hard times in the early 1990s. Reflecting broader trends in the jeanswear business, CKI was buried in excess inventory and unable to keep up with interest payments on debt secured for the Puritan acquisition. [70] Klein blamed himself for losing touch with the younger customer, reflecting that he "had become too isolated." [82 p. 1] In 1992, Klein turned to longtime friend David Geffen, who bought $62 million of CKI's debt and advised Klein to get out of manufacturing and back to his core competencies. [57] In 1994, Klein's underwear business was sold to Warnaco for $62 million, and a jeanswear license was negotiated with Designer Holdings. The moves proved highly successful in turning the company around. Klein's underwear empire soared with the support of Warnaco's marketing and distribution prowess, and jeanswear sales increased under Designer Holdings' eye, from $59 million in 1994 to $472 million in 1996. [57] Jeanswear gains were attributed to improved manufacturing efficiencies that enabled price decreases [83 p. 1] from $60 to $45 and expanded distribution, namely to discounters such as Marshall's and Loehmann's, which comprised a full 30% of accounts. [79 p. 86]

Unfortunately, Designer Holdings entered a tumultuous period precipitated by the loss of its Donna Karan jeans license, thus threatening CKI. With Designer Holdings' stock price falling, Warnaco seized the opportunity to buy the company and its cK Calvin Klein jeanswear license for $354 million in a hostile takeover in 1994. [70] By this time, the Calvin Klein underwear business ad grown to $300 million, [70] and Warnaco was anxious to capitalize on its success with the brand. Klein, concerned about having too many eggs in one basket, initially objected to the acquisition but subsequently noted the value that expanded partnership could provide through enhanced stewardship of the brand.

By the end of the 1990s, CKI had been transformed from a manufacturer to a design and licensing empire[8] that generated $5 billion annually at retail. [70] The Calvin Klein and cK Calvin Klein logos could be found in over 40 product categories including shoes, fragrances, handbags, home furnishings, hosiery, watches, eyewear, and bedding, among others. [84] Klein's royalty stream as believed to be

---

[8] As of 2000, the only products CKI manufactured in-house were the cK women's and men's bridge sportswear lines. (68)

among the highest in the industry, percentage-wise,[9] with licensing revenue representing 90% of CKI's total revenues of $175 million in 1999, [64] up from $45 million, or 25% of total revenues, in 1994 [76 p. 22] (see Exhibit 5). Klein commented: "People describe us as a licensing company. We're truly a design company that designs products for a particular lifestyle." [68] A 1999 marketing review defined the lifestyle positioning of the Calvin Klein brand: "Calvin Klein embodies a lifestyle with simplicity at its core. The design aesthetic is simple, innovative, and modern. The clothes reflect the pure sensibility of American functionalism: clean lines, rich colors and textures create distinctive, understated looks with an eye toward the future." [85]

Exhibit 5 CKI Sales History, 1992–1999

Year	Revenue
1999	$175MM
1998	$160MM
1997	$150MM
1996	$141MM
1995	$127MM
1994	$177MM
1993	$280MM
1992	$220MM

Source: "Calvin Klein Inc. Company Profile," available at Hoover's Online, <http://www.hoovers.com>, accessed July 30, 2001.

In October 1999, Klein retained investment firm Lazard Freres to initiate a search for a buyer for CKI "in order to develop the many opportunities for growth now before us, building on the strength of our brand name and competitive position in the industry." [86] Allegedly, none of the interested parties—including Tommy Hilfiger Inc., Liz Claiborne, and Warnaco—met CKI's rumored asking price of $1 billion, [87 p. 1] and on April 18, 2000, Klein took CKI off the market. Klein commented: "What it came down to is we wanted to align ourselves with people

---

[9] As points of comparison, in FY2000, Ralph Lauren had $236 million in licensing income, 12% of total revenues. Tommy Hilfiger had $62 million in licensing income, or 3% of total FY2000 revenues. Sources: Polo Ralph Lauren Corporation, June 26, 2001 10-K (New York, NY: Polo Ralph Lauren Corporation, 2001), p. 45, available from Hoovers Online <http://www.hoovers.com>, accessed October 10, 2002; and Tommy Hilfiger USA, Inc, March 31, 2001 10-K (New York, NY: Tommy Hilfiger USA, Inc., 2001), p. 17, available from Global Access <http://www.globalaccess.com>, accessed October 18, 2002.

who appreciated and respected the brand. It wasn't a question of getting the biggest number; it was a question of finding the right people." [88 p. 1]

The Calvin Klein Brand

The Calvin Klein brand was heralded as "the most globally recognized in fashion." [89 p. 1] Awareness levels were nearly universal, [90 p. 40] and consumers' brand impressions were generally positive and often glowing. [91] General agreement existed regarding the core set of associations characterizing the brand (see Exhibit 6 and Exhibit 7). Calvin Klein had fallen in its ranking among teens as one of the market's "hottest brands," however, with user imagery perceptions trending older. [92]

Exhibit 6 Calvin Klein Brand Image

In response to question: "Please tell me the degree to which you feel the words in the list below capture the meaning and spirit of the Calvin Klein brand."

Attributes	Mean Rating[a]
Run of the mill, ordinary	1.8
Distinctive	3.5
Fits my needs/lifestyle	2.7
Held in high regard	3.8
Heat/popularity	4.0
Hip	3.9
Stylish	4.1
In vogue, trendy	4.0
See it everywhere	3.3
Premium	3.9
Premium brand	4.1
Known for high-end fashion	3.9
Fashion leader	4.1
Rarely on sale	3.5
Aspirational	3.6
Aspired to	3.0
Prestigious	3.7
Exclusive	3.6
Upscale	4.0
For the masses	2.6
Classic	3.3
Timeless	3.2
Refined	3.1
Classic	3.4
Sophisticated	3.4
Miscellaneous	
Smart	3.1
Simple	2.7
Modern	3.9
Sexy	3.9
Practical	2.7

Source: Expert Report of Susan M. Fournier, submitted to Boies Schiller & Flexner with regard to 00 CIV 4052 filed in the U.S. District Court, S.D.N.Y, Table 1.1.

Note: Respondents were women 25–44 years old. N=299.

[a] As rated on a five-point scale where (1) does not describe brand at all and (5) describes brand perfectly.

Exhibit 7 Top-of-Mind Associations for Calvin Klein Brand

In response to the question: "What comes to mind when you see or hear the brand name Calvin Klein?"

Category of Association	Number of Mentions	Percentage of Total Mentions
Style/Fashion	102	14%
Price	93	13%
Quality	83	11%
Advertising	71	10%
Fit/Cut	60	8%
Body Type/Model[a]	35	5%
Product Evaluations[b]	19	3%
Brand and User Imagery:		
Youthful	27	4%
Gender-related	22	3%
Sexy, sensual	13	2%
Snobbish, elitist	13	2%
Product Exemplars :		
Jeans	88	12%
Fragrance	29	4%
Fashion	27	4%
Underwear	21	3%
Miscellaneous	20	3%
Total Mentions	**723**	**100%**

Source: Expert Report of Susan M. Fournier, submitted to Boies Schiller & Flexner with regard to 00 CIV 4052 filed in the U.S. District Court, S.D.N.Y., Table 1.2.

Table to be read as follows: For the attribute "style/fashion" there were 102 mentions out of a total of 723 coded text responses that concerned the topic of style/fashion. These 102 mentions comprised 14% of the total mentions.

Note: Multiple mentions per respondent were possible and likely. Respondents were women aged 25–44; total sample N=299. Percentage totals may not add to 100 due to rounding.

[a]For example, "need to be thin to wear," "skinny models," "Brooke Shields," "Kate Moss."

[b]For example, "nice perfume," "appealing jeans."

The reach of the Calvin Klein brand had been broadened over time through pursuit of a subbranding strategy enabled by the haute couture line that fueled the brand's credibility and cachet.[10]

CKI's ready-to-wear line, the Calvin Klein Collection, was available through limited distribution to specialty and premium department stores and provided top-of-the-line, high-quality fashions consistent with the ethos and aesthetic of the Calvin Klein brand. The cK Calvin Klein sub-brand, established in 1992, served as a bridge or diffusion line (e.g., similar to DKNY by Donna Karan or Emporio Armani by Giorgio Armani) that interpreted the Calvin Klein core values with an "easier and more casual sensibility": [93] "cK speaks to a trendy, modern, urban lifestyle . . . cK is body conscious, wear-now, use-now style for young individuals who demand newness and uncomplicated aesthetics . . . cK Calvin Klein is a lifestyle brand trusted for contemporary hip fashion." [85] While sharing the modern, sexy, minimalist aesthetic characterizing the brand overall, the cK aesthetic was updated, playful, youthful, and adaptive: essentially a "trendier, more youthful takedown of the Collection ethos." [94 pp. 12–13] cK Calvin Klein Jeans existed as a sub-brand of the cK Calvin Klein sub-brand and focused especially on the youthful, sexy, innovative, forward, and fresh components of the overall brand essence while adding an edgy, raw, American aesthetic and an ethos of casual popular culture. [95] cK Calvin Klein Jeans exhibited high awareness (94% among females, 84% among males), strong repeat purchase levels (in the range of 60%), [90 p. 40] and a solid purchase conversion rate (see Exhibit 8), though qualitative research suggested that the sub-brand was perhaps becoming "over commercialized and too accessible." [96] When evaluated alongside its competitors, cK Calvin Klein Jeans performed especially well (see Exhibit 9).

---

[10] As with most fashion houses, the Klein brand architecture included a couture brand on the top, "the griffe," which was applied to one-of-a-kind, customized products handmade for celebrities and socialites and featured in fashion shows and the media. Couture collections typically consisted of no more than 100 pieces, each designed specifically by the designer (as opposed to a design team). The griffe served as the image engine that legitimized sub-brands through fashion credibility and the establishment of aspirational qualities for the brand and was not held to profitability requirements. Source: Jean-Noel Kapferer, "Managing Luxury Brands," *The Journal of Brand Management* 4, no. 4 (1998): 251–260.

Exhibit 8 cK Calvin Klein Awareness-Purchase Conversion Index[a]

	1996	1998	2000
Men:			
<30 years old	41%	43%	52%
30–39 years old	27%	33%	37%
40–49 years old	35%	34%	33%
50–64 years old	31%	32%	30%
Women:			
<30 years old	52%	62%	65%
30–39 years old	49%	47%	54%
40–49 years old	41%	38%	58%
50–64 years old	39%	45%	48%

Source: Expert Report of David T. Scheffman, submitted to Williams & Connolly with regard to 00 CIV 4052 filed in the U.S. District Court, S.D.N.Y., Exhibits 8 and 9.

[a]To be interpreted as follows: In 2000, 52% of men under 30 years old who were aware of cK Calvin Klein Jeans purchased the product.

Exhibit 9 Brand Quality Ratings for Jeans Brands

Jeans Brand	Rating[a]
cK Calvin Klein Jeans	4.3
DKNY	4.3
Donna Karan	4.4
Guess	4.1
Lauren by Ralph Lauren	4.3
Levi's	4.3
Liz Claiborne	4.3
Nautica	4.2
Polo/Ralph Lauren	4.2
The Gap	4.0
Tommy Hilfiger	4.3

Source: Expert Report of David T. Scheffman, submitted to Williams & Connolly with regard to 00 CIV 4052 filed in the U.S. District Court, S.D.N.Y., Exhibit 13.

[a]As rated on a five-point scale where (5) is excellent and (1) is poor.

Consumer confusion and polarization surrounding the Calvin Klein brand hierarchy was evident. While some claimed to distinguish the brands along intended lines, others failed to register these differences: [91] "I think ['cK' is] a cheaper brand"; "They're targeting different markets . . . cK is for younger people"; "It is all basically the same thing just under a different name"; "cK is a sexier line of clothing compared to Calvin Klein"; "I just figured 'cK' stood for Calvin Klein so it was all Calvin Klein." The brand confusion issue was noted in a 1998 memo from CKI President Gabriella Forte to Calvin Klein and prioritized as a core marketing initiative for the year 2000:

As we grow our jeans business and other categories we have been encountering serious problems with people confusing cK with Calvin Klein. Furthermore, the entire portfolio of products under the cK label (accessories, etc.) and its distribution has created serious effects on the Calvin Klein label. . . . I think the time has come to analyze the labels and consider if we want to drop Calvin Klein from the cK Jeans label. [97 p. 9]

Warnaco Group, Inc. and Ms. Linda Wachner

Warnaco (originally Warner Brothers) was founded in 1874 by doctors Dever and Warner, who designed a "healthful corset" as an alternative to the "restrictive garb" of the time. [98 p. 185] The business quickly grew, and soon the doctors were manufacturing girdles and brassieres, which constituted the core business for the next 75 years. As the 1960s ushered in an era of more comfortable lingerie, the company capitalized on an opportunity to provide more fashionable styles for a younger, upscale clientele and began to manufacture and market sportswear, hosiery, and sweaters. While this highly successful strategy earned Warner Brothers a slot on the *Fortune* 500 list, Warnaco (the new company name) watched its sales roller-coaster up and down throughout the 1970s and 1980s as it tried—with mixed results—to predict fashion trends.

In April 1986, Warnaco was taken over in a hostile leveraged buyout by a private investment group led by Linda Wachner. At the time of the buyout, the company manufactured its own brands, including top sellers Warner's and Olga in women's innerwear and Hathaway and White Stag in men's sportswear. The company also held exclusive licenses for the manufacture and distribution of well-respected brand names such as Christian Dior, Chaps by Ralph Lauren, Speedo, Jack Nicklaus, Geoffrey Beene, and others. [99]

Wachner, known in some circles as the "Marie Antoinette of Management," [100 p. 1)] was a fierytempered, aggressive manager who credited her "take-no-prisoners" style to a childhood battle against scoliosis that confined her to a plaster cast for one year. "When you want to walk again, you learn how to focus on that with all your might and you don't stop until you do it," she said. [101 pp. 102–108] After graduating from college, Wachner joined the Manhattan buying division of Federated Department Stores and made an immediate impression. "Linda used to come flying through my door every morning hitting me with ideas on how we could run the business better," recalled a former colleague. "She wanted to tell our manufacturers how they could do more business with the stores. It was the right move, but she was making lots of people angry because she was going about it so forcefully. I thought, 'Either they are going to run this girl right out of here or she's going to be running the place.'" [101] Wachner made no apologies for her managerial style: "I'm not very long on patience . . . I've yelled at people, and I am not ashamed of it. If you don't like it, leave. It's not a prison." [102 p. 38] Wachner began her career as a bra and girdle buyer at Macy's in the early 1970s. There, Wachner originated several celebrated product innovations in innerwear, including the Merry Widow (a strapless bustier with garters for thigh-high stockings), the Wonderbra, and the stretchy shoulder strap. She also introduced numerous merchandizing innovations that quickly became industry standards, including the alphabetized measurement system for bra cup sizes and the fashion-oriented display of bras on hangers versus boxes. [70] After Macy's, Wachner joined the marketing department at Warnaco, the company she would run 12 years later. In 1978, she was recruited from Warnaco to mastermind the turnaround of troubled cosmetic company Max Factor. "Wachner [was] a real problem-solver," said David Mahoney, CEO of Max Factor's parent company. "If she gave you numbers for the business, you could go to bed at night and be able to sleep because you knew she'd make them." [70] Another executive was more blunt: "A lot of people have been run over by Linda. She will do anything, just anything, to get to the bottom line." [101]

When Wachner heard that Warnaco's CEO was planning to take his company private, she left   Max Factor, found financing, and started a bidding war for the firm. Wachner prevailed and purchased Warnaco in 1986 for $46.50 a share, or $550 million, 90% of which was borrowed. Newly installed as Warnaco's CEO, Wachner sold the women's apparel and hosiery businesses along with other unprofitable lines to focus the company on its two mainstays: intimate apparel (namely the Olga and Warner's labels) and menswear. Wachner also jettisoned Dior, which commanded a significant licensing fee. After cutting the company's debt by 40% and doubling operating cash flow, Wachner took Warnaco public in October 1991. When Warnaco's stock price rose 75% in the nine months following the IPO, Wachner was hailed as "America's most successful businesswoman." Numerous product innovations followed, notable among them Wachner's introduction of the bustlifting Miracle Bra for Victoria's Secret. A license deal with Fruit of the Loom that established Warnaco squarely in the rapidly growing discount chains further enhanced firm performance. [103 pp. 102–108]

By 1996, Wachner was the highest paid woman executive in the United States, earning over $10 million yearly. [104 pp. 26–39]

One of Wachner's most notable business successes involved the cK Calvin Klein underwear line. By broadening the women's product line and investing in 1,500 in-store shops in department stores, Wachner grew sales from $55 million at the time of the license and trademark acquisition in 1994 to $350 million in 1999. [105 p. 1] Gabriella Forte, president of CKI, credited Wachner with building the underwear business "by expanding markets, [increasing the] flow of products in stores, putting fixtures in place, and making sure the infrastructure dealt with the expansion of the business." [106 p. 9] For further sales growth, Wachner moved to expand distribution across geographic and channel bounds.

Freestanding cK Calvin Klein underwear stores were opened in Asia, which met with great success. In the United States, distribution was expanded in January 1999 to include the J.C. Penney's chain, a strategy that met with mixed response. Reflecting the role that expansion to Penney's played in the demise of the Halston brand in 1983, [107 p. 11] Bloomingdale's CEO claimed: "This does not enhance the Calvin Klein brand. When you want to expand the distribution that much, to basically a chain store, you have hurt your brand. . . . The underwear has been a spectacular performer. But this dulls the luster of the brand." [108 p. 1] CEO of online off-pricer Bluefly.com disagreed: "[It is] a bold move, but I believe a correct one for the brand. It's a home run for Penney's, an absolute win for Calvin Klein consumers, and a smart move for Warnaco. Traditional retailers will live with it, because there is nothing to replace it with." [108] Several retailers, including Dillard's, Saks, and May Co., dropped or significantly cut back the presence of cK Calvin Klein underwear in their stores in response to the move. [109 p. 1]

Wachner's signature business model was replicated with other brands, including Speedo, White Stag, Chaps from Polo/Ralph Lauren, and Oscar de la Renta, all of which were grown from niche contenders to mass-market leadership positions through channel-expansion strategies, merchandizing prowess, and fashion flair. Analysts applauded Wachner's success in rebuilding Catalina, the chaste swimsuit brand of Miss America fame, from its position as a tired department store label to a superstar performer at Wal-Mart, which accounted for 10% of all swimsuits sold.

"Previous management had broadened Catalina to the point that we couldn't make any money on it in department stores," said Wachner, "so we put it in a new channel of distribution." [110 p. 196] With exclusive sales through Wal-Mart, Catalina was up 133% over the prior year, with operating margins of 24%. [110] With several strong brands sold through the mass channels, Wachner's brand portfolio garnered powerful advantages with the trade, such as favored-partner status and channel discounts, which propelled company sales.

Wachner's strategy in handling the Hathaway men's dress shirt brand was less successful, however. At the time of the Warnaco LBO, the Hathaway brand was regarded as one of the company's "most valuable assets." [111 p. 1] Founded in 1837, the brand became popular through a legendary ad campaign created in 1951 by advertising genius David Ogilvy that depicted a man in a black eyepatch and a white dress shirt. [112] Wachner harbored hopes for the brand: "Although dress shirts are essentially a commodity, Hathaway has been able to differentiate its products by producing dress shirts with golf logos and denim dress shirts for office wear on casual Fridays." [113 p. 4] By 1995, however, Hathaway had lost $5 million on sales of $43 million [114 p. 58] to become a "promotional line" [115 p. 1] that could be found at off-price retailers for $12.99. [116 p. 22] Critics blamed the brand's downfall on limited advertising support, expanded distribution, and general declines in product quality stemming from the use of cheaper fabric blends and slimmer fits. [117] Warnaco sold the Hathaway brand in 1996 to an investment group, which attempted to restore the brand by doubling specialty store distribution, increasing advertising and new-product development investments, and improving materials sourcing. [118] By mid-1999, the label was "well on its way to once again becoming a department store darling." [116] Warnaco's Dior licensing agreement, terminated by the company under similar circumstances in 1994, was also later relaunched with a lineup of prestigious license partners and increased distribution in department and specialty stores. [119 p. 2]

In the years leading up to the CKI v. Warnaco case, Wachner focused on diversifying beyond innerwear and championed a string of acquisitions that included Designer Holdings, ABS Women's Sportswear, and Authentic Fitness. The strategy was costly and increased the company's debt load to $1.3 billion, or 70% of market capitalization in 1999. [120] In April 2000, Warnaco was valued at $600 million, below its $2.8 billion peak in June 1998 and just above its IPO price. [109] Warnaco was elected to *Fortune's* "America's Worst Boards" list. [121 pp. 241–248] (See Exhibit 10 for sales history.)

Exhibit 10 Warnaco Group Sales History, 1986–1999

Year	Net Revenues
1999	$2,114.2MM
1998	$1,950.3MM
1997	$1,435.7MM
1996	$1,063.8MM
1995	$916.2MM
1994	$788.8MM
1993	$703.8MM
1992	$625.1MM
1991	$562.5MM
1990	$548.1MM
1989	$518.1MM
1986	$425.0MM

Source: Compiled by the casewriters from "Wachner Group Profile" and Wachner Group SEC filings, both available from Hoover's Online, <http://hoovers.com>, accessed May 7, 2002; and Karyn Monget, Thomas J. Ryan, and Lisa Lockwood, "Wachner's Challenge: Win Back the Street," *Women's Wear Daily*, April 3, 2000, p. 1.

Details Concerning the Warnaco/CKI Jeanswear Relationship

Through their 40-year term jeanswear license, Warnaco and CKI had further intertwined their growing businesses and created a situation of mutual interdependency. By year-end 1999, cK Calvin Klein Jeans volume represented a quarter of the total Calvin Klein branded sales and comprised roughly 25% of Warnaco's sales. [122 p. 1] Wholesale volume of cK Calvin Klein Jeans was $700 million, up from $472 million in 1996 when Designer Holdings sold the license, [123 p. 1] and cK Calvin Klein Jeans held title as the best-selling junior jeans brand in department stores. [124] Wachner attributed the growth in part to better, trend-right product: "We're doing new, innovative things to improve our Calvin Klein business, and it's paying off. We're working with CKI on embellished jean product, not just in terms of washes but in terms of different types of abrasions to make the product feel softer, look older." [125 p. 2]

At the time of Warnaco's acquisition of the jeanswear license in 1997, CKI President Gabriella Forte stated that she expected "Wachner to apply the same growth strategy to jeans as she did with underwear, which would include thorough attention to points of sale, deeper penetration within existing points of sale, and expanded fixturing in shop-in-shops. One of the good things she's done in underwear is protect the brand." [106 p. 9] Wachner herself publicly promised to eliminate the lower-priced distribution channels that Designer Holdings had been relying on:

[cK Jeans] were sold to many people who handle off-price, but at the end of the day, we're in the designer business. . . . Calvin Klein is concerned about diversion and jobbers having stuff. We gave him our word that this is over. . . . We don't want to be in the business of jobbers. Merchandise shows up in places we can't control. . . . There will be no more mass merchandisers. We really don't want to go in that direction anymore. [83]

To help Warnaco ingest the significant excess inventory it acquired with the jeanswear license, CKI allowed a one-time clearance of jeans valued at $32.5 million to Costco in 1997, the largest single sale of jeanswear ever. [126] As noted in an October 1998 letter from Forte: "We did approve, on a onetime basis only, and subject to all the controls and parameters required under the license, a sale by [Warnaco] of certain excess and close-out products which was on hand last winter, at the time Warnaco acquired Designer Holdings, Inc." [127] Sales of cK Calvin Klein Jeans were down in 1998, nonetheless, to $457 million. [125] Wachner moved quickly to strengthen the brand in department stores; over $40 million was invested in new fixtures for shop-in-shops, 161 which lost their "edgy, industrial-looking pipe racks" and took on "the minimal look reminiscent of Klein's Collection stores—white walls and slate floors, but punctuated with large-scale lifestyle imagery." [123] Sales for cK Calvin Klein Jeans topped $700 million in 1999, [122] despite "markdowns on cK juniors jeans in the highly promotional department store climate of the time." [128 p. 2]

The cK Calvin Klein Jeans retail distribution mix had shifted significantly over the course of the CKI/Warnaco relationship. Department store sales had grown at about 5% a year from 1997 to 1999 [129] but had decreased as a percentage of total cK Jeans sales (see Exhibit 11).

Exhibit 11 cK Calvin Klein Jeans Sales by Channel

Channel	1997	1998	1999
Department Stores	39.6%	44.2%	36.0%
Warehouse Clubs	8.2%	10.3%	23.4%

Source: Expert Report of David T. Scheffman, submitted to Williams & Connolly with regard to 00 CIV 4052 filed in the U.S. District Court, S.D.N.Y., Exhibit 18.

By 1999, off-priced outlets such as T.J. Maxx accounted for a full 47% of sales in the top 50 CKI/Warnaco accounts. [79 p. 88] Warehouse c`lub sales, which dated as far back as 1984,[11] had tripled during the 1997–1999 period.Including the one-time authorized sale of excess inventory, sales to Costco alone were about $46 [130 pp. 407–411] million in 1998. [131 p. 170] In 1999, Warnaco reports showed $150 million in warehouse sales; [79 p. 88] three of the top six customers of cK Calvin Klein jeanswear were Costco, Sam's Club, and BJ's club stores. [122] Whether these sales concerned diverted or legitimate distribution placements was debated. Klein contended he had sent 94 letters to Warnaco to stop club store sales but that his calls had been unheeded. [132] Wachner countered that Warnaco had instituted greater attention to channel management issues than had existed under either CKI's or Designer Holdings' management of the brand. [133 pp. 33–34] CKI's assertion that "the company had no documents or other information about its own distribution practices prior to 1994" made it difficult to validate Wachner's claim. [79 p. 91] "He's the dogthat did not bark. He knew about, and profited from these mass merchandizing sales for years. The lawsuit is a request to recover for being made rich," Wachner said of Klein. [79 p. 86]

On the eve of the trial, the press reflected on the significant risks that each party would face in the litigation: "They're like Siamese twins stabbing each other in their mutual heart. Both, then, have a lot to lose. While Klein is fighting for his identity, Wachner is fighting for her survival." [70]

---

[11] Expert Report of David T. Scheffman, Exhibit 18.

Exhibit 12 Excerpts from Calvin Klein Jeanswear Licensing Agreement

Section 1.4 [Warnaco] agrees to use its best efforts to exploit the rights herein granted . . . and to sell the maximum quantity of Articles . . . consistent with the high standards and prestige represented by the Licensed Marks.

Section 4.3 In order to maintain the reputation, image and prestige of the Licensed Marks, [Warnaco's] distribution patterns (a) shall consist of those retail outlets whose location, merchandising and overall operations are consistent with the quality of Articles and the reputation, image and prestige of the Licensed Marks, and/or (b) shall be consistent with [CKI's] past practices, and (c) may include those authorized distribution channels in which apparel products manufactured by [CKI] and its licensees and sublicensees bearing the mark CALVIN KLEIN have been or are being sold and such other distribution channels as CKI shall approve.

Section 8.2(a) [Warnaco] acknowledges that the Calvin Klein Trademark Trust (the "Trust") is the owner, and that [CKI] is the beneficial owner, of all right, title and interest in and to the Licensed Marks and to the mark and logo "CK" for Products in the Territory in any form or embodiment thereof and that the Trust is also the owner of the good will attached or which shall become attached to the same and to the business and goods in relation to which the same has been, is or shall be used.

[Warnaco] will not, at any time, do or suffer to be done any act or thing, to the extent [Warnaco] controls any such act or thing, which may in any way adversely affect any rights of the Trust or [CKI] in and to the Licensed Marks or the mark and logo "CK" or any registrations thereof or any applications for registration thereof or which, directly or indirectly, may reduce the value thereof or detract from their reputation, image or prestige or that of the Trust, CKI or Mr. Calvin Klein.

Source: Calvin Klein Trademark Trust and Calvin Klein, Inc. vs. Linda Wachner, Warnaco Group, Inc., Warnaco, Inc., Designer Holdings, Ltd., Inc., Calvin Klein Jeanswear Co., and Outlet Holdings, Inc., U.S. District Court, S.D.N.Y., 00 CIV 4052, May 30, 2000.

Exhibit 13 Financial Terms of the Calvin Klein Jeanswear License

- Licensee to pay CKI 7% of net sales, with a provision for a minimum level of annual royalty payments.
- Licensee to pay CKI 3% of gross sales for advertising expenditures.
- Forty-year term (license expires in 2034), with an option to renew for 10 additional years.

Source: Adapted from Lisa Lockwood, "Calvin: The Control Question," *Women's Wear Daily*, October 6, 1997, p. 9.

Exhibit 14 Larry King Live: Calvin Klein Discusses His Fashion Empire

LARRY KING, HOST: You have filed a major lawsuit against Warnaco. . . . What's the suit about? CALVIN KLEIN, V.C., CALVIN KLEIN INCORPORATED: Warnaco is one of our licensing partners who has the rights to manufacture and distribute our jeanswear. . . . We have tried everything possible to rectify the problems that we've had with this company, in the way they manufacture the product . . . in the quality of the product. It's not up to standard. It's being compromised. And we have constantly been told that the problems will be taken care of, and this situation gets worse and worse, so we've been misled. I—it's my job, it's my responsibility . . . to protect the trademark, to protect the designs, to protect the brand. It's important when the consumer . . . [buys] any of the jeanswear product that they know that it is our design.

KING: Well, wait a minute, are you saying that for the past three years, if you bought a pair of Calvin Klein's jeans they were not up to your specifications?

KLEIN: They were not. Often the product was not up to our specifications. . . . Warnaco has disregarded our specifications. We don't even see, often, the product to approve it.

KING: Why did you wait three years?

KLEIN: In one year, we sent 94 letters to the chief executive officer [Linda Wachner], who is very

hands-on in this company. . . . I've sat with her, my partner has sat with her, the three of us have talked, and we have been lied to, and we have been told that these things will be taken care of.

KING: This is true no matter where you bought the jeans in whatever store?

KLEIN: Much of the product that's out there did not meet our specifications.

KING: But just to—are you saying to people, don't buy Calvin Klein jeans tomorrow?

KLEIN: No, I'm not saying to them don't buy Calvin Klein jeans, but what I'm saying is, honestly . . .

we have serious problems as to the quality and the value and the design of the product . . .

KING: But you realize in speaking like this, someone might hesitate in buying a jean tomorrow?

They might very well say, hey . . . it's $82, it should be $40.

KLEIN: This is a risk that I think the manufacturing company has taken, a huge risk. And I must do everything that I can do to rectify the situation.

KING: OK, now, they say that they're a major source of royalties for you and they were surprised by this lawsuit. They say they [sic] knew exactly where they were being sold, that you had the full list, all the royalty checks came to you . . .

KLEIN: We've been told repeatedly that distribution channels would be looked at and rectified . . . and it has not been.

KING: They continue to make the jeans, though?

KLEIN: They continue to make the jeans, we want our license back, and we want it to be in the hands of a responsible manufacturing company.

Source: CNN "Larry King Live," transcript from June 5, 2002 program, "Calvin Klein Discusses His Fashion Empire," from CNN Web site, <http://www.cnn.com>, accessed July 9, 2002.

International Franchising

Franchising is a specialized form of licensing in which the franchiser sells intangible property to the franchisee and insists on rules to conduct the business. [134] Franchising is similar to licensing but it gives the franchisor more control over the franchisee than the licensor has over the licensee. This form of expending is becoming more and more important. KFC operates over 11,000 Restaurants around the world, about half of which are franchises.

> **Franchisee** - The person who buys a licence to replicate a business system. The Franchisee pays fees to the Franchisor in exchange for the training and materials required to start up in business and receive ongoing training and support. They become their own boss and run their Franchise themselves.
>
> **Franchisor** - The owner of the original operation. The Franchisor decides to allow other people to replicate their system in exchange for a fee.
>
> *Scource: http://www.franchisetraining.co.uk*

A franchising contract is a written contract that states that the franchisee agrees to the requirements that the franchisor has in terms of appearance, operating procedures and financial reporting. Several companies allow the franchisee a certain degree of freedom to adapt to the local culture. McDonald's sells beer in Germany and Wine in its French restaurants.

Some historians argue that the Catholic Church developed a franchise-like system when the Vatican gave its clergy the right to collect taxes on behalf of the Vatican. But franchising in the way we know it today is a system that was originally developed in the United States around 1850. Later, English beer brewers used this system to cooperate with pub owners for exclusive sale of the their beer.

The franchisor provides the franchisee in most cases with trademarks, marketing campaigns, distribution services, training, support and quality assurance but expects to be compensated with a margin on the franchisee's sales and a royalty. The royalty fee can vary between 0 and 50 percent, but the average royalty fee is 7%. [135 p. 190] The start up fee to buy into a franchise system varies between $1,000 and $150,000. [136]

In a recent development, some independent businesses have converted their name and trade style to that of a large marketing network. This could be regarded as the emergence of a new franchise format. [137]

Cross border franchising is growing quickly and allows an independent company to run a business under the name of the franchisor.

If a company already runs a successful franchise system in its home country, it is more likely to succeed internationally as well since it already has a running system that it only needs to adopt instead of creating a new one for the foreign market. McDonald's for example already had hundreds of franchises in America before it decided to open up a franchise in overseas and since McDonald's was very successful in American suburbs they opened up their overseas restaurants in suburban areas as well. It was not until a Japanese entrepreneur convinced McDonald's to let him open up a franchise in downtown Tokyo that McDonald's realised that the downtown locations might be very successful as well. Well established franchise chains like KFC, Pizza Hut or McDonald's usually don't have a problem finding entrepreneurs or companies that want to open up a franchise.

The following paragraphs will introduce different forms of franchising:

Product Franchising is commonly used by automobile dealerships, bottling companies as well as petroleum companies. In this case, the company selling the product will obtain the identity of the supplier. The customer usually does not know whether he is buying the product through a franchise or from the original manufacturer, which is the purpose of this type of franchise.

The second and most common form of franchising is called "business format franchising". It is very popular in the United States. Almost 80% [138] of all franchise businesses are business format franchises. Using this approach, the franchisee can use the franchisor's business concept including its quality control, guidance and support processes, marketing strategy and standards. It is sometimes a bit difficult to distinguish between business format franchising and product franchising.

The most recent version of franchising is *multilevel franchising*, which is divided into three forms. The franchisor usually gives one franchisee the responsibility to develop a whole area. This can be done through a master franchisee, the franchisor model or an area development agreement. The difference between the three forms lies in the relationship between the franchisee and the franchisor.

An *area development agreement* allows the franchisee to develop the area by themselves or to partner with independent franchisees. The agreement is a contract which specifies how the development of the area is supposed to look like and when certain milestones have to be reached.

When one franchisee has to find other individual franchisees to develop the area by themselves, we are talking about a master franchisee model. The parent franchisee (master franchisee) supports the individual franchisees in its area and gets a share of the royalties that the individual franchisees have to pay.

The *sub-franchisor model* differs from the master franchisee model in the way the master franchisee is involved with the individual franchisees in its area. In this model, the master franchisee is not supporting the individual franchisees, which get training and help during setup from the sub-franchisor.

It is hard to estimate the number of failing franchises because often franchises that are in difficulties or in danger of failing get taken over by the franchisor or by another franchisee. It is also difficult to say if franchises fail because of mistakes that the franchisor made or because the franchisee himself was unable to succeed. A study by the Washington DC based company FranData says that about 4.4 percent of all franchises in the market leave their franchise system per year. [139 p. 11]

The parties entering into a franchising agreement are usually risk-averse. They want to profit from shared risk that arises from franchising agreement. However, Francine Lafontaine argued in the Rand Journal of Economics [140 pp. 263-283] that risk-sharing is only one explanation for agency-theoretic reasons of why companies choose a franchising strategy. According to him, there are also one- and two-sided moral hazards. Moral hazard occurs when one party to a contract tends to alter his or her behaviour in such a way that costs to the other party are increased. [137 p. 5] If the franchisor cannot watch the franchisee's behaviour in a sufficient way, moral hazard is one-sided. In this case, the franchising agreement is a trade-off between the need to support the franchisee and to motivate him with the right incentives. Making the franchisee the residual claimant on the firm's profit provides an incentive to maximise profits. [137 p. 5]

Where both parties to the agreement need incentives, we are talking about a two-sided agreement. This is usually the case if both parties need to make considerable efforts to contribute to the success of the business. If the franchisor for example needs to work hard on marketing the brand name and if the franchisor in turn needs to work hard to keep up with the quality and service standards, a two-sided moral hazard exists.

Advantages of Franchising

Franchising is a relatively low cost and low risk way of expanding internationally for the exporter since the financial risk is moved to the franchisee. Since the franchisee carries a lot of the initial investments he is encouraged to establish a profitable operation as soon as possible. The franchisor can rely on local managers that know their culture and do not need to adapt to other customs. It is also an easy way for the franchisor to learn about the customs and operating procedures that are necessary in the host country.

The franchisee, on the other hand, can rely on an established brand name, a proven product and support from the franchisor.

Disadvantages of Franchising

The franchisee and the franchisor must share the revenues earned. If they operated the business by themselves they would not need to share any profits. Another important fact is control. If the franchisee's business is not run according to the agreement, the franchisor has to enforce it and might even need to revoke a license. Otherwise the franchisors image might be at stake. In the case of McDonald's, if it became public that a restaurant in Spain is selling its hamburgers with dirt attached to the buns, the image of the whole company would be damaged. McDonald's therefore needs to control all of its restaurants with great care. In the case of McDonald's or other big franchises, the sheer amount of individual restaurants or stores can make the quality control process very difficult. Furthermore, what might be considered quality in one country does not necessarily mean quality in another. The perception of quality in Japan for example is considered "perfection", in France quality means "luxury", in the USA it means: "it works" and in Germany quality is perceived as "standard".[12] An international traveller visiting a Hilton hotel in Moscow will expect the same standard that he receives from a hotel in his home country and from every other Hilton Hotel in the world. If he had a bad experience in one hotel, Hilton might lose a customer and, more importantly, reputation.

A way to solve this problem would be to set up a number of fully or partially owned subsidiaries in host countries. These subsidiaries could be staffed with home country managers that ensure the quality standards in their region. Ken-

---

[12] Management Laboratory survey number: 02.2008

tucky Fried Chicken and McDonald's for example operate these subsidiaries to-gether with local companies in order to ensure quality, achieve an experience curve and to ensure a fluent reporting process.

International franchising can also be more complicated than in the home mar-ket if resources for the products or services needed are not accessible or not avail-able in the right quality.

Example: McDonald's [141]

Most Owner/Operators enter the System by purchasing an existing restaurant, either from McDonald's or from a McDonald's Owner/Operator. A small number of new operators enter the System by purchasing a new restaurant.

The financial requirements vary depending on the method of acquisition.

Financial Requirements/Down Payment

An initial down payment is required when you purchase a new restaurant (40% of the total cost) or an existing restaurant (25% of the total cost). The down pay-ment must come from non-borrowed personal resources, which include cash on hand; securities, bonds, and debentures; vested profit sharing (net of taxes); and business or real estate equity, exclusive of your personal residence.

Since the total cost varies from restaurant to restaurant, the minimum amount for a down payment will vary. Generally, we require a minimum of $250,000 of non-borrowed personal resources to consider you for a franchise. Individuals with additional funds may be better prepared for additional or multi-restaurant oppor-tunities.

Financing

We require that the buyer pay a minimum of 25% cash as a down payment to-ward the purchase of a restaurant. The remaining balance of the purchase price may be financed for a period of no more than seven years. While McDonald's does not offer financing, McDonald's Owner/Operators enjoy the benefits of our estab-lished relationships with many national lending institutions. We believe our Owner/Operators enjoy the lowest lending rates in the industry.

Ongoing Terms

During the term of the franchise, you pay McDonald's the following fees:

- Service fee: a monthly fee based upon the restaurant's sales performance (currently a service fee of 4.0% of monthly sales).
- Rent: a monthly base rent or percentage rent that is a percentage of monthly sales.

Buying an existing Restaurant through McDonald's The majority of new McDonald's Owner/Operators enter our System through buying an existing restaurant(s) from either McDonald's USA, LLC or one of the Owner/Operators.

The purchase price of an existing restaurant varies and is dependent upon a number of factors including sales volume, profitability, occupancy costs, reinvestment or improvement needs, competition and location.

Upon your successful completion of our world class Owner/Operator training program, a McDonald's Franchising Manager will present available restaurant opportunities to you. In some cases you will be competing with existing Owner / Operators and other applicants for these opportunities.

McDonald's provides potential buyers with a comprehensive guide to assist you in the evaluation and acquisition of the restaurant. You will negotiate directly with the selling Owner/Operator. Prior to any transfer, McDonald's USA, LLC must approve the transfer of the franchise from the buyer to the seller.

We require that the buyer pay a minimum of 25% cash as a down payment toward the purchase of a restaurant. The remaining balance of the purchase price may be financed for a period of no more than seven years. While McDonald's does not offer financing, McDonald's Owner/Operators enjoy the benefits of our established relationships with many national lending institutions. We believe our Owner/Operators enjoy the lowest lending rates in the industry.

Opening up a new Franchise with McDonald's

Relatively few first time Owner/Operators obtain a new restaurant. The costs associated with new restaurants are as follows:

Initial Costs

$45,000 Initial Fee paid to McDonald's
Franchise Term 20 years

Equipment and Pre-Opening Costs

Typically these costs range from $685,750 to $1,504,000. The size of the restaurant facility, area of the country, pre-opening expenses, inventory, selection of kitchen equipment, signage, and style of decor and landscaping will affect new restaurant costs. These costs are paid to suppliers.

The new Owner/Operators must pay forty percent (40%) cash of the total costs of a new restaurant, and may finance the remainder from traditional sources. While McDonald's does not offer financing, McDonald's Owner/Operators enjoy the benefits of our established relationships with many national lending institutions. We believe our Owner/Operators enjoy the lowest lending rates in the industry.

Case Study: Michael Bregman[13,14]

In July 1980 Michael Bregman was preparing a strategy to expand his fledgling Canadian restaurant business. During the last eight months, he had started pilot locations for two different restaurant concepts. The first was "Mmmuffins" (as in, "Mmm, good!"). This was a take-out bakery, offering a wide variety of fresh, hot muffins, baked on the premises, and accompanying beverages.

The second was "Michel's Baguette," a more elaborate French bakery cafe. Baguette offered a take-out counter for a variety of French croissants and breads (also baked in the restaurant) as well as an onpremises cafe with soups, salads, sandwiches on fresh bread, an omelette bar, and fresh croissants.

Michael hoped to build a substantial restaurant chain with one or both of these concepts. Even though the two pilots were just under way, a flurry of shopping center construction across Canada appeared to offer an opportunity for rapid growth. In fact, one major developer was negotiating with Michael for a package of locations. The package included some locations Michael approved, but the developer also wanted a commitment to some locations Michael found doubtful.

Such a deal would be a major undertaking for his young company and would heavily influence its direction during the crucial formative years. Yet Michael was still considering the merits of franchising versus internal growth and evaluating the relative attractiveness of the two restaurant concepts. He wanted to make conscious strategic decisions in these areas before he committed to any course of action.

Background

Michael Bregman was a native Canadian. After earning a degree in finance from Wharton at the University of Pennsylvania, he entered directly into Harvard's MBA program, graduating in 1977. Michael sought a career in the food business because

---

13 Harvard Business Press Rev. November 1, 1988
Richard O. von Werssowetz, senior research associate, prepared this case in association with Professor Howard H. Stevenson as the basis for class discussion rather than to illustrate either effective or ineffective handling of an administrative situation.
14 Copyright © 1983 by the President and Fellows of Harvard College. To order copies or request permission to reproduce materials, call 1-800-545-7685, write Harvard Business School Publishing, Boston, MA 02163, or go to http://www.hbsp.harvard.edu. No part of this publication may be reproduced, stored in a retrieval system, used in a spreadsheet, or transmitted in any form or by any means—electronic, mechanical, photocopying, recording, or otherwise—without the permission of Harvard Business School.

of an interest he had developed due to his family's long association with that industry.

Michael's grandfather had built a successful bakery as had Michael's father, Lou Bregman. In 1971 Lou Bregman purchased Hunt's and Woman's Bakery (Hunt's) division from the Kellogg Company which Lou had been supplying. The division had been losing money on annual sales of about $20 million, but under Lou Bregman's guidance it soon prospered. Hunt's sold bakery products to 130 company-owned retail stores and to 370 supermarkets. Michael had worked after school and during the summer in various restaurants and bakeries.

I joined Loblaws, a Canadian chain that was perceived as being a very stodgy supermarket company. Everybody thought I was crazy because I had offers from some of the big consulting companies and investment banks, places that I should be going. But at Loblaws I would be working for a new president with no experience in supermarketing right in the midst of a turnaround. I would call him a marketing genius and really went to work for him rather than the company.

Michael worked on corporate development projects including the launch of NO-NAME [unbranded] products in Canada which was very successful. But things were not going as smoothly at Hunt's. Lou Bregman was having disagreements with his majority partners (who were in the real estate business) as the result of some difficult financial times. The company was in a turmoil, and Lou asked Michael to join Hunt's to see if he could help out. Michael agreed in June 1978, and headed the retail division. Lou concentrated on the central bakery operations and the other partners attempted to provide overall direction. Michael quickly found himself at odds with the other managers and strongly disagreed with what he thought were stupid decisions. He stayed only at his father's urging until December 1978, then resigned.

I must say that I felt pretty defeated at the time. I'd worked so hard and had accomplished so little. I'd fought a lot, and I've never been much of a fighter, but I also can't do anything unless I believe in it. It was a difficult time. I didn't know what I was going to do. I'd always planned all along to start my own business at some time. I didn't know what or when, but I did know I wanted to do it quickly because I think it gets harder and harder as life goes on and you have all sorts of commitments.

I went out for lunch one day with my old boss from Loblaws who suggested I go back to them again. I really hadn't thought of that but had simply been keeping in touch. I told him I couldn't really make a long-term commitment because my heart was in starting my own business. He said that would be all right, that he could put me on a short-term assignment. It took about five minutes worth of convincing for me to agree.

Evolution of a Start-Up

As his first project, Michael was asked to recommend a strategy for Loblaws's in-store bakeries: Should Loblaws have them? If so, what should they be: bake-off stores of frozen products (baking pre-frozen doughs) or scratch bakeries? He prepared a similar study of the deli department. Michael was then asked to implement his recommendations in the bakery area and became director of bakery operations, a new position. He worked closely with the manager of bakery operations who was oriented to the day-to-day management more than to strategy and planning for the department. Bakeries became important to Loblaws's new super stores which were designed to provide greater variety and savings than traditional supermarkets. Fresh-baked crusty bread and rolls successfully drew in customers.

Somewhere along the way, a small businessman visited me. He thought we should sell his muffins in our stores. We had taken muffins for granted: they'd been around forever and were sort of stable and unexciting—what do you do with a muffin? All of a sudden this fellow comes in with these giant muffins, much larger than any we'd ever seen. We sold our small muffins for 15 cents each; we'd have to retail his at 45 cents.

Naturally everybody was against them just on price. But I decided to test them in two of the most affluent stores. They went like crazy. It was wild. We kept upping the orders and we could never keep them in stock. We didn't promote them, just put them in the counter, but there was immediate appeal. That triggered something in me. Seeing that here you could take a very drab product and make it exciting. And I thought you could do more with it than I saw him do.

Despite Michael's interest in the food industry and fascination with the performance of the large muffins, he really did not like the bakery business: It always seemed to be an old man's game, a tired industry that was declining and very production-oriented, very unexciting. Over 75% of the retail bakeries in North America had closed between the early 60s and mid-70s. Before that, the retail baking industry was composed of hundreds of independent skilled bakers who had come over from Europe and opened up shops and carried on as they had in Europe. The little shops handle two or three hundred items, mostly, if not all, made by hand.

You needed skilled bakers to continue who became very expensive and in short supply.

"Mom and Pop" were willing to work crazy hours and take low salaries because they wanted their own bakery. But by the mid-70s those same skilled people could get jobs in any supermarket in the country, earn $25,000, work 40 hours, have terrific benefits and no headaches. That together with the shift of customers to the shopping centers really put an end to most of that business. The pressure really began with the bakery chains, like my father's, that were serviced from central plants. But then the supermarkets started doing in-store baking, selling a fresher product at a lower price. Gas had gone crazy and it had become prohibitive to deliver fresh products from a central facility to many small shops daily or twice a day. And the supermarket had a different view of the baking business.

They were very price conscious. They weren't in the baking business to make money, but to draw customers to buy other things. The last thing they wanted to do was to draw a customer into the store and see a bakery that had prices that were too high. Their cost systems were often really rather silly and ignored investment and overhead and value of the space used by any individual area. Some supermarket departments, like the bakeries, were really much more expensive marketing tools than they thought. But the supermarkets tended to just look at the total bottom line as a contribution number. Looking at these things, it was easy to be negative about the industry.

Then I started to feel there was a massive opportunity out there! People still liked baked goods and they hadn't been supplied with them in the right fashion. As I thought in general terms of what was going to happen to the retail baking industry, I felt that the stores were going to get smaller and the industry would have to specialize in one or two lines of products. Also you'd surely have to bake on premises to create the freshness that no one else could duplicate. That's really the key component of quality in our industry. I also reminded myself that the retail baking business is primarily based on impulse sales and location is extremely important. I guess I had all of this in mind in May 1979 while my father and I were driving to a restaurant show in Chicago. For the first time it really occurred to me: Why don't we open a muffin shop? We sort of chuckled—what a stupid idea. Later I began to think, why not? There's not a lot of money to lose and a lot to gain if it worked. It was totally different than anything we'd seen in North America. During the summer, I began investigating some space in the Eaton Centre. This was Toronto's principal downtown shopping complex with over 3.7 million square feet of space.

The Eaton Centre was directly connected to three subway terminals and had 200,000 office workers within easy walking distance. It was anchored by two major department stores and two office towers. There were over 300 retail shops and restaurants in the complex. Their leasing agent was pretty skeptical, but was willing to lease some space. In August, I committed to lease 350 square feet at $15,000 a year or 8% of sales, whichever was greater, beginning December 1. Now I needed to develop my shop.

Meantime, Lou Bregman had sold his interest in Hunt's and had considered retirement. But when he had the chance to buy a downtown bagel store that had gone bankrupt, he decided to develop a new full-service restaurant and bakery called Bregman's. Michael was helping his father get started with that and Lou Bregman co-guaranteed the lease obligations with Michael for the muffin shop. Besides his duties at Loblaws, helping his father's new venture, and planning his muffin shop, Michael found himself drawn into yet another start-up:

My wife and I had honeymooned in France when we were married in May 1978. I really fell in love with their croissants. I couldn't believe how great they were. I'd never tasted a decent croissant in North America. They were all poor imitations and I thought this would be a great product to bring over here. I had seen a few French bakery stores in Chicago and New York, but very few. I knew that this wouldbe some thing to pursue in the future.

As we were settling our lease deal for the muffin shop in the Eaton Centre, I mentioned to the leasing agent that I had heard that a French bakery chain, Au Bon Pain, was coming to the center. He was surprised I'd heard of it, but said they had some problems with them. I said I was planning to get in the same business and he got very excited. He called his boss and very quickly offered to negotiate with us.

Space in the Eaton Centre was very difficult to obtain, and it seemed to me to be one of the best possible locations. So we leased the space and decided to do our French bakery too. Again, we personally guaranteed the leases.

Despite the serendipitous opening at the Eaton Centre, Michael's commitment to the French bakery restaurant was not a spur-of-the-moment decision. He had been actively investigating the possibilities of both the muffin shop and the French bakery since the Chicago show in May. Because the French bakery would require much more capital, Michael had prepared a short business plan which he circulated to three or four people he thought might invest. One was Ralph Scurfield of Calgary, president of the NuWest Group, the largest homebuilder in North America. Michael had met him while Ralph was enrolled in an executive program at Harvard. Michael had done a field study for NuWest and had kept in touch with Ralph. Now Ralph said that he knew very little about the restaurant business, but that he did know Michael Bregman and would be willing to bet some money on him. A long negotiation ensued as Michael sought locations for the muffin shop or for the French bakery.

They reached agreement in the fall: We capitalized the company with $450,000. My father and I each put in $62,500 in common stock and Ralph put in $125,000 in common stock and an additional $200,000 in preferred shares. I had a net worth of about $8,000 and got a loan for my share. I had to get my wife, mother, and father to cosign and my parents to put their house up. It scared the daylights out of me. If things went wrong, it wouldn't sink them, but I didn't know how I could live with it. I would take a salary cut to $25,000 a year, which together with my wife's income would just about let us live and cover the loan. The contract ended up sixty pages long with five pages of basics and the rest disaster clauses. I would have tiebreaking power unless things went wrong and would also have to get Ralph's approval for capital expenditures over $5,000. The initial spending requirements were approved as part of the agreement. There was also a complex redemption plan for the preferred which included penalties for not making the five-year schedule. The fall of 1979 was frantic as Michael managed to get both of his projects under way.

Although he and his father had been in the baking business, neither of them was familiar with either the special processes needed for muffins of this type nor with French baking. While Michael was working to design the stores, he had to find and test muffin recipes and learn to operate the specialized French baking equipment. Part of his strategy was to use the very best help he could find. For design, he employed Don Watt & Associates, one of Canada's premiere designers. The equipment suppliers were also very helpful in the strenuous task of laying out all of the necessary customer service and baking equipment in 350 square feet for the muffin shop. Michael also found a French baker who lived in Washington and who agreed to come up just before the bakery opened to teach several bakers how to bake French bakery products.

Somehow they got under way. Michael left Loblaws at the end of November 1979 and Mmmuffins opened on December 15. Michel's Baguette began construction at that point and opened in April, 1980. It was not a time Michael would like to repeat.

Evaluating the First Efforts

By July, the two stores were beginning to stabilize and Michael was preparing to expand. He reviewed the state of each operation to help him decide what directions he might take. He was pleased with both store designs and concepts. The extra expense and effort he had put into store planning had been well worth the investment. Both facilities were attractive and inviting. As for product selections, they had developed recipes for over 15 varieties of muffins which could be made from four different base mixtures. About 10 would be offered at any time. At Baguette, the menu appeared workable and was proving to be popular (see Exhibit 15). Sales for both stores had been encouraging, and costs were beginning to stabilize. He now had seven months of experience with Mmmuffins and three months with Baguette. Exhibit 16 records sales and variable costs for the two stores. Exhibit 17 is a year-to-date financial statement, showing the total performance and financial position.

Exhibit 15 Michel's Baguette, Product Line Highlights

Bakery		Cafe	
Bread:	Baguette	Salads:	Julienne
	Boule		Nicoise
	Alpine		Spinach
	Mini-Baguette		Side Salad
	Whole Wheat Baguette		Salad du Jour
Croissants:	Butter	Soups:	Yellow Pea with Ham
	Almond		Soup du Jour
	Petit Pain Au Chocolat		
	Raisin-Custard	Quiches:	Bacon
	Cream Cheese		Spinach
	Cheddar Cheese		Mushroom
	Ham and Cheese		
	Apple Cinnamon	Omelette Bar:	Cheddar Cheese
	Blueberry		Ham
	Cherry		Swiss Cheese
			Green Pepper
			Onion
			etc.
		Sandwiches:	Ham & Cheese
			Roast Beef
			Tuna
			Chicken Salad
			Egg Salad
			Cream Cheese
			Swiss Cheese
			Le Hero
			Le Jardin
			Roast Beef & Herb Cheese
			etc.
		Beverages:	Coffee
			Tea
			Milk
			Soft Drinks
			Juices
			Perrier
		Croissants:	(as in bakery)

Exhibit 16 Initial Store-Level Operating Results

Period Ending	# Wks	$ Sales	Avg. $ Sale Per Week	% Food, Supplies	% Labor	% Food, Supplies and Labor
Mmmuffins:						
Jan. 19, 1980	5	9,010	1,802	38.2	38.8	77.0
Feb. 16	4	10,866	2,716	36.3	29.8	66.1
March 15	4	14,901	3,725	24.5	23.9	48.4
April 12	4	17,250	4,312	28.0	22.5	50.5
May 10	4	16,696	4,174	34.6	25.6	60.2
June 7	4	17,346	4,337	38.5	25.4	63.9
July 5	4	20,602	5,150	31.1	21.0	52.1
		Highest Week's Sales, June 21—$5,574				51.4%
Michel's Baguette:						
May 10	4	44,470	11,118	37.7	33.5	71.2
June 7	4	52,921	13,230	27.4	25.4	52.8
July 5	4	65,487	16,372	25.9	23.1	49.0
		Highest Week's Sales, June 21—$17,289				48.7%

Exhibit 17 Financial Statements—Corporate Level Balance Sheet, June 30, 1980

Assets

Current Assets

Term deposit	$120,000
Receivables	1,525
Inventory	6,669
Prepaid expenses	15,345
Deferred charges	1,062
Deferred income taxes	7,250
	151,851
Equipment and Leasehold Improvements	400,741
Incorporation Expense—at cost	7,151
	559,743

Liabilities

Current Liabilities

Bankers' advances	1,436
Payables and accruals	124,736
Dividend payable	4,500
	130,672

Shareholders' Equity

Share Capital	450,000
Deficit	(20,929)
	$559,743
Sales	$269,428
Cost of sales	169,919
Gross operating profit	99,509
Store expenses	78,473
Income from store operations	21,036
Other income—interest	14,972
	36,008
Administration expenses	55,187
Net loss before income taxes	(19,179)
Deferred income taxes	7,250
Net loss	(11,929)
Dividends	(9,000)
Deficit, end of period	($20,929)

	Mmmuffins	Michel's Baguette
Sales	$106,404	$162,745
Food costs	35,090	44,861
Gross profit	71,314	117,884
Operating expense		
Supplies	6,083	7,259
Labor	29,249	52,333
	35,332	59,592
Gross operating profit	35,982	58,292
General expenses	2,228	1,992
Occupancy costs	19,411	35,609
Administrative costs	5,442	8,137
Total expenses	27,081	45,738
Net profit from operations	8,901	12,554
Add depreciation and amortization	5,367	9,005
Cash flow from operation	$14,268	$21,559

Note: Slightly different period than prior statements.

After hectic start-up periods, the operations of each store became satisfactory. As expected, they differed. The Mmmuffins store had only 350 square feet of space; this small area contained supplies storage, preparation of raw materials and mixes, baking, clean-up, and the retail service counters. Michael described how this worked:

I think our design was one of the most important reasons behind our early success. Don Watt, our designer, was able to create the magnet to draw customers in the first time. If they liked our service, they'd come back. They came in first because of the color, the lighting, the photography—it's just a different showcase. The design also worked well functionally. There's just enough space to do everything, but no extra space to become cluttered or dirty and not be corrected. The customer cannot see the preparation area, but the manager can easily keep track of all activities. The total staff complement for the store runs between six and twelve people including part-timers, depending on the part-time mix. You need one manager and one assistant to cover the shifts. There are sales people at the counter and bakers in the back; the employees can trade-off some during slack buying periods. Service at the counter is fairly simple and you can train a baker in two days from start to finish. You could almost get this down to two hours for most of the functions.

Although we didn't really know what we were doing when we opened, we soon learned better ways to do things. We got better at finding and selecting specialized preparation equipment that fit our particular needs. Since we bake from scratch using no commercial mixes, every extra efficiency helped. We learned what items we could make ahead of time and better ways to store them. This is really important when you begin baking early in the morning before opening and continue throughout the day.

I knew that if we were going to grow, we'd have to systematize the operation, so during the first months I wrote an operating manual with everything from opening procedures, to how to clean the store, to recipes, to baking procedures, to how to greet customers and work the counter—everything. I found it one of the most grueling experiences I had ever been through in my life. I was working behind the counter myself during those opening months and was learning how important those controls and procedures were. I also learned how important the manager was. As Baguette opened and I left the Mmmuffins store under the supervision of a manager I had hired, little problems started to arise—fighting among the staff, quality being a little less consistent than it should have been. I'm sure there was fault on both sides, but I found that the manager constantly needed attention. But all in all, I was very pleased.

As a much larger and more complete bakery and restaurant, Michel's Baguette was much more complex: Baguette had 2,500 square feet of space which was really a bit too tight. This had a larger food preparation, baking, and storage area, a take-out bakery counter, the cafeteria-style serving line, and an on-premises eating area with seats for 35. Once again, our physical design was an important asset. Our store helped attract customers at the same time that it worked well functionally in a very tight space.

With a larger menu, there were many more tasks to perform. There was a total staff of 55 to 60 people, including part-timers. You really need a very qualified head manager to be the general manager of the overall business as well as two assistant managers who have the capability to be the acting general manager when the general manager isn't there. You need a head baker who is quite skilled and who can guide the whole production area of the store. There are kitchen prep people, two kinds of service people, cafeteria counter people who actually prepare the portions, the salads, and sandwiches. Most of these jobs are more complex than those at Mmmuffins and the baking is particularly difficult. It takes 20 steps to make croissants and the breads also have more steps and are more demanding than making muffins. There are many delicate areas where you can ruin the product, but I must say that we brought in the right equipment from France and, with care, can consistently make excellent products. All of the baked goods and other items are made from scratch and are baked continuously throughout the day I began to spend most of my time at Baguette once it opened and again had to learn as we went. This would take more effort to systemize, and I hadn't written a manual here yet. I was lucky in hiring some good bakers and restaurant managers to help me out. I went after managers that I had heard did a good job for other restaurants in the city and was able to get two to join me. They both worked out very well.

The primary appeal of each concept was absolute freshness and quality of baked goods. As Michael looked at the two operations, he was satisfied that they each properly reflected the key conceptual definitions he felt were critical to their success: hard-to-replicate standards of quality with costs kept to acceptable levels by careful specialization, organization, and store design. Michael described how these worked together:

For superior quality our recipes are based on using fresh eggs, buttermilk, and other very perishable items—very expensive, very hard-to-handle items. Bakeries don't use fresh eggs; they use powdered or frozen. But we had decided we would use fresh: we didn't care about any of the rules; we would be better than anybody. But this created very difficult production problems. You can't make too much at once, and you can't make too little because it's a waste of time. The mixes and products aren't very storable, you can't freeze it, and you can't keep them for more than one day.

Besides ingredients, we control our quality by specializing. This means making limited types of baked goods in the best possible way and then providing only those menu items needed to support the specialized baking operation. With Mmmuffins this is practically absolute: there are only muffins and beverages. The bakery for Baguette is simply too capital intensive for the menu to remain that simple. So we combine the bakery with a restaurant. Having the fresh croissants and fresh bread to make sandwiches helps the restaurant, and the sampling that goes on in the restaurant spills over and helps the bakery. The restaurant and bakery counter also have different peak times, so you have better distribution for the bakery equipment and your service people can sway back and forth. But other than the baking, we do no cooking! It's just an assembly operation. We assemble salads, cut meat, cut cheese. But except for omelettes, we don't fry anything, we don't boil anything, we don't cook. Other than the baking, in terms of the back-of-the house, it's a very simple restaurant.

The stores' layouts and service delivery systems are designed to efficiently support each menu concept. Both provide efficient preparation areas. Both have ovens prominently situated in view of shoppers and passers-by—the sight and aroma of fresh baking are major merchandising tools. At Mmmuffins, we have very efficient customer handling along with some innovative packaging for quantity purchases. At Baguette, we selected a cafeteria line for the restaurant to go along with the counter service for the takeout bakery. This is one step up from the fast-food joint where you have to fight for a seat and eat from a tray with disposables. We use better dinnerware, metal utensils, and glasses. This is a step down from the full service restaurant where you are served by waitresses. We selected this because I felt strongly that in the mall environment, people want to eat quickly but in some comfort.

Considering Franchising

With both Mmmuffins and Baguette well started, Michael began to consider expansion. He felt there should be many opportunities for good restaurants and specialty food stores despite competition ranging from retail bakeries and supermarkets, to fast-food operations, to full-service restaurants. Almost all of these types of competitors would be present, clustered in large shopping areas and malls. This was true for the first Mmmuffins and Baguette locations. Yet both had held their own in the very competitive and highly visible Eaton Centre. The question was how to expand.

Michael had two concepts, limited experience, and limited resources. How could he best capitalize on his work to date to build a significant restaurant business?

One avenue of growth he could pursue was franchising. Certainly many others had chosen this method, making franchising an important factor in the Canadian and U.S. economies. A *Foodservice & Hospitality Magazine* survey estimated that franchising represented 16.5% of the total Canadian foodservice and lodging industry in 1979. This market share was increasing. Survey respondents reported a 29% increase in total foodservice franchise sales resulting from a 10.5% increase in total units operating and a 17% increase in average sales per unit (to $381,443).

For U.S. firms, franchised units accounted for approximately one-quarter of all foodservice sales.

Exhibit *18* lists several characteristics of U.S.-owned restaurant franchisors for 1978 with projections for 1979 and 1980. About 40% of all American franchised restaurants were located in California, Texas, Ohio, Illinois, Michigan, or Florida.

Exhibit 18 U.S. Dept. of Commerce Statistics

A. Statistics of U.S.-Owned Restaurant Franchisors, Restaurants (all types)[a]

				% Change	
Item	1978	1979[b]	1980[b]	1978-79	1979-80
Total number of establishments	55,312	59,928	66,672	8.3%	11.3%
Company-owned	15,510	16,781	18,549	8.2	10.5
Franchisee-owned	39,802	43,147	48,123	8.4	11.5
Total sales of products and services: ($000)	21,100,788	24,591,880	28,990,499	16.5	17.9
Company-owned	6,733,545	7,816,198	9,111,129	16.1	16.6
Franchisee-owned	14,367,243	16,775,682	19,879,370	16.8	18.5
Total sales of products and services by franchisors to franchisees: ($000)					
Merchandise (non-food) for resale	33,013	37,534	48,656	13.7	29.6
Supplies (such as paper goods, etc.)	170,889	231,017	287,379	35.2	24.4
Food ingredients	298,063	383,774	481,004	28.8	25.3
Other	46,817	53,728	40,771	14.8	−24.1
Total	548,782	706,053	857,810	28.7	21.5

[a] See Parts C and D of this exhibit.

[b] Data estimated by respondents.

B. Distribution by Number of Establishments, 1978, Restaurants (all types)[a]

	Franchising Companies Number	Establishments		Sales	
Size Groups		Number	%	($000)	%
Total	389	55,312	100.0	21,100,788	100.0
1001 and greater	12	27,750	50.2	11,400,272	54.0
501-1000	11	8,925	16.1	3,513,637	16.7
151-500	34	8,833	16.0	2,928,603	13.9
51-150	59	5,580	10.1	1,712,930	8.1
11-50	153	3,642	6.6	1,360,850	6.4
0-10	120	582	1.0	184,496	0.9

[a] See Parts C and D of this exhibit.

Source: U.S. Department of Commerce, "Franchising in the Economy 1978-1980," Jan. 1980.

C. Distribution by Major Activity, Establishments[a]

Major Activity	Firms	1978			1979			1980		
		Total	Company-Owned	Franchisee-Owned	Total	Company-Owned	Franchisee-Owned	Total	Company-Owned	Franchisee-Owned
Total	388	55,312	15,510	39,802	59,928	16,781	43,147	66,672	18,549	48,123
Chicken	31	6,708	1,870	4,838	7,193	2,011	5,182	7,826	2,197	5,629
Hamburgers, franks, roast beef, etc.	117	26,038	4,648	21,390	27,833	5,077	22,756	30,651	5,695	24,956
Pizza	66	7,542	3,042	4,500	8,355	3,288	5,067	9,434	3,577	5,957
Mexican (taco, etc.)	29	2,329	993	1,336	2,527	1,044	1,483	2,913	1,183	1,730
Seafood	11	2,297	899	1,398	2,444	901	1,543	2,704	966	1,738
Pancakes, waffles	15	1,441	363	1,078	1,577	418	1,159	1,770	491	1,279
Steak, full menu	86	7,924	3,479	4,445	8,756	3,813	4,943	9,771	4,180	5,591
Sandwich and other	33	1,033	216	817	1,243	229	1,014	1,603	260	1,343

[a] Estimated by respondents for 1979 and 1980.

D. Distribution by Major Activity, Sales ($000)[a]

Major Activity	Firms	1978			1979			1980		
		Total	Company-Owned	Franchisee-Owned	Total	Company-Owned	Franchisee-Owned	Total	Company-Owned	Franchisee-Owned
Total	388	21,100,788	6,733,545	14,367,243	24,591,880	7,816,198	16,775,882	28,990,499	9,111,129	19,879,370
Chicken	31	2,034,012	653,977	1,380,035	2,247,838	765,738	1,482,100	2,563,755	899,485	1,664,270
Hamburgers, franks, roast beef, etc.	117	10,862,837	2,589,465	8,273,372	12,961,887	3,038,923	9,922,964	15,521,446	3,595,801	11,925,645
Pizza	66	1,735,279	696,364	1,038,915	2,007,066	776,902	1,230,164	2,364,317	903,182	1,461,135
Mexican (taco, etc.)	29	602,376	304,697	297,679	648,100	315,922	332,178	766,692	377,652	389,040
Seafood	11	563,827	216,486	347,341	667,098	260,633	406,465	772,794	299,624	473,170
Pancakes, waffles	15	601,029	139,899	461,130	681,728	164,023	517,705	834,135	216,290	617,845
Steak, full menu	86	4,531,709	2,104,623	2,427,086	5,170,218	2,461,797	2,708,421	5,883,140	2,779,340	3,103,800
Sandwich and other	33	169,719	28,034	141,685	207,945	32,260	175,885	284,220	39,755	244,465

[a] Estimated by respondents for 1979 and 1980.

A January 1980 study by the U.S. Department of Commerce noted that The entry into the restaurant franchising system mostly by small companies continued in 1978 with a net gain of 38 franchisors, bringing the total to 388. During 1979, 17 franchisors with a total of 227 restaurants, 198 franchisee-owned, went out of business while 13 franchisors with a total of 168 restaurants, 84 franchise-owned, decided to abandon franchising as a method of marketing.

Big franchisors with over 1,000 units each increased to 11 in 1978 from 8 a year earlier. These 11 franchisors had 27,750 restaurants, 50.2% of all franchised restaurants, and accounted for $11.4 billion in sales, 54% of the total. Compared with 1977, the 8 franchisors with over 1,000 units each had 45% of the total units and 47% of the sales.

Menu expansion and diversification continues on the increase to meet the mounting competition from other chains and to enlarge customer counts that have been adversely affected by higher food costs and periodic gasoline shortages. The higher costs of cosmetic and structural construction changes are forcing fast-food franchisors to reevaluate their investment in design, and cast their decor changes more and more in marketing terms.

Exhibit 19 shows the growth statistics of the 25 largest franchise restaurant systems in the United States.

Exhibit 19 Top 25 U.S. Franchise Restaurant Systems

Franchise System	1974	1978	1979	'74-79 % Change	'78-79 % Change
McDonald's	$1,943	$4,575	$5,385	177%	17.7%
Kentucky Fried Chicken[a]	925.5	1,393.4	1,669	80	19.8
Burger King[a]	467	1,168	1,463	213	25.3
Wendy's	24.2	783	1,000[b]	4,032	27.8
International Dairy Queen[a]	590	823.2	926	57	12.5
Pizza Hut	232	702	829	257	18.1
Big Boy	484[b]	660[b]	750[b]	35	13.6
Hardee's[a]	280	564.6	750	168	32.8
Arby's	120	353	430	258	21.8
Ho Jo's	300[b]	425[b]	425[b]	42	0.0
Ponderosa[a]	183	328.5	406.9	122	23.9
Church's	126.9	345	405.7[b]	220	17.6
Bonanza	190	346	378	99	9.2
Tastee Freez[a]	267.9[b]	353.8[b]	350[b]	31	(1.1)
Long John Silver's[a]	45.5	283.4	342	652	20.7
Sonic Drive-ins[a]	52.1	291.7	336	545	15.2
Burger Chef[a]	250	301	335	34	11.3
Taco Bell[a]	71.1[b]	212[b]	320[b]	350	50.9
Western Sizzlin[a]	100	217.3	278.1	178	28.0
Dunkin' Donuts	163.3	249.4	283.8	74	14.0
A&W	174.4	247.5	255	46	3.0
Arthur Treacher's	48.3	191.5	226.3	369	18.2
Sizzler[a]	85.5	181.8	225.9	164	24.3
Perkins Cake n Steak	75[b]	200[b]	223[b]	197	11.5
Pizza Inn	58.6	165.8	189[b]	223	14.0

[a] Fiscal year-end figures (remaining establishments are calendar year-end figures).

[b] Estimated.

Franchise System	1974	1978	1979	'74-79 % Change	'78-79 % Change
McDonald's	3,232	5,185	5,747	78%	10.8%
Kentucky Fried Chicken[a]	4,627	5,355	5,444	18	1.7
Burger King[a]	1,199	2,153	2,439	103	13.3
Wendy's	93	1,407	1,818	1,855	29.2
International Dairy Queen[a]	4,304	4,820	4,860	8	0.8
Pizza Hut	1,668	3,541	3,846	131	8.6
Big Boy	881	1,041	1,100	25	5.7
Hardee's[a]	924	1,125	1,231	33	9.4
Arby's	439	818	928	111	13.4
Ho Jo's	922	882	867	(6)	(1.7)
Ponderosa[a]	389	588	636	63	8.2
Church's	565	970	1,125	99	16.0
Bonanza	550	700	675	23	(3.6)
Tastee Freez[a]	2,215	2,022	2,000[b]	(10)	(1.1)
Long John Silver's[a]	208	1,001	1,007	384	0.6
Sonic Drive-ins[a]	220	1,061	1,182	437	11.4
Burger Chef[a]	950	853	831	(13)	(2.6)
Taco Bell[a]	562	877	1,100	96	25.4
Western Sizzlin[a]	140	319	400	186	25.4
Dunkin' Donuts	780	956	1,007	29	5.3
A&W	1,899	1,500	1,306	(31)	(12.9)
Arthur Treacher's	250	730	777	211	6.4
Sizzler[a]	256	352	402	57	14.2
Perkins Cake n Steak	183	342	400[b]	119	17.0
Pizza Inn	336	743	760	126	2.3

Source: *Restaurant Business*, March 1, 1980. Note: Includes U.S. and foreign sales and units.

[a] Fiscal year-end figures (remaining establishments are calendar year-end figures).

[b] Estimated.

Although franchising was one means to achieve growth for Mmmuffins or Baguette, it would impose additional complexities in doing business. A franchisee is an independent businessperson with personal capital at risk and a fair amount of management flexibility. In addition to the demands inherent in such relationships, there was increasing government regulation of franchise offerings and operations. On October 21, 1979, a new U.S. Federal Trade Commission ruling required comprehensive disclosure statements for prospective franchisees. Sixteen separate states also required various types of disclosures (although some states accepted a uniform format). Canada had no such comprehensive disclosure requirement, but many felt there was a need for one and expected such a rule in the future. Some pressure for such regulation came from established franchisors, who were worried about the effect that a few incapable, overconfident, or unscrupulous franchisors might have on the industry.

The areas of disclosure required by the U.S. law illustrated the many aspects of the business and the relationship that must be considered in franchising. These included the following:

- Specific background information about the identity, financial position, and business experience of the franchisor company and its key directors and executives.
- Detail of the financial relationship including initial and continuing fees and expenses payable to the franchisor.
- Requirements for doing business with the franchisor or affiliates (such as purchase of supplies from a franchisor source) and any realty fees, financing arrangements, or other financial requirements.
- Restrictions and requirements for methods of operation placed on the franchisee.
- Termination, cancellation, and renewal terms.
- Control over future sites.
- Statistical information about the number of franchises and their rate of terminations.
- Franchisor-provided training programs and other support.

Even without disclosure requirements, it was considered a good idea to develop policies and practices for dealing with franchisees for the long term before opening the first operation. One reason for this was a general desire for consistent treatment of franchisees. Examples of current practices of Canadian franchisors are summarized in Exhibit 20.

Increased regulation was not the only change occurring in franchising. There was ever increasing competition in Canada as more U.S. franchisors sought new markets in other countries.

The need for better communication with franchisees had started a trend of franchisee advisory councils by franchisors. The ultimate role of these councils was still evolving. There was also a fairly constant trade back and forth between franchisors repurchasing franchised units for company ownership and company-owned units being franchised.

Exhibit 20 Sample Canadian Franchise Terms, February 1980

Franchisor (franchise)	History, Current Status, and Expansion Plans	Franchise Requirements and Costs	Services Offered to Franchisee
Mister Donut of Canada Ltd. (Mister Donut):	• established 1955 • 55 franchised units in Canada 715 franchised units in U.S., Japan • locations: Ont. 43, Que. 9, B.C. 2, Alta. I • Cdn. sales $10m • 10 operations to open in 1980	• initial fee $10,000 • royalty fee 4.9% of gross sales • advertising fee .5% • current equipment package $50,000	• opening supervision • field supervision • classroom training • newsletter • site selection • lease negotiation
McDonald's Restaurants of Canada Ltd. (McDonald's Restaurants)	• established 1967 in Canada • 156 franchised—168 company owned • total Cdn. sales $500m • 45 new units planned across Canada	• franchise fee $10,000 initial investment $190,000 total cost is around $400,000 • percentage rent plus royalty fee • total commitment by sole operator to run operation • 4% advertising fee	• continual consultation of operation • marketing • training • personnel • real estate
The Harvest Inn, Inc. (The Pantry Family Restaurant):	• established 1975 • 5 units company owned, 2 franchised, all in B.C. • full service restaurant for breakfast, lunch, and dinner • 4 additional units are planned for B.C.	• $20,000 initial fee • royalty fee 4% gross • advertising fee 2%	• full turnkey service incl. site selection, interior design • accounting, training, and personnel selection
Burger King Canada Ltd. (Burger King):	• established 1976 • 27 franchised units & 10 company owned; 2,650 worldwide; B.C. 2, Alta. 2, Ont. 30, P.E.I. 1, N.B. 1, N.S. 4 • 26 franchised units planned for Ont., N.B., B.C., N.S., Alta. • menu incl. hamburgers & specialty sandwiches	• initial fee $40,000 • 4% royalty fee • 4% advertising fee	• complete service package
Smitty's Pancake Houses Ltd.:	• established 1959, now has 86 franchised and 6 company owned; 3 in Hawaii • total sales $59m • 16 units planned for 1980	• initial fee $25,000 over 70 seats, $15,000 under 70 seats	
Country Style Donuts Ltd.:	• established 1962 • 66 franchised, 4 company owned, 4 in U.S., Alta. 5, Sask. 1, Man. 3, Ont. 55, Que. 5, N.S. I • total sales $15m • 14 new units planned for Alta., Ont., & Sask. • menu incl. coffee & donuts	• initial fee $85,000 ($2,500 deposit, $27,500 for construction, $50,000 equipment contract, $5,000 inventory) • royalty fee 4.5% of gross • 2% advertising fee	• turnkey operation • 4-week training course • supervisory assistance on opening • 20-year franchise term

A Question of Strategy

The question of using franchising as a means of expansion was only one aspect Michael needed to consider in planning for growth for his restaurant business. A fundamental question was how suitable were his concepts for wide use? He had started and managed both current units personally. How well would they "travel?" Both concepts depended on fresh baking which made them more demanding than many franchises. Other stores offering similar baked goods (donuts, cookies, or other items) used premixed ingredients, premade frozen products to be baked in the units, or simply distributed centrally baked products.

Michael also had to include the capital requirements and likely performance of additional units of either type in his planning. His estimates of capital requirements for new locations are shown in Exhibit *21.* His estimates of stand-alone operating results if operated by a franchisee are shown in Exhibit 22.

Finally, no matter what methods of growth he might choose, his location strategy would be critical. Where would his concepts best fit? One aspect was the type of location and surrounding demographics. Another aspect would be geographic: how far away, and Canada versus the United States. Even within Canada, there were very different demands between the more stable eastern portion and the rapidly growing western area. Should he concentrate on finding more established and stable locations in the east or should he take advantage of the many openings in new centers a construction boom in the west was creating? What differences were there between good locations for Muffins and good locations for Baguette?

Exhibit 21 Estimated Capital Requirements of Additional Stores

Mmmuffins:

Equipment package	$15,000
General construction (including fixtures and leasehold improvements)	$40,000-$60,000
Opening supplies and inventories	$ 5,000
Miscellaneous (design, insurance, permits, preopening salaries, opening promotion, landlord chargebacks, working capital)	$10,000
	$70,000-$90,000[a]

Michel's Baguette:

Equipment package	$145,000
General construction (including fixtures and leasehold improvements)	$170,000-$235,000
Furniture and supplies	$35,000-$45,000
Miscellaneous (working capital, design, permits, opening promotion, preopening salaries, advance rent)	$20,000-$40,000
	$370,000-$465,000[a]

[a] These are stand-alone estimates. If franchised, any franchise fee would be an additional requirement.

Exhibit 22 Estimated Earnings Potentials

Weekly sales	Mmmuffins Potential Annual Cash Flow[a] 350-Square-Foot Mail Location					
	$3,000		$4,000		$5,000	
Annual sales	$156,000		$208,000		$260,000	
Food cost (1)	48,360	31.0%	62,400	30.0%	78,000	30.0
Selling supplies	7,020	4.5	9,360	4.5	11,700	4.5
Labor (incl. benefits) (2)	31,200	20.0	37,440	18.0	41,600	16.0
Gross operating profit	69,420	44.5	98,800	47.5	128,700	49.5
Operating expenses:						
Royalties	9,360	6.0	12,480	6.0	15,600	6.0
Telephone	500	.3	500	.2	500	.2
Utilities	3,500	2.2	3,800	1.8	4,000	1.5
Uniforms and laundry	600	.4	600	.3	650	.3
Advertising	3,120	2.0	4,160	2.0	5,200	2.0
Repairs and maintenance	800	.5	800	.4	800	.3
Insurance	900	.6	900	.4	900	.3
Total occupancy (rent) (3)	16,800	10.8	17,500	8.4	21,000	8.1
Depreciation and amortization (4)	7,000	4.5	7,000	3.4	7,000	2.7
Miscellaneous (5)	1,560	1.0	2,080	1.0	2,600	1.0
Total operating expenses	44,140	28.3	49,820	24.0	58,250	22.4
Earnings before interest and tax (6)	25,280	16.2	48,980	23.5	70,450	27.1
Add: depreciation and amortization (7)	7,000	4.5	7,000	3.4	7,000	2.7
Cash flow before interest, tax, and franchisee compensation	$32,280	20.7%	$55,980	26.9%	$77,450	29.8%

[a] Post start-up; no operator/franchisee compensation is included.

Notes to Mmmuffins Cash Flow Projections

1. Based on prices of 60-65¢ per muffin, $3.45 for 6, and 40¢ per cup of coffee.

2. Based on 70-hour weekly selling period with hourly wages of $3.75-$4.75 for baking staff, $3.50-$4.00 for full-time selling staff, and $3.00-$3.50 for part-time staff. Owner-operator's compensation is not included.

3. Total occupancy includes all services for which landlord invoices including rent, merchants association fees, common area charges, HVAC, realty taxes, etc. Total occupancy may vary depending on location. We have assumed base rent of $40 per square foot for a 350-square-foot store or 7% of sales (whichever is greater) plus $8 per square foot in "extras."

4. Depreciation and amortization is calculated by applying the straight-line method on $70,000 over 10 years.

5. Miscellaneous expense may include cash shortages, licenses and permits, office supplies, professional fees, etc.

6. Earnings before interest, tax, and franchisee's compensation is expressed as such due to wide variances in compensations paid, amount of debt to service, individual's accounting treatment of expenses, etc.

7. Depreciation, being a noncash expense, is added back to illustrate total cash generated before interest, tax, and franchisee compensation.

| Weekly sales | Baguette Potential Annual Cash Flow[b] 3,000-Square-Foot Mail Location | | | | | |
	$14,000		$18,000		$22,000	
Annual sales	$728,000		$936,000		$1,144,000	
Food cost	232,960	32.0%	299,520	32.0%	354,640	31.0%
Selling supplies	21,840	3.0	28,080	3.0	34,320	3.0
Labor (incl. benefits) (1)	203,840	28.0	243,360	26.0	286,000	25.0
Gross operating profit	269,360	37.0	365,040	39.0	469,040	41.0
Operating expenses:						
Royalties	43,680	6.0	56,160	6.0	68,640	6.0
Utilities (2)	14,000	1.9	15,000	1.6	17,000	1.5
Telephone	700	.1	700	.1	700	.1
Uniforms and laundry	2,200	.3	2,600	.3	3,000	.3
Advertising (3)	7,280	1.0	9,360	1.0	11,500	1.0
Repairs and maintenance (4)	5,000	.7	6,000	.6	7,000	.6
Replacements (5)	3,500	.5	4,500	.5	5,500	.5
Insurance	3,000	.4	3,000	.3	3,000	.3
Total occupancy (rent) (6)	75,000	10.3	77,000	8.2	89,500	7.8
Depreciation (7)	30,000	4.1	30,000	3.2	30,000	2.6
Miscellaneous (8)	7,280	1.0	9,360	1.0	11,500	1.0
Total operating expenses	191,640	26.3	213,680	22.8	247,340	21.6
Earnings before interest and tax	77,720	10.7	151,360	16.2	221,700	19.4
Add: depreciation (9)	30,000	4.1	30,000	3.2	30,000	2.6
Cash flow before interest, tax, and franchisee compensation	$107,720	14.8%	$181,360	19.4%	$251,700	22.0%

[b] After six-month start-up; no operator/franchisee compensation is included.

Notes to Baguette Cash Flow Projections

1. Based on 70-hour weekly selling period with hourly wages of $4.00-$5.00 for baking staff, $3.50-$4.50 for full-time service food preparation, and bussing staff and $3.25-$3.75 for part-time staff. Management salaries included assistant store manager at $14,300 per year, head baker at $15,600 per year. *Owner-operator's salary is not included.*

2. Based on actual experience in Toronto store. Utility expenses may vary widely depending on location, use of gas vs. electric oven, hours of operation, etc.

3. One percent allocation is for local advertising and promotion. At this time the franchisor does not maintain a national advertising fund.

4. As most equipment is under warranty, first-year repair expenses should be lower than projections. Actual cost in future years will vary considerably due to periodic breakdowns, preventive maintenance program, use of equipment, etc.

5. Replacements include costs of replenishing supplies of utensils, dishware, cutlery, trays, etc.

6. Total occupancy includes all services for which landlord invoices: rent, merchants association fees, common area charges, heating, ventilation and air conditioning, realty taxes, etc. We have assumed a base rent of $18 per square foot for a 3,000-square-foot store or 6% of sales (whichever is greater) plus $7 per square foot in nonrent "extras." Actual total occupancy costs will vary for each location and should be evaluated individually.

7. Depreciation is calculated by applying the straight-line method on $360,000 over 12 years.

8. Miscellaneous expenses may include professional fees, licenses and permits, cash shortages, office supplies, etc.

9. Depreciation, being a noncash expense, is added back to illustrate total cash generated before interest, tax, and franchisee compensation.

An Offer of Locations

To help learn about possible locations that might be available, Michael began talking with major Canadian development companies. One important firm was Real Estate Canada (REC) which developed and controlled a large number of shopping malls across Canada. After preliminary discussions, REC offered Michael locations for Mmmuffins stores in one new mall and one mall expansion, both in Toronto suburbs. This was an important developer, and Michael felt the locations would be good for Mmmuffins, so he agreed and they shook hands on the deal.

Later, while lawyers were completing the legal paperwork, things changed. REC came back and said it wanted to include another location in Manitoba in the agreement: They said they were creating a package for me: the two Toronto locations and Manitoba in the west or nothing. And being the naive kid that I was, I got extremely upset. But we had a deal! I'd already told my partner about my plans for Toronto and that was OK but the town in Manitoba had only about 50,000 people and was a thousand miles away. It was a rural environment and difficult to reach. So I told them that we were just a young chain, and we just wanted to do a few stores at a time. They said no, that's the way it has to be. They had a brand new mall and needed to fill the space.

In the excitement of the offer of the initial two locations, Michael had been somewhat swept away with events. Now he was confronted with a more difficult situation than he had anticipated and felt he should pause to rethink his overall company strategy before reacting to this new offer. How should he make his company grow? How fast? How should he divide his efforts between the two concepts? Now he realized that he should answer these questions before going ahead with any expansion deal.

Specialised Entry Modes for International Businesses

In the following paragraphs, we want to quickly introduce some other specialised entry modes such as turnkey projects, management contracts and contract manufacturing.

Contract Manufacturing

Contract manufacturing reduces the human and financial resources that a company needs to physically produce in a host country by outsourcing the manufacturing process. Many companies like Nike for example produce parts or whole products in Asia. The factories however are not run by Nike itself, they are operated by other companies. This approach makes it possible for firms to focus on what they do best and to focus on their competitive advantages. In the case of Nike, they focus on marketing. The downside is that a company that outsources parts of its value chain also loses control over these parts. If the company that operates the factories for Nike turns out to be involved in a child labour scandal, this would definitely have a bad influence on Nike itself even though Nike has no direct control over what happens within that factory. Turning over control to another company can also lead to quality problems and dependencies. If the employees of an outsourced company decide to strike, Nike will not have many ways to influence the outcome or to lead the strike to a quick ending.

Example of Contract Manufacturing: Pepsi Cola in Iraq

PepsiCo, Inc.

PepsiCo, Inc. was founded in 1965 through the merger of Pepsi-Cola and Frito-Lay. Tropicana was acquired in 1998. In 2001, PepsiCo merged with the Quaker Oats Company, creating the world's fifth-largest food and beverage company, with 15 brands – each generating more than $1 billion in annual retail sales. PepsiCo's success is the result of superior products, high standards of performance, distinctive competitive strategies and the high level of integrity of their people.

PepsiCo, Inc. is one of the world's largest food and beverage companies. The company's principal businesses include Frito-Lay snacks, Pepsi-Cola beverages, Gatorade sports drinks, Tropicana juices and Quaker Foods. [142]

Baghdad Soft Drinks

Baghdad Soft Drinks is an Iraqi soft drinks manufacturer and is majority owned by over 30,000 private shareholders. Thirty-five per cent is controlled by state-owned institutions, and a further 10 per cent stake belonged to Saddam Hussein's son Uday. His stake has been frozen by the Finance Ministry. [143]

Contract Manufacturing between Baghdad Soft Drinks and PepsiCo An Iraqi company that has been selling fake Pepsi Cola for the past 14 years will start manufacturing the genuine article within 2007. [143]

In a deal announced recently, the Iraqi company was awarded a five-year licence as the sole distributor of Pepsi soft drinks in the central region of Iraq. Financial details are not known. "Our market is very promising and it could be one of the best in the world," Mr Jassim said. "The weather gets very hot here, but Iraqis don't drink juices - they prefer soft drinks."

Baghdad Soft Drinks had been bottling Pepsi for several years when the U.S. firm pulled out of Iraq in 1990 with the Gulf War looming. Since then, the company has been bottling and distributing non-brand cola in Pepsi bottles imported from countries such as Turkey and Iran. [143]

Management Contracts

A management contract is an agreement. The agreement is to provide some kind of technical expertise, assistance with the management or other services to a company in another country for a certain period of time. The firm renting out the expertise usually gets compensated in form of a flat fee or they might get compensated with a percentage of generated sales to motivate them.

Management Contracts are not a direct form of exporting. We want to mention them here because the company that rents out expertise can learn a lot about a foreign country and can bring this expertise back to its home country. It can therefore be used as a first step to get to know management practice in a host country and to get in touch with companies from a country that they want to enter. This approach does not inherit any significant risk and is used by British Airways and Air France for example. These two companies send senior managers to airlines from developing countries to consult them in going public or in their general business.

Example of a Management Contract: Virgin Media and BT

Virgin Media

Virgin Media is the UK's leading entertainment and communications company and offers digital TV, broadband, phone and mobile. With its 10 million customers (5m cable, 4.5m mobile, 250,000 virgin.net), Virgin Media is the UK's largest mobile virtual network operator, and the second largest home phone and pay TV provider. [144]

British Telecom

BT is one of the world's leading providers of communications solutions and services operating in 170 countries. Its principal activities include networked IT services, local, national and international telecommunications services, and higher-value broadband and internet products and services. BT consists principally of four lines of business: BT Global Services, Openreach, BT Retail and BT Wholesale. British Telecommunications plc (BT) is a wholly-owned subsidiary of BT Group plc and encompasses virtually all businesses and assets of the BT Group. BT Group plc is listed on stock exchanges in London and New York. [145]

The contract between BT and Virgin Media [146]

Virgin Media has signed a £98m fixed-line voice network management contract with BT to cut its overall communications costs to supply customers. Under the terms of the deal, BT Wholesale will manage the operation and maintenance of Virgin Media's UK fixed-line voice switching network, as well as a number of Virgin Media's existing support contracts with third-party hardware and software suppliers for transmission equipment on its behalf. Virgin Media's fixed-line voice switching network supports around 20% of all landline telephone connections in the UK, said BT. More than 180 Virgin Media employees have transferred to BT Wholesale as part of the agreement.

Paul Weir, managing director of networks for Virgin Media, said, "Our telephony switching network remains an important asset within Virgin Media, and by using BT Wholesale we gain operational cost efficiencies ahead of the network's eventual upgrade to voice over IP technology, whilst keeping guaranteed levels of service for our customers."

Turnkey Projects

Turnkey Projects are more common in the construction business. The concept of a Turnkey Project is that one company fully constructs and equips a facility and then sells it. These projects are usually over a couple years. Common Turnkey Projects are airports and power plants. Very common versions of Turnkey Projects are B-O-T projects. In this case a company designs, builds and operates the facilities for a certain time and then transfers the ownership to another company or a government. In some developing countries, freshwater cleaning facilities or power plants are built by companies from developed countries who also operate these facilities for one or two centuries and then turn them over to the local governments. Within those one or two centuries the developing country can learn how to operate the facilities and then run them by themselves.

Advantages of Turnkey Projects

Turnkey projects are very useful and common in countries where the possibilities of foreign direct investment are limited by regulations from the host government. Turnkey projects can be attractive for some companies when they would not be able to sell their technology otherwise. From a financial point of view, these projects can be attractive since the partner is often a government, whose financial credibility might be higher than those of many other business partners. Since the involvement in the project is limited in time the risk of political instabilities, an economic collapse or nationalisation is limited as well.

Disadvantages of Turnkey Projects

A company entering into a turnkey project faces two main disadvantages. First, the technology and know-how that a company provides for the turnkey project is usually a competitive advantage. When the turnkey project ends, this technology and know-how gets transferred to a competitor or a potential competitor. Many oil refining companies sold their technology to the Gulf countries and now face competition from companies that they helped to setup themselves. Second, the time that the turnkey project lasts for is limited. This can turn out to be a disadvantage if the market turns out to be a major market for the company. A solution to this problem could be to take a minority equity interest in the continuing operations.

Example of a Turnkey Project: Athens International Airport [147]

HOCHTIEF AirPort (HTA) is one of the world's leading private and independent airport investors and managers. Drawing on its long years of experience in financing, developing and operating airports, the company has built up an attractive and well-balanced portfolio of shareholdings. It has stakes in the airports of Athens, Budapest, Düsseldorf, Hamburg, Sydney and Tirana. In 2006, a total of 82.5 million passengers used HTA airports. HTA pursues an approach that is unique in this sector and distinguished by long-term commitment and active management.

The company prepares made-to measure solutions geared to each airport's specific characteristics and circumstances.

Facts and Figures:

Partners in Athens International:	55 percent Greek state
	Airport S.A. > 26.7 percent
	HOCHTIEF AirPort 13.3 percent
	HTAC < 5 percent private investors
Type of privatization:	Public-private partnership with BOOT
	contract; concession duration: 30 years
Entry of HOCHTIEF:	June 11, 1996
Airport opening:	March 28, 2001
Passengers 2006:	15.1 million
Aircraft movements 2006:	190,872
Cargo 2006:	120,177 tons
Sales revenues 2006:	EUR 357.5 million
Airport company personnel 2006:	approx. 700
Personnel of all companies:	approx. 15,000 at the airport 2006

Athens International Airport Eleftherios Venizelos

Athens International Airport – which is named after Eleftherios Venizelos, Greek prime minister in the 1930s – is not only the world's first BOOT project in the airport sector but also an outstanding example of successful public-private partnership. HTA/HTAC have a stake of just over 40 percent in the airport serving the Greek capital, with five percent held by a private investor and 55 percent by the Greek state. The Greek government is drawing up plans for a partial sale of its shares but no date for the IPO has been fixed yet.

Athens International Airport is a great credit to the motherland of the Olympic Games. In October 2007, the airport completed a hat-trick when it received the prestigious OAG Marketing Award for the third time in succession for its work in furthering cooperation with airlines. Airline marketing is one key reason why more and more airlines are including Athens on their flight schedule. In 2007 alone, the airport has acquired twelve new airlines and eleven new destinations in Europe, Asia and America.

A further basis for this airport's success is real estate development within the airport complex. The first business park was completed in 2007, and now a 50,000 square meter large convention and exhibition center is to be constructed on a second site.

Athens Airport completed

After just 51 months, the work on Athens International Airport Eleftherios Venizelos had been completed. After that came five months of trial operations before the airport was opened on March 1, 2001. The general contractor for the turn-key construction project was a consortium led by HOCHTIEF, with its partners ABB and Krantz-TKT. "The airport will be a hub between West and East, between Europe and Asia. It is creating jobs and will have a positive impact on tourism in the region", says Dr. Hans-Peter Keitel, HOCHTIEF CEO.

The four-storey main terminal with its satellites is designed in the first construction phase for a capacity of 16 million passengers a year. By expanding the central handling facilities, this can be increased to an annual volume of 25 million passengers.

At peak periods, some 5,000 people a day were employed on the construction site. 80 percent of the subcontractors, who executed a large proportion of the work, are Greek. The airport is the country's biggest infrastructure project. The fixed price agreed for the contract was around EUR 1.67 billion. For HOCHTIEF, the involvement with Athens International Airport – consisting of design and planning, construction and financing – is far from over. The company is also responsible for operating the new airport. Worldwide, this is the first and so far only example of a successful public-private partnership in the airport market in which construction and operation come from one source. In 1991, the Greek government put the airport out to tender as a B.O.O.T project, standing for "Build – Own – Operate – Transfer". This means that the private company plans and builds a project, acquires a stake in it, then operates it for a contractually agreed length of time before it is transferred to the public authorities.

HOCHTIEF will operate Athens International Airport Eleftherios Venizelos with its partner ABB and the Greek state for a period of 25 years. An operating company, Athens International Aiport S.A. (AIA), has been founded for this purpose. The private partners hold 45 percent of this, the Republic of Greece the remaining 55 percent.

Athens Airport is a milestone for HOCHTIEF on its way to a globally active airport manager. "Involving private partners at an early stage enabled this complex airport project to be realized faster and more cost-efficiently than would have been possible otherwise. We are convinced that public-private partnerships of this kind will become established in Europe and beyond", says Dr. Karl Rönnberg, member of the HOCHTIEF Executive Board.

Foreign Direct Investments

The last few paragraphs described entry modes that do not require many financial resources. One major downside of these strategies is the lack of control over the assets in the foreign country. Another approach to enter a foreign market is through investing in production and distribution facilities. This strategy is called a Foreign Direct Investment Strategy.

A foreign direct investment are funds that a firm transfers to its foreign associate. This transfer can be in the form of a takeover, a joint venture or a subsidiary that got newly set up.

The International Monetary Fund defines an FDI as "an investment that is made to acquire a lasting interest in an enterprise operating in an economy other than that of the investor, the investor's purpose being to have an effective voice in the management of the enterprise."

Foreign direct investment usually gives the firm more control and also increases the potential for higher profits. In most countries, the government defines an investment to be "direct" when a firm acquires more than 10% of a foreign firm. If this is the case, the foreign company is seen as an associate of its "parent" company.

Many governments try to promote products from their own countries. "Buy American", "100% Australian" and "Made in Germany" are examples of related slogans. In countries where the customer has a strong culture to prefer and trust its local products it makes sense to invest into local production facilities. The Australian car manufacturer Holden is a subsidiary of the American GM Corporation. Australians are very proud of their Holden cars and would probably prefer it over many other foreign manufacturers. Many customers also perceive that buying a product that gets manufactured in their own country will come with better support and quicker service. When a Jeep customer in Australia had a problem with his Jeep that the local technicians could not fix, the technicians sent the Jeep to England to get it fixed there. Three month later the customer got his car back. However, the situation has changed in most countries; but the customer's perception might take longer to change.

Foreign direct investments also come with more risks. There is for once the economic risk. In many countries the economy is predictable for the next ten years but in some countries this is not the case. Political risks are as well minimal in western countries, but especially in developing countries the government changes very often and quickly. A change in government is usually accompanied by a change in political decisions and directions. Most companies invest into foreign countries and hope that their investment will amortise over several years or even decades. These companies need to rely on political and governmental conditions to stay the same over a certain period of time.

Exchange rate changes are another risk that companies need to face when investing into foreign production facilities. Since a company cannot change the price of its products every time the exchange rates go up or down, their margin is usually the buffer for exchange rate fluctuations.

Some countries also try to minimise foreign investments into their country by controlling foreign acquisitions or by restricting the repatriation of capital and dividends. On the other hand, some countries try to encourage investments into their country by political risk insurances or by sponsoring investments with cheap credits. This was very common in the 1990s in Russia.

Why do firms go abroad?

In most cases, the reason for a company to engage in a venture to go abroad is to maximise the company's expected returns for their shareholders. A common way to achieve this goal is to lower the firm's costs by producing in a foreign country. Whenever the resources for the firm's products are cheaper in another country or when the labour to produce these products is cheaper overseas, a firm has an incentive to enter a foreign country. The country that can offer cheaper labour and resource prices has a comparative advantage over western European and the U.S. Markets. The first and most influential foreign group of investors were the great trading companies from the Netherlands and Great Britain who produced spices in Asia to ship them to Europe, where these goods where very expensive. Foreign companies usually bring experienced labour, capital and technology with them. The British East India company (1600-1858) was mainly responsible for India's industrialisation. But even until today companies such as General Electric and Alcatel have helped to lift Eastern Europe's countries to western standards. By investing in foreign markets, companies can have a significant influence on the host country and transform its environment. Japanese financial services companies, banana exporting firms in the Caribbean and most mining firms in Africa have been accused of abusing their power to influence political decisions in their favour.

A further incentive to enter another country can be to seek profits in a new market. This is particularly interesting for companies that face declining profits or increased competition in their home market. Foreign markets are especially interesting when the company has a first mover advantage. Firms like Coca-Cola, McDonalds and IBM became global market leaders because they were the first in most markets that produced a product of their kind. These companies almost had the advantages that a monopolist has in terms of setting prices. They also faced small to no competition.

A third incentive to engage in foreign direct investments is to go around tariff barriers. These barriers can prevent a company to export to a market that would be attractive to them if the government did not restrict imports to their country. Some countries such as Brazil, Mexico and Canada strictly regulated the imports for certain products to support local companies. In these countries, the only chance to enter the market can be by investing directly, by building new factories, founding subsidiaries or by acquiring a local company.

Even though most countries do not have high tariff barriers anymore, some companies still invest to protect themselves against future regimes that might raise these barriers again. Toyotas high direct investments in the United States are usually interpreted as a response to the protectionist forces over the U.S. auto industry between 1980 and 1985.

The fourth motive for a company to engage in FDI is to simply dominate another market. This view is shared by some Marxist analysts who say that some companies enter a foreign market just because they want to be present in it. According to them, the decision to enter that market is not based on costs and benefits but on opportunism. In many cases, however, a more realistic interpretation is that firms do sometimes rush into new markets without carefully considering the costs and benefits associated with the market entry. McDonald's for example opened up a new restaurant in Moscow shortly after the Berlin wall came down. This store was probably more of a symbol for the West to enter former communist Russia.

When we put all these motives and reasons for a foreign direct investment together, we get a whole web of perspectives through which managers can see a market entry and from which it can make sense for a firm to engage in a comparatively more risky and capital-intense venture.

There are three important methods of foreign direct investments: A joint venture, acquiring existing facilities (acquisition strategy) and the Greenfield strategy (building new facilities in a foreign country).

The Ground Up strategy

When a company starts a new operation from the ground up, this strategy is called the Ground Up strategy or Greenfield strategy. In this case the company owns 100% of its subsidiary. When a company uses this strategy, it first buys or leases land to build a production facility, hires staff and then launches its production. An example is Mercedes-Benz who built a new assembly plant in Alabama, USA to build its SUV.

The bigger the difference between a home culture and the culture in the foreign country the better it is to utilise the Ground Up Strategy. Even when the company can impose its own rules on the workforce, it might still run into problems. Wal-Mart for example tried to forbid its employees to have romantic relationships with each other and threatened to fire them. Even though local courts ruled that this rule was illegal and therefore could not provide a reason for terminating job contracts, Wal-Mart tried to hold on to the rule as long as possible before being forced to drop it. Disney Land Paris had problems with a painter who painted a Disney Land Hotel in pink before the Management approved the colour. The painter had considered it to be the right colour and had started painting. [1]

Advantages of the Ground Up strategy

- The company can select the construction site that best meets its needs.
- The risk to lose control over technological competences is reduced.
- Tight control that is necessary for global strategic operations can be exercised.
- Location and experience curve economies can be realised.
- Local governments or communities often sponsor companies that want to construct a business on their land because it might create jobs.
- The managers at the new site do not need to deal with old debts.
- The company does not have to deal with inflexible labour unions since the employees get newly hired with new work contracts.
- The company can learn and get used to the new culture at its own speed.

· Managers do not need to deal with cultural differences and resistance that would occur in an acquired company.

Disadvantages of the Ground Up strategy

There are also some disadvantages that managers have to take care of when approaching a new market using the Ground Up Strategy:

· Building up new facilities from scratch takes time.
· The initial investment is very high.
· Problems arising from cultural conflicts are likely.
· The required or desired land could be expensive or not available at all.
· In building new facilities, the company needs to comply with local laws and regulations.
· A new workforce needs to be hired and trained to meet the company's standards.
· Local customers might perceive the company more as a foreign company compared to the approach where the products get sold through an acquired local company or a joint venture.

The Acquisition Strategy

By acquiring another company a firm gains quick control over another firm's assets such as its brand name, its production facilities, technology, distribution networks and its labour force. Buying an established firm is a rapid way to increase a company's presence in a foreign market. Acquisitions can be done to enter a market, to gain competitiveness in terms of size or expertise to eliminate a competitor or to implement a strategy change. The German automobile maker Daimler-Benz bought Chrysler, the American number three in the automobile market, to gain quick access and market share in the U.S. market. Constructing new factories and increasing the marketing efforts in the United States would have taken years if not decades to gain a comparable market share. In this paragraph, we will focus on the advantages and disadvantages of Mergers and Acquisitions that are done to a new market.

Many acquisitions, especially in rapidly globalising industries, get done to preempt a competitor. In order to keep a competitive size and to gain customers in markets that have been formerly governmentally regulated, an acquisition can also be the only choice to stay independent.

Many managers believe that buying another company is less risky than using the Greenfield strategy. An acquired company already has a known stream of cash flows, revenue and brand name. The knowledge, logistic system, as well as other tangible and intangible assets that get acquired with a company reduce the risk of failures that would have been made by starting a new venture. However, despite the advantages that an acquisition has, many acquisitions fail. For detailed reasons, statistics and cases providing insight into why acquisitions fail, please visit the Management Laboratory website.

Advantages of the Acquisition Strategy

- The company that got bought can still generate profit while the acquirer integrates the company into its own.
- By acquiring another company no new capacity gets added to the industry, which is very beneficial in times of overcapacity.
- After a careful consolidation process economies of scale can be used in marketing, distribution and in scouring.
- An acquisition is a very quick way of gaining market share.
- Pre-emptive procedure to avoid to be taken over.

Disadvantages of the Acquisition Strategy

- The acquisition of a company in a foreign market is a very complex process. It requires expertise from M&A specialists, bankers and lawyers.
- By buying another company the acquirer acquires not only the assets but also all of its liabilities. The acquirer is financially responsible for hidden liabilities on the financial side as well as on the managerial side.
- The agreed sum for the acquisition is usually to be paid when the acquisition takes place, which does not allow spreading investments over a certain time such as the Ground Up strategy allows.
- The price for a company is often too high.

Reading: The East India Company[15]

The foundation years

The Company was founded as The Company of Merchants of London Trading into the East Indies [148 p. 9] by a coterie of enterprising and influential businessmen, who obtained the Crown's charter for exclusive permission to trade in the East Indies for a period of fifteen years. The Company had 125 shareholders, and a capital of £72,000. Initially, however, it made little impression on the Dutch control of the spice trade and at first it could not establish a lasting outpost in the East Indies. Eventually, ships belonging to the company arrived in India, docking at Surat, which was established as a trade transit point in 1608. In the next two years, it managed to build its first factory (as the trading posts were known) in the town of Machilipatnam on the Coromandel Coast of the Bay of Bengal. The high profits reported by the Company after landing in India (presumably owing to a reduction in overhead costs effected by the transit points), initially prompted King James I to grant subsidiary licenses to other trading companies in England. But, in 1609, he renewed the charter given to the Company for an indefinite period, including a clause which specified that the charter would cease to be in force if the trade turned unprofitable for three consecutive years.

The Company was led by one Governor and 24 directors who made up the Court of Directors. They were appointed by, and reported to, the Court of Proprietors. The Court of Directors had ten committees reporting to it.

---

[15] The text in this reading is available under the terms of the GNU Free Documentation License. This reading was adapted from its original source.

Picture 1: European Settlements in India from 1498 to 1739

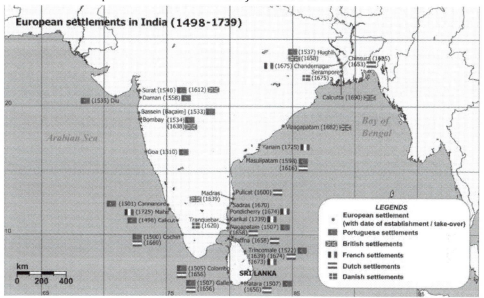

Source: This picture is licensed under the Creative Commons Attribution-ShareAlike 2.5 License

Footholds in India

Traders were frequently engaged in hostilities with their Dutch and Portuguese counterparts in the Indian Ocean. A key event providing the Company with the favour of Mughal emperor Jahangir was their victory over the Portuguese in the Battle of Swally in 1612. Perhaps realizing the futility of waging trade wars in remote seas, the English decided to explore their options for gaining a foothold in mainland India, with official sanction of both countries, and requested the Crown to launch a diplomatic mission. In 1615, Sir Thomas Roe was instructed by James I to visit the Mughal emperor Jahangir (who ruled over most of the subcontinent, along with Afghanistan). The purpose of this mission was to arrange for a commercial treaty which would give the Company exclusive rights to reside and build factories in Surat and other areas. In return, the Company offered to provide to the emperor goods and rarities from the European market. This mission was highly successful and Jahangir sent a letter to the King through Sir Thomas Roe. He wrote:

"Upon which assurance of your royal love I have given my general command to all the kingdoms and ports of my dominions to receive all the merchants of the English nation as the subjects of my friend; that in what place soever they choose

161

to live, they may have free liberty without any restraint; and at what port soever they shall arrive, that neither Portugal nor any other shall dare to molest their quiet; and in what city soever they shall have residence, I have commanded all my governors and captains to give them freedom answerable to their own desires; to sell, buy, and to transport into their country at their pleasure.

For confirmation of our love and friendship, I desire your Majesty to command your merchants to bring in their ships of all sorts of rarities and rich goods fit for my palace; and that you be pleased to send me your royal letters by every opportunity, that I may rejoice in your health and prosperous affairs; that our friendship may be interchanged and eternal." [149 pp. 333-335]

Expansion

The company, under such obvious patronage, soon managed to eclipse the Portuguese Estado da India, which had established bases in Goa, Chittagong and Bombay (which was later ceded to England as part of the dowry of Catherine de Braganza). It managed to create strongholds in Surat (where a factory was built in 1612), Madras (1639), Bombay (1668) and Calcutta (1690). By 1647, the Company had 23 factories, each under the command of a factor or master merchant and governor if so chosen, and 90 employees in India. The major factories became the walled forts of Fort William in Bengal, Fort St George in Madras and the Bombay Castle. In 1634, the Mughal emperor extended his hospitality to the English traders to the region of Bengal (and in 1717 completely waived customs duties for the trade). The company's mainstay businesses were by now in cotton, silk, indigo dye, saltpetre and tea. All the while, it was making inroads into the Dutch monopoly of the spice trade in the Malaccan straits, which the Dutch had acquired by ousting the Portuguese in 1640-41. In 1711, the Company established a trading post in Canton (Guangzhou), China, to trade tea for silver. In 1657, Oliver Cromwell renewed the charter of 1609, and brought about minor changes in the holding of the Company. The status of the Company was further enhanced by the restoration of monarchy in England. By a series of five acts around 1670, King Charles II provisioned it with the rights to autonomous territorial acquisitions, to mint money, to command fortresses and troops and form alliances, to make war and peace, and to exercise both civil and criminal jurisdiction over the acquired areas.

The road to a complete monopoly

Trade monopoly

The prosperity that the employees of the company enjoyed allowed them to return to their country and establish sprawling estates and businesses, and to obtain political power. Consequently, the Company developed for itself a lobby in the English parliament. However, under pressure from ambitious tradesmen and former associates of the Company (pejoratively termed Interlopers by the Company), who wanted to establish private trading firms in India, a deregulating act was passed in 1694. This allowed any English firm to trade with India, unless specifically prohibited by act of parliament, thereby annulling the charter that was in force for almost 100 years. By an act that was passed in 1698, a new "parallel" East India Company (officially titled the English Company Trading to the East Indies) was floated under a state-backed indemnity of £2 million. However, the powerful stockholders of the old company quickly subscribed a sum of £315,000 in the new concern, and dominated the new body. The two companies wrestled with each other for some time, both in England and in India, for a dominant share of the trade. However, it quickly became evident that, in practice, the original Company faced scarcely any measurable competition. Both companies finally merged in 1702, by a tripartite indenture involving them both as well as the state. Under this arrangement, the merged company lent to the Treasury a sum of £3,200,000, in return for exclusive privileges for the next three years, after which the situation was to be reviewed. The amalgamated company became the United Company of Merchants of England Trading to the East Indies.

In the following decades there was a constant see-saw battle between the Company lobby and the parliament. The Company sought a permanent establishment, while the Parliament would not willingly allow it greater autonomy, and so relinquish the opportunity to exploit the Company's profits. In 1712, another act renewed the status of the Company, though the debts were repaid. By 1720, 15% of British imports were from India, almost all passing through the Company, which reasserted the influence of the Company lobby. The license was prolonged until 1766 by yet another act in 1730.

At this time, Britain and France became bitter rivals, and there were frequent skirmishes between them for control of colonial possessions. In 1742, fearing the monetary consequences of a war, the government agreed to extend the deadline for the licensed exclusive trade by the Company in India until 1783, in return for a further loan of £1 million. The skirmishes did escalate to the feared war, and between 1756 and 1763 the Seven Years' War diverted the state's attention towards consolidation and defence of its territorial possessions in Europe and its colonies in North America. The war also took place on Indian soil, between the Company troops and the French forces. Around the same time, Britain surged ahead of its European rivals with the advent of the Industrial Revolution. Demand for Indian commodities was boosted by the need to sustain the troops and the economy during the war, and by the increased availability of raw materials and efficient methods of production. As home to the revolution, Britain experienced higher standards of living, and this spiralling cycle of prosperity, demand and production had a profound influence on overseas trade. The Company became the single largest player in the British global market, and reserved for itself an unassailable position in the decision-making process of the Government. William Pyne notes in his book The Microcosm of London (1808) that:

On the 1st March, 1801, the debts of the East India Company to £5,393,989 their effects to £15,404,736 and their sales increased since February 1793, from £4,988,300 to £7,602,041.

Saltpetre trade

Sir John Banks, a businessman from Kent who negotiated an agreement between the King and the Company, began his career in a syndicate arranging contracts for victualling the navy, an interest he kept up for most of his life. He knew Pepys and John Evelyn and founded a substantial fortune from the Levant and Indian trades. He also became a Director and later, as Governor of the East Indian Company in 1672, he was able to arrange a contract which included a loan of £20,000 and £30,000 worth of saltpetre for the King 'at the price it shall sell by the candle' - that is by auction - where an inch of candle burned and as long as it was alight bidding could continue. The agreement also included with the price 'an allowance of interest which is to be expressed in tallies.' This was something of a breakthrough in royal prerogative because previous requests for the King to buy at the Company's auctions had been turned down as 'not honorable or decent.'[citation needed] Outstanding debts were also agreed and the Company permitted to export 250 tons of saltpetre. Again in 1673, Banks successfully negotiated another contract for 700 tons of saltpetre at £37,000 between the King and the Company. So urgent was the need to supply the armed forces in the United Kingdom, America and elsewhere that the authorities sometimes turned a blind eye on the untaxed sales. One governor of the Company was even reported as saying in 1864 that he would rather have the saltpetre made than the tax on salt. [150]

The basis for the monopoly

Colonial monopoly

Robert Clive, 1st Baron Clive, became the first British Governor of Bengal. The Seven Years' War (1756 – 1763) resulted in the defeat of the French forces and limited French imperial ambitions, also stunting the influence of the industrial revolution in French territories. Robert Clive, the Governor General, led the Company to an astounding victory against Joseph François Dupleix, the commander of the French forces in India, and recaptured Fort St George from the French. The Company took this respite to seize Manila [151] in 1762. By the Treaty of Paris (1763), the French were allowed to maintain their trade posts only in small enclaves in Pondicherry, Mahe, Karikal, Yanam, and Chandernagar without any military presence. Although these small outposts remained French possessions for the next two hundred years, French ambitions on Indian territories were effectively laid to rest, thus eliminating a major source of economic competition for the Company. In contrast, the Company, fresh from a colossal victory, and with the backing of a disciplined and experienced army, was able to assert its interests in the Carnatic from its base at Madras and in Bengal from Calcutta, without facing any further obstacles from other colonial powers.

Military expansion

The Company continued to experience resistance from local rulers during its expansion. Robert Clive led company forces against French-backed Siraj Ud Daulah to victory at the Battle of Plassey in 1757, resulting in the conquest of Bengal. This victory estranged the British and the Mughals, since Siraj had effectively been a Mughal feudatory ally. But the Mughal empire was already on the wane after the demise of Aurangzeb, and was breaking up into pieces and enclaves. After the Battle of Buxar, Shah Alam II, the ruling emperor, gave up the administrative rights over Bengal, Bihar, and Orissa. Clive thus became the first British Governor of Bengal.

Haidar Ali and Tipu Sultan, the legendary rulers of Mysore (in Carnatic), gave a tough time to the British forces. Having sided with the French during the war, the rulers of Mysore continued their struggle against the Company with the four Anglo-Mysore Wars. Mysore finally fell to the Company forces in 1799, with the slaying of Tipu Sultan.

With the gradual weakening of the Maratha empire in the aftermath of the three Anglo-Maratha wars, the British also secured Bombay and the surrounding areas. It was during these campaigns, both against Mysore and the Marathas, that Arthur Wellesley, later Duke of Wellington, first showed the abilities which would lead to victory in the Peninsular War and at the Battle of Waterloo. A particularly notable engagement involving forces under his command was the Battle of Assaye. Thus, the British had secured the entire region of Southern India (with the exception of small enclaves of French and local rulers), Western India and Eastern India.

The last vestiges of local administration were restricted to the northern regions of Delhi, Oudh, Rajputana, and Punjab, where the Company's presence was ever increasing amidst the infighting and dubious offers of protection against each other. Coercive action, threats and diplomacy aided the Company in preventing the local rulers from putting up a united struggle against it. The hundred years from the Battle of Plassey in 1757 to the Sepoy Mutiny of 1857 were a period of consolidation for the Company, which began to function more as a nation and less as a trading concern.

Opium trade

In the eighteenth century, England had a huge trade deficit with Qing Dynasty China and so in 1773, the Company created a British monopoly of opium trading in Bengal. As opium trade was illegal in China, Company ships could not carry opium to China. So the opium produced in Bengal was sold in Calcutta on condition that it be sent to China. [152]

Despite the Chinese ban on opium imports, reaffirmed in 1799, it was smuggled into China from Bengal by traffickers and agency houses averaging 900 tons a year. The proceeds from drug-runners at Lintin were paid into the Company's factory at Canton and by 1825, most of the money needed to buy tea in China was raised by the illegal opium trade. In 1838, with opium smuggling approaching 1400 tons a year, the Chinese imposed a death penalty on opium smuggling and sent a new governor, Lin Zexu to curb smuggling. This finally resulted in the First Opium War, eventually leading to the British seizing Hong Kong and opening of the Chinese market to British drug traffickers.

Financial troubles

Though the Company was becoming increasingly bold and ambitious in putting down resisting states, it was getting clearer day by day that the Company was incapable of governing the vast expanse of the captured territories. The Bengal famine, in which one-third of the local population died, set the alarm bells ringing back home. Military and administrative costs mounted beyond control in British administered regions in Bengal due to the ensuing drop in labor productivity. At the same time, there was commercial stagnation and trade depression throughout Europe following the lull in the post-Industrial Revolution period. The desperate directors of the company attempted to avert bankruptcy by appealing to Parliament for financial help. This led to the passing of the Tea Act in 1773, which gave the Company greater autonomy in running its trade in America. Its monopolistic activities triggered the Boston Tea Party in the Province of Massachusetts Bay, one of the major events leading up to the American Revolution.

Regulating Acts

East India Company Act 1773

By this Act (13 Geo. III, c. 63), the Parliament of Great Britain imposed a series of administrative and economic reforms and by doing so clearly established its sovereignty and ultimate control over the Company. The Act recognized the Company's political functions and clearly established that the "acquisition of sovereignty by the subjects of the Crown is on behalf of the Crown and not in its own right."

Picture 2: The expanded East India House, Leadenhall Street, London

Despite stiff resistance from the East India lobby in parliament, and from the Company's shareholders, the Act was passed. It introduced substantial governmental control, and allowed the land to be formally under the control of the Crown, but leased to the Company at £40,000 for two years. Under this provision, the governor of Bengal Warren Hastings was promoted to the rank of Governor General, having administrative powers over all of British India. It provided that his nomination, though made by a court of directors, should in future be subject to the approval of a Council of Four appointed by the Crown - namely Lt. General John Clavering, George Monson, Richard Barwell and Philip Francis. He was entrusted with the power of peace and war. British judicial personnel would also be sent to India to administer the British legal system. The Governor General and the council would have complete legislative powers. Thus, Warren Hastings became the first Governor-General of Bengal. The company was allowed to maintain its virtual monopoly over trade, in exchange for the biennial sum and an obligation to export a minimum quantity of goods yearly to Britain. The costs of administration were also to be met by the company. These provisions, initially welcomed by the Company, backfired. The Company had an annual burden on its back, and its finances continued steadily to decline. (153 pp. 18- 19, 42, 45)

East India Company Act (Pitt's India Act) 1784

The India Act of 1784 (24 Geo. III, s. 2, c. 25) had two key aspects:

- Relationship to the British Government - the Bill clearly differentiated the political functions of the East India Company from its commercial activities. For its political transactions, the Act directly subordinated the East India Company to the British Government. To accomplish this, the Act created a Board of Commissioners for the Affairs of India usually referred to as the Board of Control. The members of the Board of Control were the Chancellor of the Exchequer, a Secretary of State, and four Privy Councilors, nominated by the King. The Act specified that the Secretary of State, "shall preside at, and be President of the said Board".
- Internal Administration of British India – the Bill laid the foundation of the British centralized bureaucratic administration of India which would reach its peak at the beginning of the twentieth century with the governor-generalship of George Nathaniel Curzon, 1st Baron Curzon.

Pitt's Act was deemed a failure because it was immediately apparent that the boundaries between governmental control and the Company's powers were obscure and highly subject to interpretation. The government also felt obliged to answer humanitarian voices pleading for better treatment of natives in British occupied territories. Edmund Burke, a former East India Company shareholder and diplomat, felt compelled to relieve the situation and introduced before parliament a new Regulating Bill in 1783. The Bill was defeated due to intense lobbying by Company loyalists and accusations of nepotism in the Bill's recommendations for the appointment of councillors.

Act of 1786

This Act (26 Geo. III c. 16) enacted the demand of Lord Cornwallis, that the powers of the Governor-General be enlarged to empower him, in special cases, to override the majority of his Council and act on his own special responsibility. The Act also enabled the offices of the Governor-General and the Commander-in-Chief to be jointly held by the same official.

This Act clearly demarcated borders between the Crown and the Company. After this point, the Company functioned as a regularized subsidiary of the Crown, with greater accountability for its actions and reached a stable stage of expansion and consolidation. Having temporarily achieved a state of truce with the Crown, the Company continued to expand its influence to nearby territories through threats and coercive actions. By the middle of the 19th century, the Company's rule extended across most of India, Burma, Malaya, Singapore and Hong Kong, and a fifth of the world's population was under its trading influence.

Charter Act 1813

The aggressive policies of Lord Wellesley and the Marquis of Hastings led to the Company gaining control of all India, except for the Punjab, Sind and Nepal. The Indian Princes had become vassals of the Company. But the expense of wars leading to the total control of India strained the Company's finances to the breaking point. The Company was forced to petition Parliament for assistance. This was the background to the Charter Act of 1813 (53 Geo. III c. 155) which, among other things:

· asserted the sovereignty of the British Crown over the Indian territories held by the Company;

- renewed the Charter of Company for a further twenty years but,
- deprived the Company of its Indian trade monopoly except for trade in tea and the trade with China;
- required the Company to maintain separate and distinct its commercial and territorial accounts; and,
- opened India to missionaries.

Charter Act 1833

The Industrial Revolution in Britain, and the consequent search for markets, and the rise of laissez-faire economic ideology form the background to this act. The Act:

- removed the Company's remaining trade monopolies and divested it of all its commercial functions;
- renewed for another twenty years the Company's political and administrative authority;
- invested the Board of Control with full power and authority over the Company. As stated by Kapur Professor Sri Ram Sharma, thus, summed up the point: "The President of the Board of Control now became Minister for Indian Affairs";
- carried further the ongoing process of administrative centralization through investing the Governor-General in Council with, full power and authority to superintend and, control the Presidency Governments in all civil and military matters;
- initiated a machinery for the codification of laws;
- provided that no Indian subject of the Company would be debarred from holding any office under the Company by reason of his religion, place of birth, descent or color. However, this remained a dead letter well into the 20th century;
- vested the Island of St Helena in the Crown.

Meanwhile, British influence continued to expand; in 1845, the Danish colony of Tranquebar was sold to Great Britain. The Company had at various stages extended its influence to China, the Philippines, and Java. It had solved its critical lack of the cash needed to buy tea by exporting Indian-grown opium to China. China's efforts to end the trade led to the First Opium War with Britain.

Charter Act 1853

This Act provided that British India would remain under the administration of the Company in trust for the Crown until Parliament should decide otherwise.

Indian Rebellion of 1857

The efforts of the company in administering India emerged as a model for the civil service system in Britain, especially during the 19th century. Deprived of its trade monopoly in 1813, the company wound up as a trading enterprise.

Following the 1857 insurrection, known to the British as the "Great Mutiny" but to Indians as the "First War of Independence", the Company was nationalised by the Government in London to which it lost all its administrative functions and all of its Indian possessions - including its armed forces - were taken over by the Crown.

The Company was still managing the tea trade on behalf of the British government (and supplying Saint Helena). When the East India Stock Dividend Redemption Act came into effect, the Company was dissolved on January 1, 1874. The Times reported, "It accomplished a work such as in the whole history of the human race no other company ever attempted and as such is ever likely to attempt in the years to come.

Case Study: Mannesmann / Vodafone

The following case will outline the acquisition of Mannesmann by Vodafone, a takeover that was conducted to gain a strategic advantage in the future and to beat a competitor that could have been threatening Vodafone's leading position in Europe.

Introducing the Mannesmann AG

Mannesmann was founded 1776 in Germany by Reinhardt Mannesmann. Reinhardt Mannesmann produced rasps in his first factory. His sons developed a method to produce seamless steel tubes which made the company known all over the world. After the Second World War, Mannesmann got broken up by the allies to avoid a too strong concentration of industrial power, but merged again in 1955 because the single businesses were not able to survive by themselves. Mannesmann also started to acquire a range of companies to broaden its portfolio to a company being involved in machine manufacturing, plant construction, and in automobile components.

In 1990, Mannesmann bought the license to build and run a mobile telephone system (Mannesmann D2), which was the first private one in Germany. This business unit was extremely successful, generated high earnings and dominated other business units within a couple of years. [154] In 1999, Mannesmann had 130.860 employees worldwide and a turnover of 23.27 billion Euro. [155]

Introducing Vodafone

In 1982, the British Racal Radio Group successfully purchased a mobile license by auction and started a network with the name Vodafone in 1985. Racal completely separated itself from Vodafone in 1991. From 1993 on, Vodafone started to look for an international partner and found him in Verizon. The newly formed alliance bought the American mobile operator Airtouch in 1999. With Airtouch Vodafone also acquired a minority share of Mannesmann AG. [156]

The Takeover

When the German company Mannesmann AG bought Orange, an English Telecom company, in 1999 for $36 billion U.S. Dollar, [157] it broke a gentleman's agreement [158] between Vodafone's former CEO Chris Gent and Mannesmann's

CEO Klaus Esser. This agreement was about not competing in each other's territories.

By buying the English company Orange, Mannesmann threatened Vodafone. It was only a matter of time until Vodafone would respond to this threat.

One day after Klaus Esser made its plans to acquire Orange public, the London Times reported that Vodafone was planning to take over Mannesmann. [159] At this point Vodafone already held 34 per cent of Mannesmann, the stock price was 144 Euro. On November 7th, 1999, Vodafone made its first offer with a volume of 100 billion Euro offering 43,7 of its own shares, but Mannesmann's Management declined the offer. [159] Until two weeks later the stock price was up to 209,90 billion. Vodafone offered now 53,7 of its own shares for Mannesmann, but the management declined again. Over 1000 Mannesmann employees demonstrated against the planned takeover and Esser promised to restructure the group and to focus more on the telecommunication part "D2".

A potential partnership with AOL Europe and the French telecommunication company Vivendi that could have rescued Mannesmann got rejected by Esser who agreed on the 3rd February to the takeover for 190 billion Euro in Stock. Esser became the Chef Operating Officer (COO) of Vodafone Mannesmann and received 15 million Euro special bonuses by the board of directors and another 15 million two weeks later to resign from its COO position.

In March 2001 the two lawyers Binz and Sorg filed a complaint because of possible infidelity. The Public Attorney's Office started to investigate against Esser and four other former top managers from Mannesmann. The process went on until the end of 2006 and involved high officials from consulting and accounting firms as well as the Deutsche Bank.

Two years after the takeover the last few remaining 4000 Mannesmann stock holders got offered 218 Euro per stock which cost Vodafone about 435 Million Euro [160]. This so called squeeze-out method is legal in Germany since the beginning of 2002. The squeeze-out method allows a majority shareholder to buy out the remaining shareholders for an adequate compensation if he already owns 95 per cent of a company's shares. The advantages for Vodafone were, first, that the remaining shareholders got a financial compensation instead of Vodafone's stocks, second, that the remaining shareholders could not appeal Vodafone's decision, third, that no shareholder's meeting is necessary and fourth, that no further company valuation needs to be conducted [161 p. 141]. After the squeeze-out, the former Mannesmann AG was formally deleted from the commercial register.

Since Vodafone did not have much use for all of the Mannesmann group company's businesses, it was clear that Vodafone would sell parts of it to only keep the telecommunications part (D2, Arcor, Omnitel). The industrial part Atecs was bought by a consortium of Siemens and Bosch for 9,6 billion Euro which sold parts of it later on to other companies. The luxury watches part was sold to the Swiss company Richemont for 2 billion Euro. The business with tubes and pipes was sold to Salzgitter AG for a symbolic price of 0,51 Euro. The tubes business was in deficit under Mannesmann's management. Vodafone also sold the investment in the Italian telecommunications company Infostrada for 11 billion to the energy company Enel and it had to sell the newly acquired company Orange because of cartel regulations for 48 billion to France Telecom. [158]

Business/ Company	Buyer	Price
Actes	Siemens, Bosch	9,6 billion
Luxury watches	Richemont	2 billion
Tupes and pipes business	Slazgitter AG	0,5 Euro
Infostrada	Enel	11 billion
Orange	France Telecom	48 billion
		Total: 71,1 bil.

Fiqure 8 M&A Values

Vodafone paid 180 billion Dollar for Mannesmann in stock which made it the most expensive acquisition in history [162] after the AOL/Time Warner takeover for 150 billion Euro. [163] The total value of the Vodafone group on the stock market, after paying $180billion for Mannesmann in shares, was $365bn (£228bn), making it by far the largest company on the London stock market and the fourth-largest in the world. [158] The newly formed company had 42 million customers after the merger in the year 2000 and 191.6 million in 2006. [164]

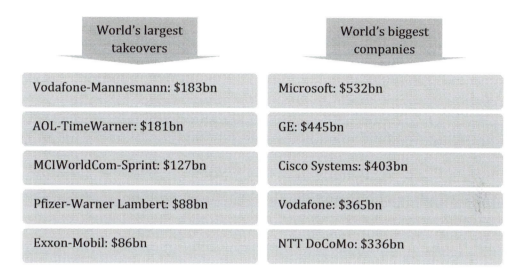

Figure 9 Takeovers

Source: BBC [158]

Conclusions from the Vodafone Mannesmann Merger

This case is relevant because it outlines different aspects of mergers and acquisitions. In a strict sense this case actually describes a takeover, starting out as a merger when Chris Gent offered the Mannesmann management to merge, to have two CEOs and two Headquarters. After Klaus Esser declined the offer a couple times, Chris Gent's goal was to take over the company and to propose a tender offer to the shareholders.

Vodafone should profit from economies of scale and economies of scope after the takeover. Economies of scale should occur because Vodafone can use its existing technique, marketing and administration to distribute its services in Germany. With only a little investment in country-specific services like customer service, it should be possible to reach a big customer base and further potential clients.

Economies of scope should occur because the products and services are related. Producing them in only one company and only one country should lower costs. Also, administration and maintenance fees should decline within a couple a years after the acquisition. Finally, research and development can be done once for the whole company and not twice as it would have been in two separate companies.

The breakoff after the takeover shows that Chris Gent was only interested in the highly profitable telecommunications part. Other branches like the original tubes and pipes business, which were primarily financed by the profitable parts, were sold to other companies. He was willing to pay an extremely high price for only one part of the Mannesmann Group. Recently Vodafone corrected the value of the former Mannesmann company down by 34.9 billion Euro, which shows that even five years later Vodafone is still digesting the enormous costs related to the takeover. But nevertheless Vodafone probably made the right choice. Even though the takeover was expensive, it was also very important for Vodafone's future. Mannesmann and especially its mobile phone operator business was becoming powerful and financially strong. [155] With the planned takeover of Orange, which had been permitted by the cartel authorities, Mannesmann would have had a very strong position in Europe. We even believe that Mannesmann would have competed head to head with Vodafone in Europe very soon. The mobile telecommunication industry has been growing since 1995 in Europe up to over 300 million customers. This number is still expected to grow up to 3,156 million wireless subscribers worldwide in the year 2011, which is partially due to a very high expected growth in the Chinese and African mobile phone industry. [165]

Figure 10 Expected growth of mobile phone users in Million

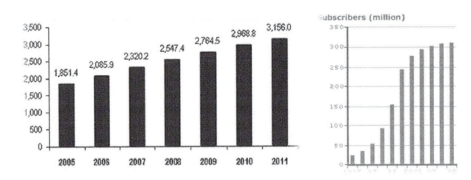

Source: [166]

By buying Mannesmann, Vodafone drew the right consequence to take over a company that could have threatened it in the near future.

Joint Ventures

A Joint Venture (JV) is a contractual agreement that joins together two or more parties for the purpose of executing a particular business undertaking. [167] All parties in the joint venture agree to share the profits and losses of the enterprise. A JV is a legal business that is separate from its parent companies and therefore has its own managers and a board of directors. However, the parent companies own the joint venture to not always equal shares, which can be managed in three different ways. In the first case, both companies owning the joint venture appoint managers to take key positions within the JV. These managers then report back to their parent company. The second possibility is that one of the parents takes primary managerial responsibility. The third and most common way is that independent managers get hired to run the company. The third approach is one that is best for the JV since independent managers are not primarily trying to satisfy the parents but the joint venture. A JV has a broad purpose that distinguishes it from other forms of strategic alliances. It might be formed to join efforts in production or to build a telecommunication network. It will survive as long as its members want it. Sometimes a joint venture with a company from the host market is the only way to enter a market. China for example severely limits the access to its market. To still enjoy the advantages of being present and producing in China, Toyota entered the Chinese market in a joint venture with China's largest automotive manufacturer - China FAW Group Corp. Since 2005, they have been manufacturing Toyota's luxury "Crown" model in Tianjin.

Joint ventures are growing more important and this is why we want to devote the whole following Chapter to this topic of international strategic alliances.

Advantages of Joint Ventures

A local partner often knows the local conditions better then a foreign company. This is especially true for the business and political system, the language and the culture as well as customer and supplier behaviour. A local partner can provide the necessary expertise to survive in a host country. The local partner might also have an interest and influence on the host government. This is beneficial to avoid nationalisation and government interference. Furthermore, financial risks and costs get shared between the partners.

Disadvantages of Joint Ventures

The issue of control over joint ventures is a major problem for joint ventures. The first and main disadvantage is that the company that enters into a joint venture risks losing part of their control over its technology. The partner firms could take advantage of this situation and copy the technology. A way to minimise this risk is to construct the joint venture agreement in a way that the company holds a majority interest in the joint venture which gives the company more control over its technology. However, most potential partners will try to have at least an equal share of control over the joint venture. The second disadvantage is that shared ownership can lead to conflicts. Even if the ownership is shared in equal proportions one partner might still be in a weaker position because of lacking experience. Once the weaker partner makes up for that lack of experience the bargaining power might shift and trigger problems that the remaining partners did not think about before. The third disadvantage is that shared subsidiaries are usually designed for a shared purpose and one purpose only. If for one company the purpose changes and the subsidiary for example becomes part of a new international strategy the company might not have enough control to convince the joint venture partner to follow that strategy. Research has shown that conflicts of interest over goals and strategy are very common in joint ventures. These conflicts tend to be greater when the venture is between firms of different nationalities, and they often end in the dissolution of the venture. [24 p. 496] Careful preparation of joint venture agreements and long term planning can avoid many control issues that arise when the circumstances for the partnering firms change.

Case Study: Milkpak Limited[16]

On January 25, 1987, Syed Babar Ali, chairman, and Syed Yawar Ali[17],1 managing director of Milkpak Limited, prepared for a meeting with a high-level team from Nestle, a multinational food company based in Switzerland. Milkpak Limited, incorporated in 1979, was a pioneer in developing a Pakistani industry for ultrahigh temperature (UHT) milk, a sterilized milk that did not require refrigeration when specially packaged. The increasing popularity of UHT milk caused company sales to increase from 96 million rupees in 1982—Milkpak's first full year of production—to 340 million rupees in 1986. The company was increasingly interested in producing value-added products and was exploring a joint venture with a foreign company.[18]

Company Background

Milkpak was part of a family group of businesses—the Ali Group—that spanned a number of interests. Considered one of Pakistan's leading industrial families, the Ali Group was involved in razor blade and textile manufacture in addition to having holdings in the insurance industry. The group had major investments in the vegetable oil and soap industries and also managed Ford's auto assembly plant prior to 1973, when the government nationalized all of these businesses. Milkpak was founded to create a market for packaging materials produced by Packages Limited, a leading company in the Ali Group. Packages Limited was established in Lahore, Pakistan, in 1956, in collaboration with AB Akerlund & Rausing of Sweden, to convert paper and board into packaging. Packages later integrated backwards into pulp and paper manufacturing. The company supplied packaging materials to a variety of industries and also provided technical assistance to packaging plants in Africa and the Middle East. Packages manufactured its own line of facial tissues

---

[16] Research Associate Afroze A. Mohammed prepared this case under the supervision of Professor John A. Quelch as the basis for class discussion rather than to illustrate either effective or ineffective handling of an administrative situation. This case contains some information from earlier cases on Milkpak prepared by the Lahore University of Management Sciences.

[17] Yawar Ali was Babar Ali's nephew.
[18] Exchange rate in 1986: Rs. 16.65 = $1.00.

and other consumer products. In 1986, Packages' total sales were approximately Rs. 633 million.

Milkpak was established following a 1976 review of the use of Packages' equipment. The Tetra Laminator, a machine designed for making packaging material for long-life milk, was used very infrequently. Packages purchased the Tetra Laminator machine in 1967 from Tetra Pak of Sweden, a company affiliated with Akerlund & Rausing. The Tetra Pak aseptic system[19] was developed to package UHT milk. The UHT process heated milk at temperatures of 130–150 degrees centigrade for 2–3 seconds. Milk thus sterilized had a shelf life of up to three months without refrigeration when packaged in Tetra Pak containers. The Tetra Pak system had special advantages for developing countries that lacked extensive refrigeration and distribution systems. Some of the packages were in the shape of tetrahedrons (a four-faced pyramid); rectangular packages that required heavier and more expensive paper were also available.

Packages found that there was one milk plant in Pakistan, at the time inoperative, designed to produce sterilized milk. The company leased the plant, with a capacity of 17,500 liters of milk per day, as a pilot project to test the market for UHT milk. Packages hoped that a successful pilot project would encourage entrepreneurs to produce UHT milk, thereby increasing the demand for Tetra Pak packaging. To implement the project, a number of challenges were surmounted, including developing a low-cost, locally produced paper for packaging and securing reliable sources of milk supply. The pilot project was deemed a success in 1978 when, with limited promotional efforts, sales reached plant capacity.

Milkpak was incorporated in January 1979 after Packages decided to invest in a 150,000 liters/day UHT milk plant, at a cost of Rs. 90 million. Financing for the new company was obtained from Tetra Pak; Danish Turnkey Dairies, the equipment supplier; and several development agencies, including the International Finance Corporation and the German Development Institute.

---

[19] An aseptic system is free from pathogenic organisms.

Exhibit 23[20] Ownership Share of Milkpak

Investor	Ownership Share
Ali family	15.7%
Packages Limited	7.1
IGI[a]	5.7
International Finance Corporation	5.7
Tetra Pak[b]	8.6
DEG[c]	5.7
DTD[d]	2.9
IFU[e]	2.9
Public shareholders	45.7%

Milkpak started commercial production of UHT milk in its new plant in November 1981.

Exhibit 24[21] Milkpak Profit-and-Loss Statements: 1981-1986

	1986	1985	1984	1983	1982	1981 (2 months)
Net sales	340,343,535	251,835,221	214,662,630	137,310,716	96,129,181	9,409,358
Cost of goods sold	296,417,357	223,485,654	185,175,145	114,742,655	85,894,230	9,986,726
Trading profit	43,926,178	28,349,567	29,487,485	22,568,061	10,234,951	(577,368)
Selling, administrative, and general expenses	30,294,796	17,980,055	14,959,910	10,723,215	8,731,245	1,413,890
Operating profit/(loss)[a]	13,631,382	10,369,512	14,527,575	11,844,846	1,503,706	(1,991,258)
Other income	1,043,295	970,458	773,190	342,738	342,021	1,194,391
	14,674,677	11,339,970	15,300,765	12,187,584	1,845,727	(796,867)
Financial charges	7,495,788	5,258,607	5,828,054	5,713,972	6,868,285	900,448
Workers' participation fund	361,500	355,970	546,389	414,430	--	
	7,857,288	5,614,577	6,374,443	6,128,402	6,868,285	900,448
Profit before taxation	6,817,389	5,725,393	8,926,322	6,059,182	(5,022,558)	(1,697,315)
Provision for taxation	3,045,000	1,603,000	4,535,000	--	--	--
	3,772,389	4,122,393	4,391,322	6,059,182	(5,022,558)	(1,697,315)

[20] Source: Company records.

a International General Insurance Company, 99% owned by the Ali family.

b The Swedish manufacturer of the equipment used to make materials for the nonrefrigerated milk containers.

c The German Development Institute, a foreign aid and development institution.

d Danish Turnkey Dairies, Limited, Milkpak's equipment supplier and the provider of Milkpak's specialized extension services to Pakistani dairy farmers.

e Industrial Fund for Developing Countries, Denmark.

[21] Source: Company records.

a The decline in operating profit as a percentage of net sales in 1985 and 1986 was primarily due to switching to an aluminum foil packaging paper that improved the shelf life of Milkpak brand milk, starting a new fruit juice plant, and increases in sales promotion expenses.

By 1987, Milkpak's product line had expanded from UHT milk to include fruit juices and other dairy products, though UHT milk still accounted for an estimated 85% of company sales. In 1984, Milkpak started marketing the Frost line of fruit juices, introduced a few years earlier by Packages. Frost juices were premixed, in contrast to existing juices on the market that were available in concentrate form.

Milkpak bought the Frost brand name and equipment from Packages, and in 1986 fruit juices accounted for 9% of Milkpak's sales. Additional products included butter, introduced in 1985. In 1986, the company launched a sterilized cream product, "balai," and also a cooking oil, "Desi Ghee." These products were sold under the brand name Milkpak.

Pakistan

Pakistan was founded in 1947, when British India was partitioned into two nation states. Pakistan, established as a Muslim country, initially had two geographically separate sections on either side of India. In 1971, the eastern wing of Pakistan separated to form Bangladesh. The western section, which remained Pakistan, had Urdu as its national language, with English widely spoken. By 1986, Pakistan had a population of over 90 million. Pakistan's GNP per capita was $380, although the country had large income disparities. *Exhibit 25* provides basic social and economic data about Pakistan. [168]

Exhibit 25[22] Pakistan Basic Country Data

Area: 803,940 sq. km.

Agricultural land (1983):   254,900 sq. km.

GNP per capita (1984): $380

Energy consumption per capita (1983):   179 kg. of oil equivalent

Population (1984):   93.3 million

Urban population (percentage of total):   30.1

Projected population in 2000:   143 million

Population density (1984):   116.0 per sq. km.

Population density of agricultural land (1984):   365.0 per sq. km.

Population growth rate (1970-84):   3.1%

Urban population growth rate (1970-84):   4.6%

Crude birthrate (1984):   41 per thousand

Crude death rate (1984):   11 per thousand

Life expectancy at birth (1984):   50.6 years

Infant mortality (1984):   116.2 per thousand

Access to safe water (1981):   34.6% of population
    Urban: 72.0
    Rural: 20.0

Population per physician (1981):   3,190

Average size of household (1979):   6.7

Secondary school enrollment (1983):   15%

Adult literacy (1979):   24%

Labor force (1984):   26.4 million

Labor participation rate (1983):   28.3%

Percentage of income received by:
    highest 5% of households (1970):   17.8
    highest 20% of households (1970):   41.8
    lowest 20% of households (1970):   8
    lowest 40% of households (1970):   20.2

---

[22] Source: Adapted from Pakistan and the World Bank, Partners in Progress (1986).
a Absolute poverty income level is the level below which a minimal nutritionally adequate diet plus essential
non-food requirements is not affordable.
b Rural relative poverty income level is one-third of average per capita personal income of the country. Urban
level is derived from the rural level with adjustment for higher cost of living in urban areas.
c Percentage of population (urban and rural) who are the "absolute poor."

In the 1980s, Pakistan had political and economic policies that promoted the role of private enterprise in the country's economy. This climate was in contrast to that prevailing from 1972 to 1977 when the government was concerned about the high concentration of industrial ownership and nationalized a number of businesses. In the mid-1980s, the rate of growth of manufacturing output was 9.1% per year, while agricultural output grew at 4.6% per year; from 1972 to 1977, these sectors

had grown each year at only 5.2% and 2%, respectively. [169 p. 115] Policy initiatives made in the 1980s offered safeguards against nationalization and sought to ensure the safety of investments.

While the overall climate for private investment was favorable, businesses had to obtain a variety of government licenses and approvals before undertaking or expanding projects. These approvals differed according to a project's source of funds and specific characteristics. The government's permission for a project would address issues such as the amount of investment allowed, procedures governing repatriation of capital and profits, the amount of raw materials that could be imported, and the location of the industrial establishment. In practice, obtaining these approvals could result in project delays, although the Pakistani government was making efforts to facilitate the process.

The Pakistani Dairy Industry

Fresh milk was traditionally supplied to urban consumers directly from farms on a daily basis. [170] Consumers obtained milk (1) directly from farmers or dairy colonies (these sources were sometimes referred to as peri-urban producers) that kept buffalos in or near the towns, and (2) from milkmen who purchased milk from farmers. Milkmen would travel the countryside by bicycle, collect milk in 40-liter cans, and then sell it to contractors, who put ice in the milk and then transported it into the city. The milk was then sold to consumers at their homes and through retail milk shops, which did not have refrigeration facilities. The entire process, from milking the buffalos to selling the milk in the city, took place each morning. While the system delivered fresh milk to consumers each day, it had drawbacks. In particular, adulteration of milk with impure water occurred at various stages in the distribution chain. In addition, the absence of a refrigerated distribution infrastructure led to milk spoilage and waste.

The problems of transporting and distributing milk resulted in shortages in major urban centers — Milkpak's target market. Shortages were exacerbated by the marked seasonality in production and consumption of milk. Milk consumption peaked during the summer. In contrast, milk production was highest during the winter months of December-March, called the "flush" season, and lowest during the "lean" season from May to August. Lower production during the summer was caused by hot weather and decreased availability of fodder. As a result of both of these factors, the Pakistani government adopted liberal policies towards the import of milk products. (Exhibit 26 provides data on Pakistani milk production and dairy imports.)

Exhibit 26[23] Milk Production and Dairy Imports, 1975-1976 to 1985-1986

Year	Estimated Milk Production (000 tons)	Dairy Imports		Imports/Production (percent)
		Value (million Rs.)	Milk Equivalent (000 tons)	
1975–76	8,348	313.0	329.2	3.94
1976–77	8,524	251.0	165.8	1.94
1977–78	8,704	391.1	448.5	5.15
1978–79	8,888	321.6	237.0	2.67
1979–80	9,075	481.9	420.4	4.63
1980–81	9,267	552.3	352.8	3.81
1981–82	9,462	522.6	275.8	2.91
1982–83	9,662	736.8	357.4	3.70
1983–84	10,242	802.1	397.4	3.88
1984–85	10,856	712.0	315.6	2.91
1985–86	11,508	779.2	282.4	2.45

Milk powder was a particularly important dairy import. Milk powder, mixed with water to make fluid milk, had an established place in the Pakistani market, especially in Karachi, where fresh milk supplies were insufficient to meet demand as a result of increases in population. In 1986, about 30% of the demand for fluid milk supplies in Karachi was met by milk powder. Demand for milk powder was met primarily by imports, which averaged 20,000–30,000 tons annually. Powder was imported both as a branded product, in tins, and also in bulk (25 kilogram bags). Bulk supplies were repackaged by retailers in 11/2 kg[24] plastic bags. Branded milk powders were typically bought by higher-income consumers while the repackaged bulk supplies were purchased by lower- and middle income consumers.

---

[23] Pakistan Economic Survey Data; imports data from Federal Bureau of Statistics. Adapted from Table 4.2 in Pakistan's Dairy Industry: Issues and Policy Alternatives.
[24] There are 1,000 kilograms in a metric ton.

Efforts had also been made to establish an indigenous local milk processing industry. Packages' decision to invest in Milkpak was made in spite of a history of failed investments in the milk processing industry. During the 1960s and 1970s, Pakistani entrepreneurs established 23 plants in the dairy processing field, including several plants for milk pasteurization. The failure of at least 15 of this "first generation" of dairy processing plants was attributed to poor management, difficulties in obtaining fresh milk supplies, and the lack of an extensive refrigerated distribution infrastructure.

Milk Collection

To ensure a reliable and high-quality supply of milk, especially during the lean season, Milkpak focused attention on developing a system for milk collection and agricultural extension. Milk collection centers were established in areas considered rich in milk production. The company taught farmers scientific techniques of livestock care and breeding, provided veterinary services, and made available high-yielding fodder seed and cattle feed. Milk was supplied to the company by traditional milk contractors who bought milk from farmers. In addition, Milkpak helped establish village cooperatives and, through them, received milk directly from farmers.

During the flush season, Milkpak often had to refuse milk supplies. Milkpak's management visited dairies in India, including Nestle's plant, to gain an understanding of how other dairies in a similar environment addressed problems of seasonality.

UHT Milk Processing

Processed milk was required by law to contain 3.5% butterfat and 8.9% solids not fat (SNF). Fresh milk usually had a higher fat content and a lower level of solids than required. As a result, before being heated to 130–150 degrees centigrade, the milk was decreamed to reduce the fat content.

To raise the SNF level, skimmed milk powder and water were added. When there was a shortage of fresh milk, milk powder could be added to increase milk production volumes, although, at prevailing

prices for imported milk powder, it was rarely economical to do so. The technology for manufacturing UHT milk was considered expensive, with processing costs accounting for about 25% of total product costs. (Exhibit 27 reports estimates of UHT processing costs, obtained from different manufacturers in the industry.) Packaging materials, which were heavily taxed, accounted for another 26% of Milkpak's production cost. [170 p. 16]

Exhibit 27[25] UHT Milk Production Costs

Cost Item	Rs./Liter
Raw milk[a]	2.66
Value of cream separated[b]	(0.45)
Net cost of raw milk	2.21
Conversion to 1 liter volume at 3.5% butter fat	2.28
Skimmed milk powder[c]	0.72
Processing cost[d]	1.72
Packaging cost	1.77
Transportation cost	0.08
Market returns/replacement[e]	0.20
Subtotal	6.77
Processor's margin	0.04
Distributor's margin	0.19
Retailer's margin	0.50
Subtotal	0.73
Retail price[f]	7.50

UHT Milk Marketing

Positioning

A major challenge facing the company was to introduce urban consumers to the idea of long-life milk. Consumers were concerned that sterilized milk contained preservatives or was somehow not genuine because, unlike fresh milk, the Milkpak brand contained no cream. In one early promotional campaign, households were given two samples of Milkpak, one for immediate consumption and the other to be consumed four days later; the goal was to demonstrate that while the milk remained packaged it did not require refrigeration. Milkpak was positioned as a pure

---

[25] Source: International Consulting Division, Chemonics. Adapted from Table 2.4 in Pakistan's Dairy Industry: Issues and Policy Alternatives (1989).
a   Price of milk at 5% butterfat and 7% solid not fats.
b   Cream (50% fat) valued at Rs. 15 per kilogram.
c   Adding 19 grams of skimmed milk powder @ Rs. 38/kg.
d   Includes depreciation and financial charges.
e   Market returns are assumed to be 3%.
f   Retail UHT milk price in Lahore zone. The price in other areas was Rs. 8/liter.

dairy product, processed in a scientific, hygienic way, and consistent in quality throughout the year.

(Exhibit 28 and Exhibit 29 show print advertisements for Milkpak brand UHT milk and butter. Sales promotion and advertising expenses for Milkpak are summarized in Exhibit 30.)

Exhibit 28 Print Advertisement for Milkpak Brand UHT Milk

Translation
Top Lines: Fresh, pure Milkpak milk——the best for the whole family.
Bottom Line: A product of Milkpak dairy. Pure, delicious, and fresh.

Exhibit 29 Print Advertisement for Milkpak Brand Butter

Translation
Top Lines: Prepared from fresh and pure milk. Milkpak butter——the best for the whole family.
Bottom Line: A product of Milkpak dairy. Pure, delicious, and fresh.

Exhibit 30[26] Milkpak Sales Promotion and Advertising Expenses

1981	778,540[a]	8.2% of sales
1982	1,517,576	1.6
1983	1,158,329	0.8
1984	900,204	0.4
1985	1,728,077	0.7
1986	8,283,452[b]	2.4

Milkpak's heavy users were "modern housewives," who were concerned about both convenience and product quality. Another target market was lower-income consumers, who were often sold relatively cheap adulterated milk by the traditional milkmen; Milkpak provided a higherquality milk than they had purchased before. (Exhibit 31 presents the results of a consumer survey sponsored by Milkpak.)

Exhibit 31[27] Results of 1986 Milkpak Survey of Middle/High Income r

- 65% of respondents used more than one source of milk (e.g., UHT milk, fresh milk, powdered milk).

- In Karachi, 9% of respondents bought UHT milk; in Lahore, 25% bought UHT milk.

- 40% of respondents had no brand preference in purchasing UHT milk, while 35% preferred Milkpak.

- Respondents' prompted recall of the Milkpak brand name was 86%. Unprompted recall was 29%.

- 56% of UHT milk purchasers bought it in general stores, 25% in bakeries, and 16% in shops that were combined general stores/bakeries.

- 58% of respondents purchased UHT milk on a daily basis; 11% bought it three times a week; 18% purchased it twice a week; 13% purchased it less frequently.

- Respondents who did not purchase UHT milk cited the following reasons: it was too expensive (18%); they thought chemicals were added to the milk (12%); they were used to fresh milk (11%); UHT milk contained no cream (10%).

- Consumers purchased family milk powder for several reasons: to feed children (40%); to make the following foods: tea (16%), desserts (11%), yoghurt (11%), drinks made from milk (10%); and for drinking (11%).

- Respondents purchased milk powder from general stores (60%), combined general/medical stores (24%), and bakeries (10%).

- 74% of respondents purchased milk powder once a month; 23% bought it twice a month; only 3% purchased powdered milk weekly.

---

[26] Source: Company records.

a   Sales promotion and advertising expenses of Rs. 778,540 were incurred in 1981, but were written off in three equal yearly instalments in 1982, 1983, and 1984.

b   Increase in sales promotion expenses was required to launch new products and sustain market share.

[27] Company Records

Packaging

Milkpak brand UHT milk was initially sold in tetrahedron shaped containers, in sizes of 1/2 liter and 1/5 liter. In 1984, a one-liter rectangular-shaped "brickpak" was introduced. The more conventionally shaped brickpak eliminated the need for special crates required to store tetra paks, but used more packaging material. In 1986, a quarter-liter brickpak was introduced.

Pricing

Table 2 shows the 1986 retail prices for Milkpak and other types of milk in two major cities in Pakistan. Milkpak competed with the traditional milk distribution system that supplied fresh, or "raw," milk to consumers each day. Milk powder competed with Milkpak as a convenience product.

Tabelle 2[28] Comparative Retail Prices of UHT Milk, Raw Milk, and Dried Milk Powder

City	Raw Milk		Whole Milk Powder[b]		UHT Milk
	Peri-Urban Producer	Milk Shop[a]	Tinned	Polythene Bags	
Lahore	5.00–6.00	4.50–5.50	7.50	6.00	7.50
Karachi	5.50–7.00	5.00–6.50	6.88	5.50	8.00

Distribution

A key success factor in Milkpak's rapid growth was the expansion of its distribution network. In 1981, there were an estimated 1,000 retail outlets selling Milkpak; by 1986, the number had grown to 13,000. Milkpak was sold in grocery stores, bakeries, general stores, and supermarkets.

The company had sales offices in Karachi, Lahore, and Islamabad, and had a nationwide network of distributors in all the major cities and towns. For Milkpak brand milk, the margin to the distributor was between 0.2 and 0.25 rupees per liter, depending on the shipping distance. The retail margin was 0.52 rupees per liter. The UHT business was viewed as similar to the soft drink business, with high turnover and low margins, requiring flexibility and fast decision making.

---

[28] Source: Adapted from Table 2.5 in Pakistan's Dairy Industry: Issues and Policy Alternatives (1986).
aIn general, the quality of milk sold by milk shops was poorer than that sold by peri-urban producers.
bIn liquid milk equivalent terms, assuming a dried milk to liquid conversion ratio of 1:8.

Evolution of the UHT Milk Industry

Milkpak's success in developing a market for UHT milk spurred the entry of several other companies. By the end of 1986, eight plants owned by different companies could manufacture UHT milk. Total sales of UHT milk grew from 11.25 million liters in 1981 to approximately 80 million in 1986. [170 p. 12] In 1986, Milkpak estimated that its share of the market was over 50%. Milkpak had a reputation for consistent, high quality, both with consumers and the trade. Some of Milkpak's early competitors were short-lived. Milkpure and Purabrand, which entered the market in 1983, competed with Milkpak by offering consumer and trade promotions such as free tea bags and raffles for free air tickets. Milkpak did not offer similar promotions in response; management felt that profit margins on UHT milk did not allow such marketing investments. Both companies had financial problems and went out of business by the end of 1985.

Other more stable competitors included Milko, the UHT plant originally leased by Packages to test the market for UHT milk. Milko returned to its original owners after Milkpak's founding. By 1986, Milko had an estimated 10% share of the market. Pakistan Dairies, the country's first producer of cheese, started manufacturing UHT milk in 1983. Because of its other dairy products, Pakistan Dairies had an extensive and effective system for milk collection and was regarded as a high- quality producer. In 1986, the company's share of the market was approximately 18%–20%. A new competitor, Chaudhuri Dairies, entered the market in June 1986 and captured a share of 15% by year end. Chaudhuri introduced its brand Haleeb in rectangular brickpak packaging, which was more convenient to store and was considered a competitive advantage.

While the sales of UHT milk grew rapidly, they still constituted a relatively small share of total consumption. It was estimated that by 1987, UHT accounted for approximately 2% of the milk consumed in Pakistan's urban areas.

The emergence of an industry to process UHT milk was fostered by government policy, notably duty exemptions on the import of machinery for dairy plants and the provision of low cost financing by government agencies. The government had sanctioned a number of additional plants that would be brought on line in coming years, and there was, therefore, concern that the industry would have substantial overcapacity. [170 p. 19]

Strategic Options for Growth

As Milkpak reviewed its growth options, management increasingly saw the development of a milk powder plant as a necessity. First, a powder plant would help smooth the seasonal mismatch between the supply of and demand for milk. During the summer (the time of peak demand), milk powder would be combined with liquid milk to extend the supplies of UHT milk. The growth potential for UHT milk had been limited by seasonality; Milkpak's marketing managers were reluctant to promote UHT milk heavily during the flush season because they felt they were creating demand that could not be satisfied in the lean season. While Milkpak's managers were very committed to increasing UHT milk sales, they knew that the UHT business was inherently a high volume, low margin business. As a result, the company wanted to explore the possibility of producing other value-added foods, such as milk powder, cereal, and infant formula, among other products.

In addition to using milk powder as an ingredient in UHT milk, Milkpak could sell milk powder, which competed with UHT milk, as a convenience product. In 1986, 25,002 tons of milk powder, with a value of Rs. 406 million, were imported. Only two domestic companies manufactured milk powder, one of which produced solely for the military. The other company, Noon Ltd., established with the technical assistance of Cow & Gate, a U.K company, had an output of 600 tons/year. The Pakistan Dairy Association, chaired by Yawar Ali, argued that the government's low tariffs on milk powder imports (which historically had been subsidized by European producers) impeded the development of a domestic dairy industry. In 1986, the government imposed a 16% tax on imports of milk powder, which improved the viability of domestic production.

About 20% of milk powder imports were branded. The major brands, with estimated market shares, were NIDO, produced by Nestle (24% market share); Red Cow, manufactured by Cow & Gate (25% of market); and Safety, manufactured by Friesland—of the Netherlands—(24% market share.) NIDO's prices were the highest (Rs. 107 per 1800 gram tin), followed by Red Cow (Rs. 92–102/tin) and Safety (Rs. 93–97/tin.) The demand for branded milk powder was forecast to increase to 18,000 tons/year by 1996.

Milkpak's management had to decide whether to acquire foreign technology and management assistance to develop its own plant. Alternatively, Milkpak considered the possibility of finding a foreign joint venture partner.

Independent Study

Milkpak prepared a feasibility study for a milk powder plant. Exhibit 32 provides a summary of the project costs, financing sources, and projected profits. Milkpak estimated that by the third year of operation the plant would produce 2,400 tons of milk powder. A locally manufactured product could be competitively priced relative to imports. In addition, a Milkpak plant would use buffalo milk, a familiar taste for local consumers. A study of the milk powder market commissioned by Milkpak recommended that Milkpak produce a branded product to capitalize on Milkpak's name and reputation. In addition to producing milk powder, the plant would also manufacture infant formula, butter oil, and butter.

Milkpak expected to hire an experienced expatriate production manager. While Milkpak executives thought it was feasible for the company to develop a powder plant without a joint venture partner, they were concerned about the technical difficulties of doing so. For example, they felt that producing products such as infant formula required technical knowledge and expertise that the company did not have.

Exhibit 32[29] Milkpak Limited Milk Powder Plant Financial Feasibility Analysis

	Rs. '000

1. Cost of Project and Sources of Finance

1.1 Cost of Project

Building	2,640
Plant and machinery (including construction)	37,245
Trial run cost and interest during construction	3,100
Contingencies	4,515
	47,500
Working capital	7,500
	55,000

	Foreign Currency	Local Currency	Total
1.2 Sources of Finance			
Issue of preferential shares (one for every three shares)	—	11,667	11,667
Loan sanctioned by Agricultural Development Bank of Pakistan	16,000	2,000	18,000
New loan required	15,000	5,000	20,000
Bank overdraft	—	5,333	5,333
	31,000	24,000	55,000

	First Year	Second Year	Third Year
2. Profit and Loss Projections			
Sales 67,357	104,703	137,860	
Cost of sales	57,928	86,798	111,407
Operating profit	9,429	17,905	26,453
Financial cost/tax etc.	6,259	6,024	12,140
Net Profit	3,170	11,881	14,313
3. Payback period is three years and two months.			
4. Additional sales of UHT milk from increased availability of milk supplies as a result of project.	2,985	3,506	4,298

Joint Venture Partners

A joint venture partner could provide both the necessary technology and a reputable brand name that could be attached to locally manufactured, value-added products. Milkpak's managers debated the advantages and drawbacks of conduct-

---

[29] Company records.

ing a joint venture. Some thought Milkpak should seek out a joint venture partner that currently exported branded products to Pakistan and already had some brand recognition in Pakistan. Others were concerned that a company with established brands would expect high royalties that would leave too little profit for Milkpak to warrant the investment risk.

Another concern was that a large multinational joint venture partner might dominate Milkpak. Chairman Babar Ali, however, felt very comfortable with the prospect of a joint venture; Packages Limited, where he had worked for much of his career, was itself a joint venture.

A major challenge was to identify appropriate joint venture partners and find ways to approach them. Danish Turnkey Dairies and Tetra Pak, companies Milkpak and Packages already had ties with, could help in identifying and providing introductions to potential joint venture partners. As a result, Friesland and Nestle emerged as particularly interesting prospects for a joint venture partnership.

Friesland

Friesland, established in 1913 as the "Cooperative Condensed Milkfactory Friesland," was founded by farmers in the Friesland province of Holland. Over 12,000 Dutch farmers supplied milk for the production of a variety of dairy products, including condensed and powdered milk and infant foods. In 1986, Friesland's net sales were 1,807 million guilders.[30]

Friesland's products were sold in 130 countries, primarily through exports. Friesland exported Safety brand milk powder and Omela brand condensed milk to Pakistan. The company also operated some manufacturing facilities and dairies overseas, usually in partnership with a local company. These included manufacturing plants in Guam, Indonesia, Lebanon, Malaysia, Nigeria, Taiwan, Thailand, Saudi Arabia, and Yemen. Friesland provided technical assistance to its affiliated companies as well as management assistance on a contract basis.

Nestle S.A.

Nestle was founded in 1867 by Henri Nestle, a chemist who developed the first milkbased food for babies. In 1905, the company merged with the Anglo-Swiss Condensed Milk Company, a former competitor. From a base in dairy products, Nestle's product line grew to encompass chocolate and confectionery, instant and

---

[30] Exchange rate in 1986: 2.45 Guilders = $1.00.

roasted coffee, culinary products, frozen foods, and instant drinks. By 1986, Nestle's consolidated sales were 38,050 million francs.[31]

Early in its development, Nestle established production facilities outside of Switzerland. By 1986, Nestle had plants in 60 countries. In determining whether to set up production facilities in a particular country, the company considered several factors, including the availability of raw materials, the overall economic climate, and consumer tastes and purchasing power. Nestle's approach to foreign operations was summarized as follows: "The Company is guided in this respect by long-term goals and not by short-term objectives. It is essential for Nestle that an industrial operation be in the reciprocal and lasting interests of both the Company and the host country." [171 p. 10]

A hallmark of Nestle was decentralization, which enabled the group's overseas subsidiaries to develop their own identity and the flexibility to respond to local market conditions. At the same time, Nestle provided research, development, and technical assistance to these subsidiaries. This assistance could be used, for example, to develop products suited to local tastes and to improve the productivity of land and livestock.

Nestle in Pakistan

Since 1974, Nestle products had been imported and sold by the Burque Corporation, a small Pakistani distributor. In 1975, Burque decided to introduce Nestle's NIDO brand of powdered milk, which accounted for an increasing share of Nestle sales in Pakistan. Nestle products were supported by an intensive distribution network and were also heavily advertised ontelevision.

In 1983, Nestle stationed a marketing advisor, Erwin Wermelinger, in Pakistan. Wermelinger's role was to investigate investment opportunities in addition to providing assistance to Nestle's distributor. During the mid-1980s, Nestle staff conducted a tour of the Punjab region of Pakistan to assess the potential for collecting milk to be used in local production of Nestle products.

---

[31]Exchange rate in 1986: 1.80 Swiss Francs = $1.00.

Joint Venture Negotiations

Discussions with Nestle

Milkpak's management was aware of Nestle's growing interest in the Pakistani market, as indicated by Wermelinger's presence in Pakistan. One of Milkpak's managers, formerly with Packages, knew Wermelinger from an earlier posting in Tanzania. As a result, there was an informal channel of communication between the two companies, which Milkpak viewed as a means of keeping Nestle apprised of Milkpak's progress.

Milkpak approached Nestle's senior management in 1986, when Babar Ali visited Nestle's headquarters in Switzerland. During these conversations, Ali received the impression that Nestle would want majority ownership in a joint venture and might also require sizable royalties and technical fees. In addition, Ali was concerned that Nestle's attitude toward Milkpak seemed overbearing.

Discussions with Friesland

Milkpak first approached Friesland in November 1985, through a mutual contact. Several factors made Friesland an attractive candidate for a joint venture, including extensive experience in the dairy industry and an established position in the Pakistani milk powder market. Milkpak's management also felt that a company of Friesland's size would be more responsive to Milkpak's concerns than a larger multinational.

An initial meeting between Babar Ali and a Friesland marketing director was followed by the visit of a three-member Friesland team to Pakistan in March 1986. The team included representatives from the marketing, finance, and technical areas. They spent two weeks studying both Milkpak and the Pakistani market. After the team's visit, Friesland made several requests for additional information. Company representatives next met in October 1986, when both Babar Ali and Yawar Ali visited the Friesland headquarters in Holland to meet the company's chairman and directors and tour the corporate plant and R&D facilities. Milkpak's executives were not shown the milk powder factory.

Friesland planned to follow the October meeting by sending a team to prepare a detailed feasibility study that would consider the milk powder project and other possible product introductions, such as cheese and ice cream. Friesland's tentative plans were to buy 25% of Milkpak's shares, obtain technical fees and royalties for their brands, and increase equity to 49% over a five-year period. Friesland targeted the end of March 1987 as the date for making a final decision about the proposed joint venture.

A number of issues remained to be resolved. Milkpak needed to determine what government policies were with respect to technical fees and royalties on consumer products, assuming that Friesland made an initial equity investment of 25%. Friesland wanted to obtain royalties on its products in the range of 3%–5%. In addition, for Friesland to be able to increase share holdings beyond 25%, changes in the ownership structure of Milkpak could be required, such as the divestment of some of the existing foreign shareholders.

While Friesland was an attractive candidate for a joint venture, Milkpak had some reservations. Milkpak's executives were concerned that Friesland had not let them tour Friesland's milk powder factory on two separate occasions, which suggested that Friesland might be withholding certain information. Milkpak attributed Friesland's many requests to Milkpak for information to Friesland's relatively limited experience in establishing production facilities overseas.

The time period within which Friesland expected to obtain a return on its investment was uncertain. Some managers at Milkpak also felt that, in light of Friesland's history as a dairy cooperative, the company would always be more interested in finding markets for products produced in Holland than in developing the Pakistani dairy industry.

Rudolf Tschan's Visit

In January 1987, Babar Ali was apprised of the forthcoming visit of Rudolf Tschan, Nestle's new executive vice president for Asia Zone II, to Pakistan. According to Erwin Wermelinger, Nestle's marketing representative in Pakistan, Tschan wanted to come to Lahore to meet Ali, tour Milkpak's Sheikhupura factory, and visit the company's milk collection centers.

On January 25, Yawar Ali led Rudolf Tschan and the Nestle team on a tour of Milkpak's plant and milk collection areas. Ali was struck by Tschan's quick assessment of the surroundings: "This side looks a lot like the other side [Indian Punjab], but your buffalo are better and your land is more fertile." As Tschan toured the milk plant, he noted that "we will have one milk powder plant here and
one there [India]."

When Yawar Ali briefed Babar Ali about the Nestle team's tour, he noted Tschan's evident interest in the Milkpak operation. Later in the day, top executives from Milkpak and Packages were scheduled to meet with Tschan and Wermelinger to discuss the prospect of Nestle and Milkpak working together. As Milkpak's team prepared for the meeting with Nestle, they considered the major issues that would arise. In addition, they considered the benefits to each company of working together.

Assessing a Nestle Joint Venture

For Milkpak, the possibility of a joint venture with Nestle was appealing. The fact that Nestle had a successful manufacturing operation, including a milk powder plant 80 miles across the border in Moga, India, gave Milkpak confidence that Nestle knew how to operate in a very similar environment. Milkpak's management also believed that Nestle typically took a long-term approach toward developing its operating companies. In addition, Milkpak might benefit from Nestle training for its staff and from increased sales by other companies in the Ali Group. For example, Nestle products could use packaging made by the group's companies.

At the same time, management felt that Milkpak offered a number of advantages as a joint venture partner. Milkpak knew that its extensive milk collection infrastructure provided access to a key raw material for Nestle products. Milkpak's government contacts would facilitate obtaining the requisite licenses for establishing new production facilities. The Ali Group had a successful history of implementing other joint ventures. Through a joint venture with Milkpak, Nestle would eliminate a potential future competitor that knew the Pakistani market. The fact that Tschan had come to Pakistan to see Milkpak's operations indicated that Nestle already had a favorable impression of the company's capabilities.

Retaining majority ownership was important to Milkpak's management because Milkpak executives wanted to ensure that any joint venture partner paid attention to their ideas about the business. Babar Ali's earlier meeting with Nestle management suggested that coming to mutually agreeable terms on topics such as majority ownership could present a challenge. However, Tschan seemed to be more flexible.

In addition to the question of ownership, both companies were likely to be concerned about management control of the operation. For example, Nestle might want to appoint the milk powder plant manager. In addition, Nestle already had an effective existing system for distributing its products in Pakistan, which would need to be integrated with Milkpak's marketing system.

Another agenda item concerned the products to be produced and sold by the joint venture and the location of their manufacture. Some Nestle products currently imported could be manufactured locally in the new plant; others would continue to be imported. The new plant might also permit local manufacture of other Nestle products not currently exported to Pakistan. Finally, there existed the possibility of introducing new products tailored more precisely to the consumption preferences of Pakistani consumers.

Conclusion

As Milkpak's management approached the meeting with Rudolf Tschan, they contemplated the key issues that would be addressed. Milkpak's objective was to increase its penetration of and success in the Pakistani market. The company was already involved in an extended negotiation with Friesland, a fact they would tell Nestle, and one that gave Milkpak some additional leverage. At the same time, they needed to carefully evaluate what terms would make a joint venture with Nestle more appealing than one with Friesland. The Milkpak executives had to decide what negotiating positions to adopt. Milkpak's executives were aware that, should they conduct a joint venture with Nestle, today's meeting would set the foundation for a relationship that was likely to change and evolve over time.

Strategic Alliances

International Corporate Cooperation

An International Corporate Cooperation is an agreement between two or more organizations to cooperate in a specific business activity, so that each benefits from the strengths of the other, and gains competitive advantage. The formation of strategic alliances has been seen as a response to globalisation and increasing uncertainty and complexity in the business environment. Strategic alliances involve the sharing of production facilities, co-founding or research projects, knowledge and expertise between partners as well as the reduction of risk and costs in areas such as relationships with suppliers and the development of new products and technologies. A strategic alliance is sometimes equated with a joint venture, but an alliance may involve competitors and generally has a shorter life span. Strategic partnering is a closely related concept. [172] Each partner of a strategic alliance will follow its own interest but agrees that cooperating with another company is the best way to reach its goals. Strategic Alliances are managed more casually than joint ventures and usually do not have an own management team or board of directors but a coordinating committee whose appointed members are employees of the alliance partners. A strategic alliance is usually of a short-term nature with a very narrow purpose and is designed to overcome a common problem that its members have.

Example: Star Alliance - "The way the Earth connects" [173]

The Star Alliance network has been created to better meet the needs of the frequent international traveller, and currently consists of 19 airlines.

Picture 3 Star Alliance Airplanes

Facts

Combined Total of the 19 Star Alliance member airlines and 3 regional carriers:

Total revenue:	U.S. $ 122.79 bn
Revenue Passenger Km:	931.89 bn
Daily departures:	17,000
Annual Passengers:	455.47 m
Countries served:	160
Number of employees:	377,321
Airports served:	897
Fleet:	3087
Lounges:	740

Creating the future of air travel today

When the Star Alliance network was founded 10 years ago it was the beginning of a new era in air travel. Five leading international airlines linked their networks in order to serve the needs of business travellers in the age of globalisation. Much earlier than others, they recognised that in order to meet the needs of a new type of traveller in a globalised economy they had to go well beyond traditional ways of cooperation among airlines. Their vision was that in the future, there would be a network stretching over all continents, where travel is seamless and passengers can be sure to be recognised and superbly served wherever they are. The basis of this cooperation should be trust and partnership, not economic dominance.

The power of this vision created an alliance that today is the undisputed industry leader in terms of size, quality, passenger service and innovation. Today Star Alliance has 17 international member airlines and three regional members. Every six seconds somewhere on the globe a Star Alliance member carrier airplane takes off or lands – 16,000 times every day. The 406 million passengers every year represent well above a quarter of the total air travel of the world. And the numbers are growing. Within the next 12 months, Air China, Shanghai Airlines and Turkish Airlines will join the alliance. Ten years after its inception there are only a few "white spots" left on the map of the alliance.

With 855 airports in 155 countries, Star Alliance has the largest network of any alliance. For travellers this means that though the Star Alliance network they are more likely to find connections to their target destinations and lounges to relax in while on the road.

Focus on convenience and speed

Connecting people across the globe so they can meet face-to-face is what air travel is all about. Consequently Star Alliance focuses on innovations that make travel more convenient and in the end, help people do business more effectively. For passengers travelling with Star Alliance carriers today it is a matter of course to do a one-stop check-in for themselves and their luggage no matter how often they might need to change flights to reach their final destination. They have access to 650 airport lounges around the world, they can earn frequent flyer miles regardless which member airline they are flying with and they are able to redeem them for upgrades on nearly any member carrier.

The alliance's Connection Centres identify alliance customers who are at risk of missing their onward flight well ahead of their arrival and takes the necessary steps in order to guarantee the connection or transfer the customer and their luggage to other member carrier's flight. Thanks to this, very often a passenger, who otherwise might lose a full day, will in most cases have a delay of a couple of hours.

As the business world is evolving every day the alliance and its members have to make sure they are adapting to the changing needs of their customers, which means helping them to be successful in a competitive environment by supporting their requirements in the best possible way. Special programmes such as Company Plus and Corporate Plus help businesses to reduce their travel expenses and deliver a tailored service. With Conventions Plus, Star Alliance has created a service that facilitates the global exchange of thoughts and ideas by making it easier to organise and attend international conferences.

Exploiting the full potential of information technology

In the digital world of today, the extensive use of information technology is the cornerstone of the service strategy of Star Alliance. The website of the alliance - www.staralliance.com - and sophisticated e-services ensure travellers always have convenient and fast access to all relevant data. Crucial information such as flight status, baggage tracing and information about visa requirements for travel between all countries of the world is available on the website.

The StarNet infrastructure links the different airline computer systems of the carriers so that they can exchange information. The development of a common IT platform – where participating carriers use the same infrastructure - is the next step in creating efficiencies for airlines and their customers.

To make seamless travel a reality Star Alliance and its members work closely with airport authorities. Creating the airport of the future where passengers are not forced to move from queue to queue requires fundamentally-improved airport processes. At more and more key airports the member carriers are collocated in the same terminal often used exclusively by the alliance and its customers. Passengers no longer have to waste their valuable time covering long distances on the ground. The effect on connecting times is dramatic. In some cases, transfers between international flights have been cut in half.

The member airlines have the most advanced aircraft in their fleets. Star Alliance is in close dialogue with the major airplane manufacturers to make sure next generation passenger jets offer even more comfort, better economics and have a much lower impact on the environment. The operational experience of the airlines and their detailed knowledge about the future needs and desires of their customers help the industry design the right aircraft for tomorrow's passengers.

Benefits of Strategic Alliances

There are several benefits that international businesses can realize from strategic alliances such as an easier market entry, shared risk, shared knowledge and expertise as well as synergy and competitive advantage. These benefits are outlined below.

Ease of Market Entry

Many countries put heavy regulations on foreign companies that want to enter their market. Partnering with a host company can often help the home company to get around regulations. Many governments such as China or Namibia are very concerned about foreign companies entering their market. They are usually afraid that local companies could be put out of business and therefore require foreign companies to partner with local companies. In China for example all big car companies had to partner with local companies to produce and sell their cars in China.

A strategic alliance can also help a company to quickly enter a market by benefiting from existing distribution networks and marketing. Furthermore it helps the company to keep its costs down and to enjoy economies of scale.

Example: General Motors in China [174]

In July 1994, when the Chinese authorities began the task of making China's automotive sector one of the country's strongest industries, the automobile market was opened to foreign companies. But the access to the market came with a rider – technology transfer to the local companies. General Motors (GM) entered the Chinese automotive market through joint ventures with seven Chinese companies. Eventually, GM got the permission to set up a manufacturing unit investing between $1 billion and $2 billion to manufacture mid-sized cars in China. But the company's Chinese odyssey has not been very smooth. It not only had to deal with fluctuating car demand but also with its joint venture partners who proved to be tough negotiators.

Shared Risk

Shared Risk is important to consider for a firm that wants to enter a market that has just opened up or that is instable or uncertain. To overcome this problem, strategic alliances can help to control or to overcome a companie's risk. Boeing for example formed a strategic alliance with Fuji, Mitsubishi and Kawasaki who built 20% of the airplanes' frame. Boeing also hoped that these Japanese Companies would help to sell the airplane to Japan's big airlines. The alliance has been so successful that it alliance got renewed to build Boeing's 787. Sometimes companies even team up with their competitors to develop products or standards together. By researching a standard together with a company in the same business, the cost can be lowered and the standard that comes out of this alliance can be marketed by both companies instead of two companies developing two different standards and then fighting each other. The risk that one company will lose the battle and will therefore not be able to repay its investment in research and development is very high. Sony for example lost the battle for its own Betamax standard against the more common VCR standard. However, Sony went on with developing their own standards such as the Sony Memory Stick, which was competing with Compact Flash cards and SD Memory cards.

Shared Knowledge and Expertise

A firm that enters a strategic alliance has the opportunity to learn and gain expertise from the other company. The host company will know a lot better how to deal with government regulations, suppliers, human resources and it will know the environment better. These are advantages that a company can observe and acquire for itself by working together with a host company. The local company can then decide if it wants to use this knowledge for other purposes or if it wants to open up their own standalone business in the host country. An example of a very successful partnership is the joint venture between Toyota and General Motors in the U.S.. In 1984, both companies started a car production plant in Fremont, California. The plant was managed by Toyota but equally owned by both partners. The purpose for Toyota was to learn how to deal with suppliers in the United States as well as with labour. General Motors on the other side wanted to learn about Toyota's management style. Both companies used their newly gained information out of this joint venture to successfully open up and operate separate production plants. GM for example doubled its productivity in its own plants shortly after.

Synergy and Competitive Advantage

By combining efforts a lot of companies are achieving better results than by working by themselves. This advantage is a combination of the other ones mentioned above. For example, when entering a new market by building a factory together with a competitor, the risk of failing is be shared between the partners. Also, fixed production cost would be shared and therefore be lowered for each partner's share. Economies of scale and sharing of information and management techniques are further examples. Each partner's ability to compete effectively can be increased by entering into a partnership. At the end of 2007, the Daimler AG was looking for a potential partner to produce its troubled A-Class and Smart models. Shared research and development as well as buying parts together with a partner would reduce production costs. An alliance with BMW, VW or another car company would probably achieve synergies that would lower Daimler's costs.

Scope of Alliances

Alliances between companies can have different scopes. Two companies might choose to only cooperate in their marketing efforts or only in their research and development of products and standards. Fuji and Kodak where only cooperating to develop a new standard of film. The result is the Advantix system, which lets the customer take pictures in different sizes. But companies might also choose to cooperate in more than one element of their business. These alliances are called comprehensive alliances.

Comprehensive Alliances

When companies cooperate in different business units, this is called a comprehensive alliance. In a comprehensive alliance, two or more companies are joining their efforts for R&D, production, marketing and/or distribution. Such alliances can be difficult to manage since they need a formal organisational structure and that is why most comprehensive alliances are joint ventures. As an independent entity, the joint venture can operate to suit what is best for itself instead of pleasing one parent more than another. The firms that join a joint venture are usually able to achieve great amounts of synergy, economies of scale and might save resources.

Functional Alliances

When two one or more firms are only cooperating in one functional business area, these alliances are called functional alliances. Functional alliances can be R&D alliances, marketing alliances, production or finance alliances. Since these alliances are easier to manage than comprehensive alliances they can take different forms. A joint venture is not always necessary.

Production alliances

Production alliances happen when two or more companies decide to produce a product together in order to take advantage of economies of scale or because one company is better in one part of the production process and the other company is better in another part. BMW for example formed an alliance with PSA Peugeot Citroen to build new car engines. BMW on its part is responsible for designing the engines while PSA Peugeot Citroen is responsible for the engineering and the procurement. [24] Not always do both companies build the production facilities together. Sometimes one company already owns them but lets them be operated by another company in the alliance, like in the case of General Motors and Toyota. General Motors already owned the facility in Fremont California. In fact, they closed the facility in 1982 and reopened the plant two years later to let Toyota manage the production.

Marketing Alliances

Marketing Alliances are alliances between two or more companies that focus on pushing their products into a market. Usually one company already has a presence in the desired market and offers its marketing and distribution channels to another company. The compensation can either be a fixed sum, a percentage of the profits or if the host company wants to distribute their products in the local country, it might be possible that both companies use each other's channels to enter each other's market. A classic example is the airline industry. The Star Alliance case above demonstrated how international airlines work together to serve more customers. Each airline has one or more home airports from where it organises its flights. However, through its alliance partners, Lufthansa can for example offer flights from Hamburg in Germany to Brisbane in Australia, even though they do not actually fly that route. In that case an alliance partner would fly to Brisbane.

Financial Alliances

Financial Alliances are formed to reduce the partner's financial risk that comes with a project. In financial alliances the partners contribute equal financial resources to the project. In other cases one partner may substitute its financial contribution with expertise or other kinds of contributions.

An example of an international financial alliance is General Electric Co. and China Life Insurance Co. GE, the world's second-largest company by market capitalisation, is involved in a wide range of businesses including manufacturing, financial services and media. China Life also owns 20 percent of Guangdong Development Bank, which is controlled by Citigroup. [175] Both companies are cooperating on a wide range of financial businesses.

Research and Development Alliances

Research and Development Alliances are formed between two or more companies to undertake research together and to develop new services, products or standards. Research findings and knowledge can be transferred through teachings, patents, and conferences as well as through scientific papers. R&D alliances are usually not organised as joint ventures, since the participating companies might not join all their research efforts with another company. If only a part of the R&D department is working for the alliance, the separation into a joint venture and in-house research might cause complications. In this case a better way would be to allow the partner access to the desired research findings by cross-licensing the findings or by sharing patents. There is usually also an agreement between the partners that no partner will fall behind, that is, to ensure that really all related findings or developments will be shared and to keep the partners from suing each other over ownership of patents and copyrights.

Some countries support research and development consortia to develop new products for the world market. Governments can do this to push a country's research and to make it known for its products. The European Union is supporting some programs called SCIENCE, JOULE, ESPRIT and BRITE, but there are others as well in the United States, Japan and other countries.

Implementation of Strategic Alliances

On the following pages, we want to address some critical issues that can arise when forming an international alliance.

Selection of Partners

The better the partners in an alliance fit together the more likely is their success. The choice of the right partner for an alliance is therefore very important and can be vital for the participating companies. One very important aspect is therefore the compatibility of its partners. The joining companies need to be able to trust each other in order to be able to work efficiently. Without trust an alliance will most likely fail. But another aspect of the compatibility of the partners is that the operating philosophy is similar. When one firm is run by managers with a finance background, financial issues such as short term profits, or bottom line issues will probably also drive their way of doing business. If the other company in the partnership is managed by engineers, problems could arise because of their different way of doing business and because their short and long term goals might be different.

Another important issue in finding the right party for a partnership is the nature of the firm's products or services. It is beneficial if the products and services of the companies in the partnership are complementary but not directly competing with each other. Moreover, it can be very hard to compete with a partner in one market and to cooperate in another. This would probably lead the partners to withhold information that would be beneficial for the other.

Another aspect that the partners should examine is how safe the alliance will be, that means that both partners should check out what the partner'sd strengths and what his weaknesses are. But they should also try to find out how successful former alliances were and how the deal looks from the partner's side. The partnership is likely to be more successful if it is beneficial for all companies involved. IBM for example has 90,000 business partners worldwide, including consultants, integrators, software vendors, value-added resellers and distributors. [176] The sheer amount of partners that IBM has can also be a sign of a good and professional alliance partner.

A further consideration is what a company can learn by entering into a partnership with another firm. The learning aspect can be very general like how to manage a factory more efficiently like in the case of the joint venture between General Motors and Toyota or it can also be very specific like how to use systems more effectively.

However, all parties involved need to value their own information that they are bringing into the partnership in order to be able to negotiate the right terms before entering the partnership. For more information and example partnership contracts visit the Management Laboratory Website.

A good partner has the following three characteristics. First, the partner needs to share the same vision. When the goals and expectations of the alliance members differ from each other, the alliance is doomed to fail. Substantial conflicts will most certainly arise from these differences. This point leads us to the second characteristic: Good partners help each other to achieve their goals. The partners need to complement each other in reaching a better market share, lower costs, access to markets or whatever else the goals are. The third characteristic is that the partners should not try to opportunistically exploit the alliance for their own good. This would for example be the case if one company tries to find out as much as possible about their partner's technology and know-how while not giving the equal amount back in return.

To find a partner with the characteristics mentioned above, a company needs to do extensive research on possible candidates. To increase the probability of selecting a good partner, the firm should [24 p. 501]

- collect as much pertinent, publicly available information on potential allies as possible.
- gather data from informed third parties. This includes firms that have had alliances with the potential partners, investment bankers who have had dealings with them, and former employees.
- get to know the potential partner as well as possible before committing to an alliance. This should include face-to-face meetings between senior managers (and perhaps middle-level managers) to ensure that the chemistry is right.

Alliance Structure

When a partner has been selected, it is important to secure the firm's technology as well as other competitive advantages against unwanted access. The risk that the partner might abuse the alliance to get access to confidential information needs to be minimised. The first step is to design the alliance in a way that reduces opportunism. Sensitive information and technology can be walled off by giving the partner only access to final products that the company contributes to the alliance. Technology that is not needed for the purpose of the alliance should be restricted. The next step is to write safeguards into the alliance agreement that reduce opportunistic behaviour. An example would be to include a paragraph that permits the alliance partners to compete with each other on the same market or for the same clients. By doing this, the company shields itself off from being abused by a partner in order to enter their market. Third, both parties to an alliance can agree in advance to swap skills and technologies, thereby ensuring a chance for equitable gain. [24 p. 502] A possible way to achieve this would be by cross-licensing the technology contributed to the joint venture. The fourth possibility to reduce the risk that an alliance partner takes unfair advantage of the alliance is to get the alliance partners to make major initial commitments before the start of the joint venture to ensure their good intentions. This could for example be the investment in production facilities or long term contracts that are necessary for the joint venture to be successful.

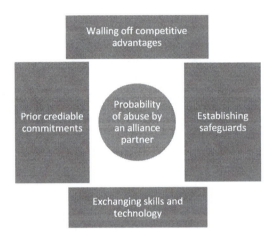

Figure 11 Protective Shield

Form of Ownership

A joint venture is usually to a certain country. However, for tax benefits, some corporations choose to incorporate their company in Switzerland, the Bahamas or other countries that are considered to be a "tax heaven". The form of a corporation enables the partners to better secure their assets in the parent company in case the joint venture gets sued for breach of contract or negligence. It can also be better for a joint venture that the staff is hired by the joint venture itself and not sent from the parents to manage the JV and to report back to the parents. The facilities of a joint venture should provide a neutral setting in order to avoid conflicts between the joining parties that could arise if the joint venture is on the premises of one of the partners. However, if one partner has a very good reputation in a field that the joint venture will be doing business in, it might be reasonable to have the partner's name or logo as a part of the joint venture's name.

Where an incorporation might not be optimal, the partners might choose to form a limited partnership. A limited partnership usually has one managing partner who is fully financially responsible for the partnership, regardless of how high his initial investment was. The other partners in a limited partnership have only limited liability, which means that they are financially only responsible up to the amount of their investment. Famous limited partnerships are Bloomberg L.P., Carnegie Steel Company and CNN.

Public Private Venture

The public private venture (PPV) is a special form of a joint venture. In this case, the partnership exists between a private company and the government or a government agency. This type of joint venture is common in the oil industry. Often governments do not have the technical expertise that companies like Shell, British Petroleum or other big oil companies have. These companies on the other hand often do not have the necessary rights to drill in a country where rich oil fields are. In this case, the government provides the drilling rights and the oil company the expertise and the necessary capital for this public private venture. Some countries don't allow foreign firms to operate on their own. If in this case a suitable local partner is not available, the foreign company might ask the government to join the operations. Exxon Mobil and Total for example cooperate with the Nigerian government to drill for oil and to export oil from Nigeria.

To assess the possible success of a public private venture, the company needs to carefully evaluate the political environment and the legal environment in the host country. This partnership depends a lot on the government. If this government gets replaced, the new government might not consider the partnership as important or in a worse case might even end the partnership because it considers it to be too much associated with the old government.

Therefore a stable government is very important for this type of venture. Often the government does not interfere with the operations and lets the private company operate by itself. Some governments even try to protect their investment into the public private venture by restricting the access to the market and thus the venture does not have much competition. However, it is very important for a firm to understand the financial and political motivations of a foreign government to enter into a PPV. But a PPV is not only common in the oil industry, it can also be an attractive way to enter the Chinese market. Sometimes it is the only way, as we have seen in the example of General Motors and Volkswagen.

Joint Management Considerations

The following paragraphs will introduce three different management styles of a strategic alliance.

Shared Management Agreement

In a shared management agreement the partners are equal in their responsibility and power to manage the alliance. In this case, the alliance gets run by managers in the parent companies which pass on instructions to the alliance. The alliance managers therefore do not have much authority since they are mainly executing the decisions made by the partners. This type of alliance is the most difficult to manage and to maintain. Conflicts can easily arise because of equal power of the parents. Decisions need to be made by all partners, which can lead to the alliance becoming temporally paralysed if the partners cannot agree on a decision.

Assigned Agreement

In the case of an assigned agreement, one parent has the primary managerial responsibility for the alliance. This could be because the partners agree on this term in the partnership agreement to avoid conflicts or because one partner owns more shares than another, which gives him the power to dominate other partners and to even overrule them if necessary. This management style can cause conflict, but it has the advantage that decisions can be made quicker. However, all partners should take care that no partner is left out in the decision making process and that all partners have at least the possibility to convince others of their opinion.

Delegated Arrangement

This is a form of management arrangement that is utilised in joint ventures. The partners send managers or hire new managers to create a new management for the joint venture. The joint venture's management runs the daily business of the joint venture and has enough authority to make decisions that are best for the joint venture. However, this is only feasible if the managers are independent from the parent companies.

Pitfalls of Strategic Alliances

The literature and real life cases provide us with five common problems that can damage or even cause a partnership to fail. A common reason that we already mentioned is the incompatibility of partners; a second one is the limited access to information; a third problem might be the conflict over how earnings will be distributed; fourth, one partner might lose its autonomy; and last, a change of circumstances may occur.

Incompatibility of Partners

This is the main reason for partnerships to fail, but it can also lead to bad performance and conflicts that can damage the relationship between the partners. Incompatibility can arise if the objectives and goals are different, if the corporate culture is too different or for any other reason that is a link between the alliance partners. If one company's management style is more financially driven and the partner's management is engineerially driven, problems can arise because the goals might be different. Other alliances ran into problems because the partners' corporate cultures were different. This can be overcome by intensive meetings between managers of both companies to discuss the values, goals and the expectations that all partners have from the alliance. It is also important to evaluate the strategy of all partnering firms and their reasons to enter into the partnership. Another possible and more inexpensive way to overcome incompatibility problems is the Management Exchange Program, which is outlined below.

Management Exchange Program

The Management Exchange Program is a program that permits managers from one company to spend a couple of days assisting managers in the company that they want to form an alliance with. In this way, they can get to know the culture and can gain valuable information that might help them to understand each other's culture and to make connections that might help them to overcome possible problems during the partnership.

If this is not possible because both companies are related, there are independent consulting companies that evaluate all companies involved from the inside and then advise the partners on how to form that alliance and what problems they might run into. So far not many companies take advantage of this service which could lead to less alliances failing.

217

Access to Information

Often companies are not aware that they need to share information with the alliance partner that might be important for their competitive advantage or that might be secret for another reason. However, for an alliance to work all partners need to share information that is best for the alliance. It is therefore important to discuss required information before the joint venture is formed. An alliance between Mazda and Ford in 1988 [177] to produce the Mazda 626 / Ford Telstra was almost compromised because Mazda did not want to allow Ford engineers to visit their research facilities. After several weeks, Mazda agreed to let the Ford engineers visit its laboratories, though only for a limited time.

Conflict over Distributing Earnings

How the profits should be distributed between the alliance partners needs to be part of the partnership agreement. Some partners distribute profits on an equal basis if all companies are also distributing to the alliance in the same way, others choose to distribute profits on a more unequal basis if a company is distributing more to the alliance than another one does. Another important issue of the partnership agreement should be how profits and transfer prices should be calculated. Variations in accounting standards or calculation methods can cause conflicts later on during the alliance. Some companies forget to include in their agreement whether and how much of the profits should be reinvested into the joint venture. One firm might have the goal to get as much out of the alliance as possible in order to end it in the short term while another company is planning on reinvesting profits to make the alliance competitive in the long run.

Loss of Autonomy

Just like sharing profits and risks, firms also share control in an alliance. This topic has been addressed earlier, but we want to mention it here because it can also be a reason for a strategic alliance to fail. By sharing control over the alliance, the partners are also limiting themselves in what they can do because every change in organisation, change in strategy or product launch needs to be discussed and negotiated. To overcome this issue, some companies decide to buy their partners. A study of alliances that involved Japanese firms showed that 75% of all alliances examined in that study ended because the Japanese firm took over their partner.

Changing Circumstances

A change of circumstances can have various economic, financial or political reasons. But what problematic changes have in common is that, for at least one partner in the alliance, it is not beneficial any more to keep the partnership alive. Some alliances get terminated because the demand for the venture's product or service decreased or because exchange rates make it impossible to keep an international alliance alive. But it can also happen that a private public partnership gets terminated when a new government gets elected and the new politicians have other plans or other partners in mind.

Case Study: FreeMove

(Creating Value Through Strategic Alliances in the Mobile Telecommunications Industry)[32]

"This is an alliance in which the winners will be not just the partners but all their customers, because they will benefit from better products and services, as well as from better prices, which we will achieve by translating the advantages we obtain into cost savings. By working jointly to initiate seamless services in voice, data and mobile Internet, and extending them to all the countries where the three operators are present, we will create a truly world-class service offering."

Antonio Viana-Baptista, Chairman and CEO of Telefónica Móviles; April 20031

Introduction

On April 7, 2003, Telefónica Móviles (TEM) of Spain, T-Mobile International (TMO) of Germany and TIM (Telecom Italia Mobile) signed a memorandum [178] of understanding to set up an alliance to provide their customers with the opportunity to access all their products and services abroad. They were joined by Orange, France's incumbent mobile operator, in July 2003 [179], thus creating a network with access to over 170 million mobile subscribers in Europe. The TTTO-Alliance – named after the initials of its members – combined its product and service offering under the joint FreeMove brand.

The foundation of FreeMove[33] had been greeted by industry observers and the press as a challenge, if not a declaration of war [180] on Vodafone Plc., the world's leading mobile operator with 122.5 million [181] customers worldwide at the time. The initial focus of the newly created alliance was the highly attractive Multinational Corporations (MNCs) segment. The FreeMove partners only had a combined

---

[32] This case was prepared by Frank Riehl, MBA student, and Professor Africa Ariño, as the basis for class discussion rather than to illustrate either effective or ineffective handling of an administrative situation. October 2004. This case was written with the support of Anselmo Rubiralta Center for Globalization and Strategy. Copyright © 2004, IESE. To order copies or request permission to reproduce materials, call IESE PUBLISHING 34 932 534 200, send a fax to 34 932 534 343, or write Juan de Alós, 43 - 08034 Barcelona, Spain, or iesep@iesep.com No part of this publication may be reproduced, stored in a retrieval system, used in a spreadsheet, or transmitted in any form or by any means - electronic, mechanical, photocopying, recording, or otherwise without the permission of IESE. Last edited: 7/19/05
[33] The FreeMove brand was introduced almost a year later, in March 2004.

market share of 25% in this €4bn market segment, although 87% of Europe's MNCs were located within the alliance's footprint [182] (see Exhibit 33; see also Vodafone's footprint in Exhibit 34).

Exhibit 33 FreeMove's European and worldwide footprint[34]

Exhibit 34 Vodafone and its partners' worldwide footprint[35]

Creating value for each of the alliance members as well as their current and future customers was FreeMove's prime objective. However, in the competition with Vodafone and Starmap, an alliance launched by Europe's smaller operators after the foundation of FreeMove, chances for differentiation were slim. Would Free-Move be able to create unique customer value, or was its strategy doomed to fail

---

[34] Source: http://www.freemovealliance.net
[35] Source: http://www.vodafone.com

because Vodafone had too much of a head start in the trans-national telecommunication business?

History of Mobile Telecommunications in Europe

The history of mobile telecommunications in Europe was one of simultaneous developments across different dimensions.

Technology

In the technological dimension, there were first (1G), second (2G) and third (3G/UMTS) generation technologies. While the first generation was still analogue, the second and third were digital, which enabled the transmission of data services such as SMS, MMS and mobile gaming. The main differences between 2G and 3G were the speeds with which data could be transmitted.

The First Generation

Europe's first generation (1G) of mobile networks differed substantially across countries (see overview in Exhibit 35). In 1981, the first cellular service was introduced when the Nordic Mobile Telephone System or NMT450 began operating in Denmark, Sweden, Finland and Norway. Other countries followed in 1985, but using different technologies such as the TACS (Total Access Communications System) in Great Britain, the "C-Netz" in Germany, Radiocom 2000 in France or RTMI/RTMS in Italy, leaving Europe with a total of nine different and incompatible analogue radio telephone systems.

Exhibit 35 Overview of mobile technologies (not exhaustive)

Generation	Name	Explanation
1	AMPS	Advanced Mobile Phone System. Developed by Bell Labs in the 1970s and first used commercially in the United States in 1983. It operates in the 800 MHz band and is currently the world's largest cellular standard.
1 1	C-Netz N-AMPS	Older cellular technology found mainly in Germany and Austria. Uses 450 MHz. Narrowband Advanced Mobile Phone System. Developed by Motorola as an interim technology between analogue and digital. It has some three times greater capacity than AMPS and operates in the 800 MHz range.
1	NMT450	Nordic Mobile Telephones/450. Developed specially by Ericsson and Nokia to service the rugged terrain that characterises the Nordic countries. Range 25 km. Operates at 450 MHz. Uses FDD FDMA.
1	NMT900	Nordic Mobile Telephones/900. The 900 MHz upgrade to NMT 450 developed by the Nordic countries to accommodate higher capacities and handheld portables. Range 25 km. Uses FDD FDMA technology.
1	RC2000	Radiocom 2000. French system launched November 1985.
1	TACS	Total Access Communications System. Developed by Motorola and similar to AMPS. It was first used in the United Kingdom in 1985, although in Japan it is called JTAC. It operates in the 900MHz frequency range.
2	CDMA	Code Division Multiple Access. There are now a number of variations of CDMA, in addition to the original Qualcomn-invented N-CDMA (originally just "CDMA", also known in the US as IS-95. See N-CDMA below).
2	GSM	Global System for Mobile Communications. The first European digital standard, developed to establish cellular compatibility throughout Europe. It's success has spread to all parts of the world and over 80 GSM networks are now operational. It operates at 900 MHz.
2.5	EDGE	UWC-136, the next generation of data heading towards third generation and personal multimedia environments builds on GPRS and is known as Enhanced Data rate for GSM Evolution (EDGE). It will allow GSM operators to use existing GSM radio bands to offer wireless multimedia IP-based services and applications at theoretical maximum speeds of 384 kbps with a bit-rate of 48 kbps per timeslot and up to 69.2 kbps per timeslot in good radio conditions.
2.5	GPRS	GSM's new GPRS (General Packet Radio Services) data transmission technology is optimized for "bursty" datacom services such as wireless Internet/intranet and multimedia services. It is also known as GSM-IP (Internet Protocol) because it will connect users directly to Internet Service Providers.
3	B-CDMA	Broadband CDMA. Now known as W-CDMA (see below). To be used in UMTS.
3	UMTS	Universal Mobile Telephone Standard, the next generation of global cellular which should be in place by 2004. Proposed data rates of <2Mbps, using combination TDMA and W-CDMA. Operates at around 2GHz.
3	W-DCMA	One of the latest components of UMTS, along with TDMA and CDMA2000. It has a 5Mhz air interface and is the basis of higher-bandwidth data rates. Click HERE for more technical details...
fixed mobile	CTS	GSM Corldless Telephone System. In the home environment, GSM-CTS phones communicate with a CTS Home Base Station (HBS), which offers perfect indoor radio coverage. The CTS-HBS hooks up to the fixed network and offers the best of the fixed and mobile worlds: low cost and high quality from the Public Switched Telephone Network (PSTN), services and mobility from the GSM.
fixed mobile	DECT	Digital European Corldless Telephone. Uses 12-timeslot TDMA. This started off as Ericsson's CT-3, but developed into ETSI's Digital European Cordless Standard. It is intended to be a far more flexible standard than the CT2 standard, in that it has more RF channels (10 RF carriers x 12 duplex bearers per carrier = 120 duplex voice channels). It also has a better multimedia performance since 32kbit/s bearers can be concatenated. Ericsson has developed a dual GSM/DECT handset.

Source: http://mobileoffice.co.za

The Second Generation - GSM[36]

Truly European Mobile Telecommunications began with the development of GSM, Europe's first digital uniform mobile communications standard. As early as 1982, a task force within the CEPT (Conference Européennes des Administrations des Postes et Télécommunications) was launched to develop a uniform standard. In 1987 this Groupe Speciale Mobile decided on the final specifications of the standard and its acronym GSM, previously derived from the group's name, stood now for Global System for Mobile Communications. Thirteen European countries committed to introducing the GSM standard in September 1987. The first GSM network was launched in January 1992 in Finland by Oy Radiolinja Ab. By 2004, 143 mobile operators had launched GSM networks in 50 European countries or areas [183].

The Third Generation - UMTS[37]

By the end of the 1990s, most European markets had three to four mobile network operators and the national champions were looking for further opportunities for growth. Based on the unprecedented growth of GSM subscribers, which rose from zero to 442.3 million in 10 years [183], the introduction of UMTS or third generation (3G) networks was generally perceived as the next gold mine. Licenses to operate a 3G network were seen as entrance tickets into foreign markets and as a means to bolster the average revenues per subscriber (ARPU) by the additional revenue streams from data services (e.g. mobile Internet). UMTS technology promised to raise transmission speeds for data from 9.6 kbps[38] to up to 2 mbps in the most optimistic scenarios. However, this was very unrealistic, and the maximum speed was thought to be around 150 to 300 kbps once the networks were fully rolled out. An intermediate level of between 2G and 3G were GPRS services (2.5G). They could be pictured as a "turbo" on existing 2G infrastructure and increased performance (speed) from 9.6 kbps to around 50 kbps. With this mobile broadband technology, mobile operators hoped to introduce products such as video-telephony and a multitude of other multi-media applications. As governments realized the enormous pressure on operators to get UMTS licenses in order to be positioned competitively and raise their market value, they increasingly switched from traditional "beauty-contests" (may the best win) to auctions (may the richest win). Especially in Germany (€50.5bn) [184 p. 26] and the UK (€37.1bn) [184 p. 23] govern-

---

36 GSM = Global System for Mobile Communications.
37 UMTS = Universal Mobile Telecommunications Service.
38 kbps = kilobits per second.

ments raised huge amounts of money from the licenses. The total burden (not including the additional investment of building the 3G networks) placed on the industry by 3G licenses amounted to approximately €125bn. The UMTS euphoria waned quickly for a number of reasons. To begin with, the collapse of the stock markets hit the telecommunications industry particularly hard (see Exhibit 36) and many operators struggled to reduce their debt burden, which became overwhelming with shrinking market capitalization. Furthermore, the introduction of

UMTS services was delayed by technological difficulties in providing UMTS handsets and services soon after the auctions in 2000. Most important, however, was the lack of demand for any wireless broadband offerings. Operators only expected the UMTS market to pick up, slowly, by 2004/2005 [179]. The main victims of the UMTS hype were new entrants to the market, like Mobilcom and Quam in Germany, who were sponsored by incumbents of neighbouring countries, France Telecom and Telefónica Móviles/Sonera, respectively, and who had to say goodbye to their UMTS ambitions in the face of substantial license and network costs and insufficient revenues. In Spain, the Xfera consortium, which had acquired a UMTS license in the Spanish "beauty contest", had not even started the roll-out of its UMTS network by 2004 because of the great uncertainties in cost, technology and market demand [185]. The only new entrant to survive was "3", owned by the Hutchison Whampoa conglomerate, which launched Europe's first UMTS networks in Austria, Italy and the UK by 2003.

Exhibit 36 Share price performance, January 2000 to July 2004

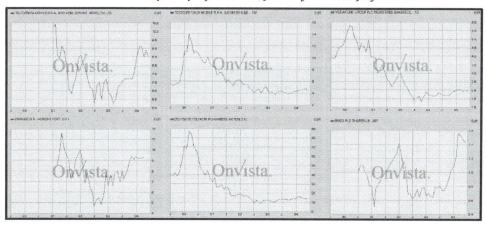

Source: www.onvista.com; 5 July, 2004

Regulation

Regulatory decisions and government actions towards the liberalization of the national telecommunication markets constituted a major force in the proliferation of mobile communication in the 1990s. Liberalization was triggered by the European Commission, which set up a regulatory framework through various directives, starting with the 1987 Telecommunications Green Paper. Since then, the European Commission had required its then 15 EU Member States to take appropriate measures at a national level in order to create a competitive environment for telecommunication networks and services and to end the control of the telecommunication sector by national monopolies. One key element inthe Commission's push for liberalization was the establishment of independent regulators[39] for telecommunications in each country.

In Germany, the UK, France and Spain, as well in many other European countries, this led to the issuing of at least two mobile GSM licenses, extended to include third and even fourth licenses at later stages (see Exhibit 37). The launch of the second, third and even fourth mobile operators often preceded the issue dates for the licenses by less than six months. In Great Britain and Scandinavia, regulators took an even more radical approach to liberalization by issuing licenses to mobile operators without a network – known as MVNOs (Mobile Virtual Network Operators) – and obliging existing mobile operators *with* a network to sell capacity (minutes) to their competitors at regulated prices.

---

[39] National Regulatory Authority (NRA).

Exhibit 37 Overview of launch dates for GSM networks

FRANCE	Bouygues Telecom	BOUYGUES TELECOM	France	GSM 900/1800	Jan 1996
FRANCE	Bouygues Telecom Caraibe	Bouygues Telecom Caraibe	Martinique, Guadelopue, French Guyana	GSM 900	Dec 2001
FRANCE	Orange France	France Telecom Mobile	FRANCE	GSM 1800	Nov 1996
FRANCE	Orange France	Orange F	FRANCE	GSM 900/1800	Jul 1992
FRANCE	SFR - CEGETEL	SFR	France	GSM 900	Apr 1993
GERMANY	E-Plus Mobilfunk	E-Plus	Germany	GSM 1800	May 1994
GERMANY	O2 (Germany) Gmbh & Co. OHG	O2 (Germany) GmbH & Co. OHG	GERMANY	GSM 1800	Oct 1998
GERMANY	T-Mobile Deutschland GmbH	D1	Germany	GSM 900/1800	Jul 1992
GERMANY	Vodafone D2 GmbH	Vodafone	GERMANY	GSM 900/1800	Jun 1992
SPAIN	Retevision Movil S.A.	Retevision Movil	SPAIN	GSM 1800	Jan 1999
SPAIN	Telefonica Moviles España S.A.	MOVISTAR	Spain	GSM 900/1800	Jul 1995
SPAIN	Vodafone España S.A.	Vodafone	SPAIN	GSM 900/1800	Oct 1995
UNITED KINGDOM	O2 (UK) Limited	O2	UK	GSM 900/1800	Dec 1993
UNITED KINGDOM	Orange PCS Ltd	Orange	UK	GSM 1800	Apr 1994
UNITED KINGDOM .	T-Mobile (UK) Limited	T-Mobile UK	UK	GSM 1800	Sep 1993
UNITED KINGDOM	VODAFONE Ltd	Vodafone	UK	GSM 900/1800	Jul 1992

Note: The operators listed as network owners were not necessarily the companies that received the licenses at the time they were issued. The table refers to current ownership structures as of June 2004. Vodafone Germany was, at the time of the license issuing, Mannesmann Mobilfunk (D2-brand).

Source: www.gsmworld.com

Internationalization

With the proliferation of third and fourth GSM licensees in the second half of the 1990s, many European Telcos sought to broaden their geographical footprint. The most commonly used means was the acquisition of equity stakes in the newly emerging operators. As many mobile operators were still fully owned subsidiaries of their cash rich former monopolist parents, these bought together a portfolio that would also make their subsidiaries more interesting to potential investors.

British Telecom (BT), Deutsche Telekom (DTAG), France Telecom (FT), Telecom Italia and Telefónica all bought equity stakes in targeted markets for their mobile subsidiaries. The main differentiation in their portfolios became apparent outside Europe: Telefónica and Telecom Italia focused on Latin America, while DTAG covered most Eastern European markets and Russia and became, after the acquisition of Voicestream, one of the then largest GSM mobile operators in the U.S. and the first truly international mobile operator. FT concentrated on strengthening its European portfolio and achieved market leadership under its Orange brand in two of the largest European markets: France and the UK. BT stretched its resources to acquire stakes in a number of European, U.S. and even Japanese mobile operators.

After the burst of the Internet bubble, and under the pressure of reducing debt, many of these portfolios had to be consolidated. The operator hit hardest was BT, which sold most of its stakes in Japan, Spain and other markets and divested its mobile operations under the new mmO2 brand in 2001. The main beneficiary of this development was Vodafone, as BT's demise provided it with the opportunity to expand its international footprint and increase its existing equity stakes. In 2004, most mobile subsidiaries of these Telcos had been floated in IPOs, with the exception of T-Mobile, which nevertheless enjoyed great independence from DTAG. Also, Orange's shares – originally floated – had been bought back by France Telecom in 2003 in an attempt to gain full control of Orange's cash flow generation [186]. All of them had significant international equity holdings; however, market leadership in Europe was mostly confined to their respective home markets[40].

The FreeMove Alliance

The launch of FreeMove in April 2003 heralded the beginning of an unprecedented level of cooperation between European mobile operators. For the first time, operational integration would take place without prior equity investments in the respective partners.

Benefits

Under the FreeMove alliance, four of the largest European mobile operators decided to enhance their products and services portfolio through stronger interoperability and cooperation among their networks. By doing this, they would be

---

[40] Telefónica Móviles was also market leader in most markets where its Latin American shareholdings operated. Source: annual report 2003

able to offer their customers a "Virtual Home Environment" where they could access the same high quality services internationally as they did at home. This "seamless international experience" would mean that business travellers or tourists abroad could use their short-numbers as at home and access mailboxes and other data services without any problems. Moreover, the pricing of voice and data services (like SMS) would be unified[41] across countries for the customers of each company individually, enabling greater transparency for customers (see Exhibit 38). This focus on the interoperability of networks to enable seamless voice and data roaming (that is, the utilization of partner networks abroad) at transparent prices earned FreeMove the title of a "roaming-alliance" (see inlay on FreeMove roaming).

---

[41] Under a unified pricing scheme, a Telefónica Móviles customer would pay the same tariff independently of her location, i.e. a call from the UK to Spain would cost the same as a call from Germany to Spain. Unified tariffs would be applied within different zones, e.g. the Euro-zone countries Germany, Andorra, France, Monaco, Portugal, Great Britain, Austria, Belgium, Denmark, Finland, Greece, Netherlands, Ireland, Italy, Luxembourg, San Marino, Sweden, Vatican, Switzerland, Liechtenstein, Iceland, Norway and Morocco (only with Medi-Telecom). www.movistar.com

Exhibit 38 Comparison of roaming tariffs: Vodafone and Orange in the UK

Source: www.orange.co.uk

Zone If you're in...	Calling the UK & same country	Calling Zones 1 & 2	Calling Zones 3,4,5, & 6	Receiving a call	Sending a text
1 Republic of Ireland, Channel Islands & Isle of Man	60p *75p*	60p *75p*	150p	50p	35p†
2 France, Germany, Italy, Spain, Switzerland, The Netherlands...	75p *99p*	75p *99p*	150p	75p	35p†
3 Czech Republic, Hungary, Croatia, Poland, Estonia...	99p *125p*	150p	150p	75p	35p†
4 Australia, New Zealand, South Africa, Singapore, Taiwan & Thailand	79p *99p*	195p	195p	75p	35p†
5 USA & Canada	*149p*	195p	195p	99p	35p†
6 Rest of World...	149p *169p*	195p	195p	125p	35p†

Prices shown in bold RED are on a Vodafone preferred network.
Prices shown in *BLUE* italics are for any other network.

Source: www.vodafone.co.uk

On the customer side, FreeMove vowed to "exploit (its) synergies and size in order to achieve cost efficiencies and to allow (them) to offer exclusive products, including higher-end handsets that are more accessible to all." [187] Around 6 million handsets had already been acquired under the alliance by 2004, and plans had been made to increase the procurement of handsets to 25% of the alliance's total handset requirements, thus achieving overall cost savings of around 10% [182]. Finally, joint product development would be the last step in the ever-closer cooperation among FreeMove members. From allowing their members' own customers to access their services abroad to developing *joint* services, product development would evolve with time. As member networks had large technological commonalities, FreeMove enjoyed a competitive advantage in this field.

Other benefits would be achieved through the increase in the overall growth of subscribers, especially in the business customer segment. For example, corporate lines would grow by 5% per year over the following three years through integrated bid cooperation. Providing "one-stop-shop" services to multinational corporations (MNCs) was intended to raise the alliance's market share significantly in the €4bn MNC market, where it covered 87% of the market but owned only 25% of the customers [182]. In the mass market, the alliance hoped to grow voice traffic on its networks above the European average of 3.5% [188] by 10% annually over the next three years and to double the GPRS[42] data traffic every year in the same period [189].

Vis-à-vis its suppliers, the alliance sought to gain additional advantages through coordinated handset specification, and thus influence the development of new 3G handsets according to their requirements. Also, the possibility of gaining access to FreeMove-branded handsets would be higher, although no concrete plans were envisaged in the near future [182]. Finally, the increased purchasing power would enable the alliance to gain exclusive access to newly released handset models for a limited time.

Organization and Scope

When T-Mobile, Telefónica Móviles, TIM and Orange launched the FreeMove Alliance, they stressed that the alliance was "a brand rather than an actual company" [182], which would reinforce the partners' brands and make the most of their pooled expertise. In this sense, FreeMove had established a strong virtual organization, as

---

[42] GPRS = General Packaged Radio Services (see Exhibit 3) are an enhanced generation (2.5G) in digital mobile telephony that provided master transmission rates for data.

all experts working for FreeMove remained employed by the partner organizations and were halfor full-time dedicated to FreeMove tasks.

FreeMove was registered as a legally incorporated entity and had defined a clear corporate governance structure consisting of both a Management Board and a Supervisory Board with a semi-annually rotating presidency. The Supervisory Board included the CEOs of all four member operators, who would meet regularly. FreeMove had several functional working groups of which some are operational groups on issues like roaming, devices or MNCs and other support groups on issues such as PR, brand and legal affairs, were each staffed with three to four experts per company. The total FreeMove organization thus comprised of more than 100 people. All working groups met at least once a month and members kept in continuous contact. In the first year of its existence, 20 projects had already been successfully launched, establishing crucial processes on roaming, joint purchasing and business customer sales [179].

Operationally, the integration of networks to support joint enablers and the design of unified tariffs and services would be pursued by coordinated task forces within each member company. A specific set of key performance indicators were established to monitor the progress of the alliance. With respect to broadening the alliance, targets and admission criteria had been formulated. New members should add value to the alliance, have a complementary footprint, be leaders in their respective home markets and have high quality networks that could support the products and services of the other FreeMove members [179].

The FreeMove product and service offerings targeted primarily the 170 million existing European customers of the alliance. Worldwide, the alliance had an additional 60 million customers, mainly through TEM and TIM shareholdings in Latin America and T-Mobile USA, which would be targeted at a later stage, according to Nikesh Arora, chief marketing officer at T-Mobile [182]. With regard to purchasing, the initial target for the joint purchasing volume of handsets would be 25% of the total.

FreeMove Partners

T-Mobile (TMO)

T-Mobile International was one of the world's largest mobile operators, with approximately 61 million subscribers at the end of 2003 [190] (see Exhibit 39 for a comparison of all members of FreeMove and Vodafone). Its German operations were the largest in Europe, with 26.45 million subscribers [191], giving it a small lead over Vodafone's 22.82 million. At 42%, T-Mobile's market share was strongest in its home market of Germany (see Exhibit 40 Market shares in key European markets in 2003Exhibit 40), but in the UK it had also managed to establish a strong presence, with a market share of 24.7%.

Majority-owned subsidiaries in the U.S., Great Britain, the Netherlands, Austria, Hungary and the Czech Republic operating under the T-Mobile brand gave TMO a strong European footprint and made it the only European operator with fully integrated U.S. operations. There were further minority shareholdings in Croatia, Poland and Slovakia. Moreover, all its operations were based on GSM technology, enabling seamless roaming between the various networks, even in the U.S..

In contrast to most of its competitors, T-Mobile was still fully owned by its parent company: Deutsche Telekom AG (DTAG). The T-Mobile group's total revenue amounted to €22.8bn, up 15.4 percent from €19.7bn in 2002. As a result, T-Mobile accounted for nearly 40 percent of the Deutsche Telekom Group's net revenue in 2003. From 2002 to 2003, adjusted EBITDA grew by 32.4 percent from €5.0bn to €6.7bn [192].

Exhibit 39 Companies' key data in 2003, overview

	Telefónica Móviles	T-Mobile	Telecom Italia	Orange	Vodafone
Revenues (million €)	10,070.3	22,778	11,782	17,941	50,338.5
EBITDA (million €)	4,462.9	6,671	5,502	6,578	18,960
EBITDA Margin	44.3%	29.3%	46.7%	36.7%	37.7%
Net profit (million €)	1,607.8	na	2,342	4,409	-13,522.5
Employees	12,384	41,767	18,888	7,619	60,000
Customers	52 million	61 million	44.5 million	49 million	133 million
as of	Dec 2003	Dec 2003	Dec 2003	Dec 2003	March 2004

Source: Company websites / annual reports

Exhibit 40 Market shares in key European markets in 2003

Country	Brand	Market share	Country	Brand	Market share
Germany	T-Mobile Germany	42.9%	U.K.	Orange	26.7%
	Vodafone	36.3%		T-Mobile UK	24.7%
	E-Plus	12.2%		Vodafone	24.4%
	O2	8.6%		O2	24.3%
		100.0%		"3" (Hutchinson 3G)	0.0%
					100.0%
Italy	Telecom Italia Mobile	48.2%	France	Orange France	48.6%
	Vodafone Omnitel	34.7%		SFR	35.7%
	Wind incl. Blu	17.1%		Bouygues Telecom	15.7%
		100.0%			**100.0%**
Spain	Telefonica Moviles	54.0%			
	Vodafone	25.8%			
	Amena	20.2%			
		100.0%			

Sources: www.cellular.co.za; company websites

History and Strategic Outlook

T-Mobile was founded in 1992, and formally took over the mobile telephony business of DTAG in July 1993. At that point it solely controlled its German operations, where the GSM network went on air in July 1992 as one of Europe's earliest GSM networks.

The next eleven years saw a continuous race for new subscribers, driving penetration levels in Germany from zero up to 75.2% in December 2003 [193]. TMO's fierce rivalry with its main competitor Mannesmann Mobilfunk, which was acquired by Vodafone in April 2000, was one of the main drivers of innovation. Other drivers included the introduction of prepaid, used by 52% of all subscribers in 2003 [193], and mobile data services, used by 62.4% of all subscribers [193].

With regard to its products, TMO – along with all of its major European competitors – acquired UMTS licenses in all the markets its subsidiaries were operating in. Enabling the company to provide its customers with mobile Internet products was regarded as a priority given the potential of data to restore profits lost during the price erosion and rise of the less profitable prepaid segment among its customers. Roaming services, one of the most profitable services in mobile telephony were improved through increased interoperability among the subsidiaries' networks and a preferred tariff structure for customers roaming with T-Mobile.

To tackle the most important issues facing the company, TMO increasingly acted in alliances. To reduce costs in the build-up of UMTS networks in the UK and Germany, TMO and British Telecom signed a memorandum of understanding in 2001 in which they agreed on shared antenna-sites and the right to share each other's data networks [194]. For the provision of content on their mobile platforms, T-Mobile and Sony Music announced a "broad, global, strategic partnership" in 2004 [195]. Likewise, for the provision of handsets, TMO engaged in bilateral alliances with handset makers to gain exclusive access to certain models in order to achieve greater differentiation [196]. With regard to increasing its geographical scope, TMO co-founded the FreeMove alliance in 2003. In this alliance, its major assets were its strong and complementary footprint in Eastern Europe and the U.S. and its large buying power with suppliers of handsets and network equipment. As the largest of the four operators, it would also be able to wield significant influence in joint decision-making.

Telefónica Móviles (TEM)

Telefónica Móviles was the fifth largest mobile operator in the world, with more than 52 million subscribers in December 2003 [190]. This represented an increase of 25.7% over 2002 and also made it the fastest growing operator in the alliance. In Spain, it served 19.7 million subscribers or 54% of the market (see Exhibit 40) and was the undisputed market leader. Its other operations were concentrated in Latin America and the Mediterranean Basin. By the end of 2003, TEM had a presence in Brazil, Mexico, Argentina, Peru, Chile, Guatemala, El Salvador, Puerto Rico and Morocco. In 2003, TEM earned €10bn in revenues (10.2% up from 2002) and made a net profit of €1.6bn. Its parent, Telefónica S.A., owned 92.44% of TEM, which went public in 2000. With a market capitalization of €37.4bn [197], it was less than a third of the size of its main competitor, Vodafone, at €120.9bn.

History and Strategic Outlook

Telefónica S.A. started its Mobile GSM operations in 1995, trailing other big European operators by two to three years. However, due to the widespread popularity of prepaid services (which accounted for 61% of all Spanish subscribers in 2003 [193]), the less extensive fixed-phone line system in Spain and two vigilant competitors, Airtel (later acquired by Vodafone) and Amena, mobile penetration picked up fast, and by 2003, was 88% —higher than in Germany [193].

Telefónica S.A. bundled its mobile operations in its Telefónica Móviles division and issued about 8% of the division's shares in an IPO in 2000. One of the cornerstones of its corporate strategy was the launch of UMTS services in Spain and other European countries. Together with different partners, such as Sonera of Finland, TEM acquired UMTS licenses in Germany, Italy, Austria and Switzerland and tried to internationalize

further by building operations from scratch. However technological difficulties experienced by handset and network equipment manufacturers in the provision of UMTS handsets and equipment, strong competition from existing 2G operators and the lack of a customer demand for UMTS services lead to a reassessment of the UMTS strategy at TEM.

As the first European operator, it wrote off its UMTS investments abroad and concentrated instead on the home market and expansion in Latin America. In contrast to its efforts to expand in Europe, TEM's Latin American expansion was very successful. Buying existing operators minimized the risk of failure and added new subscribers immediately.

On the product side, TEM increased its efforts to generate own content by cooperating with a multitude of other small content generators as well as the Telefónica group subsidiaries, TerraLycos and Endemol. The number of small partnerships, alliances and shareholdings in this content-network very much resembled the approach of most other European operators. One big difference, however, was TEM's strategy of striking an alliance with NTT DoCoMo of Japan and adopting its "i-mode" technology [198]. This technology for providing mobile data-services to customers was difficult to replicate on partner networks and worked only within TEM's network.

The FreeMove alliance provided TEM with the opportunity of finding a new way into Europe, after it was unable to establish a presence of its own in the key markets of Germany, France or the UK. Its own Latin American footprint, with more than 30 million subscribers, on the other hand, provided the alliance with the opportunity to expand on a larger scale in the future.

Telecom Italia Mobile (TIM)

The Italian market, at 97.5%, was one of the most penetrated markets in Europe. 26.1 million subscribers made TIM the undisputed leader in this market, with a market share of almost 50%. In 2003, the TIM Group posted revenues of

€11,782m (8.4% up from 2002), gross operating profits of €5,502m (9.2% up) and an operating income of €3,786m (12.7% up from 2002) [199]. Its market capitalization of €39.7bn gave it approximately the same value as TEM [200].

Internationally, TIM had a presence in Greece, Turkey, Brazil, Venezuela and Peru. In particular, its majority stakes in mobile operators in Latin America and Greece accounted for the additional 18 million subscribers who TIM could contribute to the alliance.

History and Strategic Outlook

TIM was set up in July 1995 following the spin-off of Telecom Italia's mobile division. With over 44% public ownership, it had the least concentrated ownership structure within the alliance.

TIM had launched a mobile radio service in April 1990 on an analogue network (TACS 900 MHz) and in April 1995 it introduced the service on GSM standard. In October 2000, TIM was awarded one of the UMTS licenses (at a price of approximately €2,417m), put up for auction by the Italian government.

In an effort to reduce competition in its home market, TIM participated in one of the most unique transactions in the mobile phone industry: the buy-out of Italy's fourth GSM operator Blu. Together with the number 2 and 3 operators in the market, and with regulatory approval, TIM bought Blu, dissolved its operations and distributed its assets and customers among the three remaining operators.

In the development of the mobile market, TIM was, like TEM, one of the most innovative operators. Early adoption of prepaid cards pushed penetration levels to close to 100%. However, internationally, TIM was not able to gain a strong foothold in other European markets and instead focused on Latin America, Greece and Turkey. Its current focus was on the enhancement of its brand in Greece, the consolidation of newly acquired operations in Turkey and the introduction of new products and services in Latin America [201].

The FreeMove Alliance was another cornerstone of TIM's strategy, giving it access to the Northern European markets. Its chairman, Marco de Benedetti, headed the alliance in March 2004, and stressed the alliance's focus on driving up lucrative roaming revenues [202]. Italy, as one of Europe's primary tourist locations, would have a lot to gain in this respect.

Orange

Unique among the partners of the alliance, Orange had managed to gain market leadership in two of the biggest European markets: France (with over 20 million subscribers) and the UK (with over 13.6 million subscribers), by the end of 2003. In total, it had 49 million subscribers [190]. As one line of business within France Telecom (FT), Orange earned €17.9bn in 2003, up by 9% from 2002 [203], more than a third of FT's total revenues of €46.1bn.

Orange had, by the end of 2003, a strong European as well as international presence, with subsidiaries operating under the Orange brand in UK, France, Switzerland, Romania, Denmark, Slovakia, Luxemburg, the Netherlands, Thailand, the Ivory Coast, the Dominican Republic, Cameroon, Botswana and Madagascar. It also had stakes in operators in Belgium, Egypt, Portugal, Austria and India [190].

History and Strategic Outlook

The history of Orange was one of the most interesting of all the European mobile operators: after launching its GSM services in the UK as the fourth operator in 1994, Orange went public two years later, having already achieved an 8.5% share of the UK market. One year later it had gained additional 6% of the UK market, and in 1999 it opened its first international operations in Switzerland. In 1999, it became part of the battle between Mannesmann and Vodafone. Mannesmann bought Orange in 1999.

When Vodafone acquired Mannesmann after long negotiations in 2000, it had to sell Orange again. France Telecom bought Orange in May 2000, and merged its French "Itineris" branded operations under the Orange brand in 2001. In the following years, the internationalization of Orange gained momentum, adding operators in 19 additional countries to its network by June 2004. France Telecom owned Orange completely by the end of 2003, after repurchasing the remaining minority interest of 14% earlier that year.

Orange suffered its biggest defeat when, like Telefónica, it tried to establish a market presence in Germany by acquiring one of the six UMTS licenses in 2000. Its investment in the German service provider MobilCom, which had acquired the German license for €8bn, was finally written off in 2002.

In the field of data services, Orange decided, along with T-Mobile, TIM and Vodafone, against the introduction of i-mode services. The websites specifically designed for this mobile service created a "parallel Internet" that was considered likely to become obsolescent once transmission speeds over the mobile network were sufficient to surf the real Internet.

Orange joined the FreeMove alliance in June 2003, two months after the three founding members had announced its launch. Solomon Trujillo, the then newly appointed CEO of Orange, made the alliance a central part of the group's strategy [204]. From the alliance's standpoint, Orange's decision to join allowed it to close gaps – most notably France – in the alliance's geographical footprint.

Competition

The foundation of FreeMove was driven by the objective of enhancing its members' product and service portfolios in the roaming area, and providing attractive alternatives to Vodafone's roaming products. Likewise, many of Europe's smaller operators had joined forces under the leadership of Great Britain's mmO2 to form Starmap, the second European alliance. Combined, these three competitors, serving 170 million (FreeMove), 90 million (Vodafone), and 46 million (Starmap) European subscribers by March 2004, controlled over 90% of the European market.

Vodafone

With over 133 million proportionate[43] subscribers in 26 countries at the end of March 2004, Vodafone was the world's second largest mobile operator after China Mobile (with over 150 million subscribers). However, in terms of market capitalization, with €120.4bn [205] it was by far he largest pure-play mobile operator – larger than China Mobile (€33.9bn), Telefónica Móviles (€37.4bn) and Telecom Italia (€39.6bn) put together. In the financial year ending March 31, 2004, it had revenues of €50.34bn (up 10%) and an operating profit before goodwill, amortization and exceptional items of €16.05bn (up 17%) [164].

History

Vodafone was originally the name for the analogue network of Racal Radio Group, UK. It was launched on 1 January 1985 as the first analogue network in the UK, and had 19,000 subscribers by the year's end. Over the following years, Vodafone expanded its coverage to reach 80% of the UK population by 1987. In 1991,

---

[43] Proportionate subscribers were calculated according to the percentage of Vodafone interests in their shareholdings. In total, the companies of which Vodafone either had control or invested in had 340.1 million subscribers by March 2004. Source: www.vodafone.com

the highly successful Vodafone division fully de-merged from its parent and registered on the London and New York Stock Exchanges as Vodafone Group. In the same year, it launched the first GSM network in the UK.

The next eight years saw Vodafone grow at high speed in the UK and internationally through the acquisition of equity stakes. Product innovations such as the introduction of SMS (over the GSM network in 1994) and pre-paid (first implemented in the analogue network in 1996), the strengthening of its distribution network (500 specialist retail outlets and seven high street chains by 1995) and a radical restructuring, after CEO Chris Gent took over in 1997, helped to fuel its growth and profitability.

In 1999, a merger with AirTouch Communications Inc. of the U.S. created Vodafone AirTouch PLC, then the largest mobile operator in the world, considered to be "an engine for growth in the 21st Century". Vodafone AirTouch and Bell South of the U.S. created Verizon Wireless, a new wireless business with a national footprint, composed of Bell Atlantic's and Vodafone AirTouch's U.S. wireless assets. Verizon Wireless, with Vodafone holding a 45% stake, became the largest mobile operator in the U.S., although operating on a different technology (CDMA) to Vodafone's European operations (GSM) (see Exhibit 41).

Exhibit 41 Overview of the U.S. mobile market Q3 2003

	Verizon Wireless	Cingular Wireless	AT&T Wireless	Sprint PCS	Nextel Communications	T-Mobile USA
Market Dynamics						
Subscriber Market Share	23.9%	15.5%	14.5%	10.2%	8.2%	8.0%
Year-to-year Subscriber Growth	14.3%	5.9%	8.4%	6.6%	22.1%	36.1%
ARPU	$50	$51	$61	$63	$71	$54
Business Model						
Year-to-year Revenue Growth	18.2%	4.6%	7.7%	5.8%	26.7%	66.1%
Profitable	Yes	Yes	Yes	No	Yes	No
Cash Position	**	$1,3 billion	$4.2 billion	$1.5 billion	$3.5 billion	$195 billion
Long-term Debt	**	$12.7 billion	$10.6 billion	$14.2 billion	$10.7 billion	$7.6 billion
2G Network	CDMA	TDMA/GSM	TDMA/GSM	CDMA	WIDEN	GSM/GPRS
2 5/3G Migration Path	edma2000	EDGE/UMTS	EDGE/UMTS	edma2000	WIDEN	EDGE/UMTS
Investors	Verizon Comm and Vodafone	SBC Comm and BellSouth	NTT DoCoMo	Sprint FON	Motorola	Deutsche Telekom

Source: www.tbri.com/News/PressRelease/TBR.NBQ.3Q03.MobileOperatorBenchmark.pdf

In the period from 2000 to 2003, Vodafone grew even faster than before. The biggest transaction took place in 2000, when Vodafone acquired Germany's Mannesmann, a conglomerate combining operations in steel, automation, electronics and telecommunications, to control D2, Germany's successful competitor to T-Mobile, with a market share at the time of 42%. To comply with EU regulations, Vodafone sold Orange to France Telecom after the merger and also voluntarily shed all non-telecom related activities.

In 2001 and 2002, Vodafone added more international shareholdings and increased its ownership in existing ones to achieve at least majority ownership, if not 100% control, by these companies. At the same time, it divested equity stakes in companies where it was not able to gain influence in the corporate strategy. Vodafone also followed a strategy of establishing partner network agreements[44] in markets which it could not enter through equity stakes, and thus managed to cover most of Europe by 2003. Within each country, Vodafone concentrated heavily on customer growth, but as markets saturated it was among the first companies to refocus on profitability or average revenue per user (ARPU). This led to a temporary decline in pre-paid users, the most unprofitable segment in the market. In terms of revenue and profit, however, it put Vodafone in a leading position, as the example of the UK demonstrated.

Product innovations were another cornerstone of Vodafone's organic growth. In 2002, it introduced key innovations such as Vodafone Remote Access (as part of

---

[44] Under these agreements, partner networks took over Vodafone's brand and benefited from Vodafone's

the mobile office for business customers) and Vodafone Live! (as an entertainment platform for consumers). With Eurocall Platinum, Vodafone created a new roaming tariff option offering greater value to high volume roaming customers.

Vodafone also engaged in a number of strategic alliances in 2003 that exceeded the scope of its previous partnerships. With Orange, Telefónica Móviles, and T-Mobile it formed a new association to drive interoperable mobile payments [206]. With British Telecom [207] it cooperated in the further development of the area of fixed-mobile conversion[45]. Together with Microsoft [208], Vodafone worked on the development of a proprietary operating system for mobile phones. This was a significant deviation from the industry consensus as it threatened the agreement reached on a technical standard

for mobile phones established by the Symbian consortium [209]. However, Vodafone thus increased its pressure on handset developers to respond to its wishes in handset design and exclusivity deals, while for Microsoft it presented the opportunity to gain a foothold in the mobile market. Last but not least, Vodafone announced a letter of intent with SAP AG and HP to work together in order to develop new business applications, and agreed with Sony Music on the distribution of content through its Vodafone Live! service. These content relationships were very profitable for Vodafone as it managed to pay only 60% of revenues, compared to the 91% of revenues paid in i-mode relationships to content providers (see Exhibit 42).

---

45 Fixed-mobile conversion targeted the integration of fixed and mobile telephony in the field of tariffs and billing. In a best-case scenario, customers would get one bill for both their mobile and fixed line and pay reduced rates when they phoned from their "home zone", i.e. close to their fixed line access. A similar pricing scheme had already been offered by mmO2 to its customers in the UK and Germany).

Exhibit 42 Key features of i-Mode, early WAP and Vodafone Live! in comparison

Elements of a winning proposition	i-Mode	Early WAP Services	Vodafone live!
Colour display	Colour	Monochrome	Colour
Effective marketing to consumers	No mention of technology "Fun" NOT the Internet	Too much focus on technology ("WAP", "GPRS")	No mention of technology "Fun and entertainment"
Compelling package of services	Low-cost mobile messaging (email) + colour browsing + downloads	Limited monochrome browsing only SMS already well established	Low-cost mobile messaging (instant messaging/email) + colour browsing + pictures + downloads
Third-party relationships which stimulate innovation	Mass of third-party content providers 91% of premium service revenues to content providers (NNT DoCoMo retains just 9%)	Initial focus on internal development of content Operators too greedy in relationships with content providers	60% of premium service revenues to content providers
Control of terminals and user experience	Control over available handsets	Range of handsets with differences in WAP implementation	Control over limited number of handsets

Source: Analysis Research, 2003.

Strategy

In June 2004, Vodafone had formulated six strategic goals for its business:

1. Provide superior shareholder returns.
2. Delight our customers.
3. Leverage global scale and scope.
4. Expand market boundaries.
5. Build the best global Vodafone team.
6. Be a responsible business.

While the first two goals were in line with Vodafone's historical track record of increasing profitability and innovating its product portfolio, the third goal included new aspects, such as the development, implementation and commercialization of 3G services in all member countries. It also focused on achieving speed to market, enhanced customer experience, strategic cost advantages and growth opportunities for employees. The fourth goal was the most decisive in determining the interactions of Vodafone with other market players. It set the agenda for further geographical and functional growth.

Geographically, Vodafone indicated that its main interest would be in increasing its stakes in France (minority shareholding in SFR) and Italy (majority shareholding in Vodafone Italy) [210]. However, its failed bid for AT&T Wireless in the U.S. showed that it strove to get access to a fully/majority-owned mobile operator in this market as well.

Some industry observers expected Vodafone to strive for a deal with its shareholding partner in Verizon, Bell South, in order to gain control over Verizon. In a "big bang" scenario, Vodafone could even take over Bell South and divest everything apart from its wireless interests as it did with Mannesmann in 2000 [211].

Functionally, Vodafone defined strategic relationships in the mobile ecosystem (see Exhibit 43) in order to position itself best in a rapidly changing environment. Except for the field of telecommunications, where it followed primarily a full control strategy, it sought partners in the IT/wireless productivity and Infotainment fields. Vodafone's fifth and sixth goals took into account the ever increasing requirements for companies to create and maintain motivated workforces and comply with the high standards of socially responsible business conduct and impeccable corporate governance.

Starmap Alliance

The Starmap alliance was the smallest and youngest competitor in the European market. It had been launched in October 2003 under the leadership of mmO2, the former British Telecom mobile subsidiary. It typically comprised the third or fourth largest operators in its members' respective countries, with the exception of Norway, where incumbent and market leader Telenor, who served 58% of the market, joined the alliance (see Exhibit 44).

Exhibit 43 Vodafone's strategic relationships in the Mobile Ecosystem (March 04)

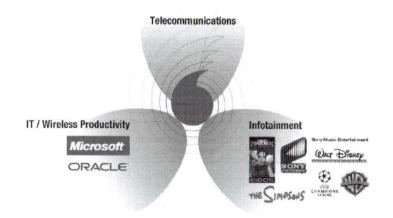

Source: Company websites and annual reports.

Exhibit 44 Starmap's European footprint

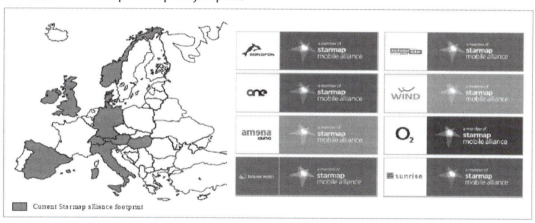

Source: http://www.starmapalliance.com; casewriter's analysis

Members

By July 2004, the Starmap Mobile Alliance had ten members: Amena (Spain), O2 (Germany, the UK and Ireland), One (Austria), Pannon GSM (Hungary), SONOFON (Denmark), sunrise (Switzerland), Telenor Mobil (Norway) and Wind (Italy), covering a subscriber base of more than 46 million. Its last member, SONOFON of

Denmark, joined the alliance in June 2004 which showed Starmap's ambition to increase coverage and scale across Europe.

With revenues of £4.874bn (€7.311bn) in FY 2003, and 11,750 employees, mmO2 was the largest member of the alliance. Its 18.7 million customers in the UK, Germany and Ireland benefited from its sophisticated technological standards – it was the first European operator to launch a commercial GPRS data network and offered innovative pricing schemes. In Germany and the UK, O2 was the fourth operator in the market (see Exhibit 40).

Amena of Spain was also positioned in last place in its home market, behind incumbent Telefónica Móviles and Vodafone. Nevertheless, it achieved significant growth rates through innovative products and could capture 42.8% of new subscribers in the still growing market, leaving it with 8.2 million customers and revenues of €3.858bn by the end of 2003.

The third large operator in the alliance was Wind of Italy. In the highly penetrated Italian market, Wind reached 10 million mobile subscribers and revenues of €2.238bn [212]. In contrast to the other alliance members, Wind had introduced i-mode services in June 2003 and gained 100,000 subscribers at the end of the promotional period. Innovative pricing schemes in the MNC segment such as free communication between company phones under the "Leonardo" tariff brought Wind a market share of 43% in new customer acquisitions.

Most other members of the alliance were approximately of the same size in terms of subscribers (Telenor 2.3 million; sunrise 2.6 million; ONE 1.8 million; SONOFON over 1 million) and operated in small or medium-sized European markets such as Norway, Switzerland and Austria.

Objectives and Organization

The objectives of Starmap were similar to those of FreeMove: cooperation in the areas of sourcing, technology and sales to large corporate customers to increase competitiveness. Starmap members agreed in February 2004 on a joint brand and developed joint pricing schemes for MNCs. Under a rotating presidency, the management board coordinated the joint activities of its members. It consisted of representatives of each operator. Further cooperation took place in bi- or multilateral working groups to avoid additional administrative or operational integration.

The Mobile Telecommunication Market in 2004

The global mobile telecommunication market developed very differently in its three major regions: Europe, the U.S. and Asia. Of a worldwide 1.5 billion mobile users in July 2004, 320 million lived in Europe, 140 million in the U.S., 295 million in China and around 90 million in Japan. 1.25 billion subscribers used the GSM standard while only 300 million used the competing CDMA / TDMA standards [213].

The Western European market had the highest penetration levels of mobile subscribers. With 85% penetration by the end of 2003, it had a significant lead over both Japan (66%) and the U.S. (53%). In this more saturated environment, factors such as the share of prepaid versus contract, business versus private and "mobile data" versus "voice only" users became more important for operators, because they influenced the development of the average revenue per user (ARPU) (see Exhibit 45). With increasing market penetration, the share of the less profitable prepaid users had continuously grown to reach around 62% in 2003. These figures differed widely across countries; for example Italy led with approximately 93% of prepaid users at the European scale, while in Finland only around 4% of subscribers used prepaid services. Mobile data users became crucial to mobile operators who hoped to compensate for eroding prices in the voice segment with increased revenues from mobile data services such as SMS, MMS, video telephony and mobile online gaming.

Exhibit 45 Mobile market data and forecasts, Western Europe

		2002	2003	2004	2005	2006	2007	CAGR
Key Market Indicators								
Population	Thousands	378,874	379,008	379,156	379,318	379,495	379,688	
Installed Base Penetration by Population	*Percent*	*82.0%*	*84.9%*	*88.1%*	*90.3%*	*91.8%*	*92.8%*	
Total Installed Base	Thousands	310,862	321,650	333,999	342,536	348,287	352,197	2.5%
YOY net adds	Thousands	18,075	10,787	12,350	8,536	5,751	3,910	
growth	*Percent*	*6.2%*	*3.5%*	*3.8%*	*2.6%*	*1.7%*	*1.1%*	
Prepaid Share of Installed Base	*Percent*	*63%*	*62%*	*59%*	*57%*	*55%*	*53%*	
Total Monthly ARPU per Installed Base	€ Units	31	31	32	32	33	33	1.5%
Total Revenue	€ Millions	112,254	118,664	125,322	131,524	136,471	140,177	
growth	*Percent*	*12.6%*	*5.7%*	*5.6%*	*4.9%*	*3.8%*	*2.70%*	
Voice and Data Market Segmentation								
Voice Monthly ARPU per Voice User	€ Units	27.1	26.4	25.6	24.8	24.3	24.0	-2.4%
Share of Installed Base Using Voice Services	*Percent*	*100%*	*100%*	*100%*	*100%*	*100%*	*100%*	
Mobile Data Montly ARPU per Data User	€ Units	7.3	8.4	10.2	11.9	13.1	14.0	14.0%
Share of Installed Base Using Voice Services	*Percent*	*56%*	*60%*	*63%*	*65%*	*66%*	*67%*	
Mobile Data Revenue Share of Total Revenue	*Percent*	*13%*	*16%*	*20%*	*23%*	*26%*	*28%*	
Users by Generation								
1G	Thousands	546	71	0	0	0	0	-86.9%
2G	Thousands	283,774	248,896	200,093	145,484	104,991	77,981	-22.8%
2.5G/3G	Thousands	26,543	72,682	133,906	197,052	243,296	274,215	59.5%
Total users (installed base)	Thousands	310,862	321,650	333,999	342,536	348,287	352,197	
Handset Sales by Generation								
1G	Thousands	0	0	0	0	0	0	
2G	Thousands	90,343	61,868	31,285	5,451	0	0	-60.8%
2.5G/3G	Thousands	25,224	56,757	92,142	122,872	132,586	135,122	39.9%
Total handset sales	Thousands	115,567	118,625	123,427	128,323	132,586	135,122	

Sources: Yankee Group 2003; www.nfo-bi.com

At the bottom line, operators tried to control their subscriber acquisition costs (SAC) by reducing the free provision of handsets to new customers. They also curbed costs for handsets by forming larger purchasing groups. Through the introduction of 3G / UMTS services and the necessity to promote new 3G handsets it was, however, expected that overall SAC would rise again. The design and availability of handsets also played a crucial role in operators' strategies as they strove to increase their influence over suppliers such as Nokia, Siemens, SonyEricsson and Motorola and deliver customized handsets exclusively in sufficient numbers – especially for the ongoing roll-out of 3G services in 2004.

With the introduction of 3G services the mobile industry was transforming itself into an eco-system that included not only operators and handset and network suppliers, but also content providers for the mobile Internet and software companies like Microsoft who tried to gain a foothold in the market for mobile operating systems. Operators had to position themselves not only against each other but also against other players in the mobile value chain if they did not want to end up as commoditized mobile voice and data providers.

Alliance Outlook: Set for Success?

The history of alliances in the telecommunication industry had not been encouraging. All of the former alliances in the fixed-line business set up in the early 1990s had failed due to emerging rivalries between national operators whose European participants were mostly similar in size and backed by their respective governments. FreeMove showed similar characteristics with regard to its composition. However, growing liberalization and internationalization of the telecom markets and the presence of a powerful competitor, Vodafone, mitigated national rivalries. It would be interesting to see if the operators in FreeMove could achieve similar successes in integration and value generation to Vodafone's without any equity exchange. In order to achieve maximum cohesion in the alliance, potential candidates had to fulfil certain criteria in order to join. But in the existing constellation, many challenges already needed to be addressed. Who would get the roaming customers of a partner network such as Telefónica if two other members had networks in the same country, such as T-Mobile and Orange in Great Britain? Promotion of the alliance varied across websites and ranged from a small link to widely visible banners. Shouldn't it be better unified? And how would the members' cultures work together given their strong national roots?

In moving forward, the alliance also faced a number of difficult choices: should it deepen its operational ties or maintain a loosely integrated entity? Should it allow new members in or first expand within the alliance's existing footprint (U.S./Latin America)? Finally, should it correspond to the changing mobile market by integrating other key players from the mobile eco-system?

Case Study: Budweiser in Japan

Introduction

The main focus of this case study is to outline the key factors which contribute to the success of launching an alcoholic beverage product in the Japanese market. This market differs vastly from domestic European or North American markets. Systemic cultural, social, and political phenomena combine to make Japan a uniquely challenging place for foreign firms to do business. Thus, studying the Japanese market provides an excellent opportunity to explore how cultural and societal differences impact business decision making. Japan is the second largest economy in the world, and will continue to play an important role in international trade and serve as an important market for western firms into the near- and medium-term future. It is also one of the three Triad regions (the U.S. and Europe being the other two), which are the three leading economic clusters in the world. [214] Learning about this market is thus beneficial for anyone seeking to work for a multinational business. The alcoholic beverages market was selected principally because of the interesting issues encountered by the firm Budweiser. As Budweiser entered Japan, they shifted their business model several times in order to accommodate the unique characteristics of the Japanese business environment. The alcoholic beverages market exemplifies many of these unique characteristics, which are prevalent in other industries and indeed are inherent to doing business in Japan. Thus, the discussion of the alcoholic beverages industry in Japan, with Budweiser as an example, provides an excellent opportunity to analyze in practical terms the complexities of doing business in Japan. As well, assessing the key success factors for a launch in this industry provides general insights for launches into other industries in Japan, and suggests a framework for analyzing foreign product launches in general.

Procedure

References for this case were gathered from a variety of resources. Principally, academic journals, expert interviews, industry-specific case studies, and theoretical texts were used.

Conceptual framework

The framework of this case study is as follows. First, a theoretical discussion of the main considerations that should be accounted for when planning a product launch in a foreign consumer goods market is presented. This discussion is lengthy and exhaustive, covering more than what is directly important to the specific case of Budweiser in Japan. Next, a discussion of the Japanese market is given, with specific attention to cultural, social, economic, and political issues which impact business decision making of foreign firms entering the alcoholic beverages industry. At the end of this discussion, a summary is given, which determines which of the above considerations are important to such firms given the specifics of the Japanese business climate, i.e. the key success factors for firms entering the Japanese alcoholic beverage industry. Next, a discussion of the specific example of Budweiser in Japan is given. This discussion draws on the previous conclusions and assesses Budweiser's performance in light of the important key factors identified for the Japanese alcoholic beverages industry. Finally, the results of the entire analysis are summarized, and recommendations are given which are applicable to firms entering both the alcoholic beverages industry in Japan and other Japanese segments in general.

The product launch of alcoholic beverages in the Japanese market

Companies that want to enter the Japanese alcoholic beverages market need to understand their business model abroad. They need to know how their company will create value in the Japanese market, and what their competitive advantage will be. To determine this, it is necessary to evaluate the business model according to established key considerations of an international product launch. As well, it is vital that the model incorporate the specifics of the Japanese business climate, as these can affect the company's traditional sources of competitive advantage and may significantly impact the way they do business in Japan. This section deals first with the established key considerations of an international product launch that any consumer goods manufacturing company would have to explore when launching abroad. Next, the business climate of the Japanese alcoholic beverages market is evaluated, including a discussion on important cultural, legal, and political issues that affect this market. Finally, drawing on these two discussions, a set of key success factors is given for companies choosing to launch into the Japanese alcoholic beverages market.

Key considerations of an int. product launch and market entry

As mentioned above, when companies launch abroad, they must evaluate their business models according to several key considerations. These factors can be grouped into three categories: physical access factors, commercial access factors, and legal and political access factors. [214] Each group will now be dealt with in turn.

Physical access factors

Physical access factors concern the products themselves and their delivery to the end consumer. Three key issues that the company must consider when evaluating its business model are the nature of the products they plan to sell, the infrastructure of the country into which they plan to sell, and the transportation costs inherent in the delivery of their products to the end consumer.

Nature of the products

Different countries can exhibit widely different tastes and preferences in the consumer goods they purchase. As well, cultures, traditions, and values differ greatly across borders. As a result of these differences, some products will inherently not be successful in some markets. For example, a frozen-hamburger manufacturer will not be able to sell its products in India, where cows are revered and beef is not eaten on a large scale. Similarly, American toy manufacturers may not be able to sell many of their products in countries with strong anti-American sentiments. In many cases, attributes of products can be changed to adapt them and make them saleable in local markets (see discussion below). However, companies must first evaluate whether the very nature of the products they plan to sell will be suitable for the new market they are entering, given the differences mentioned above.

Country infrastructure

Country infrastructure is also not consistent across borders. Different levels of road and rail systems can make delivery of goods more challenging in some countries than in others. Similarly, a less developed electrical utility system can make local production much more expensive and risky. Even telephone and communication systems can vary greatly, imposing varying degrees of costs depending on the type of entry strategy selected (i.e. producing locally versus exporting). A company must analyze all such infrastructure in the market they wish to enter and determine the costs associated with each possible entry method. [214] These costs will then help influence the decision of entry method, or sometimes whether to enter at all. Of course, strategic considerations may favour an entry mode that is disadvantageous with respect to infrastructure costs. However, such costs must still be considered in the business model, and the model should be altered so as to minimize costs resulting from differing levels of country infrastructure.

Transportation costs

Linked in part to infrastructure, transportation costs are essentially the costs associated with delivering the product to the end consumer. These costs do not only depend on infrastructure, but also depend on the nature of the distribution channels and sophistication of transportation services in the target market. These costs may also vary according to the entry mode selected. For instance, by producing locally, a company may be able to locate near a major distributor, potentially reducing shipping costs from the nearest shipping dock. However, these savings need to be considered as part of a total cost-benefit analysis of the entry mode decision, as obviously other costs will vary depending on the mode chosen. Nevertheless, the business model must be evaluated as to its efficiency in transportation costs, and should be altered to reduce these costs wherever possible.

Commercial access factors

Commercial access factors concern the interactions of the product and company with the business environment. This environment includes all customers throughout the supply chain, from distributors through to end consumers (i.e. marketing factors), suppliers of inputs (i.e. operational factors), and competitors. Accordingly, these factors are divided into the above three sub-groups.

Marketing factors

Price

Price is a vital success factor for three reasons. [215] First and foremost, it is one-half of the equation that establishes the company's margin in the new market. However, it also supports the company's overall growth strategy. Thus, a company must not only decide what margin it requires to achieve its desired return; it must first decide what type of growth strategy it thinks is feasible or optimal, and then structure its desired return around this strategy. The two broad growth strategies are penetration and niche [10]. In a penetration strategy, a company usually believes its product will be well received by a large portion of the market, and thus can price its product low to achieve profits through large volume. Returns in this strategy will be lower, but contribution margins will be very high if sales proceed as expected. In a niche strategy, a company usually believes that a select market segment exists to which its product specifically appeals. This segment will typically pay a premium to obtain the unique value that the company's product delivers. Thus, pricing under such a strategy will be high, as will margins. However, contribution margin will be low because sales will be limited. The growth decision must be based on a careful analysis of the foreign market, including customer tastes and preferences, as well as their likeliness to prefer the unique qualities of the new product being launched.

The Price is also important for a third reason: it acts as a signal to competitors insofar as it can be used to deter entry or force a price war.

Product

As mentioned above, consumer preferences and tastes can vary greatly from country to country. It is often beneficial for a manufacturer to adapt its products to these local differences when entering a new market. For example, changing an ingredient in a brand of soup to accommodate a preference for a local seasoning may help sales of that brand. However, not all accommodations can be made, as some may sacrifice the core competency or source of competitive advantage of the company in question. Therefore, a company must ask itself what are the key attributes of its product that make it successful in its current markets, what are the key differences in preferences and tastes of consumers in the new market, and can any of the key attributes be changed to accommodate these key tastes without sacrificing competitive advantage. Any attributes which pass this test should be changed to accommodate the local preferences.

Promotion

Promotion refers to activities which communicate the product directly to consumers. These activities cover both traditional advertising campaigns (television, radio, print), as well as non-traditional methods such as public events, displays, sponsorship, product placements, and a slew of other initiatives. [215] All of these activities are used to build, enhance, or reposition a company's or product's brand in the new market. Thus, before launching a successful promotional campaign, a company must first assess what its brand equity is in the new market. Depending on the level of awareness and/or positive reputation, the company will decide whether it needs to build, enhance, or reposition its brand in order to maximize positive customer opinion and therefore sales.

Packaging

Like promotion, packaging can be seen as a form of communication to the end consumer – consider the use of bright colours, attractive pictures, and persuasive messages on prominently displayed boxes in a retail store. However, packaging also plays a functional role in that it transports the goods from the point of purchase to the place of use. Thus, companies must not only think of packaging their product to appeal to new consumers with potentially differing ideals of aesthetics; they must also consider how the consumer will arrive at the retail store (or shop online?), carry goods around the store, check-out from the store, and transport the goods back home (i.e. via car, transit, walking). All these considerations must be explicitly accounted for in the packaging decision, as they can vary greatly from market to market.

Distribution and market entry

The very nature of the distribution model selected, or market entry model in the case of a company that is introducing itself for the first time to the foreign market, can significantly impact the success of the foreign venture. Distribution models vary from simple exporting to a third party, to partnering exclusively with an import company, to licensing domestic production, to entering jointly with a local manufacturer, to a merger or acquisition, to launching a wholly-owned subsidiary to produce locally [216]. In the case of the latter three models, the choice of wholesalers and/or retailers is an added decision that needs to be included in the distribution model analysis. Many factors will influence which model is optimal for the given product in the given market. Customer power plays a role, as one would like to avoid ceding too much negotiating power to purchasers. Knowledge of the local market is also very important, as often local companies will be better able to meet customer demands than foreign ones. As well, cultural, political, and legal issues specific to the new market can be vital, as countries vary widely in the ease with which foreign companies can set up shop locally. Lastly, the company's own financial resources may dictate which model will yield the best results for them, since each model requires a different level of risk.

Operational factors

Material Inputs

Consumer goods companies need to procure physical inputs to the products they produce. Thus, upstream supply lines need to be evaluated prior to entry into the foreign market. The availability of inputs, as well as the concentration and state of the industries that supply them, can impact both the overall choice to enter a foreign market, and the choice of entry method, discussed above. For example, a soap company that finds that the necessary chemicals are very expensive to procure locally or import from abroad may decide simply to export its finished goods to the new market. Thus, an evaluation of supplier power and the availability or cost-effectiveness of local supplies must be considered in shaping the business model of the foreign launch. [10 p. 71]

Physical Capital

Like physical inputs, physical capital is necessary to produce consumer goods. Depending on the local cost to operate such capital and transport it into the facility and the technological knowledge of local workers, producing locally may be more or less suited to the particular market being considered. Thus, an analysis of the physical capital requirements and the costs associated with operating the equipment should be factored into the business model.

Human Capital

The availability of skilled labour can vary widely from country to country, and the labour requirements of companies can differ widely from segment to segment. Companies therefore need to assess the fit of their own labour requirements – dependent on the entry model they select – with the state of the labour supply in the local country. Another consideration is the prevailing equilibrium wage in the new market. Wage costs could prove to be economically prohibitive, and thus may also influence the entry model. All such factors must be included in the design of the business model.

Financial Capital

Entry into foreign markets incurs risk that varies from market to market and from business segment to business segment. The availability of capital, and its requisite cost, will thus also vary. Companies must therefore adapt their business model so that the expected returns will be sufficient to cover the risk-adjusted returns that their suppliers of financial capital will expect.

Competition factors

(For further discussion on topics in this section, see Porter, M., The McKinsey Quarterly, 1980)

Rivals

The degree of rivalry within the selected foreign market is a crucial determinant of success for the company at hand. Some industries are too mature and exhibit too low growth and too low margins for a new company to enter and be profitable over the long-term. The degree of rivalry can be assessed by the number and concentration of competitors (more competitors with lower concentration means more rivalry), the size of margins, the growth in sales, the level of advertising dollars spent, as well as other indicators. Overall, mature industries that are slowly-growing should be avoided, unless the company can alter the industry dynamics to spur new growth in a unique and inimitable way. [217]

Substitutes

The degree to which substitute products exist in the new market which can pose threats to the new company's market share is also an important factor in the success of the new company. For example, a cola beverage company may find it difficult to compete against products such as tea in countries where tea is a traditional staple. Thus, the degree to which substitute products pose a credible threat in the new market should be assessed in the business plan. Though this may not affect the go/no-go decision, it will impact the marketing strategy and/or the distribution strategy (discussed above).

Entrants

Ease of entry is an important consideration for two reasons. First, it will determine how efficiently the new company can enter the market. However, it will also determine how easily future competitors will enter the market. Ideally, barriers to entry would be present which the company at hand has the ability to overcome, but other competitors likely do not. For instance, a particular country may have stringent entry laws in a particular segment, but a foreign company may have a unique historical tie with a local manufacturer. Such a company may be able to set up a joint-venture that few other foreign companies would have the ability to, and thus would be able to take advantage of this barrier to entry. Such barriers, acting as both deterrents to entry and hedges against future competition, must therefore be assessed in the formulation of the business model.

Legal and political access factors

Legal and political access factors are those factors exogenous from the direct players in the commercial environment but nevertheless exert influence on that environment by affecting market dynamics. Three important factors are now discussed.

Entry barriers

Entry barriers include all deterrents which serve to dissuade companies from entering a market. In the context of legal and political access factors, such barriers include government regulations in certain industries limiting the number of participants, intractable legal guidelines which prove prohibitive for new entrants to learn to abide by, [218] and political taboos against increased competition in certain segments, among others. Such barriers can be assessed by analyzing a country's legal system and business climate, especially pertaining to the industry or sector at hand. As in the case mentioned above – where a more general class of entry barriers was discussed – If entry barriers prove sufficient to deter certain entrants, but can be somehow subverted by the company at hand, such a company would benefit by entering and using the barriers as a hedge against further competition. However, the converse is also true, and so these factors must be evaluated with respect to the business model.

Legal and fiscal environment

The legal and fiscal environment describes the atmosphere of doing business in a particular country or sector within a country. Though not necessarily deterrents to entry, issues such as long term growth and stable legal frameworks can impact the long-term prosperity of a company entering a new market. These issues need to be assessed a priori in order to determine whether the market will support the new product well into the future, and whether the rules of the game are likely to remain stable. Since both these issues affect the success of the company in the long run, they are important success factors and warrant sufficient study.

Political issues

In a similar vein, political issues can serve to hinder or assist both entry and the long-term profitability of the foreign venture. As regards posing a barrier to entry, this issue was discussed above. In the latter respect, a stable political environment will greatly enhance the ability of a foreign venture to raise financial capital and, more importantly, draw sustainable revenues. Moreover, a pro-business political environment will ensure that profits can be earned efficiently and will reduce the risk of new anti-business legislation being enacted which may hinder future prospects. Thus, political issues in the foreign market must be assessed and the business model must be adapted to take into account the risks they pose.

The launch of an int. alcoholic beverage product in Japan

As mentioned at the beginning, companies entering Japan must understand the specifics of the Japanese business climate. This is vital because doing business in Japan is very different from doing business in most western economies. Specifically, cultural, social, and political qualities differ greatly from the West, and impact the business environment in ways to which western companies must learn to adapt in order to succeed. This section will first describe the Japanese economy in the context of these cultural, social, and political differences. Next, the discussion will narrow to the alcohol market in Japan, and describe the peculiarities of this market that are important for foreign firms to understand. Finally, an analysis will be presented to determine those of the considerations discussed in above which, given the discussion herein, are key success factors for entering the Japanese alcoholic beverages market.

The Japanese economy

Potentials and risks

At the end of World War II, Japan was in ruins and lagged far behind the industrialized and experienced western nations. However, it has managed to rebuild and compete against almost all other countries in a relatively short time, pulling out of its economic slump and showing clear signs of an emerging recovery. Close government-industry cooperation, a strong work ethic, mastery of high technology, and a comparatively small defence budget have helped Japan advance with extraordinary speed to become the second largest economy in the world in terms of nominal GDP, placing right behind United States and third after the United States and China if purchasing power parity is taken into account. GDP growth for the year 2005 was 2.8%, with an annualized fourth quarter expansion of 5.5%, surpassing the growth rates of the U.S. and the European Union during the same period. Domestic consumption has been the dominant factor in leading the growth. Hence, the Japanese government predicts that recovery will continue in 2006.

Japan is the country with the greatest amount of liquid savings per capita – and, therefore, purchasing power – and ranks as one of the most highly developed industrialized countries in the world. Japan is among the world's largest and most technologically advanced producers of motor vehicles, electronic equipment, machine tools, steel and nonferrous metals, ships, chemical, textiles, and processed foods, and is home to some of the largest and most well-known multinational corporations and commercial brands in technology, machinery, and finance. It is also one of the leading research nations in these sectors. Japan's service sector accounts for about three-quarters of its total economic output. Banking, insurance, real estate, retailing, transportation, and telecommunications are all major industries in Japan. [219] Besides London and New York, Tokyo is the most important banking centre in the world. The Tokyo Stock Exchange is the second largest in the world, with a market capitalization of more than $4 trillion. Altogether, these industries make Japan a major global economic power. Due to its high level of global participation in many industries, Japan is a market that may prove to be integral in the future success of several companies.

In the mid 1980s, the Japanese market was often characterized as being excessively regulated and difficult to penetrate. Japan still is a very bureaucratic country in many ways, with a dense network of regulations, permissions, certifications, procedures, and authorities with approval procedures for many things. Numerous documents are devoted to Japan's standards and regulations concerning import procedures, quarantine periods, technical requirements, etc. Many of these restrictions are designed as entry barriers against newcomers to existing industries. Slowly these regulations are eased and seldom eliminated. Several factors have contributed to the easing of these regulations and to opening up the economy. Changes brought through technology and the internet, restructuring within the Japanese economy, and bilateral negotiations have opened the Japanese market in many sectors where U.S. companies are globally competitive. As a result of the Economic Partnership for Growth, launched by President Bush and Prime Minister Koizumi in June 2001, the U.S. and Japanese governments continue to exchange reform recommendations on key sectors every fall. [220] These days thousands of

U.S. companies have established successful operations in Japan and even more export to Japan on a regular basis. Despite the liberalisation of the import system in Japan, it is still difficult to penetrate the Japanese market because of its structure. As a rule, most of the goods are freely authorised to be imported. However, some products are subject to a license, especially products restricted by quotas. A certain number of agricultural products are also subject to a license (animals, plants, perishable foodstuffs). This system is supervised by the Ministry of Economy, Trade and Industry. All products affecting consumers' health have to go through the preliminary request of a license to be launched on the market, and have to do so before they are able to be imported into Japan. The Ministry of Health is in charge of assessing the goods included in this category. It is very difficult, even today, to import, for example, cosmetics in Japan, and pharmaceutical products are very highly regulated.

Japan has very limited natural resources to sustain economic development, since most of the islands are volcanic and mountainous. As a result it is dependent on other nations for most of its raw materials. Japan is an extremely accessible country due to its position directly on long-established global trade routes and its proximity to the important emerging markets within Asia. [221 p. 62] The country's dependence on trade necessitates a highly integrated and efficient transport network both domestically and internationally. Since the end of World War II, the United States has been the most important trading partner with Japan. Their bilateral trade volume amounts for around one-fourth of Japan's total trade. All the East and Southeast Asian countries (except Korea) maintain more extensive trade relations with Japan than with other Asian countries. With a trading volume of around 15 percent, the European Union is an important trading partner as well. [222 p. 211]

Japan shows extensive market potential but the country is facing several problems and challenges as well. The weak business cycle, the high indebtedness of the state and of many companies, and the reluctance to restructure prevalent in many sectors of the "Old Economy" are weak points of the Japanese economy. The central bank is facing the dilemma of needing to break a new credit expansion with an increase in interest rates without harming the longed-for cyclical upturn – an "artwork of monetary policy" that is not likely to work. [223] In the long run, Japan needs to cut public spending and cope with a declining population and a shrinking workforce. Worries about inequality are also surfacing, and a rise in the undervalued yen could create problems for Japan's exporters. [224]

Cultural issues of the Japanese market

When doing business in Japan, it is important to be aware of the cultural issues that affect the economy. The distinguishing cultural characteristics of the Japanese economy include the cooperation of manufacturers, suppliers, distributors, and banks in closely-knit groups called keiretsu (examples include Mitsubishi, Sumitomo, Fuyo, Mitsui, Dai-Ichi Kangyo and Sanwa); the powerful enterprise unions and shuntō; cozy relations with government bureaucrats; and the guarantee of lifetime employment (shushin koyo) in big corporations and highly unionized blue-collar factories. The Japanese attach a high degree of importance to personal relationships, and these take time to establish and nurture. Patience and repeated follow-up are required to clinch a deal. In most Asian business cultures, harmony is valued above everything else. [225] Problems can arise out of the international cooperation and misunderstandings due to language and gestures. Very few Japanese people (less than 3% - 5%) speak good English, and as a consequence there has been a certain amount of intellectual isolation from the rest of the world. When it comes to a faux-pas, it can have serious consequences: the image of the company can be destroyed, the contract will probably not be settled, and the cooperation can be deranged. It is not different manners, but rather different mindsets, that make international cooperation difficult: far-eastern "distance" hits the western "backslapping" mentality. [226] In Japan, building relationships should emphasize mutual trust, confidence, loyalty, and commitment for the long term, both among individuals and companies. Recently, Japanese companies have begun to abandon some of these norms in an attempt to increase profitability. But for now, the future success of firms entering Japan rests on their ability to adapt to these norms. Regarding cultural issues Hofstede's dimensions should also be considered when doing business in or with Japan. According to Hofstede, Japan's business culture can be characterized by a high power distance, high masculinity, high uncertainty avoidance and high long-term orientation. Furthermore, it has a high-context culture. We will discuss the differences between cultures in a later chapter.

The Japanese alcohol beverage market

If an alcoholic beverage company wants to expand to the Japanese market, it is not just necessary to have a broad knowledge about the Japanese economy in general but also about the Japanese alcoholic beverage market in particular. The following discussion seeks to give an overview of the characteristics of the liquor market in Japan and their implications for companies that want to enter the Japanese alcoholic beverage market.

Sales volumes of alcohol beverages are widely regarded in Japan as one measure of overall consumer sentiment. There are striking differences in the market development between different categories of alcoholic beverages. [227] The different categories are beer and happo-shu, sake, whiskey, wine and scho-chu. These will each be dealt with in turn.

Japanese alcoholic beverages categories

Beer & Happoshu

The favourite liquor of the Japanese is beer. Consumption of sake was overtaken by that of beer around the beginning of the 20th century and now beer - or its close relation, happoshu - accounts for over 75% of alcohol consumption. The beer market in Japan is an oligopoly, essentially controlled by the two most prominent brands, Kirin (from Kirin Beverages) and Asahi (from Asahi Breweries, Ldt. with 39% market share), along with two other important brands, Sapporo and Suntory. [228] Japanese beer brands such as Kirin, Asahi and Sapporo are known worldwide. Consumers are also served by many of the world's major beer brands that compete in Japan as well.

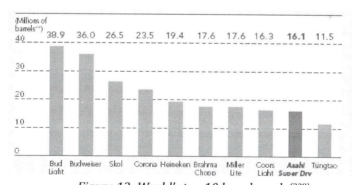

Figure 12: World's top 10 beer brands [228]

	1990	1995	2000	2001	2002	2003	2004
China	59.0	132.4	190.2	193.8	203.2	211.2	240.6
United States	193.0	185.9	196.1	196.3	197.8	197.4	198.9
Germany	96.8	94.6	87.9	86.0	85.5	82.8	81.1
Brazil	46.4	68.2	70.4	71.5	73.9	72.4	74.4
Russia	28.5	16.8	47.1	52.0	57.2	63.1	70.1
Japan**	56.7	60.8	60.5	60.7	59.1	55.4	53.6
United Kingdom	55.5	50.4	48.2	48.3	48.7	48.6	49.2
Mexico	31.5	34.8	42.9	43.6	43.2	44.7	45.8
Spain	24.1	23.0	24.8	26.5	26.2	28.5	29.4
Poland	9.6	12.9	19.0	20.7	22.8	24.2	24.9

Figure 13: Beer market: beer consumption, top 10 countries [228]

Consumer preferences in alcoholic beverages have diversified greatly over the past ten years and within each sector the market is tending to polarize. This means that in the beer business premium beers are selling well, yet at the same time new-genre products are enjoying a boom in the more price-conscious end of the spectrum. Some consumers are purposely switching between the poles, choosing premium beers during the weekend and lower-cost drinks and new-genre alcoholic beverages during the week. One response to consumer demand at the low end of the market has been the development of new-genre products that attract lower rates of liquor tax because of the low malt content. [227] The new-genre beers are not classified as beer according to the Japanese tax system. Malt beverages with 67% or more malt content are classified as beer; but the new beers, with less than 25% malt content, are not taxed as beer, and sell for 1/3 the price of regular beer. [229] Japanese consumers have responded enthusiastically to *happoshu*: a cheap low-malt drink that has gained popularity in Japan as an alternative to regular-priced, heavily-taxed beer. Happoshu, which means "fizzy liquor," made its debut about eight years ago, and now holds more than 40% of the Japanese beer market. Happoshu looks like beer, and has an alcohol content that is about the same, approximately 5% a.b.v. But it is generally half the price of beer. Malted barley usually makes up about 25% of the ingredient mix, and the rest is a witch's brew of adjuncts that can include rice, potatoes, corn syrup, starch and sugar. This is where the cost savings derive, because in Japan, tax on beer is based on the percentage of malt the beer contains. [229] Happoshu accounted for over a fifth of the beer market in 2000.

The so-called "third-generation beer-taste beverages," are a new trend. They use neither barley nor barley malt and thus are subject to a lower liquor tax rate than *happoshu*. The pioneer in this field was Draft One, launched by Sapporo Breweries in February 2004. This product has had a major impact on the market. There is a definite possibility that home market users who initially switched from beer to *happoshu* because of lower prices may switch from *happoshu* to third-generation beer-taste beverages for the very same reason. Consequently, marketing for imported beer (which makes up less than 1% of the market) and for domestically produced foreign brands of beer is increasingly targeting the commercial market. Foreign brand-makers and importers are focusing on beverage establishments consistent with the unique characteristics of the country and the brand, with special emphasis on draft beer. The World Cup-inspired surge in demand, beginning in 2002, has come to an end, but there are excellent prospects for growth in exploring beverage establishments, especially in smaller cities in the provinces. (230 pp. 1-24)

Despite fast-growing demand for third generation beer, however, it is still unable to hold the decline among total beer sales in 2005. The Japanese beer market peaked in 1994 and has been on the decline ever since. Consumers are drinking less beer and the price of beer remains expensive compared to other alcoholic drinks such as chu-hai. (230 p. 8) Although overall beer sales are declining, the premium beer category is growing. (227 p. 11)

Whiskey

The Japanese whiskey market has been hit harder by the recessions in the 1990s than other alcoholic beverages. Both domestic and imported whiskies continue to post weak sales. Both domestic distillers and importers responded to the major liquor tax reductions by cutting retail whiskey prices significantly. They have also aggressively introduced new products, including smaller bottles of whiskey to encourage young adult drinkers to try the product, and whiskies that go better with Japanese style home-cooked meals. However, from 2001 onward annual consumption has been dropping. Market leader Suntory, along with Asahi Breweries and Kirin Brewery, began targeting young adults between the ages of 25 to 35 in the second half of 2003 with a variety of promotional sales strategies. These included advertising new ways of drinking whiskey and opening direct outlet bars. As a result, the whiskey market is regaining its vitality for the first time in a long time. Discount liquor stores sell brands of imported whiskey that once were considered strictly luxury items, at prices that are comparatively affordable. As a result, these brands have become much more available and accessible. (230)

Sake

Sake is a traditional Japanese drink made from polished rice, with around 15% alcohol content. Produced in Japan for more than 2,000 years, sales volumes of Sake have been gradually falling over the last fifty years as consumer tastes diversify. [227]

Wine

The wine market in Japan was particularly vibrant in the late 1990s. Numerous TV shows and magazine articles have touted the health benefits of drinking red wine. Since then wine has taken its spot as a routine part of Japanese lifestyles. It is no longer something people drink only on special occasions. Now it is something that people drink routinely, with their daily meals. Consumers' wine knowledge seems to have grown markedly in Japan. Consumers increasingly are choosing imported wines over domestic wines if they are priced similarly, and this is significantly undermining the position of domestic wines. Japanese wine is aiming now for a higher profile in premium class wines, which depend on carefully selected grapes, and in plumb, apple, and other fruit wines. Many imported wines have been forced to revise retail prices due to the strong Euro and to the higher cost imposed by the liquor tax increase. After the licensing system of general liquor retailers relaxed in 2003, more stores are carrying wines, but it is also expected that expanded wine distribution channels will greatly intensify price competition. [230 p. 19]

Schochu

Schochu is a clear, grain-based distilled liquor with around 25% alcohol content, and is sold on premises and for home consumption. [227 p. 62] With its volume overtaking that of sake in 2003, volume sales of schochu are expected to continue growing in 2005, as it remains popular among consumers in Japan. Shochu is being widely accepted by both young and old consumers, as well as males and females. The media continues to promote the health benefits of drinking shochu, while manufacturers continue to push for new products to entice consumers' interest. [231]

Chu-hi

Chu-hi is a sparkling distilled liquor with fruit juice, with around 5-7% alcohol content. It differs from the RTD (ready to drink) cocktails of overseas markets in that chu-hi has been a staple of the Japanese market for more than 25 years, it is sold primarily in cans, and more than 90% of sales are for home consumption. Industry sales have grown dramatically, headed by market leader Kirin Chu-hi Hyoketsu, since Kirin's reinvented the category in 2001. [227 p. 62] Many consumers are looking for beverages with lower alcohol content, with chu-hai containing on average 5% alcohol. The launches of healthier variants of chu-hai also helped boost sales. Low-calorie, reduced-sugar and increased-juice chu-hai all helped to increase its popularity. Furthermore, with manufacturers launching new flavours every season, consumers are pampered with numerous choices of different flavours to select according to their own preference. [231]

Imports and licensing

Japan has a lot of domestic liquor products and brands but the more than 100 million people aged 20 and over are not served only by the four large brewers, but also by many of the world's major liquor brands who compete in Japan as well. There are several imported products. The leading imported alcoholic beverage is wine, which accounts for 36.9% of all imports. The leading exporter of wine to Japan is France with 39.3% of the imported wine market in 2003, followed by Italy (19.0%), the United States (11.8%), Chile (7.2%), and Spain (6.0%). The next leading imports on a volume basis are other distilled liquors (38.9%), and beer (17.9%). On a value basis the next leading imports are whisky (15.9%) and brandy (8.4%). [230]

(Note) Beer includes " happoshu. "

Figure 14: Breakdown of imported alcoholic beverages [230 p. 2]

The World Cup Soccer tournament held in Japan during June of 2002 lifted consumer awareness of imported beer and led to more widespread channel availability. However a lot of leading world brand (Heineken (the Netherlands: Kirin Brewery), Miller Special (U.S.A.: Asahi Breweries), Löwenbräu (Germany: Asahi Breweries), Carlsberg (Denmark: Suntory) are produced under license in Japan now, and with only small size cans still being imported from the respective home countries.

Consequently, import volume growth has been very small. Since the all-time high recorded in 1994, the imported beer market has shrunk to just one-tenth its former size. The resultant import market comprises high-volume imports of ultra-cheap beer. Imported beer has yet to recover its status in the minds of consumers from the 1994 high. [230]

Laws and regulations

The alcoholic beverage market is not just characterized by products that are highly cultural, but it is also a highly regulated market. Alcoholic beverage imports are subject to the provisions of the Food Sanitation Law and the Liquor Tax Law. Under the provisions of the Food Sanitation Law, an import notification is required for alcoholic beverages being imported for the purpose of sale or for other commercial purposes. Importers are required to submit the completed "Notification Form for Importation of Foods", etc. to the Quarantine Station at the port of entry. Prior to importing, the importer may take a sample of forthcoming imports to laboratories registered with the Minister of Health, Labour, and Welfare, or the competent government agency of Japan. [230] The Liquor Tax Law requires a business license from the competent tax office in order to manufacture or sell liquor. Any person or entity may import liquor without restriction, but without a liquor vendor's license, it is not permitted to ship imported liquor out of the bonded area. In Japan, the Liquor Tax Law subjects all forms of beverages with an alcohol content of 1% or higher to taxation. Beer, wine, and other beverages containing less than 1% alcohol are not classified as alcoholic beverages under the Liquor Tax Law. These products are sold as soft drinks instead, and are thus not subject to the Liquor Tax Law. [230 p. 9]

The domestic sale of liquor is subject to the Liquor Tax Law, the Liquor Business Association Law, the Food Sanitation Law, the Measurement Law, and the Act against Unjustifiable Premiums and Misleading Representations. Products that infringe intellectual property rights are regulated by the various intellectual property laws (Trademark Law, Patent Law, Unfair Competition Prevention Law, etc.). Prospective exporters to Japan must be aware of these considerations, as rights holders may initiate legal action. [230 p. 10] In addition to the compliance with laws and regulations for liquor companies, the compliance with ethical standards to gain the trust of the society and the business community is important as well. [230]

Recent trends and challenges

With a rising average age and a low birth-rate, the Japanese market has matured over the last quarter-century. At the same time, total alcoholic drinks volume sales are expected to continue declining as consumers drink less because they are getting more health-oriented. There is a considerable demand for products that cater to health conscious consumers or those looking for lighter, cleaner tastes. Health-conscious consumers will also become more selective in the types of alcoholic drinks they consume. Shochu, which is seen as beneficial to health, is expected to see positive growth. Niche products will also increase in popularity, such as still light grape wine with high polyphenol content. Alcoholic drinks that are lower in calories or carbohydrates will also support growing sales, and newly developed products fortified with anything beneficial to health will continue to sell well in the near future. [231]

At the same time, consumer tastes and drinking styles have diversified. Younger consumers in particular may have a beer after work on Friday, enjoy a glass of wine on Saturday, then sip a cold chu-hi while watching a Sunday night video. The boundaries separating the segments of the alcoholic beverage market have eroded, with consumer satisfaction across a broad product range growing in importance. The diversification of consumer preferences has caused major brewers to adopt new business models to develop as comprehensive alcohol beverage companies. Managing a collection of strong brands in all the core and growth categories has become a necessity to survive in this diversified market. [227]

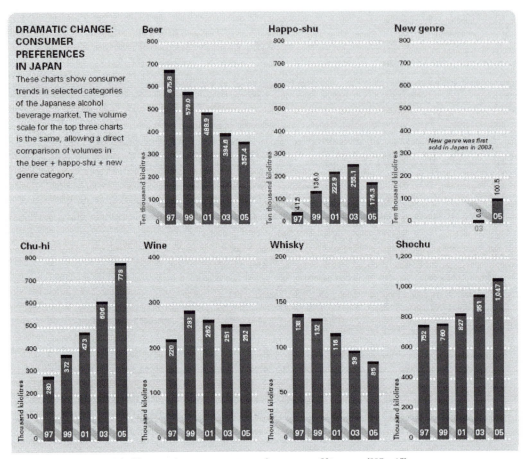

Figure 15: Change in consumer preferences of liquors [227 p. 15]

While there is little prospect for dramatic growth in demand in the alcoholic beverage market as a whole, expanded liquor distribution channels (gasoline stations, home delivery service, pizza delivery chains, video rental stores) greatly intensified competition. To respond to this new environment, leading beer makers are transforming themselves into comprehensive alcoholic beverage providers, adding wine, shochu, spirits, chuhai, liqueur, and other beverages to their mainstay beer and happoshu, or even as general beverage providers. They are moving rapidly on strategic alliances and acquisitions both inside and outside Japan in an effort to solidify their positions. Also, there is a noteworthy trend toward alliances and mergers between food and liquor wholesalers, in an effort to acquire comprehensive wholesaling capabilities. [230]

Key success factors for entering the Japanese alcoholic beverage market

After having analysed different access factors when entering a new market and considered Japan as an entrance market with all its given conditions (see: cultural and environmental aspects), in this part of the book the key success factors for entering the Japanese alcoholic beverage market will be explored. Table 1 summarizes the different categories of access factors. In the following discussion, a selection of these factors, the key success factors, will be highlighted and specified for the Japanese alcoholic beverage market. A clear distinction between the three categories under this analysis is no longer possible, because the factors relate to and overlap with each other. The aim of this part is therefore to give an integrated view of the aspects which have to be regarded when entering the Japanese alcoholic beverage market.

Physical access factors	Commercial access factors	Legal and political access factors
Nature of products	Marketing factors (price, product, promotion, packaging, distribution & market entry)	Entry barriers
Country infrastructure	Operational factors (material inputs, physical capital, human capital, financial capital)	Legal and fiscal environment
Transportation costs	Competition factors (rivals, substitutes, entrants)	Political issues

Table 2: Overview of the categories of access factors [214]

A company that wants to enter the Japanese market and especially the alcoholic beverage sector must first have a wide and broad knowledge of the product or service they want to introduce in the foreign market. But not only the full understanding of the product itself is essential; in addition, knowledge about customers and their consumption and buying habits, market dynamics and competitors, and country conditions and laws are crucial for success.

Physical access factors

Physical access factors comprise the nature of the product, country infrastructure, and transportation costs. The nature of the product – for liquor, therefore, the taste - can differ extremely from country to country. Japanese tastes are different than the ones of the United States or Europe, see for example the introduction of Kirin Ice Beer in Japan. [232] [233] Because of different tastes in Japan, companies sometimes have to adapt their products for Japanese customers. As it was shown above, the trend in the Japanese alcoholic beverage market is towards low calories, reduced sugar, and different variations of flavours. Furthermore, healthier drinks are becoming more and more popular. [231] This argument should not be overlooked, especially when considering that Asian people in general have less natural enzymes which digest alcohol, and therefore retain alcohol longer in their bodies. [234]

Country infrastructure and transportation costs are the other components of the physical access factors. Regarding Japan's highly developed infrastructure (roads, airports, ports etc.) and position as a technology leader, entry into the Japanese market causes no infrastructural difficulties. But one point that has to be looked at is the geography of Japan, which is formed out of four (volcanic) islands. This geographical fact requires ship or airplane transportation for the last kilometres in getting a product to Japan. On the other hand, Yokohama has one of the biggest ports in the world, [235] which is used to handle high volumes efficiently. Because of the high geographical transportation costs when exporting out of or importing into Japan, the particular entry strategy for Japan must be well-conceived. As well, for companies producing in Japan transportation costs are an important subject, because of the rare resources that Japan owns.

Commercial access factors

There are different market entry strategies: [236] distributing over a general trading organization; licensing agreement; strategic partnerships with Japanese companies still acting in the industry; and mergers and acquisitions. Concerning the Japanese market, a success factor in distributing the products is the direct contact to the customer, because this interaction allows the company to improve their products and services. This direct contact is achieved readily through strategic partnerships and M&A. Analysing the alcoholic beverage market, which is strictly regulated by different legal and tax systems, a strategic partnership between the foreign company who wants to enter and a Japanese partner makes sense. On the other hand, there is still the language barrier encountered when negotiating contracts and also when getting in contact with suppliers, customers, authorities, and other Japanese actors, who still do not all speak English. [237] This situation is changing, as more and more young people are learning English. But older people in companies and seniors in general do not know or speak English. This fact makes doing business with Japan more complicated. In addition, although lots of books were written about Japan and its culture and attitudes, business environment "faux-pas" are still a major problem in doing business in Japan. [237] As well, Japan's strict organizational hierarchy could lead to problems when foreigners (young and not Japanese-speaking) partner with Japanese companies (i.e. in case of an M&A). But not only language could cause problems. Getting access to the desired channels is not ensured with a licensing agreement or partnership. As discussed above, the huge level of competition in the Japanese alcoholic beverage market has put pressure on old distribution channels.

Besides product placement, price plays an important role when entering a new market. In Japan, the price is seen as an index of quality. An example from the alcoholic beverage market was Johnny Walker, who reduced prices. The price reduction was perceived as a quality reduction and harmed not only sales but also the company's image. [238 p. 160] The country of origin of the product also plays into the price setting. For example, a product from China which is considered to be a low quality product in Japan is better off setting its price lower than a Swiss product, which is seen as a high quality product and therefore can set prices higher than the average in Japan.

Similar to price setting, promotion is a vital success factor and has to consider cultural and social facts in Japan. Knowledge of the customers, rituals, traditions, and also religion is essential for launching successful ads. Budweiser, for example, had in the mid 1990's an advertisement series showing Budweiser girls who induced Japanese men to drink beer in crowded bars after work. This ad flopped totally because 70% of all beer is consumed at home, so the link between beer-drinking and girls at bars made no sense in Japan. [239]

Packaging is a subpart of promotion, and is also a key success factor for entering Japan. For the Japanese alcohol beverage market, it is essential to know about the way Japanese people live and how they consume alcohol in order to make effective packaging decisions. For example, refrigerators are smaller than in the United States. Therefore packaging and sizes must be adapted when entering the Japanese market. As we have seen above, Japanese customers drink beer mostly at home. For this habit small cans would be more suitable than one litre bottles. As an example, Budweiser changed their can sizes and now offers 24 x 350mml cans. [240]

Another category of access factors are operational factors. Material resources are restricted because of the size of Japan and its geographical conditions (volcanic, islands). Japan is therefore strongly dependent on imports of raw material. On the other side their human capital is good, because education levels are high. But as the aging population poses more and more of a problem in Japan, the question remains as to whether they will have enough skilled working-age people in the future. In addition, as we have seen in above, financial capital is a potential risk for the Japanese market. The Japanese economy suffers from a weak business cycle, high indebtedness of the state and also of companies, and the need of getting a new credit expansion and to cut public spending. [224] These risks may make financing Japanese ventures more costly for foreign firms.

The alcoholic beverage market and players were analyzed above. When entering a new market a company must do more than define its optimal entry strategy; it is essential that the company also take analyze the nature of competition in the new market and adapt its positioning and strategy accordingly. As a foreign entrant, it can be hard to build entry barriers. But when it ever becomes possible to erect such barriers – for example, by changing standards in a market – a company must definitely make every effort to do so. The trends in the alcoholic beverage market are strategic alliances and acquisitions inside and outside Japan to increase the market share and encourage strong positions. Not only are alliances and mergers between liquor companies popular, but so are mergers with food and beverage wholesalers. These latter strategies are part of an effort to acquire comprehensive wholesaling capabilities and gain greater control over distribution channels. [230]

Legal and Political access factors

Political problems are not very highly weighted for entering the Japanese market – except for the relationship between Japan and China and perhaps the sometimes still-existing hostility to the U.S. because of the Second World War. However, because these factors play a lesser role in doing business in Japan, for simplification it is recommended that foreign firms not prioritize political considerations when developing their strategies to enter the Japanese market.

Lastly, before entering the Japanese liquor market, prospective importers and domestic sellers must also make sure that all necessary business licenses for sale of liquors under the liquor tax laws have been obtained. A profound knowledge of the tax system is therefore essential. For example is the tax on beer regulated by the percentage of malt it contains. [229]

Budweiser in Japan

The first move for Anheuser-Busch into the Japanese market was in 1981 when it formed an alliance with the Japanese brewery, Suntory Ltd. Company. Anheuser-Busch was the first foreign company to enter the Japanese beer market and the first new beer company in 30 years. [241] At that time, there were four Japanese brewers who had a license to brew and distribute beer in Japan. Suntory Ldt. had been the weakest one. The distribution and advertising for Anheuser-Busch was left up to Suntory's marketing team, who marketed "Bud" as an expensive upscale foreign beer that American actors and stars drink. Therefore, it was mainly sold in certain exclusive bars. However, Suntory believed that Bud would not need much promotion and would somehow sell by itself. [242]

Within a couple of years Budweiser grew to be the favorite foreign beer of Japanese consumers, but did not reach more than 1.2% of Japan's beer market in 1992, which is about 10 million cases. [243] At this time Budweiser's U.S. market share was 21.6%, which amounts to about 330 million cases. [242] Like previously discussed, beer is the most preferred alcoholic drink in Japan, and therefore Budweiser felt it could do better to penetrate this large market. However, to accomplish this, a change in strategy and/or a new strategic partner had to be found.

In 1993, Anheuser-Busch formed an alliance with the Japanese beer manufacturer Kirin. Kirin was Japan's biggest beer company. [241] Holding a 90% share of this alliance, Budweiser was able to brew the beer in Kirin's facilities and to use Kirin's distribution and marketing channels as well as building their own networks. 30% of the beer demand was supposed to be produced in Kirin's facilities and 70% in Budweiser's Los Angeles facilities. [241] Kirin's return out of this venture was to learn about the worldwide beer market.

Budweiser was planning on distributing its beer through 600 wholesalers [241] in big Japanese cities, of which most had special contracts with Kirin. The usual distribution channel for other Japanese beer manufactures comprises a small network of exclusive wholesalers that are allowed to distribute the beer to supermarkets, restaurants and bars throughout the whole country. [242]

Under the new venture agreement, Anheuser-Busch was able to start aggressive marketing campaigns. They brought in American sales managers who trained Japanese salesmen to hand out bowtie-shaped neon signs to bars and restaurants in big Japanese cities. These neon signs are characteristic for Budweiser. Big horses pulled cartfuls of Bud through Tokyo in an effort to raise public awareness about the brand. American TV ads were translated and published on Japanese TV. The major slogan at that time was: "Bud, makes you drink more and more". Taking a look at the Japanese alcoholic beverages market, this is a slogan which does not really fit with Japan's culture. Japanese believe they cannot handle too much alcohol well, and the trend is therefore not to drink too much alcohol at one time. In part due to this ineffective campaign, the sales of Budweiser dropped to 1.19 billion gallons, which is 2.2% less than under the Suntory partnership. [242]

Facing these problems, the new formed alliance between Kirin and Budweiser, Budweiser Japan Ltd., came to the conclusion that it would be best to change the image of Budweiser and to market its beer to a new customer group. The new focus was on middle-aged heavy drinkers, who consumed more beer then the customers of high-fashion bars. In addition, Budweiser was now sold in aluminum bottles and advertised in newspapers and magazines, saying that the "age when beers became trends and fashion is over". [242]

To this day, Budweiser is working closely together with Kirin. Kirin is selling its beer over Budweiser's distribution channels in the U.S. and Budweiser is using Kirin's channels and advice to increase their market share to an aspired level of 10%. [242]

After 1994 Anheuser-Busch realized that the American-style ads did not appeal effectively to many customers in Japan. American-style ads were mainly featuring three frogs sitting on lily pads, each one saying, "Bud"-"wei"-"ser". These ads did not need much translation and were understood everywhere where they were shown in Italy, Ireland, the U.K. and Japan.

Translation and interpretation were more difficult with ads in which Lizards saying, "Enjoy it while you can, hotshots. Your days are numbered!" [244] But even more important is that lizards in the U.S. are easily recognizable and are considered funny. This is not the case in Japan. So the ad could be misunderstood and might not be perceived as humorous, like it would in the U.S.

Therefore, more and more Japanese ads for Budweiser today are featuring young Japanese people smiling and holding a Bud in their hand. In recent years, Budweiser has also started promotions where Japanese girls gave away Budweiser bottles for free in bars in clubs. The girls are usually dressed in special Budweiser clothes.

In 1994, Budweiser agreed to launch Anheuser-Busch's Iced Beer in Japan. The beer has been published under the name "Kirin Ice Beer" and is supposed to reinforce the cooperation between Kirin and Anheuser-Bush after they set up their cooperation. Kirin Iced Beer is canned in the United States and is adapted to the slightly different Japanese taste. The cooperation between the two companies is expected to move towards joint supply and purchasing deals and expansion into other areas of Asia. [245]

In 1995, Budweiser entered a lower price segment by producing Anheuser Extra Dry. This drink is a carbonated beverage and has lower malt content then traditional beers. This allows Anheuser to sell its drink under a lower liquor tax under Japan's liquor tax law, which was discussed in more detail above. [246]

In 2002, when the FIFA World Cup came to Japan, Budweiser was one of the main sponsors, using promotions and various multi-media advertising channels like the official website and Yahoo! Networks to receive visibility in Japan and worldwide. Millions of soccer fans recognized Budweiser as a global sport-supporting company. [247]

Hence, Budweiser encountered different cultural and strategic problems when they entered the market in 1981. Since that time, however, they have improved and adapted their overall strategy to fit with the local differences in the Japanese market.

Conclusions and suggestions

In this section, Budweiser's entry into the Japanese market is evaluated and recommendations for other companies who want to enter the Japanese market are given.

Budweiser tried in the beginning to enter the Japanese beer market by a licensing agreement with Suntory – the fourth biggest beer producer. After 12 years of disappointing sales resulting in a market share of only 1.2%, Anheuser-Bush decided to do a joint venture with Kirin Beer – Japan's biggest brewery – instead. This joint venture opened for Budweiser the doors to more Japanese retailers and allowed them to conduct their own marketing and promotional campaigns.

Licensing arrangements are quick and relatively easier to set up than other entry methods. However, there is the potential to lose protected information to the licensee, as their interests may not be aligned with the licensor. A solution to this is the strategic partnership, where two companies help each other enter their respective home markets. Strategic partnership is a good option to enter a market when distribution channels are different than known in the home market or their access is restricted. Through a partnership not only access is given; as well, further knowledge of the market, customers, and legal system is provided. Also, an agreement such as the one Budweiser formed with Kirin gives both companies the possibility to share resources, save costs, and learn from each other.

M&A's have the same advantages as the strategic partnerships, but there are several problems surrounding the integration of the two companies. For a merger of a foreign company with a Japanese one, organizational structures are possibly different. Japanese companies are known to be very hierarchical, whereas American companies tend to have a very flat hierarchy. This difference could cause conflicts between the two ways of managing. The language barrier is another problem for American firms merging with Japanese ones. As we have seen, English is not yet spoken widely in Japan.

Thus, Budweiser's tactic to enter the market through an alliance was well founded. However, their example shows that it is very difficult to find the right partner. In Budweiser's case, it took 12 years to find a partner that fit the company well. Japanese culture is very different from American culture, and is not well-suited to the American way of selling and promoting aggressively. These tactics may be understood as rude and as an aggressive attempt to push Japanese brands out of the market. Japanese culture is based on great respect among individuals and businesses alike. Hence, for Budweiser to become accepted by Japanese consumers, they first had to earn their respect. Perhaps a public apology to the Japanese people would have helped Budweiser recover more quickly from its early advertising blunders push sales into the right direction. Even today, Budweiser needs to earn the respect of its consumers continually. Otherwise, it may take them another 12 years to become fully accepted and start generating sales that are acceptable for the biggest American beer company.

Access Factors	Specifications
Physical	
Nature of the product	What is the taste of the new customer? What is trend on the market?
Country's infrastructure	Geography? Technology development? Infrastructure: roads, airports, ports etc.
Transportation costs	Different ways? Cost effectiveness? Handling of transport, bureaucratic/easy?
Commercial	
Marketing	Price setting? Quality measurement? Values? Promotion activities? Brand image? Access to distribution? Knowledge about customer, market, competitors?
Operational	Human capital? Education? Evolutionary trend? Finacial capital – country's currency strength? Indebtedness?
Competition	Positioning on the market? Market growth? Tactics of main competitors? Market leader?
Legal & Political	
Entry barriers	Changing standards?
Legal and fiscal environment	Knowledge about laws and taxes? Benefits?
Political issues	Secure? Difficult relationships? Historical remedies?

Figure 16 Key Success Factors for an alcoholic product market entry in Japan

The main lessons that other firms entering the Japanese market can learn from Budweiser's example are the following. First, choosing a strategic partner to gain local access can be a big advantage in Japan, if the partner is selected carefully. Japan's economy is highly regulated, which makes entering markets and gaining access to distribution channels very difficult. As well, distribution channels are often governed by long-standing traditional relationships between networks of firms that can be exclusive to new entrants. Thus, picking the right local partner can give a firm access to the distributors it needs to reach its consumers. Second, knowing the particular tastes, values, and culture of the Japanese people is vital to implementing an effective marketing strategy in Japan. It is often a mistake made by foreign firms to assume Japanese consumption behaviour is similar to that in their own countries. This assumption must be tested because the consequence could be a value proposition that not only does not appeal to the Japanese consumer, but can go so far as to repel the consumer and severely harm the image of the foreign firm. Lastly, one particular cultural value must always be at the top-of-mind of decision makers in foreign firms that enter Japan: respect. The Japanese espouse respect for each other and they expect businesses to act similarly. This manifests itself in how a company treats its employees, its customers, its suppliers, and even its competitors. In today's world, with easily accessible information just a mouse-click away, companies' images are under a microscope. Thus, in a nation like Japan where corporate behaviour is scrutinized by the public and held to a high moral standard, foreign firms must take extra care to ensure they incorporate the value of respect in all that they do.

Appendix A: Interview with Makiko Masuko

Monday, November 27th 2006; phone interview Paris-Lausanne, 18.00-18.15
(The following is not a word-word transcript, but a summary of the essentials what was discussed)
What should a company consider when entering the Japanese market?
First of all, a company has to know Japan as country and the different values and traditions. Japan is a well developed country and one of the technology leaders on the world - but it has its own conditions for example the ways Japanese people communicate and behave in different relationships (business, private, family etc). Politeness is one success factor when acting with Japanese. This politeness is to some extent shown by the appropriate use of language.

So, foreign companies will face problems when entering the Japanese market, when they do not speak Japanese?

Yes and no. Japanese is a language that more and more foreigners learn. But the Japanese that they speak is not adapted to all the politeness forms that Japanese people use. But this fact is not a problem, because Japanese people appreciate it, when a foreigner knows some Japanese. But foreigners are never seen as one of them. On the other hand, Japanese people know English and used it more and more – especially in business context. But still not every Japanese person knows English and their grammar and written skills are much better than their spoken English.

What do companies further has to consider when establishing business relations with Japanese?

Don't forget to respect Japanese companies' strong hierarchy. It will be difficult for a foreign young manager to work in a hierarchical Japanese company. Senior managers are still older, experienced men – for a young graduate it is nearly impossible to have a cadre position in a Japanese company.

Market Entry Strategies

Chapter 4

The Influence of Culture on Market Entries

Market Entry Strategies

Chapter 4:

The Influence of Culture on Market Entries

It is very important for managers that are involved in an internationalisation project to understand that people in another culture can be very different in terms of their personality, their goals and their motives. Each person perceives their environment differently. People in another country can have different values, priorities and expectations from a product, a service or their work. Employees might also respond differently to supervision, motivation and feedback. International managers face the difficult task to manage different nationalities and cultures. The effect of these cultural differences on a business expansion is the topic of this chapter. To gain a basic understanding we first want to discuss the nature of individual differences and then introduce some aspects of behaviour which are very important for multinational businesses that are involved in a new market entry.

Individual Behaviour in International Businesses

Individual Behaviour is anything that an organism does involving action and response to stimulation. [248] Organisational behaviour refers to attitudes and behaviours of individuals and groups in organisations. The discipline of organisational behaviour systematically studies these attitudes and behaviours and provides insight about effectively managing and changing them. It also studies how organisations can be structured more effectively and how events in their external environment can affect organisations. [249 p. 7] Companies that enter a new market often need to deal with employees that sometimes show a very different set of organisational behaviour. Organisational behaviour is important to managers, employees and consumers, and understanding it can make us more effective managers [249 p. 9] and lead to a more successful market entry.

Culture

Culture is considered as one of the most difficult English words to define. It is seen either as academic knowledge, the intellectual aspect of a civilisation or the behaviour forms. [250 p. 11] An anthropological approach defines culture as the integration of values that are gained in a social system. [251] The transmissible character of culture implies a consideration of the process by which individuals of society acquire culture. Culture determines what we perceive, how we react to situations, and how we relate to other people. [252] It can be seen as commonly shared code of behaviour and information that can be read and understood by members of the same culture. People from another culture often cannot understand this code without a method to decrypt the information received. This is especially true for information that gets transmitted by other means than verbal communication. It is estimated that about 90% of all communication is nonverbal. This represents a difficult task for multinational companies and especially for companies that are entering a market and getting in touch with different behaviours from another culture for the first time. On the following pages, we want to focus on non-verbal components that are important for internationally operating managers by discussing the fundamental patterns of behaviour in different countries.

High and Low Context

"A high context (HC) communication or message is one in which most of the information is already in the person, while very little is in the coded, explicit, transmitted part of the message. A low context (LC) communication is just the opposite; i.e., the mass of the information is vested in the explicit code. Twins who have grown up together can and do communicate more economically (HC) then two lawyers in a courtroom during a trial (LC), a mathematician programming a computer, two politicians drafting legislation, two administrators writing a regulation." Edward T. Hall, 1976 [252]

About Edward T. Hall's ideas:

Human resource management, at home and abroad, means assisting the corporation's most valuable asset - its people - to function effectively. Edward T. Hall and Mildred Reed Hall offer new insights and practical advice on how to manage day-to-day transactions in the international business arena.

Source: http://www.edwardthall.com

Context is the circumstance in which an event occurs. [253] The elements that produce a certain meaning vary in different cultures. Variations in the level of context can have different meanings.

High Context Cultures

Countries where people are involved in close personal relationships with their families, colleagues, friends and sometimes clients are high context cultures. These cultures have wide-ranging information networks with the people that surround them. Their networks keep them up to date about everything important going on within their network. Therefore, normal meetings are not required to be the source of background information since they are already informed about

High Context Countries:

Japan
Italy
Turkey
Dubai
Mexico
Arabian Countries
Spain
South France

the prior status of processes and developments and are more seen as the source of first-hand updates. Information flows freely. Everybody constantly tries to give and seek as much information as possible. This way everybody in the business is informed about everything important going on. Differences in high and low context cultures also exist in the form of how executive offices are arranged. The highest person in an office room can easily be found because he or she sits in the middle of the room in order to be in the middle of the information flow. The management of a company is usually situated in the middle of the office building and not like in low context cultures on the top levels.

Shifts in context levels can lead to the following interpretations: In Japan, it is very common to start negotiations by addressing the colleagues in a more formal way, a more informal version gets used when the negotiations are going well. Very typically for high context cultures is also to give more importance to people than to actual activities. In Japan, it is more important who is going to be at a meeting than what the meeting is actually about. Attendance of high officials gives a meeting immediately a very high and important status. Since high officials often need to change their plans on short notice, it is common that important meetings will be called for on short notice as well. It is expected that everybody else works around this issue and makes time for an appointment that is more important.

Furthermore, High Context people from France, Italy or Turkey like to evaluate new ventures by themselves; they keep asking questions until they have all the information they need.

Low Context Cultures

Low context cultures divide their work, their personal relationships and other aspects of their life. Hence each time people meet or talk to each other they need very detailed information. In a low context culture the variation of the amount of context communicated can have the following affect: When more context is given it can mean that the relationship between two or more people is starting to warm up. If less amounts of context are communicated it can mean that the relationship is starting to cool down. For example, if in Germany a boss is usually communicating with an employee on an informal high context level, then the shift to a low context conversation can mean that the employee did something wrong by kind of punishing him with a more superficial way of communicating. Another characteristic of low context cultures is the factor of planning ahead. In low context countries, it is common to schedule important meetings or appointments a long time ahead. In only very rare occasions will meetings be cancelled because something else came up. Another important characteristic is that high executives or officials are usually shielded by consultants or secretaries around them. The information flow to the high executive gets filtered through these few people that are in direct contact with them. Their offices are in the corner shielded with doors which are sometimes even soundproof. What gets talked about in the office does not get shared with many people. The information flow is strictly controlled.

Low Context Countries:

Germany
Switzerland
Sweden
Finland
Denmark
Norway
USA
England

Problems between high and low context cultures

People from high context cultures might feel talked down to if a low context person tries to tell them in detail about every little aspect. They might feel bored to hear the background to every aspect and decision made. Low context people on the other hand might feel lost or do not exactly know what to do if a high context person does not give them all the information they need. A high context person will also expect the low context person to participate in the overall information flow by contributing and by keeping themselves up to date. If this expectation is not met by the low context person, this could lead to the low context person being left out even more. It can also look like the low context person is not interested in the overall information flow or has something to hide.

One of the biggest challenges is to find the right level of contexting when communicating with employees or partners from another culture.

The Perception of Space between Cultures

Perception of Space can be very different between cultures. Every living being is surrounded by visible and invisible boundaries. The most obvious one is the skin followed by invisible boundaries whose distance to us can vary significantly. The closest area around us is called the personal space followed by the territory that a person claims to be his.

The invisible personal space around a person is a very intimate area. It can vary significantly between a couple of centimetres and up to one or two meters. How big it is depends on the culture, the people nearby and the mood that a person is in as well as the activity that the person is engaged in. Only a few people, usually people that we know very well, are allowed to enter this personal space. We are a lot more comfortable to let a wife or girlfriend for example stand 20cm in front of us than a person that we do not know or is on a hierarchy level above us. People from southern European countries usually have a smaller personal space than people from northern European countries. But the same goes for Arabic countries and southern American cultures. They usually have a smaller personal space around them than Americans, Australians or Europeans. In countries like Sweden, Germany or Norway it is very common to apologise even if only two coats of two passing people barely touched each other. In these countries touching somebody is not allowed at all.

Followed by the personal space is what a person claims to be his or her territory. In some countries like Germany and America, this territory can be quite extensive and even an evidential violation of this territory can be seen as an invasion and trigger discomfort. In Germany, this territory even extends to all possessions like someone's car, desk or books. If these possessions are touched by another person the German might feel like he himself was touched.

It is very important that space and territory are perceived by more than one sense, in fact they can be perceived by all senses. In America as well as northern European countries for example, space can also mean a certain atmosphere or noise. To concentrate these cultures often need silence around them. French and Italians might be more open to interruptions and to constant noise while working. In America, it is also more common to say hi to everyone when you enter an office for the first time than in Germany, Finland or Denmark.

Problems that can arise because of differences in space

As mentioned above, personal space can be perceived as something very intimate. It is therefore very important to respect and to be aware of other cultures' personal spaces and territories. If a German person sees somebody leaning against his car, he might see it as a personal offence. If somebody borrows his book or just takes a pen without asking him or her first, he might interpret it as disrespect. An American that finds himself in a conversation with an Italian person might feel pressured because the Italian stands a lot closer to him than he is used to from other Americans. Most people do not think about personal distance and therefore easily touch a person in a very personal way that might not be intended.

The Perception of Time between Cultures

Many kinds of time systems exist in the world today, but the two systems that are important in international business are the polychronic time and the monochronic time. These two systems describe different attitudes towards time. Monochronic means that a person is only doing one thing at a time and only gives his attention to this one thing. People living by a monochronic system tend to be punctual and have a long lead time. The saying: "Time is money" describes their attitude towards time pretty well; it is treated as something that can be saved or lost. It is very important to be aware of the differences because both time systems do not mix very well. Every culture has its own speed and perceives time differently. If somebody from another culture is moving too fast, he can be interpreted as pushing which might lead the slower culture to work even slower or to sabotage the faster ones. If we enter a foreign market and expect the local workforce "tick" in the same way we do, then we will most likely run into problems. It is therefore important to be aware of the different speed and to consider it in the own plans.

Monochronic Time

Monochronic time is divided into segments; the schedule may take priority above all else and be treated as sacred and unalterable. [252 p. 13] An example of monochronic cultures are the U.S. and Germany. People in a monochronic culture tend to do only one thing at a time. People who live by the monochronic time system do not like to be

Monochronic Cultures:

Sweden
Germany
Switzerland
USA

interrupted and often do things by themselves hence they do not interact as much. Some relationships get more intense while there is simply no time for others. This time system is a by-product of the industrialisation in England, where it was for the first time important to be on time and to work in shifts around the clock. To-day, Switzerland and Germany are representative examples of this time system. In these two countries, you are late once you are one minute later than the exact scheduled time. Northern European countries also follow this system nowadays. They tend to take deadlines, schedules and commitments very seriously. They are focused on their work, show great respect for property that does and does not be-long to them and adhere princely to plans. They also tend to be low-context people that need a lot of information at once since they do not absorb a lot of information while they are working. Hence, information does not flow as freely as in high-context polychronic cultures. It is typical for monochronic cultures to have sepa-rate offices. Even big offices in the U.S. or Germany with twenty or thirty employ-ees in it still have dividing walls between them in order to give the employee more privacy and to shield them from distractions. However, in recent years there has been a tendency to group at least a couple of people together without barriers be-tween them in order to allow more information to flow within a team.

Polychronic Time

Polychronic cultures tend to be less rigid to-wards time. They do several things at once and an exact planning of events is not seen as a require-ment for good performance. These cultures tend to see business as a form of socialising with oth-

Polychronic Cultures:

France, Italy, Spain
Brazil, Portugal
Mexico

ers in a work place environment. They are constantly involved with other people. Two Brazilians that meet by coincidence would rather chat a little bit with each other than just saying hi even if it means that both of them will be late for a meeting. Hence, they are much more time-flexible. The interaction with people is seen as more important than schedules. Thus, polychronic people are more distractible then their monochronic partners, they change their plans often and they are high-context people that constantly absorb information through the many interactions with others. A time commitment is more seen as something that should be met if possible and they tend to lend things out more easily. The lead time in these cultures is very small. If a person is important, an Italian or French person will always make time on short notice, even though he or she might have had other plans. Lifetime relationships are more often formed than in monochromic cultures.

Appointments and Meetings

Another important aspect of time between cultures in the context of meetings is the waiting time. If a person is expected to a meeting and needs to wait in order to see the other person that he or she has the meeting with, his responses depend on what culture he or she is from. Since in a monochronic culture everything is exactly timed, one expects everybody attending the meeting to be in time. As mentioned above, even one or two minutes delay might cause irritation. We have talked with a French manager who was consulting a German aircraft manufacturer and whose car broke down on the way to the meeting. Hence he was about two hours late to the meeting. He said himself that it took him almost two years to prove to the Germans that he is not unorganised and unreliable. In Germany, a presenter can have a very good presentation, but if he is late nobody will be overwhelmed. In America, if a businessman does not take the time for some superficial small talk before a meeting he might be seen as impolite.

In a monochronic culture, letting somebody wait in front of an office before an appointment can be interpreted as putting somebody down. The person that is waiting could also see the other one as being unorganised. Since these signals can be interpreted as insults, it is very important to try to avoid these situations. In other countries like Hispanic countries, that is in polychronic cultures, a waiting time does not carry any message.

If an interpreter is necessary, then especially in Japan, Germany and the U.S. it is important that the interpreter himself is well educated, familiar with the local customs and speaks the language very well. If he is not, it might get interpreted as a weakness or as being careless.

The Importance of Print Media

To find the right communication media can be difficult between cultures. Edward T. Hall compares this dilemma with sending numbers when words are wanted, and words when the recipient only feels comfortable with numbers. This can release a negative or even frustrated response. Germans for example are print-oriented, which explains in part why there is so little advertising on German TV. Also, Germans are always looking for what is "true", and to them the numbers are a way of signalling that a product is exactly as it has been presented. Germans demand facts, facts, and more facts. [252 p. 30] French people are more conversation-oriented. When there is a problem, they talk about it instead of writing each other formal letters. Human contact is very important for them: If things do not work as expected, a personal meeting will be a better solution than a letter or phone call. For the French, it is also very important to keep their rituals of form. If an outsider uses the wrong form to transmit a message, it might not trigger the intended response in the French person. It can be understood as the outsider being not very well mannered or ignorant since he or she does not seem to care about the proper form. Paying attention to the detail and being correct in everything you do is the only tactic that brings about the right response in France.

Problems that can arise between Polychronic and Monochronic Cultures

The differences between managers that grew up in a polychronic culture and managers that grew up in a monochronic cultures becomes obvious in business meetings. The monochronic manager usually has a very strict time line that he will try to keep. Sometimes it is even planned how many minutes a conversation will last until a decision needs to be made. The polychronic manager would see the timeline as a pressure or even insulting. In polychronic cultures, a business meeting can be seen as chaotic for a monochronic person because the information flow is very high. Often many people talk at once and it is almost expected that people can read other people's thoughts, since everybody is informed about everything and should therefore know the other people's position on a certain topic. In a polychronic country, everybody already has pretty good knowledge of what will be discussed at the meeting. The meeting has the purpose of reaching an agreement more than a decision. Another problem that can arise is based on the different lead times in these cultures. In Germany and in the USA, important appointments get scheduled very far in advance. A short lead time means that the business or the appointment is not very important. In France and Japan however there will always be time for an important appointment at short notice. If a Japanese person tries to make an appointment with an American manager and the American declines the appointment, the Japanese manager could think that he is simply not important enough. In Arab countries on the other hand, scheduling an appointment two weeks ahead is unusual. A couple of days before would be more common.

It is very important to be aware of these differences. Some French managers can use this knowledge to their advantage. When American or German managers come to France to negotiate a contract or certain terms they usually have an exact schedule of what they want to achieve and by what date or time. The closer their own deadline gets they might be more likely to give in to reach a consensus instead of going home without an achievement. The French managers could take advantage of this situation.

Another common problem that arises when polychronic and monochronic people work together is that polychronic people like to change things while they happen. Since they are used to being always up to date, they rather adjust a contract or project once the information becomes available instead of trying everything possible to stick to the old plan like a monochronic person. This can be difficult when a Japanese company wants to constantly renegotiate terms of a contract but the American partner is making their own plans based on the original contract. Uncountable alliances and partnerships broke because of this reason. Everybody involved needs to be cautious, open minded and understanding. He should have the strength not to value actions with standards from the own culture. As it is a lot more difficult to succeed in another country, the importance of local experts cannot be overstressed.

Power Distance

Power distance resolves out of the society. Geert Hofstede, Mauk Mulder, David Kipnis and many more studied the influence between a supervisor and his subordinate from the subordinates' point of view. Mauk Mulder defined power in 1977 as "the potential to determine or direct (to a certain extent) the behaviour of another person or other persons more so than the other way around," and "power distance is the degree of inequality in power between a less powerful Individual (I) and a more powerful Other (O), in which I and O belong to the same (loosely or tightly knit) social system" [254 p. 30] In his book, he says

> **About Geert Hofstede's ideas:**
>
> His ideas were first based on a large research project into national culture differences across subsidiaries of a multinational corporation (IBM) in 64 countries. Subsequent studies by others covered students in 23 countries, elites in 19 countries, commercial airline pilots in 23 countries, up-market consumers in 15 countries, and civil service managers in 14 countries. These studies together identified and validated five independent dimensions of national culture differences.
>
> (source: Geert Hofstede in A Summary of My Ideas About National Culture Differences)

that having power is addictive: "Having power feeds [a] need [in humans], making it comparable to the need for hard drugs. An individual can become addicted to power distance reduction" [254 p. 46] How much power a person can acquire and how much power a person can exercise is to a great extent determined through culture and the social environment of that person. Agreeing with Mulder, I will borrow his definition of power distance: "The power distance between a boss B and a subordinate S in a hierarchy is the difference between the extent to which B can determine the behaviour of S and the extent to which S can determine the behaviour of B." [255 p. 83] Hofstede conducted a study of IBM employees working in various countries all over the world. His survey contained different "questions [that] dealt with perceptions of subordinates' fear of disagreeing with superiors and of superior's actual decision making styles, and with the decision-making style that subordinates preferred in their bosses." [255 p. 79] Each country that Hofstede covered in his study was given a score. Out of these scores, he developed a scale which is called the Power Distance Index and makes it possible to compare the different countries with each other. The Power Distance Index examines the need for dependence compared to interdependence within a culture. A country that is very low on the power distance scale sees inequality as something that is not good and should be avoided or at least minimised. People from these such a country tend to be less involved in the daily business and organise more in unions or parties to have some form of influence on the business, but rarely get consulted for advice by superiors.

A country with a high score on the power distance scale sees inequality as something that is the basis for their social order. It follows that in a high PDI country a hierarchy within a company is seen as something existential and that a boss is really somebody superior. The Power Distance Index can also have significant influence on management techniques. The management by objectives (MBO) technique, which is very popular in the United States and in Germany, can only be successful if there is room for discussion and bargaining between the subordinate and its supervisor. In a culture where subordinates are not used to bargaining with their bosses this MBO technique would probably fail since it is based on the employee committing to achievements that will be determined by negotiation. The following table describes key differences between countries with a low Power Distance Index and countries that are high on the power distance scale.

Table 3 PDI Ranks

Rank	Country	Rank	Country
1	Malaysia	27/28	South Korea, Greece
2/3	Guatemala	29/30	Iran
2/3	Panama	29/30	Taiwan
4	Philippines	31	Spain
5/6	Mexico	32	Pakistan
5/6	Venezuela	33	Japan
7	Arab countries	34	Italy
8/9	Ecuador	35/36	Argentina
8/9	Indonesia	35/36	South Africa
10/11	India	37	Jamaica
10/11	West Africa	38	United States
12	Yugoslavia	39	Canada
13	Singapore	40	Netherlands
14	Brazil	41	Australia
15/16	France	42/44	Costa Rica
15/16	Hong Kong	42/44	Germany
17	Colombia	42/44	Great Britain
18/19	Salvador	45	Switzerland
18/19	Turkey	46	Finland
20	Belgium	47/48	Norway
21/23	East Africa	47/48	Sweden
21/23	Peru	49	Ireland
21/23	Thailand	50	New Zealand
24/25	Chile	51	Denmark
24/25	Portugal	52	Israel
26	Uruguay	53	Austria

Source: adapted from Geert Hofstede; Cultural Consequences, 2nd edition

Differences in Work Organisation[46]	
Low PDI	**High PDI**
Decentralised decision structure; less concentration of authority.	Centralised decision structures; more concentration of authority
Flat organisation pyramids.	Tall organisation pyramids.
Small proportion of supervisory personnel.	Large proportion of supervisory personnel.
Hierarchy in organisations means inequality of roles, established for convenience.	Hierarchy in organisations reflects the existential inequality between higher-ups and lower-downs.
The ideal boss is a resourceful democrat; sees self as practical, orderly, and relying on support.	The ideal boss is well-meaning autocrat or good father; sees self as benevolent decision maker.
Managers rely on personal experience and on subordinates.	Mangers rely on formal rules.
Subordinates expect to be consulted.	Subordinates expect to be told.
Consultative leadership leads to satisfaction, performance, and productivity.	Authoritative leadership and close supervision lead to satisfaction, performance, and productivity.
Employees want to be in control of their career.	Employees feel less in control of their career.
Preference for "blue collar" (manual) work.	Strong preference for "white-collar" (office) work.
Privileges of superiors need to be earned to be accepted	Privileges ("private laws") are normal for superiors.
Subordinate-superior relations are pragmatic.	Subordinate-superior relations polarized, often emotional.
Institutionalised grievance channels in case of power abuse by superior.	No defence against power abuse by superior – treated as bad luck.
Subordinates influenced by bargaining and reasoning; MBO is feasible.	Subordinates influenced by formal authority and sanctions; MBO cannot work.
Innovations need good champions.	Innovations need good support from hierarchy.

---

46 Adapted from Hofstede p.105-108

Low PDI	High PDI
Managers involved in relevant purchasing decisions.	Managers not involved in relevant purchasing decisions.
Narrow salary range between top and bottom organisation.	Wide salary range between top and bottom of organisation.
Mangers feel adequately paid.	Mangers feel underpaid.
Mangers (increasingly) satisfied with career.	Managers dissatisfied with career.
Possibilities to escape from role ambiguity and overload.	Frequent role ambiguity and overload.
Openness with information, also to non-superiors.	Information constrained by hierarchy.

Table 4 PDI Differences in Work Organisation

Uncertainty Avoidance

Richard M. Cyert and James G. March introduced the term of uncertainty avoidance in their book A Behavioural Theory of the Firm in 1963. Geert Hofstede arrived though his studies at mean scores for countries by three survey questions dealing with stress employment stability and rule orientation. As for the Power Distance Index, Hofstede classified each country into a scale and assigned them an Uncertainty Avoidance Index.

Uncertainty Avoidance deals with a society's tolerance for uncertainty and ambiguity; it ultimately refers to man's search for truth. It indicates to what extent a culture programs its members to feel either uncomfortable or comfortable in unstructured situations. Unstructured situations are novel, unknown, surprising, different from usual. Uncertainty avoiding cultures try to minimize the possibility of such situations by strict laws and rules, safety and security measures. People in uncertainty avoiding countries are also more emotional, and motivated by inner nervous energy. The opposite type, uncertainty accepting cultures, is more tolerant of opinions different from what they are used to; they try to have as few rules as possible. People from these cultures are more phlegmatic and contemplative, and not expected by their environment to express emotions. [256] It is important to not get uncertainty avoidance confused with risk avoidance. Uncertainty avoiding cultures shun ambiguous situations. People in such cultures look for structure in their organisations, institutions and relationships which makes events clearly interpretable and predictable. Paradoxically, they are often prepared to engage in risky behaviour in order to reduce ambiguities. [255 p. 148] A multinational company that enters a market with a high UAI needs to take care that their strategy is very well defined and explained in detail to the employees since they want to be led and want to know that the people that tell them what to do actually know what they are doing. If this is the case, the employees will follow the strategy and will not break the company's rules even if they think it would be in the interest of the company.

Countries with weaker uncertainty avoidance tendencies demonstrate a lower sense of urgency, expressed, for example, in lower speed limits. In such countries not only familiar but also unfamiliar risks are accepted, such as changing jobs and starting activities for which there are no rules. [255 p. 148] In these countries, it is acceptable for an employee to break the rules if he truly believes that he is acting in the best interest for the firm.

Interesting is that countries that are high on the uncertainty avoidance scale change, and innovation is not as easily to implement, but once they are, they are taken more seriously than in countries that are lower on the UA scale. In these countries, innovations are more welcome and easier to implement, but their application might lack some determination.

The following table summarises the key differences between low- and high uncertainty avoidance cultures.

Table 5 UDI Ranks

Rank	Country	Rank	Country
1	Greece	28	Ecuador
2	Portugal	29	Germany
3	Guatemala	30	Thailand
4	Uruguay	31/32	Iran
5/6	Belgium	31/32	Finland
5/6	Salvador	33	Switzerland
7	Japan	34	West Africa
8	Yugoslavia	35	Netherlands
9	Peru	36	East Africa
10/15	Spain	37	Australia
10/15	Argentina	38	Norway
10/15	Panama	39/40	South Africa
10/15	France	39/40	New Zealand
10/15	Chile	41/42	Indonesia
10/15	Costa Rica	41/42	Canada
16/17	Turkey	43	United States
16/17	South Korea	44	Philippines
18	Mexico	45	India
19	Israel	46	Malaysia
20	Colombia	47/48	Great Britain
21/22	Venezuela	47/48	Ireland
21/22	Ireland	49/50	Hong Kong
23	Italy	49/50	Sweden
24/25	Pakistan	51	Denmark
24/25	Austria	52	Jamaica
26	Taiwan	53	Singapore
27	Arab countries	Source: adapted from Geert Hofstede; Cultural Consequences, 2nd edition	

301

Differences in Work Organisation [255 pp. 169-170]	
Low UDI	**High UDI**
Weak loyalty to employer; short average duration of employment.	Strong loyalty to employer, long average duration of employment.
Preference for smaller organisations but little self-employment.	Preference for larger organisations, but at the same time much self-employment.
Scepticism toward technological solutions	Strong appeal of technological solutions.
Innovators feel independent of rules.	Innovators feel constraint by rules.
Renegade championing.	Rational championing.
Top managers involved in strategy.	Top managers involved in operations.
Power of superiors depends on position and relationships.	Power of superior depends on control of uncertainties.
Tolerance for ambiguity in structures and procedures.	Highly formalised conception of management.
Appeal of transformational leader role.	Appeal of hierarchical control role.
Many new trademarks granted.	Few new trademarks granted.
Innovations welcomed but not necessarily taken seriously.	Innovations resisted but, if accepted, applied consistently.
Precision and punctuality have to be learned and managed.	Precision and punctuality come naturally.
Relationship-orientation.	Task-orientation.
Flexible working hours not appealing.	Flexible working hours popular.
Belief in generalists and common sense.	Belief in specialists and expertise.
Superiors optimistic about employees' ambition and leadership capacities.	Superiors pessimistic about employees' ambition and leadership capacities.

Table 6 UDI Differences in Work Organisation

Individualism and Collectivism

Individualism and Collectivism describe how much an individual is integrated into a group. "Individualism stands for a society in which the ties between individuals are loose: Everyone is expected to look after him/herself and her/his immediate family only." [255 p. 225] In some cultures, individualism is regarded as something to be admired while other cultures interpret it as alienating.

"Collectivism stands for a society in which people from birth onwards are integrated into strong, cohesive in-groups, which throughout people's lifetime continue to protect them in exchange for unquestioning loyalty." [255 p. 225] The word 'collectivism' in this sense has no political meaning: it refers to the group, not to the state. [256]

A lot of things that must be explicitly said in cultures that are low on the IDV scale can be self evident in cultures that are high on the IDV scale. That is why in some countries like Japan business contracts are a lot shorter than they are in Germany or in the United States. Germans, since they are print-oriented, but also Americans and Australians tend to write as much as possible into a contract to cover every possible scenario that could follow from of it. Managers that are new to a country must be careful because these explicit contracts could be seen as mistrust which could lead the other party from a collectivist country to break off the negotiations associated with the contract. Collectivist cultures on the other hand need to understand that an explicit contract is only the result of careful planning and an exact print of what is expected from all parties signing the contract. Countries that are low on the IDV scale tend to have more unwritten implied rules that managers from high IDV cultures often do not know. It is important when doing business with a low IDV culture to ask for implied rules and to try to get to know them through local advice.

People from a collectivist culture tend to create family-like ties with people that are not biologically in their family but who are very close to them. These people are socially integrated into a person's group of people that surround them. Collectivist people are more integrated into society vertically and horizontally which means that they stay very close to their families and close friends throughout their whole life. People from individualist cultures tend to not be as much vertically or horizontally integrated into society. The circle of friends changes a couple of times throughout their lives and even the contact to the parents is not as intense after they move out. This difference in cultures has also some effect on the way these cultures do business. In an individualist country, employees are expected to perform according to their own interest. They expect that the job they have to do somehow match with their self interest.

In a collectivist country, employers look for employees who belong to the same social group so that the employee acts in the interests of this group over his own. Hiring people from the same family or friends is considered preferable over hiring a stranger. A person from the same social group would try to live up to the expectations in order to stay in the social group and to not let a friend or family member down. However, a bad performing employee will not be fired as quickly since he is tied to the company for more than professional reasons. The employee repays this form of protection with loyalty.

A Dutch delegation was shocked and surprised when the Brazilian owner of a large manufacturing company introduced his relatively junior accountant as the key co-ordinator of a $15m joint venture. The Dutch were puzzled why a recently qualified accountant had been given such weighty responsibilities, including the receipt of their own money. The Brazilians pointed out that this young man was the best possible choice among 1,200 employees since he was the nephew of the owner. Who could be more trustworthy than that? Instead of complaining, the Dutch were supposed to consider themselves lucky that he was available. [257 p. 163]

In an individualist culture hiring family members or close friends could be considered as cronyism and is not desired. One would get blamed to choose a person out of personal interest and not because of professional reasons. The individualist culture sees an employer-employee relationship as a business transaction for which the best one will get the job. The loyalty to the employee is smaller and an employee is more likely to change jobs for a better salary or better career chances. An interesting experiment was done by Early in 1989 with a group of 48 Chinese management trainees and 48 management trainees from the United States. The Chinese, coming from a collectivist culture, performed best when told that their performance would be measured for groups of 10 and when their names were not marked on the documents they handled. [255] The American, that is individualist, participants performed best when told that their performance would be measured individually and with their names marked, and abysmally low when operating a group target anonymously. [255 p. 238]

Throughout his studies, Hofstede assigned Individualism scores to each country that he investigated. The country scores on his Individualism Index (IDV) are as flows:

Table 7 IDV Ranks

Rank	Country	Rank	Country
1	United States	28	Turkey
2	Australia	29	Uruguay
3	Great Britain	30	Greece
4/5	Canada	31	Philippines
4/5	Netherlands	32	Mexico
6	New Zealand	33/35	Yugoslavia
7	Italy	33/35	Portugal
8	Belgium	33/35	East Africa
9	Denmark	36	Malaysia
10/11	Sweden	37	Hong Kong
10/11	France	38	Chile
12	Ireland	39/41	Singapore
13	Norway	39/41	Thailand
14	Switzerland	39/41	West Africa
15	Germany	42	Salvador
16	South Africa	43	South Korea
17	Finland	44	Taiwan
18	Austria	45	Peru
19	Israel	46	Costa Rica
20	Spain	47/48	Pakistan
21	India	47/48	Indonesia
22/23	Japan	49	Colombia
22/23	Argentina	50	Venezuela
24	Iran	51	Panama
25	Jamaica	52	Ecuador
26/27	Brazil, Arab countries	53	Guatemala

Source: adapted from Geert Hofstede; Cultural Consequences, 2nd edition

Key differences between collectivist and individualist societies in the work environment [255 p. 244]	
Low IDV	**High IDV**
Employees act in the interest of their in-group, not necessarily of themselves.	Employees supposed to act as "economic men"
Hiring and promotion decisions take employees' in-group into account.	Hiring and promotion decisions should be based on skills and rules only.
Relatives of employer and employees preferred in hiring.	Family relationships seen as a disadvantage in hiring.
Employer-employee relationship is basically moral, like a family link.	Employer-employee relationship is a business deal in a "labour market".
Poor performance reason for other tasks.	Poor performance reason for dismissal.
Employee commitment to organisation low.	Employee commitment to organisation high.
Potential emotional commitment to union.	Relationship with union calculative.
Employees perform best in groups.	Employees perform best as individuals.
Training most effective when focused at group level.	Training most effective when focused at individual level.
Preferred reward allocation based on equality for in-group, equity for out-group.	Preferred reward allocation based on equity for all.
Relationships with colleagues corporative for in-group members, hostile for out-group.	Relationships with colleagues do not depend on their group identity.
Treating friends better than others is normal and ethical: particularism.	Treating friends better than others is nepotism and unethical: universalism.
In business, personal relationships prevail over task and company.	In business, task and company prevail over personal relationships.
Organisational success attributed to sharing information, openly committing oneself, and political alliances.	Organisational success attributed to withholding information, not openly committing, and avoiding alliances.
Belief in collective decisions.	Belief in individual decisions.

Low IDV	High IDV
Innovation champions in organisations want to involve others.	Innovation champions in organisations want to venture out on their own.
Innovations within existing networks.	Innovation outside existing networks.
Fewer invention patents granted.	More invention patents granted.
Entrepreneurs claim contribution of others to their results.	Entrepreneurs claim own results without depending on others.
Emplyees and managers report team-work, personal contacts and discrimi-nation at work.	Employees and managers report work-ing individually.
Less control over job and working conditions; fewer hours worked.	More control over job and working conditions, longer hours worked.
Less social mobility across occupa-tions.	Greater social mobility across occupa-tions.

Table 8 Differences Between Collectivist And Individualist Societies

Masculinity and Femininity

Masculinity versus femininity refers to the distribution of roles between the genders which is another fundamental issue for any society to which a range of solutions are found. Hofstede studied which implications the biological difference between masculinity and femininity for social roles within different countries. According to him, it is very important for women to help others, and to put a lot importance on relationships and other social goals. Men on the other hand value their career, money as well as ego goals very high. The importance of masculinity and femininity varies across different countries. Hofstede developed a scale for 53 countries varying from very high masculinity to very low masculinity which equals femininity. The results for the masculinity index values for 50 countries and three regions are shown below:

Table 9 MAS Ranks

Rank	Country	Rank	Country
1	Japan	28	Singapore
2	Austria	29	Israel
3	Venezuela	30/31	Indonesia
4/5	Italy	30/31	West Africa
4/5	Switzerland	32/33	Turkey
6	Mexico	32/33	Taiwan
7/8	Ireland	34	Panama
7/8	Jamaica	35/36	Iran
9/10	Great Britain	35/36	France
9/10	Germany	37/38	Spain
11/12	Philippines	37/38	Peru
11/12	Colombia	39	East Africa
13/14	South Africa	40	Salvador
13/14	Ecuador	41	South Korea
15	United States	42	Uruguay
16	Australia	43	Guatemala
17	New Zealand	44	Thailand
18/19	Greece	45	Portugal
18/19	Hong Kong	46	Chile
20/21	Argentina	47	Finland
20/21	India	48/49	Yugoslavia
22	Belgium	48/49	Costa Rica
23	Arab Countries	50	Denmark
24	Canada	51	Netherlands
25/26	Malaysia	52	Norway
25/26	Pakistan	53	Sweden
27	Brazil		

Source: adapted from Geert Hofstede; Cultural Consequences, 2nd edition, p. 286

The difference between a high MAS country and a low MAS country has a big influence on the way business is done in the respective countries. A more general difference is that people from a high MAS culture see their work as something that is a reason to live. Material rewards, a high salary and good performance are goals to be achieved. In a low MAS culture, people tend to think of work as something that has to be done to live. A study from the Commission des Communautés Européennes in 1978 revealed that if employees could improve their work/life situation, high MAS country inhabitants would increase their salary while people form low MAS countries would decrease their working hours. [255 p. 317] The concern for a high quality of life is therefore higher in a feminine culture.

Feminine cultures tend to see their superiors differently from masculine cultures. In low MAS countries a manager is seen as an employee like everybody else. The status difference is not as high as in high MAS countries. Also, it seems that in feminine cultures women have more opportunities to reach high level jobs. Both cultures have different perceptions of the ideal manager. A good manager in a masculine culture is more aggressive, self-confident and important. Only the fittest will survive. [258 p. 256] He is expected to encourage others to follow a career path and to develop its subordinates. Women can develop if they adapt to the masculine culture. A manager in a feminine culture is more intuitive, not so aggressive and less visible. Corporate ventures are feminine in their form of doing business since the partners are equal and contribute in a cooperating way.

The way of handling conflicts in a business environment is also different between masculine and feminine cultures. In Britain, the United States as well as other countries that are high on the MAS scale, managers believe that a conflict should be solved by confrontation. In low MAS cultures, a conflict is more likely to be solved by compromising or by negotiating a solution. Each country has its own institutional context of conflict resolution. In France, which scored moderately feminine in the IBM studies (MAS 43), there is occasionally a lot of verbal insult, both between employers and labour and between bosses and subordinates, but there is also a particular sense of moderation that enables parties to continue working together while agreeing to disagree. [259 pp. 32, 60-61]

Hofstede furthermore argues that industrially developed masculine cultures have a competitive advantage in manufacturing, especially in large volume – doing things efficiently, well, and fast. They are good at the production of big and heavy equipment and in bulk chemistry. Feminine cultures have a relative advantage in service industries such as consulting and transportation, in manufacturing according to customer specifications, and handling live matter, such as high-yield agriculture and biochemistry.

Key Differences Between Feminine and Masculine Societies in the Work Situation[47]	
Low MAS	**High MAS**
Work in order to live.	Live in order to work.
Meaning of work for workers: relations and working conditions.	Meaning of work for workers: security, pay, and interesting work.
Stress on equality, solidarity, and quality of work life.	Stress on equity, mutual competition, and performance.
Managers are employees like others.	Managers are culture heroes.
Managers expected to use intuition, deal with feelings, and seek consensus.	Managers expected to be decisive, firm, assertive, aggressive, competitive, just.
Successful managers seen as having both male and female characteristics.	Successful managers seen as having solely male characteristics.
More women in management.	Fewer women in management.
Smaller wage gap between genders.	Larger wage gap between genders.
Women choose female boss.	Women choose male boss.
Career ambitions are optional for both men and women.	Career ambitions are compulsory for men, optional for women.
Managers hold modes career aspirations.	Mangers hold ambitious career aspirations.
Managers less prepared to uproot their families for career reasons.	Managers more prepared to uproot their families for career reasons.
Women in management take having families for granted and adapt their careers.	Women in management take having careers for granted and adapt their families.
Job applicants undersell themselves.	Job applicants oversell themselves.
Humanisation of work through creations of work groups.	Humanization of work through provision of task challenge.

47 Adapted from Hofstede p. 318

Low MAS	High MAS
Resolution of conflicts through problem solving, compromise, and negotiation.	Resolution of conflicts through denying them or fighting until the best "man" wins.
More sickness absence.	Less sickness absence.
Lower job stress: fewer burnout symptoms among healthy employees.	Higher job stress: more burnout symptoms among healthy employees.
Preference for smaller companies.	Preference for lager companies.
Preference for fewer hours worked.	Preference for higher pay.
Competitive advantage in service industries, consulting, live products, and biochemistry.	Competitive advantage in manufacturing industries, price competition, heavy products, and bulk chemistry.

Table 10 Key Differences Between Feminine and Masculine Societies

Long- Versus Short-Term-Orientation

This fifth dimension was found in a study among students in 23 countries around the world, using a questionnaire designed by Chinese scholars. It can be said to deal with virtue regardless of truth. Values associated with long-term-orientation are thrift and perseverance; values associated with Short-Term Orientation are respect for tradition, fulfilling social obligations, and protecting one's 'face'. [256] As for the other dimensions mentioned in this chapter, there is a long-term-orientation scale. A country that scored a very high index on this scale is long-term-oriented and a country with a very low index is more short-term-oriented. According to this study, East Asian countries such as Hong Kong, South Korea, China, Taiwan and Japan are very high on the long-term-orientation Scale and Western countries are on the lower half. The lowest indexes are occupied by third world countries like Pakistan, Zimbabwe, the Philippines and Nigeria which shows that this index does not only divide the west from the east. There are obviously not only cultural but also economic factors that influence a country's long-term-orientation which we will not discuss in this book. For further reading on this, we recommend Geert Hostede's Book "Culture's Consequences". In this text, we want to focus on what is important to know when a company wants to enter a market that is either short term or long term orientated. Businesses in long-term-orientated cultures are accustomed to working towards building up strong positions in their markets; they do not expect immediate results. In Japan, corporate strategies are often designed to last centuries. Short term losses are accepted if it fits to the long term strategy.

In short-term-orientated cultures the "bottom line" (the results of the past month, quarter, or year) is a major concern; control systems are focused on it and managers are constantly judged by it. [255 p. 361] Low LTO countries tend to have an analytic way of thinking but seem to solve problems fuzzily. High LTO countries also put more emphasis on building long-lasting business relationships. Sometimes they are even prepared to make a loss at first if they think that a business contact could turn into a profitable long lasting relationship in the future. When a business partnership is going well, the business partner can also be invited to family events. This only happens on very rare occasions in a Low LTO country like Great Britain or Australia. Here, one's business world is strictly separated from one's private life and managers are not very interested in their partner's private lives. Unless both are friends, the question about the health of the partner's wife or family could be misunderstood.

To summarise, a long term orientated country is a bit more focused on the future. Presents are given to children to prepare them for the future, income will be saved for future purposes and when investments are made, they will be made in long-term investments like real estate. Short term oriented countries focus more on the past and the present. Short risky decisions are acceptable if they increase the short term profit. Short term relationships get explored if they provide a good opportunity.

The main differences are summarised in the following table:

Key Differences Between Short- and Long-Term-Oriented Societies in the business environment[48]	
Low LTO	**High LTO**
Parents' gifts to children for their self-concept and love.	Parents' gifts to children for their education and finances.
Lower performance in basic mathematical tasks.	Higher performance in basic mathematical tasks.
The bottom line.	Building a strong position.
Analytic thinking.	Synthetic thinking.
Fuzzy problem solving.	Structured problem solving.
In business, short term results important.	Building of relationships more important.
Family and business sphere separated.	Vertical coordination, horizontal coordination, control, and adaptiveness.
Meritocracy: economic and social life to be ordered by abilities.	People should live more equally.
Leisure time important.	Leisure time not so important.
Most important events in life occurred in the past or occur in present.	Most important events in life will occur in the future.
Small share of additional income saved.	Large share of additional income saved.
Investment in mutual funds.	Investment in real estate.

Table 11 Key Differences Between Short- and Long-Term-Oriented Societies

Conclusion

To mention all possible conclusions that one can draw out of these dimensions would go far beyond the scope of this book. We should also be very careful with predictions about individuals from different cultures. Values, talents and the way of doing things can vary widely within a country. Some countries even overlap in some areas. A generalisation is never a good thing when it comes to intercultural

---

48 Adapted from Hofstede p. 366-367

management, but research has provided us with tendencies that can be very help-ful if we know and understand them. Given this caution, a few propositions can still be made:

- If people are to work together in hierarchical relationships, differences in power distance are the most likely source of trouble (more so than differences on the other dimensions).[49]

- Among colleagues, differences in power distance and individualism / collectiv-ism are especially problematic for the interaction process.[50]

- For ambiguous tasks (e. g., strategic planning), people from low-UAI cultures perform better than those from high-UAI cultures. If an ambiguous task is given to a group, the chairperson should preferably be chosen from a low-UAI cul-ture.[51]

- For clearly defined and urgent tasks, people from high-UAI cultures are likely to perform better. [255 p. 443]

- Other factors being equal, people from low-UAI cultures can more easily acquire cross-cultural sensitivity than can those from high-UAI cultures. [260 p. 36] How-ever, personal factors play a crucial role: Persons who grew up or have lived abroad, who have parents from divergent nationalities, who have cross-national marriages, or who have studied foreign languages are more likely to be cultur-ally sensitive regardless of their passports. [255 p. 443]

- Latin Europeans ("dependent individuals") do not function well in non-hierarchical peer groups with their own compatriots. They easily engage in fights for leadership, or they concentrate on avoiding such fights; either comes at the expense of task performance. Latin Europeans function well in non-hierarchical multicultural groups in which their initial reactions are not rein-forced. [255 p. 443]

- Civic action groups are more likely to be formed in low-PDI, low UAI cultures than elsewhere. [255 p. 443]

---

[49] Merritt (1995) illustrated this for the case of commercial airline crews.
[50] This proposition is based on the findings in a Ph.D. dissertation by Noonan (1995), who held in-depth interviews with23 U.S. and 17 non-U.S. managers and professionals about successful and unsuccessful interactions across cultures.
[51] Hofstede made the experience at INSEAD in the 1970s, discussion groups with British chairman did better on average than those with chairman of other nations.

- Business corporations will have to be more concerned with informing the public in low-PDI, low-UAI cultures than elsewhere.[52]
- Public sympathy and legislation on behalf of economically and socially weak members of society are more likely in low MAS countries. (255 p. 444)
- Public sympathy and both government and private funding for aid to economically weak countries and in the case of disasters anywhere in the world will be stronger in affluent low-MAS than in affluent high-MAS countries. (255 p. 444) You can compare this to the number that countries donate to 3rd world countries from the country profiles in the back of this book.
- Public sympathy and legislation on behalf of environmental conservation and maintaining the quality of life are more likely in low-PDI, low MAS countries. (255 p. 444)

International Encounters and Important Considerations

The language

The question of who to send abroad is very difficult to solve. Since the culture in another country can be completely different, the time a person needs to adapt to this culture can vary significantly.

The language is a very important component of international business. Even though English is the world trade language, not all managers speak it well enough to negotiate in it. Some countries even expect you to speak their own language if you want to be treated as an equal partner. France and Japan are examples of two countries where the language in which you approach a manager from that country is extremely important. The French language has many different dialects and a French person can quickly see what custom you are from. The old nobleness who surrounded the king centuries ago is still present today. They are usually very conservative and guarded. They have their own dialect, which distinguishes them from other customs. Then there is also the new nobleness which are people form rich families as well as grand ecole students, lawyers and doctors, people that are much

---

[52] This inference is inspired in part by a comparative study of corporate social reporting in France, Germany and the Netherlands by Schreuder (1978) (255)

respected in society and who have their own dialect as well. Of course, there is also the working class that speaks a dialect that distinguishes them from the other more educated classes. Even today it is sometimes hard for the classes to mix. The grand ecoles are very expensive and therefore often only accessible for students with higher income parents. Not many very good students from the working class get into one of these elite schools which can be seen as the entry ticket into the upper class. In these upper classes the accent you speak and the way you express yourself is extremely important to be respected.

In France, a rich man does not need to drive a big car or wear an expensive suit, he will always be recognised by the way he talks. This is different in Germany for example, where the car and the house are seen as a representation of one's status in society. The language itself is not as important in terms of being a status symbol. Another aspect of language that international managers need to be aware of is humour. Many managers do not recognise that the sense of humour differs in different cultures. What is funny in one culture might not be funny in another. In fact, some jokes might even be offending. A manager that goes into another country should therefore be careful with telling jokes in public. Only if he is very sure about the way the joke will be understood, he can go on with it.

The following extract from Cardel Gertsen's and Martine Söderberg's book "Cultural Dimensions of International Mergers and Acquisitions" points out what consequences a foreign management can have on local employees:

Even though most Danes are good at foreign languages, we ... have examples of employees with seven to nine years of schooling who ... were unable to communicate freely and advance beliefs on behalf of their colleagues because the foreign management fixed the agenda in their [the foreign] language, unaware that active participation and exchange of views in a discussion ... needs a standard of English that is so high that it is mastered by only very few Danish employees. We also have examples of engineers who can easily communicate in German as long as they talk with German engineers about ... the development of a product. But they have never learned how to discuss and argue in German in order to defend their interests when cooperation problems arise between a Danish and a German project group.
(261 p. 193)

Culture Shock

It is very hard to pick the right employees to send to another country to build up a new branch or a line of business. Some intercultural consulting companies claim to have developed tests to evaluate people that are adequate to manage in another country. However, there is no proven statistic that these tests are really as good as they claim to be. In fact, these tests are usually made

Kwintessential
www.kwintessential.co.uk/

Advance
http://www.advance.org

Synergy Associates
www.synergy-associates.com

Management Laboratory
www.management-laboratory.com

by companies from the home country and not by people that are actually from the foreign country. A management quality that is regarded as being beneficial like extrovertism in the United States will probably not be very valuable in China where understatement and self-effacement are qualities of a good leader. The best guarantee seems to be to send somebody who has already lived in one or more other countries besides his home country. These people have already experienced what it means to adapt and to face the culture shock. However, even for these experienced people, the culture shock will come every time they go to another country that they have not been to before.

The culture shock itself can be classified into four stages. The first one is the euphoric stage. The manager leaves his home country with a positive attitude and optimism. Exciting new things can be explored and some kind of holiday feeling puts you in a good mood.

The second phase is the culture shock after a couple weeks or month. The holiday feeling is gone and first problems and confrontations with the new culture arrive. Since culture is partially defined as a set of "distinctive techniques of a group and their characteristic products" [262] we start realising that our system and our techniques are not always working. Expectations that are not met can lead to unsatisfying performance or frustration.

The third phase is the acculturation phase. This phase starts when the visitor is starting to adapt and learns how to function in the new culture. He needs to learn how to integrate into the society and social networks. Until the acculturation phase starts it usually takes a couple of months but can also take one or two years, depending on how open-minded the visitor engages the new culture, how different the culture is and if the manager has gained experience in other countries before.

The stable state is the fourth phase after the main part of adaption is done. The attitude towards the host country may remain negative, positive or equal compared to his home culture. If it remains negative towards the host culture it would probably be wise to exchange the manager since an adaption and enthusiasm towards the host culture is necessary to build a successful business. Otherwise business partners or employees will feel that the manager is not happy or comfortable. Many cultures require a foreigner to adapt; if he does not he will always be an outsider or maybe even discriminated against.

If the manager feels equal between the two cultures he can be considered bicultural which is the ideal state. The manager can be brought back to the home country if necessary but also does not mind to stay as long as he is needed.

Sometimes managers even feel more comfortable in the host country after they have gone through the acculturation phase. They can be described as native and will be happy to stay. However, all states depend strongly on the business environment and the social network that the employee finds in the new country. Also, an accompanying spouse has a big effect on the manager's attitude towards the new culture. Often managers return because their spouses where not able to adapt. Some companies offer an intercultural training which can prepare the manager and their spouse for the challenges they will face in the other country. Another good way to accompany a manager sent to another culture is to assign a sponsor from the top management to motivate him and to give the manager the feeling of still being incorporated into his company.

One of the biggest dangers confronting a company that goes abroad for the first time is the danger of being ill-informed. International businesses that are ill-informed about the practices of another culture are likely to fail. Going international requires a company to adapt to the values, norms and culture of the host country. [24]

To avoid the danger of being not well enough or misinformed, multinational companies should think about employing local citizens. Local employees can help them to do business in that particular culture. It is also very important that home country managers are cosmopolitan. They need to understand how the differences between the home and the host country can affect their business. One way of confronting this challenge is to send home country employees to different cultures and to build a management team that is cosmopolitan and experienced in international business issues.

Another danger that international businesses are facing is ethnocentric behaviour. Ethnocentric managers believe that their own culture or ethnic group is superior to another. Sometimes this behaviour is a sign of insecurity and of being uncomfortable with another culture. Ethnocentrism is very common, but an international manager should not exhibit this behaviour.

Negotiations

Negotiations in another culture can be very different from negotiations in your home country. The outlined dimensions of national culture above can help you to understand and prepare negotiations better. The following paragraphs give you an example how these dimensions can affect negotiations with other cultures:

- Power distance affects the degree of centralisation of the control and decision-making structure, and the importance of the status of the negotiators.
- Uncertainty avoidance affects the (in)tolerance of ambiguity and (dis)trust in opponents who show unfamiliar behaviours and the need for structure and ritual in the negotiation procedures.
- Collectivism affects the need for stable relationships between (opposing) negotiators. In a collectivist culture replacement of a person means that a new relationship will have to be built, which takes time. Mediators (go-betweens) have an important role in maintaining a viable pattern of relationships that allows negotiators to discuss problem content.
- Masculinity affects the need for ego-boosting behaviour and the sympathy for the strong on the part of negotiators and their supervisors, and the tendency to resolve conflicts by a show of force. Feminine cultures are more likely to resolve conflicts through compromise and to strive for consensus.
- Long-term orientation affects the perseverance with which desired ends are pursued, even at the cost of sacrifices.[53]

International Acquisitions, Mergers, and Joint Ventures

As we have shown in Chapter 3, there are six different ways of doing business on the global market. The first and classic approach is by licensing or exporting the

---

[53] Affects taken from (255 p. 436)

goods manufactured in the home country to local agents that handle the export by themselves. In the last couple of decades, more companies started to enter foreign markets by direct foreign investment (DFI). By using this approach, a company is involved in a lot of intercultural interactions which involves different national cultures but also the different organisational cultures.

The discussed Greenfield approach in which a company starts setting up another branch or subsidiary on a green field, which means from scratch has a very high success rate. This is because the local home company only sends a few managers to the other country in order to hire local employees who are from that country but who also fit into their organisations culture. However, this strategy is very slow and requires a lot of initial capital investments, but the risk to fail because of cultural reason is minimal. Many international organisations have used this approach successfully, including Daimler, Nike and IBM.

The approach where a company buys another foreign company is called foreign acquisition. The cultural risks associated with this approach are very high because the home company does not only buy the host companie's physical assets; it also purchases its employees, corporate culture and its national culture. Hence the risks that come with this approach are very high. I recommended keeping the acquired organisation at an arm's length and treating it as an investment instead of integrating the company into its acquirer. However, this is only possible in rare cases where the home company's interests in the host company are purely financial. In most cases, companies get bought to eliminate a competitor, to gain market share or to exploit synergies. In this case, conflicts are often solved with force, which means that the top management and key employees are replaced with employees and managers from the home company in order to implement the new culture as fast as possible and to eliminate adverse winds. However, often these key people leave by themselves. The downside is that these key employees and managers are human capital that has considerable value to both companies. It is important to remember that problems start after the purchasing price is established and the contracts are signed. The cost associated with the integration can be significant and sometimes even more than the purchasing price for the company.

From a cultural management point of view, the most risky way to enter a foreign market is a merger. Many business commentators are now acknowledging that failure does not have its roots simply in financial, monetary and legal issues, but also in a lack of intercultural synergy. Research suggests that up to 65% of failed mergers and acquisitions are due to 'people issues', i.e. intercultural differences causing communication breakdowns that result in poor productivity. [263] The author of Managing Cultural Differences, Piero Morosini, writes in his book that "misunderstood national cultural differences have been cited as the most important factors behind the high failure rate of global JVs and alliances."

DaimlerChrysler, Sprint-Nextel and CBS/Viacom are only some of the more popular cases. It is very difficult if not impossible to eliminate differences by showing power since both companies are of equal size or are equally important. As long as executives base their merging decision purely on financial or power reasons, mergers will continue to fail at a very high rate. However, there are also popular international mergers that have been very successful such as Vodafone/D2 and HP/Compaq. Characteristics of a successful merger are two separate head offices even though organisation comes with inefficiencies, but the benefit that the signal of two head offices sends out can be an important criterion for the survival of the merged companies. One head office could give the employees the impression that the new company is not merging but actually got taken over. Strong and charismatic leaders are also a very important factor in merging two companies.

A joint venture is a form of business in which two or more companies contribute resources to found a new company together. The contribution can be resources, know-how, labour or finances. As soon as a company is transferring management and employees to the joint venture it is transferring its culture as well. As long as it is clear which partner contributes which resources to the joint-venture, the cultural risk is not as high as in the case of a merger. These joint ventures have the highest chances for succeeding if only one partner provides the entire management. The chances for cultural differences are limited if only one partner manages the daily business matters. Overall, a joint-venture is a risk-limited way of entering a new market. Some joint-ventures are only temporary because one partner usually wants to intensify its business and then buys the other partner out. However, since the purpose for at least one partner in the joint venture is usually to start a business in a new country, the buyout process is not conflicting with these intentions.

The safest way to enter a new market is to entering into a strategic alliance with a company from the host country. The partners agree to work together on a certain project and get to know each other. An alliance can usually be called off without ruining one of the partners. If an alliance turns out to be a merger later on, both companies already know each other's culture. Employees and managers on both sides are prepared and know what to expect from their counterparts in the foreign country.

It is crucial for a company that wants to enter a foreign market to be aware of cultural differences. Two scientists Li and Guisinger found in 1991 that foreign entries into the United States from culturally distant countries were more likely to fail than were those from culturally close countries.[54] One year later, Li and Guisinger also found that the levels of foreign investment were inversely related to the cultural distance between parent and host country. (255 p. 446) Bell, Barkema and Pennings found in 1996 that the survival rates decrease with cultural distance, but more for joint ventures and acquisitions than for greenfield entries, and more for partially owned subsidiaries, whatever the entry mode. They also showed that the effect of learning, as the number of previous foreign entries into the same country or region decreased the risk. (255 p. 447) I strongly suggest that a company that wants to expand into a new country professionally manages the integration process. Whatever the mode of entry is, all involved companies and countries should be carefully analysed by all partners. This analysis should be the basis for an integration plan.

The integration process takes time, a lot of money and should be overseen by all partners. The contributions from a partner to the integration process can be very valuable and time-saving. Often financial experts are not able to foresee how much money, time and energy the integration will actually cost. This can be a reason why a lot of mergers and acquisitions fail. Not all problems can be foreseen and not all problems can be prepared for, only be minimised by a professional integrations management. Such an integration management cannot be overestimated and should be actively supported by the highest organisational level.

---

54 Li and Guisinger's Study covered the period 1978-88 (255 p. 446)

Ethics and Social Responsibility in International Business

Ethics and Social Responsibility are a core topic of international business. However, in this book I only want to introduce you to the challenges that a company going international might face. A company should not only thrive for success regardless of the ethical and social costs. Some people argue that what is considered ethical depends on the culture were the person is from. This is probably right, because what is seen as ethical is different from culture to culture. In Asian cultures for example it would be considered normal to bring presents to a negotiation. To invite the other party to a luxury hotel and pay their bills would be considered graceful. While this behaviour is right and considerate to Asian cultures, western cultures could understand these actions as bribery which would be unethical to them.

Another situation a company might face that is operating in a third world country in order to produce its products cheaper than it could in its home country is the following: A manager from a Canadian company visits his new production plant in a very poor country. While he is there, he finds out that the local manager hired a 13 year old girl to clean oily machines. When he faces the responsible local manager who hired the girl the local manager does not see anything unethical in what he did. He replies that the girl does not have any guardians to take care of her and her little brother. Therefore, she needs to earn money in order to support herself and her brother. In fact he even replies that he saved the girl from prostitution by giving her a job that she would not have gotten anywhere else.

This example is representative of many cases that have really happened in big international companies. The question here is what ethical standard to apply. If the company continues to hire under-aged children, they will probably face heavy reproaches in their home country. If they fire the girl, they practically send her to prostitution.

Many of the ethical issues and dilemmas in international business are rooted in the fact that political systems, law, economic development, and culture vary sig-

MCI WorldCom background case:
http://www.scu.edu/ethics/dialogue/candc/cases/worldcom-update.html

Arthur Anderson background:
http://www.commondreams.org/views02/0712-02.htm

Enron background:
http://news.bbc.co.uk/2/hi/business/1780075.stm

nificantly from nation to nation. Consequently what is considered normal practice in one nation may be considered unethical in others. [24 p. 126] Managers that work for an internationally operating organisation need to be very sensitive to differences between cultures and differences in ethical standards. Most problems that result from of ethical issues have to do with human rights, moral obligations, environmental regulations and corruption.

The existence of a business can only be justified with the purpose to create value for its owners. Employees of a company are working in order to earn a salary that supports them. Most decisions that are made on behalf of a company or an employee within the company are to maximise its income or to reduce expenses. In most cases, the decisions made are tolerable to society. However, in the last few years, cases like Enron, Arthur Anderson and WorldCom have shown that either managers are increasingly involved in unacceptable business practices or that these cases can be detected better due to increased anti fraud regulations and practices. Whatever the reason might be, fact is that business ethics are of increased importance in the international business environment. Business ethics can be defined as one of the following: The study of standards which businesses should observe in their dealings, over and above compliance with the law. [264] Over 500 business-ethics courses are currently taught on American campuses; fully 90% of the nation's business schools now provide some kind of training in the area. [265]

The concept has come to mean various things to various people, but generally it is coming to know what is right or wrong in the workplace and doing what is right - this is in regard to effects of products/services and in relationships with stakeholders. Business ethics has come to be considered a management discipline, especially since the birth of the social responsibility movement in the 1960s. In that decade, social awareness movements raised expectations of businesses to use their massive financial and social influence to address social problems such as poverty, crime, environmental protection, equal rights, public health and improving education. An increasing number of people asserted that because businesses were making a profit from using a country's resources, these businesses owed it to the country to work to improve society. Many researchers, business schools and managers have recognized this broader constituency, and in their planning and operations have replaced the word "stockholder" with "stakeholder", meaning to include employees, customers, suppliers and the wider community.

Today, ethics in the workplace can be managed through use of codes of ethics, codes of conduct, roles of ethicists and ethics committees, policies, procedures to resolve ethical dilemmas, ethics training, etc. [266] For more information on business ethics please see the Resources Section on the Management Laboratory website.

Ethical behaviour refers to a behaviour that conforms to social values and norms that are generally established and tolerated. Unethical behaviour is therefore not conforming to these norms and values.

Market Entry Strategies

Country Profiles [55]

The Management Laboratory Press thanks
Neil Payne from Kwintessential for the
resources in this section.

[55] These country profiles are taken and adapted with kind permission from Kwintessential. For more
information on other countries as well as Intercultural Communication, Cross Cultural Training, Translation Services & Interpreters, visit: http://www.kwintessential.co.uk

Market Entry Strategies

Country Profiles

Australia

Facts and Statistics

Location:	Oceania, continent between the Indian Ocean and the South Pacific Ocean
Capital:	Canberra
Climate:	generally arid to semiarid; temperate in south and east; tropical in north
Population:	19,913,144 (July 2004 est.)
Ethnic:	Make-up: Caucasian 92%, Asian 7%, aboriginal and other 1%
Religions:	Anglican 26.1%, Roman Catholic 26%, other Christian 24.3%, non-Christian 11%, other 12.6%
Government:	democratic, federal-state system recognizing the British monarch as sovereign

Languages in Australia

English is the primary language used in Australia. Yet their colourful vocabulary, accent, phonetics system and slang ('Strine') can take a lot of getting used to. In 1788, there were about 250 separate Aboriginal languages spoken in Australia, plus dialects. Today, only two thirds of these languages survive and only 20 of them (eight per cent of the original 250) are still strong enough to have chance of surviving well into the next century. In addition to these there are also the languages of immigrants from Europe, the Middle East and Asia.

Australian Society & Culture

Aussie Modesty

- Australians are very down to earth and always mindful of not giving the impression that they think they are better than anyone else.
- They value authenticity, sincerity, and loathe pretentiousness.
- Australians prefer people who are modest, humble, self- deprecating and with a sense of humour.

- They do not draw attention to their academic or other achievements and tend to distrust people who do.
- They often downplay their own success, which may make them appear not to be achievement-oriented.

Mates

- Australians place a high value on relationships.
- With a relatively small population, it is important to get along with everyone, since you never know when your paths may cross again.
- This leads to a win-win negotiating style, since having everyone come away with positive feelings helps facilitate future business dealings.

A Multi-Cultural Society

- The initial population of Australia was made up of Aborigines and people of British and Irish descent.
- After World War II there was heavy migration from Europe, especially from Greece, Italy, Germany, the Netherlands, Yugoslavia, Lebanon, and Turkey.
- This was in response to the Australian policy of proactively trying to attract immigrants to boost the population and work force.
- In the last thirty years, Australia has liberalised its immigration policy and opened its borders to South East Asia.
- This has caused a real shift in self-perception as Aussies begin to re-define themselves as a multi-cultural and multi-faith society rather then the old homogenous, white, Anglo- Saxon, Protestant nation.

Meeting Etiquette

- Australians are not very formal so greetings are casual and relaxed.
- A handshake and smile suffices.
- While an Australian may say, 'G'day' or 'G'day, mate', this may sound patronizing from a foreigner. Visitors should simply say, 'Hello' or 'Hello, how are you?'
- Aussies prefer to use first names, even at the initial meeting

Gift Giving Etiquette

- Small gifts are commonly exchanged with family members, close friends, and neighbours on birthdays and Christmas.
- Trades people such as sanitation workers may be given a small amount of cash, or more likely, a bottle of wine or a six-pack of beer!
- If invited to someone's home for dinner, it is polite to bring a box of chocolates or flowers to the hostess. A good quality bottle of wine is always appreciated.
- Gifts are opened when received.

Dining Etiquette

- Many invitations to an Aussies home will be for a 'barbie' (BBQ).
- Guests to a barbeque typically bring wine or beer for their personal consumption. In some cases, very informal barbecues may suggest that you bring your own meat!
- Arrive on time if invited to dinner; no more than 15 minutes late if invited to a barbeque or a large party.
- Contact the hostess ahead of time to see if she would like you to bring a dish.
- Offer to help the hostess with the preparation or clearing up after a meal is served.

Watch your table manners!

- Table manners are Continental -- hold the fork in the left hand and the knife in the right while eating.
- Indicate you have finished eating by laying your knife and fork parallel on your plate with the handles facing to the right.
- Keep your elbows off the table and your hands above the table when eating.

Relationships & Communication

- Australians are very matter of fact when it comes to business so do not need long- standing personal relationships before they do business with people.
- Australians are very direct in the way they communicate.
- There is often an element of humour, often self-deprecating, in their speech.
- Aussies often use colourful language that would be unthinkable in other countries.

Business Meeting Etiquette

- Appointments are necessary and relatively easy to schedule.
- They should be made with as much lead time as possible.
- Punctuality is important in business situations. It is better to arrive a few minutes early than to keep someone waiting.
- Meetings are generally relaxed; however, they are serious events.
- If an Australian takes exception to something that you say, they will tell you so.
- If you make a presentation, avoid hype, making exaggerated claims, or bells and whistles.
- Present your business case with facts and figures. Emotions and feelings are not important in the Australian business climate.

Negotiating and Decision Making

- Australians get down to business quickly with a minimum amount of small talk.
- They are quite direct and expect the same in return. They appreciate brevity and are not impressed by too much detail.
- Negotiations proceed quickly. Bargaining is not customary. They will expect your initial proposal to have only a small margin for negotiation.
- They do not like high-pressure techniques.
- Decision-making is concentrated at the top of the company, although decisions are made after consultation with subordinates, which can make decision making slow and protracted.

What to wear?

- Business dress is conservative in Melbourne and Sydney.
- Men should wear a dark coloured, conservative business suit.
- Women should wear a smart dress or a business suit.
- In Brisbane or other tropical areas, depending on the job function and company culture, men may wear shirts, ties and Bermuda shorts.

Business Cards

- Business cards are exchanged at the initial introduction without formal ritual.
- If you are not given a business card, it is not an insult; the person simply may not have one. China

China

Facts and Statistics

Location:	Eastern Asia bordering Afghanistan 76 km, Bhutan 470 km, Burma 2,185 km, India 3,380 km, Kazakhstan 1,533 km, North Korea 1,416 km, Kyrgyzstan 858 km, Laos 423 km, Mongolia 4,677 km, Nepal 1,236 km, Pakistan 523 km, Russia (northeast) 3,605 km, Russia (northwest) 40 km, Tajikistan 414 km, Vietnam 1,281 km
Capital:	Beijing
Climate:	extremely diverse; tropical in south to subarctic in north
Population:	1,298,847,624 (July 2004 est.)
Ethnic Make-up:	Han Chinese 91.9%, Zhuang, Uygur, Hui, Yi, Tibetan, Miao, Manchu, Mongol, Buyi, Korean, and other nationalities 8.1%
Religions:	Daoist (Taoist), Buddhist, Muslim 1%-2%, Christian 3%-4%
Government:	(former) Communist state

The Chinese Language

Chinese is a family of closely-related but mutually unintelligible languages. These languages are known variously as fˈ¡ngyˈ¢n (regional languages), dialects of Chinese or varieties of Chinese. In all over 1.2 billion people speak one or more varieties of Chinese.

All varieties of Chinese belong to the Sino-Tibetan family of languages and each one has its own dialects and sub-dialects, which are more or less mutually intelligible.

Chinese Society & Culture

The Importance of "Face"

- The concept of 'face' roughly translates as 'honour', 'good reputation' or 'respect'.
- There are four types of 'face':
  1) *Diu-mian-zi*: this is when one's actions or deeds have been exposed to people.
  2) *Gei-mian-zi*: involves the giving of face to others through showing respect.

335

3) *Liu-mian-zi:* this is developed by avoiding mistakes and showing wisdom in action.

4) *Jiang-mian-zi:* this is when face is increased through others, i.e. someone complementing you to an associate.

- It is critical you avoid losing face or causing the loss of face at all times.

Confucianism

Confucianism is a system of behaviours and ethics that stress the obligations of people towards one another based upon their relationship. The basic tenets are based upon five different relationships:

- Ruler and subject
- Husband and wife
- Parents and children
- Brothers and sisters
- Friend and friend

Confucianism stresses duty, sincerity, loyalty, honour, filial piety, respect for age and seniority. Through maintaing harmonious relations as individuals, society itself becomes stable.

Collectivism vs. Individualism

- In general, the Chinese are a collective society with a need for group affiliation, whether to their family, school, work group, or country.
- In order to maintain a sense of harmony, they will act with decorum at all times and will not do anything to cause someone else public embarrassment.
- They are willing to subjugate their own feelings for the good of the group.
- This is often observed by the use of silence in very structured meetings. If someone disagrees with what another person says, rather than disagree publicly, the person will remain quiet. This gives face to the other person, while speaking up would make both parties lose face.

Non-Verbal Communication

- The Chinese' Non-verbal communication speaks volumes.
- Since the Chinese strive for harmony and are group dependent, they rely on facial expression, tone of voice and posture to tell them what someone feels.

- Frowning while someone is speaking is interpreted as a sign of disagreement. Therefore, most Chinese maintain an impassive expression when speaking.
- It is considered disrespectful to stare into another person's eyes. In crowded situations the Chinese avoid eye contact to give themselves privacy.

Meeting Etiquette

- Greetings are formal and the oldest person is always greeted first.
- Handshakes are the most common form of greeting with foreigners.
- Many Chinese will look towards the ground when greeting someone.
- Address the person by an honorific title and their surname. If they want to move to a first-name basis, they will advise you which name to use.
- The Chinese have a terrific sense of humour. They can laugh at themselves most readily if they have a comfortable relationship with the other person. Be ready to laugh at yourself given the proper circumstances.

Gift Giving Etiquette

- In general, gifts are given at Chinese New Year, weddings, births and more recently (because of marketing), birthdays.
- The Chinese like food and a nice food basket will make a great gift.
- Do not give scissors, knives or other cutting utensils as they indicate the severing of the relationship.
- Do not give clocks, handkerchiefs or straw sandals as they are associated with funerals and death.
- Do not give flowers, as many Chinese associate these with funerals.
- Do not wrap gifts in white, blue or black paper.
- Four is an unlucky number so do not give four of anything. Eight is the luckiest number, so giving eight of something brings luck to the recipient.
- Always present gifts with two hands.
- Gifts are not opened when received.
- Gifts may be refused three times before they are accepted.

Dining Etiquette

- The Chinese prefer to entertain in public places rather than in their homes, especially when entertaining foreigners.

- If you are invited to their house, consider it a great honour. If you must turn down such an honour, it is considered polite to explain the conflict in your schedule so that your actions are not taken as a slight.
- Arrive on time.
- Remove your shoes before entering the house.
- Bring a small gift to the hostess.
- Eat well to demonstrate that you are enjoying the food!

Table manners

- Learn to use chopsticks.
- Wait to be told where to sit. The guest of honour will be given a seat facing the door.
- The host begins eating first.
- You should try everything that is offered to you.
- Never eat the last piece from the serving tray.
- Be observant to other peoples' needs.
- Chopsticks should be returned to the chopstick rest after every few bites and when you drink or stop to speak.
- The host offers the first toast.
- Do not put bones in your bowl. Place them on the table or in a special bowl for that purpose.
- Hold the rice bowl close to your mouth while eating.
- Do not be offended if a Chinese person makes slurping or belching sounds; it merely indicates that they are enjoying their food.
- There are no strict rules about finishing all the food in your bowl.

Tipping Etiquette

- Tipping is becoming more commonplace, especially with younger workers although older workers still consider it an insult. Leaving a few coins is usually sufficient.

Relationships & Communication

- The Chinese don't like doing business with companies they don't know, so working through an intermediary is crucial. This could be an individual or an organization who can make a formal introduction and vouch for the reliability of your company.

- Before arriving in China send materials (written in Chinese) that describe your company, its history, and literature about your products and services. The Chinese often use intermediaries to ask questions that they would prefer not to make directly.
- Business relationships are built formally after the Chinese get to know you.
- Be very patient. It takes a considerable amount of time and is bound up with enormous bureaucracy.
- The Chinese see foreigners as representatives of their company rather than as individuals.
- Rank is extremely important in business relationships and you must keep rank differences in mind when communicating.
- Gender bias is nonexistent in business.
- Never lose sight of the fact that communication is official, especially in dealing with someone of higher rank. Treating them too informally, especially in front of their peers, may well ruin a potential deal.
- The Chinese prefer face-to-face meetings rather than written or telephonic communication.
- Meals and social events are not the place for business discussions. There is a demarcation between business and socializing in China, so try to be careful not to intertwine the two.

Business Meeting Etiquette

- Appointments are necessary and, if possible, should be made between one-to-two months in advance, preferably in writing.
- If you do not have a contact within the company, use an intermediary to arrange a formal introduction. Once the introduction has been made, you should provide the company with information about your company and what you want to accomplish at the meeting.
- You should arrive at meetings on time or slightly early. The Chinese view punctuality as a virtue. Arriving late is an insult and could negatively affect your relationship
- Pay great attention to the agenda as each Chinese participant has his or her own agenda that they will attempt to introduce.

- Send an agenda before the meeting so your Chinese colleagues have the chance to meet with any technical experts prior to the meeting. Discuss the agenda with your translator/intermediary prior to submission.

- Each participant will take an opportunity to dominate the floor for lengthy periods without appearing to say very much of anything that actually contributes to the meeting. Be patient and listen. There could be subtle messages being transmitted that would assist you in allaying fears of on-going association.

- Meetings require patience. Mobile phones ring frequently and conversations tend to be boisterous. Never ask the Chinese to turn off their mobile phones as this causes you both to lose face.

- Guests are generally escorted to their seats, which are in descending order of rank. Senior people generally sit opposite senior people from the other side.

- It is imperative that you bring your own interpreter, especially if you plan to discuss legal or extremely technical concepts as you can brief the interpreter prior to the meeting.

- Written material should be available in both English and Chinese, using simplified characters. Be very careful about what is written. Make absolutely certain that written translations are accurate and cannot be misinterpreted.

- Visual aids are useful in large meetings and should only be done with black type on white background. Colours have special meanings and if you are not careful, your colour choice could work against you.

- Presentations should be detailed and factual and focus on long-term benefits. Be prepared for the presentation to be a challenge.

Business Negotiation

- Only senior members of the negotiating team will speak. Designate the most senior person in your group as your spokesman for the introductory functions.

- Business negotiations occur at a slow pace.

- Be prepared for the agenda to become a jumping off point for other discussions.

- Chinese are non-confrontational. They will not overtly say 'no', they will say 'they will think about it' or 'they will see'.

- Chinese negotiations are process oriented. They want to determine if relationships can develop to a stage where both parties are comfortable doing business with the other.

- Decisions may take a long time, as they require careful review and consideration.
- Under no circumstances should you lose your temper or you will lose face and irrevocably damage your relationship.
- Do not use high-pressure tactics. You might find yourself outmanoeuvred.
- Business is hierarchical. Decisions are unlikely to be made during the meetings you attend.
- The Chinese are shrewd negotiators.
- Your starting price should leave room for negotiation.

What to Wear?

- Business attire is conservative and unpretentious.
- Men should wear dark coloured, conservative business suits.
- Women should wear conservative business suits or dresses with a high neckline.
- Women should wear flat shoes or shoes with very low heels.
- Bright colours should be avoided.

Business Cards

- Business cards are exchanged after the initial introduction.
- Have one side of your business card translated into Chinese using simplified Chinese characters that are printed in gold ink since gold is an auspicious colour.
- Your business card should include your title. If your company is the oldest or largest in your country, that fact should be on your card as well.
- Hold the card in both hands when offering it, Chinese side facing the recipient.
- Examine a business card before putting it on the table next to you or in a business card case.
- Never write on someone's card unless so directed.

Market Entry Strategies

France

Facts and Statistics

Location:	Western Europe, bordering Andorra 56.6 km, Belgium 620 km, Germany 451 km, Italy 488 km, Luxembourg 73 km, Monaco 4.4 km, Spain 623 km, Switzerland 573 km
Capital:	Paris
Climate:	generally cool winters and mild summers, but mild winters and hot summers along the Mediterranean; occasional strong, cold, dry, north-to-northwesterly wind known as mistral
Population:	60,424,213 (July 2004 est.)
Ethnic Make-up:	Celtic and Latin with Teutonic, Slavic, North African, Indo chinese, Basque minorities
Religions:	Roman Catholic 83%-88%, Protestant 2%, Jewish 1%, Mus lim 5%-10%, unaffiliated 4%
Government:	republic

Languages in France

French, the official language, is the first language of 88% of the population. Most of those who speak minority languages also speak French, as the minority languages are given no legal recognition. 3% of the population speak German dialects, predominantly in the eastern provinces of Alsace-Lorraine and Moselle. Flemish is spoken by around 90,000 people in the northeast, which is 0.2% of the French population. Around 1m people near the Italian border, roughly 1.7% of the population, speaks Italian. Basque is spoken by 0.1% and mainly along the French-Spanish border.

Catalan dialects are spoken in the French Pyrenees by around 260,000 people or 0.4% of the French population. The Celtic language, Breton, is spoken by 1.2% and mainly in the north west of France. These three languages have no official status within France.

In the South of France, over 7m speak Occitan dialects, representing 12% of the population of France, but these dialects have no official status. Nor too does Corsu, the dialect of the island of Corsica that is closely related to Tuscan and is spoken by 0.3%. Arabic, the third largest minority language, is spoken by around 1.7% of the population throughout the country. Other immigrant languages from the former French colonies include Kabyle and Antillean Creole.

French Society & Culture

Cuisine

- Food is one of the great passions of the French people.
- French cooking is highly refined and involves careful preparation, attention to detail, and the use of fresh ingredients.
- It varies by region and is heavily influenced by what is grown locally.

French Family Values

- The family is the social adhesive of the country and each member has certain duties and responsibilities.
- The extended family provides both emotional and financial support.
- Despite their reputation as romantics, the French have a practical approach towards marriage.
- Families have few children, but parents take their role as guardians and providers very seriously.

Relationships - Public vs. Private

- The French are private people and have different rules of behaviour for people within their social circle and those who are not.
- Although the French are generally polite in all dealings, it is only with their close friends and family that they are free to be themselves.
- Friendship brings with it a set of roles and responsibilities, including being available should you be needed. Friendship involves frequent, if not daily, contact.

Meeting Etiquette

- The handshake is a common form of greeting.
- Friends may greet each other by lightly kissing on the cheeks, once on the left cheek and once on the right cheek.
- First names are reserved for family and close friends. Wait until invited before using someone's first name.

- You are expected to say 'bonjour' or 'bonsoir' (good morning and good evening) with the honorific title Monsieur or Madame when entering a shop and 'au revoir' (good-bye) when leaving.
- If you live in an apartment building, it is polite to greet your neighbours with the same appellation.

Gift Giving Etiquette

- Flowers should be given in odd numbers but not 13, which is considered unlucky.
- Some older French retain old-style prohibitions against receiving certain flowers: White lilies or chrysanthemums as they are used at funerals; red carnations as they symbolize bad will; any white flowers as they are used at weddings.
- Prohibitions about flowers are not generally followed by the young. When in doubt, it is always best to err on the side of conservatism.
- If you give wine, make sure it is of the highest quality you can afford. The French appreciate their wines.
- Gifts are usually opened when received.

Dining Etiquette

If you are invited to a French house for dinner:

- Arrive on time. Under no circumstances should you arrive more than 10 minutes later than invited without telephoning to explain you have been detained.
- The further south you go in the country, the more flexible time is.
- If invited to a large dinner party, especially in Paris, send flowers the morning of the occasion so that they may be displayed that evening.
- Dress well. The French are fashion conscious and their version of casual is not as relaxed as in many western countries.

Table manners

- Table manners are Continental -- the fork is held in the left hand and the knife in the right while eating.
- If there is a seating plan, you may be directed to a particular seat.
- Do not begin eating until the hostess says 'bon appetit'.

- If you have not finished eating, cross your knife and fork on your plate with the fork over the knife.
- Do not rest your elbows on the table, although your hands should be visible and not in your lap.
- Finish everything on your plate.
- Do not cut salad with a knife and fork. Fold the lettuce on to your fork.
- Peel and slice fruit before eating it.
- Leave your wineglass nearly full if you do not want more.

Relationships & Communication

- French business behaviour emphasizes courtesy and a degree of formality.
- Mutual trust and respect is required to get things done.
- Trust is earned through proper behaviour.
- Creating a wide network of close personal business alliances is very important.
- If you do not speak French, an apology for not knowing their language may aid in developing a relationship.
- It is always a good idea to learn a few key phrases, since it demonstrates an interest in a long-term relationship.
- The way a French person communicates is often predicated by their social status, education level, and which part of the country they were raised.
- In business, the French often appear extremely direct because they are not afraid of asking probing questions.
- Written communication is formal. Secretaries often schedule meetings and may be used to relay information from your French business colleagues.

Business Meetings Etiquette

- Appointments are necessary and should be made at least 2 weeks in advance.
- Appointments may be made in writing or by telephone and, depending upon the level of the person you are meeting, are often handled by the secretary.
- Do not try to schedule meetings during July or August, as this is a common vacation period.
- If you expect to be delayed, telephone immediately and offer an explanation.
- Meetings are to discuss issues, not to make decisions.
- Avoid exaggerated claims, as the French do not appreciate hyperbole.

Business Negotiation

- French business emphasizes courtesy and a fair degree of formality.
- Wait to be told where to sit.
- Maintain direct eye contact while speaking.
- Business is conducted slowly. You will have to be patient and not appear ruffled by the strict adherence to protocol.
- Avoid confrontational behaviour or high-pressure tactics. It can be counterproductive.
- The French will carefully analyze every detail of a proposal, regardless of how minute.
- Business is hierarchical. Decisions are generally made at the top of the company.
- The French are often impressed with good debating skills that demonstrate an intellectual grasp of the situation and all the ramifications.
- Never attempt to be overly friendly. The French generally compartmentalize their business and personal lives.
- Discussions may be heated and intense.
- High-pressure sales tactics should be avoided. The French are more receptive to a low-key, logical presentation that explains the advantages of a proposal in full.
- When an agreement is reached, the French may insist it be formalized in an extremely comprehensive, precisely worded contract.

Dress Etiquette

- Business dress is understated and stylish.
- Men should wear dark-coloured, conservative business suits for the initial meeting. How you dress later is largely dependent upon the personality of the company with which you are conducting business.
- Women should wear either business suits or elegant dresses in soft colours.
- The French like the finer things in life, so wear good quality accessories.

Business Cards

- Business cards are exchanged after the initial introductions without formal ritual.

- Have the other side of your business card translated into French. Although not a business necessity, it demonstrates an attention to detail that will be appreciated.
- Include any advanced academic degrees on your business card.
- French business cards are often a bit larger than in many other countries.

Germany

Facts and Statistics

Location:	Central Europe, bordering Austria 784 km, Belgium 167 km, Czech Republic 646 km, Denmark 68 km, France 451 km, Luxembourg 138 km, Netherlands 577 km, Poland 456 km, Switzerland 334 km
Capital:	Berlin
Climate:	temperate and marine; cool, cloudy, wet winters and summers; occasional warm mountain (foehn) wind
Population:	82,424,609 (July 2004 est.)
Ethnic Make-up:	German 91.5%, Turkish 2.4%, other 6.1% (made up largely of Greek, Italian, Polish, Russian, Serbo-Croatian, Spanish)
Religions:	Protestant 34%, Roman Catholic 34%, Muslim 3.7%, unaffiliated or other 28.3%
Government:	federal republic

Languages in Germany

The official language of Germany is German, with over 95% of the population speaking German as their first language. Minority languages include Sorbian, spoken by 0.09% in the east of Germany; North and West Frisian, spoken around the Rhine estuary by around 10,000 people, or 0.01%, who also speak German. Danish is spoken by 0.06%, mainly in the area along the Danish border. Romani, an indigenous language is spoken by around 0.08%. Immigrant languages include Turkish, which is spoken by around 1.8%, and Kurdish, by 0.3%.

German Society & Culture

A Planning Culture

· In many respects, Germans can be considered the masters of planning.

· This is a culture that prizes forward thinking and knowing what they will be doing at a specific time on a specific day.

· Careful planning, in one's business and personal life, provides a sense of security.

· Rules and regulations allow people to know what is expected and plan their life accordingly.

- Once the proper way to perform a task is discovered, there is no need to think of doing it any other way.
- Germans believe that maintaining clear lines of demarcation between people, places, and things is the surest way to lead a structured and ordered life.
- Work and personal lives are rigidly divided.
- There is a proper time for every activity. When the business day ends, you are expected to leave the office. If you must remain after normal closing, it indicates that you did not plan your day properly.

The German Home

- Germans take great pride in their homes.
- They are kept neat and tidy at all times, with everything in its appointed place.
- In a culture where most communication is rather formal, the home is the place where one can relax and allow your individualism to shine.
- Only close friends and relatives are invited into the sanctity of the house, so it is the one place where more informal communication may occur.
- There are many unwritten rules surrounding the outward maintenance of one's home.
- It is imperative that common areas such as sidewalks, pavements, corridors (in apartments), and steps be kept clean at all times.

Meeting Etiquette

- Greetings are formal.
- A quick, firm handshake is the traditional greeting.
- Titles are very important and denote respect. Use a person's title and their surname until invited to use their first name. You should say Herr or Frau and the person's title and their surname.
- In general, wait for your host or hostess to introduce you to a group.
- When entering a room, shake hands with everyone individually, including children.

Gift Giving Etiquette

- If you are invited to a German's house, bring a gift such as chocolates or flowers.
- Yellow roses or tea roses are always well received.
- Do not give red roses as they symbolize romantic intentions.

- Do not give carnations as they symbolize mourning.
- Do not give lilies or chrysanthemums as they are used at funerals.
- If you bring wine, it should be imported, French or Italian. Giving German wines is viewed as meaning you do not think the host will serve a good quality wine.
- Gifts are usually opened when received.

Dining Etiquette

- If you are invited to a German's house: Arrive on time as punctuality indicates proper planning. Never arrive early.
- Never arrive more than 15 minutes later than invited without telephoning to explain you have been detained.
- Send a handwritten thank you note the following day to thank your hostess for her hospitality.

Table manners

- Remain standing until invited to sit down. You may be shown to a particular seat.
- Table manners are Continental -- the fork is held in the left hand and the knife in the right while eating.
- Do not begin eating until the hostess starts or someone says 'guten appetit' (good appetite).
- At a large dinner party, wait for the hostess to place her napkin in her lap before doing so yourself.
- Do not rest your elbows on the table.
- Do not cut lettuce in a salad. Fold it using your knife and fork.
- Cut as much of your food with your fork as possible, since this compliments the cook by indicating the food is tender.
- Finish everything on your plate.
- Rolls should be broken apart by hand.
- Indicate you have finished eating by laying your knife and fork parallel across the right side of your plate, with the fork over the knife.
- The host gives the first toast.
- An honoured guest should return the toast later in the meal.
- The most common toast with wine is 'Zum Wohl!' ('good health').
- The most common toast with beer is 'Prost!' ('good health').

Relationships & Communications

- Germans do not need a personal relationship in order to do business.
- They will be interested in your academic credentials and the amount of time your company has been in business.
- Germans display great deference to people in authority, so it is imperative that they understand your level relative to their own.
- Germans do not have an open-door policy. People often work with their office door closed. Knock and wait to be invited in before entering.
- German communication is formal.
- Following the established protocol is critical to building and maintaining business relationships.
- As a group, Germans are suspicious of hyperbole, promises that sound too good to be true, or displays of emotion.
- Germans will be direct to the point of bluntness.
- Expect a great deal of written communication, both to back up decisions and to maintain a record of decisions and discussions.

Business Meeting Etiquette

- Appointments are mandatory and should be made 1 to 2 weeks in advance.
- Letters should be addressed to the top person in the functional area, including the person's name as well as their proper business title.
- If you write to schedule an appointment, the letter should be written in German.
- Punctuality is taken extremely seriously. If you expect to be delayed, telephone immediately and offer an explanation. It is extremely rude to cancel a meeting at the last minute and it could jeopardize your business relationship.
- Meetings are generally formal.
- Initial meetings are used to get to know each other. They allow your German colleagues to determine if you are trustworthy.
- Meetings adhere to strict agendas, including starting and ending times.
- Maintain direct eye contact while speaking.
- Although English may be spoken, it is a good idea to hire an interpreter so as to avoid any misunderstandings.
- At the end of a meeting, some Germans signal their approval by rapping their knuckles on the tabletop.

There is a strict protocol to follow when entering a room:

- The eldest or highest ranking person enters the room first.
- Men enter before women, if their age and status are roughly equivalent.

Business Negotiation

- Do not sit until invited and told where to sit. There is a rigid protocol to be followed.
- Meetings adhere to strict agendas, including starting and ending times.
- Treat the process with the formality that it deserves.
- Germany is heavily regulated and extremely bureaucratic.
- Germans prefer to get down to business and only engage in the briefest of small talk. They will be interested in your credentials.
- Make sure your printed material is available in both English and German.
- Contracts are strictly followed.
- You must be patient and not appear ruffled by the strict adherence to protocol. Germans are detail- oriented and want to understand every innuendo before coming to an agreement.
- Business is hierarchical. Decision-making is held at the top of the company.
- Final decisions are translated into rigorous, comprehensive action steps that you can expect will be carried out to the letter.
- Avoid confrontational behaviour or high- pressure tactics. It can be counterproductive.
- Once a decision is made, it will not be changed.

Dress Etiquette

- Business dress is understated, formal and conservative.
- Men should wear dark coloured, conservative business suits.
- Women should wear either business suits or conservative dresses.
- Do not wear ostentatious jewellery or accessories.

Market Entry Strategies

Hong Kong

Facts and Statistics

Location:	Eastern Asia, bordering the South China Sea and China
Population:	6,855,125 (July 2004 est.)
Ethnic Make-up:	Chinese 95%, other 5%
Religions:	eclectic mixture of local religions 90%, Christian 10%

Language in Hong Kong

English and Chinese are Hong Kong's two official languages. The Cantonese dialect is the most commonly spoken language in the territory, though English is the language of the business and service industries; hotel employees, many urban Hong Kong residents, most young people and shop and service personnel understand and speak it to some degree. Other Chinese dialects such as Mandarin (Putonghua), Shanghainese, and Chiu-Chow can be heard as well.

Major hotels have employees with knowledge of other languages, such as French, German, Japanese and Mandarin. Translation services in many languages are also available from major hotels' business centres.

Hong Kong Society & Culture

The Concept of Face

- Face is an intangible quality that reflects a person's reputation, dignity, and prestige.
- You may lose face, save face, or give face to another person.
- Companies as well as individuals have face and this is often the rationale behind business transactions.
- You give someone face by complimenting them, showing them respect, or doing anything that increases their self-esteem.
- Such actions must be done with the utmost sincerity. Doing them in a patronizing manner causes both parties to lose face.
- Humiliating people by publicly reprimanding them, insulting them publicly, or contradicting them in front of someone else causes them to lose face.

Confucianism / Hierarchy / Family Values

- The teachings of Confucius describe the position of the individual in Hong Kong Chinese society.
- Confucianism is a system of behaviours and ethics that stress the obligations of people towards one another based upon their relationship. .Confucianism stresses duty, loyalty, honour, filial piety, respect for age and seniority, and sincerity.
- These traits are demonstrated by the Hong Kong Chinese in their respect for hierarchical relationships.
- Although not readily apparent to the casual observer, there are strict rules about appropriate behaviour and the manner in which people must act in order to respect the hierarchy.

Meeting and Greeting

- The handshake is commonly used when greeting westerners.
- The Hong Kong Chinese handshake is rather light.
- During the greeting, many Hong Kong Chinese lower their eyes as a sign of respect.
- There is no need for you to emulate this gesture, although prolonged eye contact should be avoided during the greeting.
- If you are at a large function, you may introduce yourself to other guests.
- At smaller functions, it is polite to wait for your host or hostess to introduce you.
- The Chinese traditionally have 3 names: The surname, or family name is first and is followed by two personal names. The first personal name is their father's name and the second personal name is their own name.
- Address the person by an honorific title and their surname.
- If they want to move to a first name basis, they will advise you which name to use.
- Some Chinese adopt more western names and may ask you to call them by that name.

Gift Giving Etiquette

- A gift may be refused one or two times before it is accepted.

- If you are invited to someone's home, bring good quality sweets, fruit, flowers, or imported spirits to the hostess.
- Do not give red or white flowers.
- Do not give scissors, knives or other cutting utensils, as they indicate that you want to sever the relationship.
- Do not give clocks, handkerchiefs or straw sandals, as they are associated with funerals and death.
- Do not wrap gifts in white, blue or black paper.
- Gold and red are lucky colours, so they make excellent gift wrapping.
- Elaborate gift wrapping is important.
- Do not give odd numbers as many are considered unlucky.
- Never give a quantity of four items.
- Eight is a particularly auspicious number, so giving eight of something bestows good fortune on the recipient.
- A small gift for the children is always appreciated; however, do not give green hats.
- Always present gifts with two hands.
- Gifts are not opened when received.

Dining Etiquette

- Table manners are rather relaxed in Hong Kong, although there are certain rules of etiquette. When in doubt, watch what others do and emulate their behaviour.
- Wait to be told where to sit. There is often a seating plan.
- Wait for the host to tell you to start eating or for him to begin eating.
- Food is served on a revolving tray.
- You should try everything.
- Never eat the last piece from the serving tray.
- Burping is considered a compliment.
- Chopsticks should be returned to the chopstick rest after every few bites and when you drink or stop to speak.
- Always refuse a second serving at least once if you don't want to appear gluttonous.
- Leave some food in your bowl when you have finished eating.
- When you have finished eating, place your chopsticks in the chopstick rest or on the table. Do not place your chopsticks across the top of your bowl.

- The host offers the first toast. You may reciprocate later in the meal.

Building Relationships & Communication

- Although businesspeople in Hong Kong do not require long-standing personal relationships to do business, many businesses are family- owned, so personal relationships are an integral part of the enterprise.
- Once you have begun to work with a Hong Kong businessperson, it is important to maintain the relationship.
- When you first meet, expect a fair amount of small talk. Your Hong Kong colleagues will want to get to know you well enough that they are comfortable working with you.
- Do not be surprised if you are asked questions that might be considered extremely personal in your home country.
- The Hong Kong Chinese are generally sophisticated and cosmopolitan.
- They are quite familiar and comfortable with people from other countries.
- Although some businesspeople may overlook poor behaviour for the sake of the business deal, many will not.
- The Hong Kong Chinese take a long-term view of business relationships.
- Hong Kong Chinese are direct communicators, although they also make use of non-verbal communication.
- In general, businesspeople are non- confrontational and will never overtly say no, so that they do not embarrass the other person.
- If someone sucks air through his/her teeth while you are speaking, it means that they are unhappy with what you have just said. If at all possible, try to restate your position or modify your request, since you have made the other person extremely unhappy.
- As in many Asian cultures, silence is a form of communication.
- Resist the urge to jump into the conversation if your Hong Kong business colleague remains silent for a minute.

Business Meetings & Negotiations

- Appointments are necessary and should be made between 1 and 2 months in advance if you are travelling to Hong Kong.
- Avoid trying to schedule meetings during Chinese New Year (late January or early February) as many businesses close for a week during that time.

- You should arrive at meetings on time.
- If you are detained, telephone and advise the person you are meeting.
- There will be a period of small talk before getting down to business discussions.
- When meeting your Hong Kong business associates, allow the most senior person in your delegation to lead the group and be introduced first.
- Business negotiations happen at a slow pace.
- Avoid losing your temper or you will lose face and damage your relationship.
- Do not use high-pressure tactics. You might be out-maneuvered.
- Decisions are usually made at the top of the company. However, the pace of decision making is swifter than in other Asian countries.
- Your starting price should leave room for negotiation. Never offer your best price initially.
- Business is more price than quality driven.
- If you are signing a contract, the signing date may be determined by an astrologer or a feng shui practitioner.

Business Card Etiquette

- Business cards are exchanged after the initial introductions.
- Have one side of your business card translated into Chinese, with the Chinese characters printed in gold, since it is an auspicious colour.
- Business cards are exchanged using both hands.
- Hand your card so the typeface faces the recipient.
- Examine business cards carefully before putting them in a business card case.
- It is important to treat business cards with respect - never write on someone's card unless directed to do so.
- Your own business cards should be maintained in pristine condition.
- Make certain your business card includes your job title. This helps your Hong Kong business colleagues understand where you fit in your company's hierarchy.

Market Entry Strategies

Hungary

Facts and Statistics

Location:	Central Europe, bordering Austria 366 km, Croatia 329 km, Romania 443 km, Serbia and Montenegro 151 km, Slovakia 677 km, Slovenia 102 km, Ukraine 103 km
Capital:	Budapest
Climate:	temperate; cold, cloudy, humid winters; warm summers
Population:	10,032,375 (July 2004 est.)
Ethnic Make-up:	Hungarian 89.9%, Roma 4%, German 2.6%, Serb 2%, Slovak 0.8%, Romanian 0.7%
Religions:	Roman Catholic 67.5%, Calvinist 20%, Lutheran 5%, atheist and other 7.5%
Government:	parliamentary democracy

The Hungarian Language

The official language of Hungarian is spoken by 98% of the 10.3m population. Minority languages have become more prominent in recent years, and they include German, Croatian, Romani, Slovak, Romanian, Serbian and Slovene. Attempts are being made to protect these languages, as many members of the ethnic groups actually do not speak them.

Hungarian Society & Culture

Nation of Horsemen

- The Ancient Hungarians lived in the Euro-Asian nomadic pastoral region, where the keeping and use of horses played an important role in their lives.
- Therefore it is not surprising that the horse and horse riding has a central place in Hungarian History, leading to Hungarians being regarded as the nation of horsemen.
- Invitations to foreigners for horseback riding are not uncommon.

Family in Hungary

- The family is the centre of the social structure.
- Generations of extended family often live together.
- The grandparents play an important role in helping raise the grandchildren.

- The family provides both emotional and financial support to its members.

Get Personal

- Hungarians expect friends to share private and intimate details of their personal lives.
- If you ever feel you are being asked personal questions, this is simply meant as part of the getting-to-know-you process.
- Hungarians will even enjoy sharing details of their romantic life with you!

Meeting Etiquette

- Both men and women greet by shaking hands, although a man should usually wait for the women to extend her hand.
- The older generation may still bow to woman.
- Close friends kiss one another lightly on both cheeks, starting with the left cheek.
- In the business context is safest to address people by their titles and surnames.

Gift Giving Etiquette

- When visiting a company it is not necessary to bring gifts.
- If invited to a Hungarian's home for a meal, bring a box of good chocolates, flowers or Western liquor.
- Do not bring wine as the Hungarians are proud of the wines they produce.
- Flowers should be given in odd numbers, but not 13, which is considered an unlucky number.
- Do not give lilies, chrysanthemums or red roses.
- Gifts are usually opened when received.

Dining Etiquette

   If in the rare case you invited to a Hungarian's house:
- Arrive on time if invited for dinner, although a 5-minute grace period is granted.
- If invited to a party or other large gathering, arrive no more than 30 minutes later than invited.
- You may be asked to remove your outdoor shoes before entering the house.
- Do not ask for a tour of the house.

Table manners

- Table manners are formal in Hungary.
- Table manners are Continental -- the fork is held in the left hand and the knife in the right while eating.
- The hostess will wish the guests a hearty appetite at the start of each course.
- Do not begin eating until the hostess starts.
- Do not rest your elbows on the table, although your hands should be visible at all times.
- Hospitality is measured by the amount and variety of food served. Try everything.
- If you have not finished eating, cross your knife and fork across your plate.
- Indicate you have finished eating by laying your knife and fork parallel across the right side of your plate.
- The guest of honour usually proposes the first toast which generally salutes the health of the individuals present.
- At the end of the meal, someone toasts the hosts in appreciation of their hospitality.
- An empty glass is immediately refilled so if you do not want more to drink, leave your glass ½ full.
- Never clink glasses if drinking beer.

Relationships & Communication

- Although Hungarians are transactional and do not require long-standing personal relationships in order to conduct business, being introduced by someone they know and trust can often help
- Hungarians pride themselves on using proper etiquette in all situations and expect others to do the same.
- Socializing is an important part of the relationship building process.
- Expect many invitations to dinner or cultural events. If you have the time, reciprocate invitations.
- Hungarians prefer face-to-face meetings rather than more impersonal vehicles of communication such as letters.
- Hungarians are emotive speakers who say what they think and expect you to do the same.
- They do not like euphemisms or vague statements.

- Hungarians often use stories, anecdotes, and jokes to prove their points.
- Hungarians are suspicious of people who are reticent and not willing to share their innermost thoughts.
- Hungarians view eye contact as indicative of sincerity and believe that people who cannot look them in the eye while speaking have something to hide.

Business Meeting Etiquette

- Appointments are necessary and should be made 2 weeks in advance and in writing.
- It is often difficult to schedule meetings on Friday afternoon or from mid July to mid August. Also avoid scheduling meetings from mid December to mid January.
- Punctuality for all social situations is taken extremely seriously. If you expect to be delayed, telephone immediately and offer an explanation. It is considered extremely rude to cancel a meeting at the last minute and could ruin your business relationship.
- Initial meetings are scheduled to get to know each other and for your Hungarian colleagues to determine if you are trustworthy.
- Expect some small talk and getting-to-know-you conversation before business is discussed. Do not move the conversation to business yourself.
- Do not remove your suit jacket without asking permission.
- If you have an agenda, it may be used as a springboard to further discussion and not followed item by item.

Business Negotiating Etiquette

- Business is conducted slowly.
- Deals in Hungary cannot be finalized without a lot of eating, drinking and entertaining.
- Hungarians are very detail-oriented and want to understand everything before reaching an agreement.
- Contracts should be clear and concise.
- Contracts function as statements of intent. It is expected that if circumstances change, the contract will accommodate the revised conditions.
- Hungarians are skilled negotiators.
- Avoid confrontational behaviour or high-pressure sales tactics.

Dress Etiquette

- Business dress is formal and conservative.
- Men should wear dark business suits with a white shirt and tie.
- Women should wear either business suits or elegant dresses, complimented with good quality accessories.
- Jeans are standard casual wear. Shorts are uncommon in the city.
- Business wear is appropriate for all formal occasions.

Business Cards

- Business cards are exchanged without formal ritual.
- Have one side of your card translated into Hungarian.
- The Hungarian side should list your surname before your first name, Hungarian style.
- Include any advanced university degrees on your business card.
- Include the founding date of your company on the card.

Market Entry Strategies

India

Facts and Statistics

Location:	Southern Asia, bordering Bangladesh 4,053 km, Bhutan 605 km, Burma 1,463 km, China 3,380 km, Nepal 1,690 km, Pakistan 2,912 km
Capital:	New Delhi
Climate:	varies from tropical monsoon in south to temperate in north
Population:	1,065,070,607 (July 2004 est.)
Ethnic Make-up:	Indo-Aryan 72%, Dravidian 25%, Mongoloid and other 3% (2000)
Religions:	Hindu 81.3%, Muslim 12%, Christian 2.3%, Sikh 1.9%, other groups including Buddhist, Jain, Parsi 2.5% (2000)
Government:	federal republic

Languages in India

The different states of India have different official languages, some of them not recognized by the central government. Some states have more then one official language. Bihar in east India has three official languages - Hindi, Urdu and Bengali - which are all recognized by the central government. But Sikkim, also in east India, has four official languages of which only Nepali is recognized by the central government. Besides the languages officially recognized by central or state governments, there are other languages which don't have this recognition and their speakers are running political struggles to get this recognition. Central government decided that Hindi was to be the official language of India and therefore it also has the status of official language in the states.

Indian Society & Culture

Hierarchy

- The influences of Hinduism and the tradition of the caste system have created a culture that emphasizes established hierarchical relationships.
- Indians are always conscious of social order and their status relative to other people, be they family, friends, or strangers.

- All relationships involve hierarchies. In schools, teachers are called gurus and are viewed as the source of all knowledge. The patriarch, usually the father, is considered the leader of the family. The boss is seen as the source of ultimate responsibility in business. Every relationship has a clear- cut hierarchy that must be observed for the social order to be maintained.

The Role of the Family

- People typically define themselves by the groups to which they belong rather than by their status as individuals. Someone is deemed to be affiliated to a specific state, region, city, family, career path, religion, etc.
- This group orientation stems from the close personal ties Indians maintain with their family, including the extended family.
- The extended family creates a myriad of interrelationships, rules, and structures. Along with these mutual obligations comes a deep-rooted trust among relatives.

Just Can't Say No

- Indians do not like to express 'no,' be it verbally or non- verbally.
- Rather than disappoint you, for example, by saying something isn't available, Indians will offer you the response that they think you want to hear.
- This behaviour should not be considered dishonest. An Indian would be considered terribly rude if he did not attempt to give a person what had been asked.
- Since they do not like to give negative answers, Indians may give an affirmative answer but be deliberately vague about any specific details. This will require you to look for non-verbal cues, such as a reluctance to commit to an actual time for a meeting or an enthusiastic response.

Meeting Etiquette

- Religion, education and social class all influence greetings in India.
- This is a hierarchical culture, so greet the eldest or most senior person first.
- When leaving a group, each person must be bid farewell individually.
- Shaking hands is common, especially in the large cities among the more educated who are accustomed to dealing with westerners.
- Men may shake hands with other men and women may shake hands with other women; however there are seldom handshakes between men and women be-

cause of religious beliefs. If you are uncertain, wait for them to extend their hand.

Naming Conventions

Indian names vary based upon religion, social class, and region of the country. The following are some basic guidelines to understanding the naming conventions:

Hindus:
- In the north, many people have both a given name and a surname.
- In the south, surnames are less common and a person generally uses the initial of their father's name in front of their own name.
- The man's formal name is their name "s/o" (son of) and the father's name. Women use "d/o" to refer to themselves as the daughter of their father.
- At marriage, women drop their father's name and use their first name with their husband's first name as a sort of surname.

Muslims:
- Many Muslims do not have surnames. Instead, men add the father's name to their own name with the connector 'bin'. So, Abdullah bin Ahmed is Abdullah the son of Ahmad.
- Women use the connector 'binti'.
- The title Hajji (m) or Hajjah (f) before the name indicates the person has made their pilgrimage to Mecca.

Sikhs:
- Sikhs all use the name Singh. It is either adopted as a surname or as a connector name to the surname.

Gift Giving Etiquette

- Indians believe that giving gifts eases the transition into the next life.
- Gifts of cash are given to friends and members of the extended family to celebrate life events such as birth, death and marriage.
- It is not the value of the gift, but the sincerity with which it is given, that is important to the recipient.
- If invited to an Indian's home for a meal, it is not necessary to bring a gift, although one will not be turned down.

- Do not give frangipani or white flowers as they are used at funerals.
- Yellow, green and red are lucky colours, so try to use them to wrap gifts.
- A gift from a man should be said to come from both he and his wife / mother / sister or some other female relative.
- Hindus should not be given gifts made of leather.
- Muslims should not be given gifts made of pigskin or alcoholic products.
- Gifts are not opened when received.

Dining Etiquette

- Indians entertain in their homes, restaurants, private clubs, or other public venues, depending upon the occasion and circumstances.
- Although Indians are not always punctual themselves, they expect foreigners to arrive close to the appointed time.
- Take off your shoes before entering the house.
- Dress modestly and conservatively.
- Politely turn down the first offer of tea, coffee, or snacks. You will be asked again and again. Saying no to the first invitation is part of the protocol.

There are diverse dietary restrictions in India, and these may affect the foods that are served:

- Hindus do not eat beef and many are vegetarians.
- Muslims do not eat pork or drink alcohol.
- Sikhs do not eat beef.
- Lamb, chicken, and fish are the most commonly served main courses for non-vegetarian meals as they avoid the meat restrictions of the religious groups.

Table manners

Table manners are somewhat formal, but this formality is tempered by the religious beliefs of the various groups.

- Much Indian food is eaten with the fingers.
- Wait to be told where to sit.
- If utensils are used, they are generally a tablespoon and a fork.
- Guests are often served in a particular order: the guest of honour is served first, followed by the men, and the children are served last. Women typically serve the men and eat later.

- You may be asked to wash your hands before and after sitting down to a meal.
- Always use your right hand to eat, whether you are using utensils or your fingers.
- In some situations food may be put on your plate for you, while in other situations you may be allowed to serve yourself from a communal bowl.
- Leaving a small amount of food on your plate indicates that you are satisfied. Finishing all your food means that you are still hungry.

Relationships & Communication

- Indians prefer to do business with those they know.
- Relationships are built upon mutual trust and respect.
- In general, Indians prefer to have long-standing personal relationships prior to doing business.
- It may be a good idea to go through a third party introduction. This gives you immediate credibility.

Business Meeting Etiquette

- If you will be travelling to India from abroad, it is advisable to make appointments by letter, at least one month and preferably two months in advance.
- It is a good idea to confirm your appointment as they do get cancelled at short notice.
- The best time for a meeting is late morning or early afternoon. Reconfirm your meeting the week before and call again that morning, since it is common for meetings to be cancelled at the last minute.
- Keep your schedule flexible so that it can be adjusted for last minute rescheduling of meetings.
- You should arrive at meetings on time since Indians are impressed with punctuality.
- Meetings will start with a great deal of getting-to- know-you talk. In fact, it is quite possible that no business will be discussed at the first meeting.
- Always send a detailed agenda in advance. Send back-up materials and charts and other data as well. This allows everyone to review and become comfortable with the material prior to the meeting.
- Follow up a meeting with an overview of what was discussed and the next steps.

Business Negotiating

- Indians are non-confrontational. It is rare for them to overtly disagree, although this is beginning to change in the managerial ranks.
- Decisions are reached by the person with the most authority.
- Decision making is a slow process.
- If you lose your temper you lose face and prove you are unworthy of respect and trust.
- Delays are to be expected, especially when dealing with the government.
- Most Indians expect concessions in both price and terms. It is acceptable to expect concessions in return for those you grant.
- Never appear overly legalistic during negotiations. In general, Indians do not trust the legal system and someone's word is sufficient to reach an agreement.
- Do not disagree publicly with members of your negotiating team.
- Successful negotiations are often celebrated by a meal.

Dress Etiquette

- Business attire is conservative.
- Men should wear dark coloured conservative business suits.
- Women should dress conservatively in suits or dresses.
- The weather often determines clothing. In the hotter parts of the country, dress is less formal, although dressing as suggested above for the first meeting will indicate respect.

Titles

- Indians revere titles such as Professor, Doctor and Engineer.
- Status is determined by age, university degree, caste and profession.
- If someone does not have a professional title, use the honorific title "Sir" or "Madam".
- Titles are used with the person's name or the surname, depending upon the person's name.
- Wait to be invited before using someone's first name without the title.

Business Cards

- Business cards are exchanged after the initial handshake and greeting.
- If you have a university degree or any honour, put it on your business card.

- Use the right hand to give and receive business cards.
- Business cards need not be translated into Hindi.
- Always present your business card so the recipient may read the card as it is handed to them.

Market Entry Strategies

Japan

Facts and Statistics

Location:	Eastern Asia, island chain between the North Pacific Ocean and the Sea of Japan, east of the Korean Peninsula.
Capital:	Tokyo
Population:	127,333,002 (July 2004 est.)
Ethnic Make-up:	Japanese 99%, others 1% (Korean 511,262, Chinese 244,241, Brazilian 182,232, Filipino 89,851, other 237,914)
Religions:	observe both Shinto and Buddhist 84%, other 16% Christian 0.7%)

The Japanese Language

Japanese is the sixth most spoken language in the world, with over 99% percent of the country's population using it. Amazingly, the language is spoken in scarcely any region outside Japan.

The origin of the Japanese language has many theories in reference to it, some believe it is similar to the Altaic languages, namely Turkish or Mongolian. It is recognized and acknowledged to be close in syntax to the Korean language.

Dialects are used in areas, particularly in Kyoto and Osaka, but standard Japanese, based on the speech of Tokyo, has become more popular through the use of television, radio and movies.

Japanese Society & Culture

The Japanese and 'Face'

- Saving face is crucial in Japanese society.
- The Japanese believe that turning down someone's request causes embarrassment and loss of face to the other person.
- If the request cannot be agreed to, they will say, 'it's inconvenient' or 'it's under consideration'.
- Face is a mark of personal dignity and means having high status with one's peers.
- The Japanese will try never to do anything to cause loss of face.
- Therefore, they do not openly criticize, insult, or put anyone on-the-spot.
- Face can be lost, taken away, or earned through praise and thanks.

Harmony in Japanese Society

- Harmony is the key value in Japanese society.
- Harmony is the guiding philosophy for the Japanese in family and business settings and in society as a whole.
- Japanese children are taught to act harmoniously and cooperatively with others from the time they go to pre-school.
- The Japanese educational system emphasizes the interdependence of all people, and Japanese children are not raised to be independent but rather to work together.
- This need for harmonious relationships between people is reflected in much Japanese behaviour.
- They place great emphasis on politeness, personal responsibility and working together for the universal, rather than the individual, good.
- They present facts that might be disagreeable in a gentle and indirect fashion.
- They see working in harmony as the crucial ingredient for working productively.

Japanese Non-Verbal Communication

- Since the Japanese strive for harmony and are group dependent, they rely on facial expression, tone of voice and posture to tell them what someone feels.
- They often trust non-verbal messages more than the spoken word as words can have several meanings.
- The context in which something is said affects the meaning of the words. Therefore, it is imperative to understand the situation to fully appreciate the response.
- Frowning while someone is speaking is interpreted as a sign of disagreement.
- Most Japanese maintain an impassive expression when speaking.
- Expressions to watch out for include inhaling through clenched teeth, tilting the head, scratching the back of the head, and scratching the eyebrow.
- Non-verbal communication is so vital that there is a book for 'gaijins' (foreigners) on how to interpret the signs!
- It is considered disrespectful to stare into another person's eyes, particularly those of a person who is senior to you because of age or status.
- In crowded situations the Japanese avoid eye contact to give themselves privacy.

Japanese Hierarchy

- The Japanese are very conscious of age and status.
- Everyone has a distinct place in the hierarchy, be it the family unit, the extended family, a social or a business situation.
- At school children learn to address other students as senior to them ('senpai') or junior to them ('kohai').
- The oldest person in a group is always revered and honoured. In a social situation, they will be served first and their drinks will be poured for them.

Meeting Etiquette

- Greetings in Japan are very formal and ritualized.
- It is important to show the correct amount of respect and deference to someone based upon their status relative to your own.
- If at all possible, wait to be introduced.
- It can be seen as impolite to introduce yourself, even in a large gathering.
- While foreigners are expected to shake hands, the traditional form of greeting is the bow. How far you bow depends upon your relationship to the other person as well as the situation. The deeper you bow, the more respect you show.
- A foreign visitor ('gaijin') may bow the head slightly, since no one expects foreigners to generally understand the subtle nuances of bowing.

Gift Giving Etiquette

- Gift-giving is highly ritualistic and meaningful.
- The ceremony of presenting the gift and the way it is wrapped is as important--sometimes more important--than the gift itself.
- Gifts are given for many occasions.
- The gift need not be expensive, but take great care to ask someone who understands the culture to help you decide what type of gift to give.
- Good quality chocolates or small cakes are good ideas.
- Do not give lilies, camellias or lotus blossoms as they are associated with funerals.
- Do not give white flowers of any kind as they are associated with funerals.
- Do not give potted plants as they encourage sickness, although a bonsai tree is always acceptable.
- Give items in odd numbers, but not 9.

- If you buy the gift in Japan, have it wrapped.
- Pastel colours are the best choices for wrapping paper.
- Gifts are not opened when received.

Dining Etiquette

On the rare occasion you are invited to a Japanese house:

- Remove your shoes before entering and put on the slippers left at the doorway.
- Leave your shoes pointing away from the doorway you are about to walk through.
- Arrive on time or no more than 5 minutes late if invited for dinner.
- If invited to a large social gathering, arriving a little bit later than the invitation is acceptable, although punctuality is always appreciated.
- Unless you have been told the event is casual, dress as if you were going into the office.
- If you must go to the toilet, put on the toilet slippers and remove them when you are finished.

Table Manners

- Wait to be told where to sit. There is a protocol to be followed.
- The honoured guest or the eldest person will be seated in the centre of the table the furthest from the door.
- The honoured guest or the eldest is the first person to begin eating.
- Never point your chopsticks.
- It will yield tremendous dividends if you learn to use chopsticks.
- Do not pierce your food with chopsticks.
- Chopsticks should be returned to the chopstick rest after every few bites and when you drink or stop to speak.
- Do not cross your chopsticks when putting them on the chopstick rest.
- Place bones on the side of your plate.
- Try a little bit of everything. It is acceptable to ask what something is and even to make a face if you do not like the taste.
- Don't be surprised if your Japanese colleagues slurp their noodles and soup.
- Mixing other food with rice is usually not done. You eat a bit of one and then a bit of the other, but they should never be mixed together as you do in many Western countries.

- If you do not want anything more to drink, do not finish what is in your glass. An empty glass is an invitation for someone to serve you more.
- When you have finished eating, place your chopsticks on the chopstick rest or on the table. Do not place your chopsticks across the top of your bowl.
- If you leave a small amount of rice in your bowl, you will be given more. To signify that you do not want more rice, finish every grain in your bowl.
- It is acceptable to leave a small amount of food on your plate when you have finished eating.
- Conversation at the table is generally subdued. The Japanese like to savour their food.

Understanding of Foreign Ways

- Japanese understand that it is very difficult for foreigners to work in Japan.
- They will not expect you to speak or read Japanese, or be conversant with their strict cultural nuances and protocol.
- Mistakes are allowed as long as genuine respect is shown at all times.
- They will usually try to help you but often feel embarrassment at their own lack of understanding or English language ability.

Relationships & Communication

- The Japanese prefer to do business on the basis of personal relationships.
- In general, being introduced or recommended by someone who already has a good relationship with the company is extremely helpful as it allows the Japanese to know how to place you in a hierarchy relative to themselves.
- One way to build and maintain relationships is with greetings / seasonal cards.
- It is important to be a good correspondent as the Japanese hold this in high esteem.

Business Meeting Etiquette

- Appointments are required and, whenever possible, should be made several weeks in advance.
- It is best to telephone for an appointment rather than send a letter, fax or email.
- Punctuality is important. Arrive on time for meetings and expect your Japanese colleagues will do the same.

- Since this is a group society, even if you think you will be meeting one person, be prepared for a group meeting.
- The most senior Japanese person will be seated furthest from the door, with the rest of the people in descending rank until the most junior person is seated closest to the door.
- It may take several meetings for your Japanese counterparts to become comfortable with you and be able to conduct business with you.
- This initial getting to know you time is crucial to laying the foundation for a successful relationship.
- You may be awarded a small amount of business as a trial to see if you meet your commitments.
- If you respond quickly and with excellent service, you prove your ability and trustworthiness.
- Never refuse a request, no matter how difficult or non- profitable it may appear. The Japanese are looking for a long-term relationship.
- Always provide a package of literature about your company including articles and client testimonials.
- Always give a small gift, as a token of your esteem, and present it to the most senior person at the end of the meeting. Your Japanese contact can advise you on where to find something appropriate.

Business Negotiation

- The Japanese are non-confrontational.
- They have a difficult time saying 'no', so you must be vigilant at observing their non-verbal communication.
- It is best to phrase questions so that they can answer yes. For example, do you disagree with this? Group decision-making and consensus are important.
- Written contracts are required.
- The Japanese often remain silent for long periods of time. Be patient and try to work out if your Japanese colleagues have understood what was said.
- Japanese prefer broad agreements and mutual understanding so that when problems arise they can be handled flexibly.
- Using a Japanese lawyer is seen as a gesture of goodwill. Note that Japanese lawyers are quite different from Western lawyers as they are much more functionary.

- Never lose your temper or raise your voice during negotiations.
- Some Japanese close their eyes when they want to listen intently.
- The Japanese seldom grant concession. They expect both parties to come to the table with their best offer.
- The Japanese do not see contracts as final agreements so they can be renegotiated.

Dress Etiquette

- Business attire is conservative.
- Men should wear dark-coloured, conservative business suits.
- Women should dress conservatively.

Business Cards

- Business cards are exchanged constantly and with great ceremony.
- Invest in quality cards.
- Always keep your business cards in pristine condition.
- Treat the business card you receive as you would the person.
- You may be given a business card that is only in Japanese.
- It is wise to have one side of your business card translated into Japanese.
- Give your business card with the Japanese side facing the recipient.
- Make sure your business card includes your title, so your Japanese colleagues know your status within your organization.
- Business cards are given and received with two hands and a slight bow.
- Examine any business card you receive very carefully.
- During a meeting, place the business cards on the table in front of you in the order people are seated.
- When the meeting is over, put the business cards in a business card case or a portfolio.

Market Entry Strategies

Mexico

Facts and Statistics

Location:	Middle America, bordering the Caribbean Sea and the Gulf of Mexico, between Belize and the U.S. and bordering the North Pacific Ocean, between Guatemala and the U.S.
Capital:	Mexico City
Climate:	varies from tropical to desert
Population:	104,959,594 (July 2004 est.)
Ethnic Make-up:	mestizo (Amerindian-Spanish) 60%, Amerindian or pre dominantly merindian 30%, white 9%, other 1%
Religions:	nominally Roman Catholic 89%, Protestant 6%, other 5%
Government:	federal republic

Language in Mexico

Spanish control of Mexico led to the dominance of Spanish, the official language. As many as 100 Native American languages are still spoken in Mexico, but no single alternative language prevails. Eighty percent of those Mexicans who speak an indigenous language also speak Spanish. The most important of the Native American languages is Nahuatl. It is the primary language of more than a million Mexicans and is spoken by nearly one-fourth of all Native Americans in the country. This is followed by Maya, used by 14 percent of Native Americans, and Mixteco and Zapoteco, each spoken by about seven percent of Native Americans. No other indigenous language is spoken by more than five percent of Mexico's Native Americans.

Mexican Society & Culture

Mexican Family Values

- The family is at the centre of the social structure.
- Outside of the major cosmopolitan cities, families are still generally large.
- The extended family is as important as the nuclear family since it provides a sense of stability.
- Mexicans consider it their duty and responsibility to help family members. For example, the will help find employment or finance a house or other large purchase.

- Most Mexican families are extremely traditional, with the father as the head, the authority figure and the decision-maker.
- Mothers are greatly revered, but their role may be seen as secondary to that of their husband.

Hierarchical Society

- Mexican society and business are highly stratified and vertically structured.
- Mexicans emphasize hierarchical relationships.
- People respect authority and look to those above them for guidance and decision-making.
- Rank is important, and those above you in rank must always be treated with respect.
- This makes it important to know which person is in charge, and leads to an authoritarian approach to decision-making and problem- solving.
- Mexicans are very aware of how each individual fits into each hierarchy--be it family, friends or business.
- It would be disrespectful to break the chain of hierarchy.

'Machismo'

- Machismo literally means 'masculinity'.
- There are different outward behaviours to display machismo.
- For example, making remarks to women is a stereotypical sign of machismo and should not be seen as harassment.
- Mexican males generally believe that nothing must be allowed to tarnish their image as a man.

Meeting Etiquette

- When greeting in social situations, women pat each other on the right forearm or shoulder, rather than shake hands
- Men shake hands until they know someone well, at which time they progress to the more traditional hug and back slapping.
- Wait until invited before using a Mexican's first name

Gift Giving Etiquette

- If invited to a Mexican's house, bring a gift such as flowers or sweets.

- Gift wrapping does not follow any particular protocol.
- Do not give marigolds as they symbolize death.
- Do not give red flowers as they have a negative connotation.
- White flowers are a good gift as they are considered uplifting.
- Gifts are opened immediately.
- If you receive a gift, open it and react enthusiastically.

Dining Etiquette

If you are invited to a Mexican's home:

- Arrive 30 minutes late in most places (check with colleagues to see if you should arrive later than that).
- Arriving on time or early is considered inappropriate.
- At a large party you may introduce yourself.
- At a smaller gathering the host usually handles the introductions.

Watch your table manners!

- Always keep your hands visible when eating. Keep your wrists resting on the edge of the table.
- When you have finished eating, place your knife and fork across your plate with the prongs facing down and the handles facing to the right.
- Do not sit down until you are invited to and told where to sit.
- Do not begin eating until the hostess starts.
- Only men give toasts.
- It is polite to leave some food on your plate after a meal.

Relationships & Communication

- The right connections facilitate business success.
- You will be judged by the person who introduces you and changing this first impression is nearly impossible.
- Since the initial meeting is generally with someone of high stature, it is important that your delegation include an upper-level executive.
- After the initial getting-to-know-you meeting, the senior executive may not attend meetings or be visible.
- This indicates you are now getting down to business and they are no longer needed to smooth the introduction.

- Demonstrating trustworthiness, sincerity, and integrity are crucial to building relationships.
- Expect to answer questions about your personal background, family and life interests.

Business Meeting Etiquette

- Business appointments are required and should be made at least 2 weeks in advance. Reconfirm the appointment one week before the meeting.
- Reconfirm the meeting again once you arrive in Mexico and make sure that the secretary of the person you will be meeting knows how to contact you.
- It is important that you arrive on time for meetings, although your Mexican business associates may be up to 30 minutes late.
- Do not appear irritated if this occurs as people often run behind schedule.
- Meetings may be postponed with little advance warning.
- Initial meetings are formal.
- Have all written material available in both English and Spanish.
- Agendas are not common. If they are given, they are not always followed.

Business Negotiation

- Since Mexicans are status conscious, you should always have someone on your negotiating team who is an executive.
- If you do not speak Spanish, hire an interpreter.
- It will take several meetings to come to an agreement.
- Face-to-face meetings are preferred over telephone, letters or email.
- Negotiations and decisions take a long time. You must be patient.
- Deadlines are seen as flexible and fluid, much like time itself.
- Negotiations will include a fair amount of haggling. Do not give your best offer first.
- Do not include an attorney on your negotiating team.

Business Dress

- Dress as you would in Europe.
- Men should wear conservative, dark coloured suits.
- Women should wear business suits or conservative dresses.

Business Cards

- Business cards are exchanged during introductions with everyone at a meeting.
- It is advisable to have one side of your business card in Spanish.
- Business cards should contain both your professional and educational qualifications.
- Present your business card with the Spanish side facing the recipient.

Singapore

Facts and Statistics

Location:	Southeastern Asia, islands between Malaysia and Indonesia
Capital:	Singapore
Population:	4,353,893 (July 2004 est.)
Ethnic Make-up:	Chinese 76.7%, Malay 14%, Indian 7.9%, other 1.4%
Religions:	Buddhist (Chinese), Muslim (Malays), Christian, Hindu, Sikh, Taoist, Confucianist

The Language

Singapore has attempted to promote a national identity in its land of immigrants since its independence in 1965. As part of this effort, Singapore has four national languages: Mandarin, Malay, Tamil and English. For business and politics, English is the language of choice.

Singapore Society & Culture

The Family

- The concepts of group, harmony, and mutual security are more important than that of the individual.
- The family is the centre of the social structure and emphasizes unity, loyalty and respect for the elderly.
- The term, 'family' generally includes extended family and close friends who are treated as family members.
- Respect for the elderly and seeing the family as the place one goes to for support, both help retain core values in this island nation.

Face & Respect

Having face indicates personal dignity. Singaporeans are very sensitive to retaining face in all aspects of their lives. Face is a prized commodity that can be given, lost, taken away or earned. It is a mark of personal qualities such as a good name, good character, and being held in esteem by one's peers. It can also be greater than the person and extend to family, school, company, and even the nation itself. Face is what makes Singaporeans strive for harmonious relationships.

Hierarchy

Singaporeans claim they are an egalitarian society, yet they retain strong hierarchical relationships that can be observed in the relationship between parents and children, teachers and students, and employers and employees. This goes back to their important cultural value, group dependence. This reliance on hierarchy is drawn from Confucianism, which emphasizes respecting age and status, ven blind obedience to one's elders. . In the workplace this is seen in the increased deference that is paid to employees who are older. The elderly are always treated with the utmost respect and courtesy. ven if you do not personally know the individual, you will be expected to give special consideration. Elders are introduced first, are given preferential seating, are given the choicest food, and in general put on a pedestal. There was a law passed in 1996 that mandated that children must assume financial responsibility for their elderly parents should the need arise. This is indicative of the high status of the elderly and the challenges facing the small country as the next generation becomes more individualistic.

Ethnic Diversity

- Singapore is a multi-ethnic society where Chinese, Malay and Indian traditions coexist beneath the veneer of a western cosmopolitan metropolis.
- The three main ethnic groups are religiously and culturally diverse.

Non-Verbal Communication

- Singaporeans are group dependent and rely on facial expression, tone of voice and posture to tell them what someone feels.
- They often trust non-verbal messages more than the spoken word.
- They tend to be subtle, indirect and implicit in their communications.
- They hint at a point rather than making a direct statement, since that might cause the other person to lose face.
- Rather than say 'no', they might say, 'I will try', or 'I'll see what I can do'. This allows the person making the request and the person turning it down to save face and maintain harmony in their relationship.
- Silence is an important element of Singaporean communication.
- Pausing before responding to a question indicates that they have given the question appropriate thought and considered their response carefully.

- They do not understand western cultures ability to respond to a question hastily and think this indicates thoughtlessness and rude behaviour.

Meeting and Greeting

- Greetings will follow a strict protocol often based on both the ethnic origin and age of the person.
- Younger people or those who work in multi-national companies may have adopted the western concept of shaking hands with everyone, but this is not the case with older or more reserved Singaporeans.
- Ethnic Chinese shake hands. Their grasp is rather light although the handshake itself can be rather prolonged.
- Men and women may shake hands, although the woman must extend her hand first. Introductions are always done in order of age or status.
- Between men, ethnic Malays shake hands.
- Men and women do not traditionally shake hands, since Muslim men do not touch women in public.
- Younger Malays may shake hands with foreign women, but it is more appropriate to use the 'salaam' (bowing the head) greeting.
- This is also the greeting to be used when two women meet.
- Ethnic Indians shake hands with members of the same sex.
- When being introduced to someone of the opposite sex, nodding the head and smiling is usually sufficient.
- As with the other groups, the elderly or the person with the most status is introduced first.

Titles/Names

Chinese:

- Chinese traditionally have 3 names. The surname or family name is first and is followed by two personal names.
- Address the person by an honorific title and their surname. If they want to move to a first name basis, they will advise you which of their two personal names to use.
- Some Chinese adopt more western names in business and may ask you to call them that.

Malay:

- Many Malays do not have surnames. Instead, men add the father's name to their own name with the connector bin. So Noor bin Isa, would be Noor, the son of Isa. Women use the connector binti, so Zarina binti Isa would be Zarina the daughter of Isa.
- The title Haji (male) or Hajjah (female) before the name indicates the person has made their pilgrimage to Mecca.
- The name Sayyed (male) or Sharifah (female) indicates that the person is considered to be a descendent of the prophet Mohammed.

Indian:

- Many Indians in Singapore do not use surnames. Instead, they place the initial of their father's name in front of their own name. The man's formal name is their name 's/o' (son of) and the father's name. Women use 'd/o' to refer to themselves as the daughter of their father.
- Since many Indian names are extremely long, they commonly use a shortened version of their name as a sort of nickname.
- At marriage, women drop their father's name and use their first name with their husband's first name as a sort of surname.
- Sikh Indians all use the name Singh to denote themselves as Sikhs.

Gift Giving Etiquette

Since there are cultural differences in how the three main ethnic groups treat gifts, they are listed separately.

Gift giving to ethnic Chinese:

- A gift may be refused three times before it is accepted. This demonstrates that the recipient is not greedy.
- Do not give scissors, knives or other cutting utensils as they indicate that you want to sever the relationship.
- Do not give clocks, handkerchiefs or straw sandals as they are associated with funerals and death.
- Do not wrap gifts in white, blue or black paper as these are mourning colours.
- Wrap gifts in red, pink, or yellow since these are happy colours
- Elaborate gift wrapping is imperative.

- Never wrap a gift for a baby or decorate the gift in any way with a stork as birds are the harbinger of death.
- Do not give odd numbers as they are unlucky.
- Do not bring food if invited to a formal dinner party as it insinuates you do not think the host will provide sufficient hospitality.
- Bring a small gift of fruit, sweets, or cakes, saying that it is for the children.
- Gifts are not opened when received.
- Flowers do not make good gifts as they are given to the sick and are used at funerals.

Gift giving to ethnic Malays:
- Never give alcohol.
- Do not give toy dogs to children.
- Do not give anything made of pigskin as Malays are Muslim.
- Give the gift when you are departing, rather than when you arrive.
- Avoid white wrapping paper as it symbolizes death and mourning.
- Wrap gifts in red or green paper.
- If you give food, make sure it is halal.
- Offer gifts with the right hand only or both hands if the item is large.
- Gifts are not opened when received.

Gift giving to ethnic Indians:
- If you give flowers, avoid frangipani as they are used in funeral wreaths.
- Money should be given in odd numbers, so give S$11 rather than S$10.
- Offer gifts with the right hand only or both hands if the item is large.
- Do not wrap gifts in white or black.
- Wrap gifts in red, yellow or green paper or other bright colours as these bring good fortune.
- Do not give leather products to a Hindu.
- Do not give alcohol unless you are certain the recipient imbibes.
- Gifts are not opened when received.
- Business in Singapore is more formal than in many western countries.
- There are strict rules of protocol that must be observed.
- The group (company or department) is viewed as more important than the individual.

- People observe a strict chain of command, which comes with expectations on both sides.
- In order to keep others from losing face, much communication will be non-verbal and you must closely watch the facial expressions and body language of people you work with.

Building Relationships & Communication

- Personal relationships are the cornerstone of all business relationships.
- Business is a matter of being tied into the proper network, which is the result of long- standing personal relationships or the proper introductions.
- This is a group-oriented culture, so links are often based on ethnicity, education or working for the same company.
- Once you are recognized as part of the group, you will be accepted and expected to obey the unwritten rules of the group.
- Relationships take time to develop.
- You must be patient as this indicates that your organization is here for the long-term and is not looking only for short- term gains.
- Always be respectful and courteous when dealing with others as this leads to the harmonious relationships necessary within business.
- Rank is always respected. The eldest person in the group is revered.
- Most Singaporeans are soft-spoken and believe a calm demeanour is superior to a more aggressive style.
- Watch your body language and facial expressions.

Business Meeting Etiquette

- Appointments are necessary and should be made at least 2 weeks in advance, whenever possible.
- The most formal way to schedule a meeting is to write to the person concerned, although most Singaporeans will schedule an appointment by telephone, fax, or e-mail.
- Do not try to schedule meetings during Chinese New Year (late January/early February), since many businesses close for the entire week.
- You should arrive at meetings on time. Punctuality is a virtue.
- There will be period of small talk before getting down to business discussions.

- Since questioning authority is a taboo, it is important to encourage questions when after making a presentation and then smile when a question is eventually asked.
- Presentations should be accompanied by backup material, including charts and figures.
- Never disagree or criticize someone who is senior to you in rank as it will cause both of you to lose face and may destroy the business relationship.
- Pay attention to non-verbal communication.

Negotiating

- Always send a list of people who will be attending the negotiations and their title well in advance.
- Always wait to be told where to sit. There is a strict hierarchy that must be followed.
- Business negotiations happen at a slow pace.
- Singaporeans are non-confrontational. They will not overtly say 'no'; likewise, their 'yes' does not always signify agreement.
- Singaporeans give a respectful pause of up to 15 seconds before answering a question. Do not start speaking too quickly or you will miss the answer.
- Be prepared with a mental list of concessions you would be willing to make that would not injure your own business.
- Singaporeans are tough negotiators on price and deadlines.
- Decisions are consensus driven.
- Avoid losing your temper or you will lose face and damage your relationship.
- If you are signing a contract with ethnic Chinese, the signing date may be determined by an astrologer or a geomancer (feng shui man).

Business Cards

- Business cards are exchanged after the initial introductions.
- Business cards are exchanged using both hands.
- If you will be meeting ethnic Chinese, it is a good idea to have one side of your card translated into Mandarin. Have the Chinese characters printed in gold, as this is an auspicious colour. Hand your card so the typeface faces the recipient.
- Examine business cards carefully before putting them in a business card case.

- Treat business cards with respect. This is indicative of how you will treat the relationship.
- Your own business cards should be maintained in pristine condition. Never give someone a tattered card.

USA

Facts and Statistics

Location:	North America, bordering both the North Atlantic Ocean and the North Pacific Ocean, between Canada and Mexico
Capital:	Washington, DC
Climate:	mostly temperate, but tropical in Hawaii and Florida, arctic in Alaska, semiarid in the great plains west of the Missis sippi River, and arid in the Great Basin of the southwest.
Population:	301,139,947 (July 2007 est.)
Ethnic Make-up:	white 81.7%, black 12.9%, Asian 4.2%, Amerindian and Alaska native 1%, native Hawaiian and other Pacific is lander 0.2% (2003 est.)
Religions:	Protestant 52%, Roman Catholic 24%, Mormon 2%, Jewish 1%, Muslim 1%, other 10%, none 10% (2002 est.)
Government:	Constitution-based federal republic

Language in the USA

The United States does not have an official language, but English is spoken by about 82% of the population as a native language. The variety of English spoken in the United States is known as American English; together with Canadian English it makes up the group of dialects known as North American English. Spanish is the second-most common language in the country, spoken by almost 30 million people (or 12% of the population).

American Society and Culture

Diversity

America is ultimately a nation of immigrants and as a result is a cultural mish-mash in every sense of the word. Not only is the country populated by people from foreign countries but all Americans in one way or another trace their ancestry back to another culture, whether Irish, German, Italian or Scottish. Looking around any major city one will notice the 'melting-pot' that it is.

Informal and Friendly

Most people who come to the United States may already know a few things about the people through TV. Although this is of course a skewed reality some of the stereotypes are true, especially American friendliness and informality. People tend to not wait to be introduced, will begin to speak with strangers as they stand in a queue, sit next to each other at an event, etc. Visitors can often be surprised when people are so informal to the point of being very direct or even rude.

Time is Money

The country that coined the phrase obviously lives the phrase. In America, time is a very important commodity. People 'save' time and 'spend' time as if it were money in the bank. Americans ascribe personality characteristics and values based on how people use time. For example, people who are on-time are considered to be good people, reliable people who others can count on.

The Family

The family unit is generally considered the nuclear family, and is typically small (with exceptions among certain ethnic groups). Extended family relatives live in their own homes, often at great distances from their children.

Individualism is prized, and this is reflected in the family unit. People are proud of their individual accomplishments, initiative and success, and may, or may not, share those sources of pride with their elders.

Meeting and Greeting

- Greetings are casual.
- A handshake, a smile, and a 'hello' are all that is needed.
- Smile!
- Use first names, and be sure to introduce everyone to each other.

Gift Giving Etiquette

- In general, Americans give gifts for birthdays, anniversaries and major holidays, such as Christmas.
- A gift can be as simple as a card and personal note to something more elaborate for a person with whom you are close.
- Gift giving is not an elaborate event, except at Christmas.

- When invited to someone's home for dinner, it is polite to bring a small box of good chocolates, a bottle of wine, a potted plant or flowers for the hostess.
- Gifts are normally opened when received.

Dining Etiquette

- Americans socialise in their homes and 'backyards', in restaurants and in other public places.
- It's not at all unusual for social events to be as casual as a backyard barbecue or a picnic in the park.
- Arrive on time if invited for dinner; no more than 10 minutes later than invited to a small gathering. If it is a large party, it is acceptable to arrive up to 30 minutes later than invited.
- Table manners are more relaxed in the U.S. than in many other countries.
- The fork is held in the right hand and is used for eating. The fork is held tines down. The knife is used to cut or spread something. To use the knife, the fork is switched to the left hand. To continue eating, the fork is switched back to the right hand.
- If you have not finished eating, cross your knife and fork on your plate with the fork over the knife. Indicate you have finished eating by laying your knife and fork parallel across the right side of your plate.
- If you are more comfortable eating in the Continental manner, go ahead. It will not offend anyone.
- Feel free to refuse specific foods or drinks without offering an explanation.
- Many foods are eaten by hand.
- Food is often served family-style, which means that it is in large serving dishes and passed around the table for everyone to serve themselves.
- Do not begin eating until the hostess starts or says to begin.
- Remain standing until invited to sit down.
- Do not rest your elbows on the table.
- Put your napkin in your lap as soon as you sit down.
- Leave a small amount of food on your plate when you have finished eating.

Greetings

- The hand shake is the common greeting.

- Handshakes are firm, brief and confident.
- Maintain eye contact during the greeting.
- In most situations, you can begin calling people by their first names.
- Most people will insist that you call them by their nickname, if they have one.
- In formal circumstances, you may want to use titles and surnames as a courtesy until you are invited to move to a first name basis, which will happen quickly.
- Business cards are exchanged without formal ritual.
- It is quite common for the recipient to put your card in their wallet, which may then go in the back pocket of their trousers. This is not an insult.

Communication Styles

Americans are direct. They value logic and linear thinking and expect people to speak clearly and in a straightforward manner. To them if you don't "tell it how it is" you simply waste time, and time is money. If you are from a culture that is more subtle in communication style, try not to be insulted by the directness. Try to get to your point more quickly and don't be afraid to be more direct and honest than you are used to. Americans will use the telephone to conduct business that would require a face-to-face meeting in most other countries. They do not insist upon seeing or getting to know the people with whom they do business.

Business Meetings

Arrive on time for meetings since time and punctuality are so important to Americans. In the Northeast and Midwest, people are extremely punctual and view it as a sign of disrespect for someone to be late for a meeting or appointment. In the Southern and Western states, people may be a little more relaxed, but to be safe, always arrive on time, although you may have to wait a little before your meeting begins.

Meetings may appear relaxed, but they are taken quite seriously. If there is an agenda, it will be followed. At the conclusion of the meeting, there will be a summary of what was decided, a list of who will implement which facets and a list of the next steps to be taken and by whom. If you make a presentation, it should be direct and to the point. Visual aids should further enhance your case. Use statistics to back up your claims, since Americans are impressed by hard data and evidence.

With the emphasis on controlling time, business is conducted rapidly. Expect very little small talk before getting down to business. It is common to attempt to reach an oral agreement at the first meeting. The emphasis is on getting a contract signed rather than building a relationship. The relationship may develop once the first contract has been signed.

Business Dress

- What is considered appropriate business attire varies by geographic region, day of the week and industry.
- In general, people in the East dress more formally, while people in the West are known for being a bit more casual.
- Executives usually dress formally regardless of which part of the country they are in.
- Casual Friday is common in many companies. High technology companies often wear casual clothes every day.
- For an initial meeting, dressing conservatively is always in good taste. Women can wear business suits, dresses or pantsuits. Men should wear a business suit unless you know the firm to be quite casual.

Recommended Reading List

Geert Hofsteede: Culture's Consequences, ISBN: 0-8039-7324-1

Fons Trompenarars, Charles Hampden-Turner: Riding the Waves of Cultures, ISBN: 978-1-85788-176-9

Edward T. Hall and Mildred Reed Hall: Understanding Cultural Differences, ISBN: 1-877864-864-07-2

Edward T. Hall: Doing Business With The Japanese, ISBN: 978-0385238847

Ricky W. Griffin, Michael W. Pustay: International Business, ISBN: 0-13-233532-8

Charles W. L. Hill: International Business, ISBN: 978-0-07-110671-9

Website: Management Laboratory: www.Management-Laboratory.com

Website: Kwintessential: www. kwintessential.co.uk

Website: Harvard Business Review: www.hbr.org

Market Entry Strategies

Works Cited

1. Griffin, Ricky W. and Pustay, Michael W. *International Business.* 5th Edition. Quebecor World-Versailles / Pheonix : Pearson Prentice Hall, 2007. 0-13-233532-8.

2. Bayer AG. Bayer Jobs & Career. [Online] Bayer AG. [Cited: 06 01 2008.] http://www.mybayerjob.de/en/entrylevel/traineeprograms/internationaltraineep rogrambhc/.

3. *IKEA.* [Online] IKEA United States. [Cited: 27 09 2007.] http://www.ikea.com.

4. Bosch GmbH. www.bosch.com. [Online] Bosch GmbH. [Cited: 01 12 2007.] http://www.bosch.com.

5. Texas Instruments. Company Info. [Online] Texas Instruments. [Cited: 12 10 2007.] http://www.ti.com/corp/docs/company/index.htm.

6. Intel . Intel's Leadership. [Online] Intel. [Cited: 12 10 2007.] http://www.intel.com.

7. Center for Business Planning. [Online] Business Resource Software. [Cited: 1 11 2007.] http://www.businessplans.org/.

8. The Disney Company. Corporate Information . [Online] [Cited: 13 12 2008.] http://corporate.disney.go.com.

9. Merck. [Online] Merck. [Cited: 12 12 2007.] http://www.merck.com/.

10. Johnson, Gerry, Scholes, Kevan and Whittington, Richard. *Exploring Corporate Strategy.* 7th Edition. Edinburgh : Prentice Hall, 2006. 0-273-71017-6.

11. International, Medion. Medion International. [Online] Medion International. [Cited: 1 11 2007.] http://www.medion.com/company.

12. Zumwinkel, Klaus. CEO. Hamburg : Manager Magazin, 10 2007. CEO Deutsche Post AG.

13. Rapoport, Carla. CNN Money. [Online] Furtune, 19 09 1994. [Cited: 01 11 2007.] http://money.cnn.com/magazines/fortune/fortune_archive/1994/09/19/79744/i ndex.htm.

14. Mager, Stefan. *HR Manager.* [interv.] Christoph Lymbersky. Cronberg, 17 09 2007.

15. Designbuild-Network. [Online] SPG Media. [Cited: 01 11 2007.] http://www.designbuild-network.com/projects/bmw/.

16. Business Week Online. [Online] Business Week, 30 05 1995. [Cited: 01 10 2007.] http://www.businessweek.com/.

17. Zhao, M.A. Xuemin. *Modeling Market Entry Mode Choice: the Case of German Firms in China.* Fakultät für Wirtschaftswissenschaften, Universität Bielefeld. Bielfeld : s.n., 2005.

18. Tchibo GmbH. Hungary. *Tchibo.* [Online] Tchibo GmbH. [Cited: 01 01 2008.] http://www.tchibo.com/corweb/servlet/content/75586/LnderstartseiteDeutsch_en/Unternehmen_en/International_en/Ungarn_en.html.

19. Adam, Ben. *Luftfahrt.net.* [Online] [Cited: 01 11 2007.] http://www.luftfahrt.net/special/airbus.php.

20. Joyner, Nelson T. Paagproducts.org. *How to Find and Use an Export Management Company.* [Online] Paagproducts. [Cited: 01 12 2007.] http://www.paagproducts.org.

21. *Webster's Online Dictionary.* [Online] Webster. [Cited: 02 12 2007.] http://www.websters-dictionary-online.org.

22. *Fortune Magazine.* July 24, 2006.

23. [Online] Adopted from: http://www.investorwords.com/2799/licensing.html.

24. Hill, Charles W. L. *International Business.* 6th Edition. New York : McGraw-Hill Irwin, 2007.

25. Warnaco, Inc., Designer Holdings, Ltd. Inc., Calvin Klein Jeanswear Co., and Outlet Holdings, Inc. *Calvin Klein Trademark Trust and Calvin Klein, Inc. v. Linda Wachner, Warnaco Group, Inc.* U.S. District Court, S.D.N.Y., 00 CIV 4052. s.l. : Warnaco, Inc., May 30, 2000. pp. 1-2.

26. Vicki M. Young and Lisa Lockwood. Calvin Klein and Warnaco Tangle Over Trademarks, Brand Dilution. *Brand Marketing.* 2000, 7.

27. Warnaco, Inc., Designer Holdings, Ltd., Inc., Calvin Klein Jeanswear Co., and Outlet Holdings, Inc. *Defendants' Amended Answer and Counterclaims, Calvin Klein Trademark Trust and Calvin Klein, Inc. v. Linda Wachner, Warnaco Group Inc.* s.l. : U.S. District Court, S.D.N.Y., 00 CIV 4052, June 26, 2000.

28. Robert Kopp, Robert Eng, and Douglas Tigert. A Competitive Structure and Segmentation Analysis of the Chicago Fashion Market. *Journal of Retailing.* 1989, December.

29. Lindquist, J. Meaning of Image. *Journal of Retailing.* 1974, 4. See also Sharon Beatty, "Customer-Sales Associate Retail Relationships," Journal of Retailing 72, no. 3 (1996): 223–247.

30. Moin, David. The Department Store Saga. *Women's Wear Daily.* Supplement, June 4, 1997.

31. PricewaterhouseCoopers. *Industry Report: Department Stores.* s.l. : PricewaterhouseCoopers, March 2000.

32. Silverman, Dick. Retail Space Wars. *Daily News Record.* January 19, 1998, Vol. 28, 8.

33. Socha, Miles. Rebuilding Calvin's Jeans. *Women's Wear Daily.* March 5, 1998.

34. Amy Merrick, Jeffrey A. Trachtenberg, and Ann Zimmerman. Idle Aisles: Department Stores Fight an Uphill Battle Just to Stay Relevant. *The Wall Street Journal.* sec. A, March 12, 2002.

35. Moin, David. Differentiate or Die- Retail. *Women's Wear Daily.* June 8, 1998.

36. Seckler, Valerie. Retail's Share Master: The Discounter. *Women's Wear Daily .* September 22, 1999.

37. Calvin Klein at a Discount? *The Toronto Star.* Life sec., January 25, 2001.

38. Bell, David E. *Costco Companies Inc.* 599-041, Boston : s.n., 1999.

39. *Total Apparel Report.* s.l. : NPD Group data, 1997–1999.

40. Moriwaki, Lee. Costco: The Empire Built on Bargains. But Where Does It Get All That Great Stuff? That's What Makers of Some Costco Merchandise Want to Know. sec. A, July 20, 1997.

41. Joel H. Steckel submitted to Williams & Connolly. with regard to 00 CIV 4052 filed in the U.S. District Court, S.D.N.Y..

42. Skipworth, Mark. Get a Load of This: Club Shopping. *Sunday Times of London.* magazine sec., September 5, 1993.

43. *Retail Market Structure: Implications for Retailers and Consumers.* Morganosky, Michelle. s.l. : International Journal of Retail & Distribution Management, 1997, Vol. 25.

44. Michael Exstein, Shirley Lee. *Brand Migration.* s.l. : U.S. Retail Equity Research Report, Credit Suisse First Boston, June 13, 2000.

45. Socha, Miles. Heritage and Pricing Outweigh Status. *Women's Wear Daily.* Supplement, January 24, 2000.

46. *Linking Brand and Retailer Images: Do the Potential Risks Outweigh the Potential Benefits?* Jacoby, Jacob and Mazursky, David. 2, s.l. : Journal of Retailing, 1984, Vol. 60.

47. *The Effects of Price, Store Image, and Product and Respondent Characteristics on Perceptions of Quality.* Wheatley, John and Chiu, John S. Y. s.l. : Journal of Marketing Research, May 1977, Vol. 14. R. Kenneth Teas and Sanjeev Agarwal, "The Effects of Extrinsic Product Cues on Consumers' Perceptions of Quality, Sacrifice, and Value," Journal of the Academy of Marketing Science 28, no. 2 (April 2000): 278–290; .

48. *Store Atmosphere and Purchasing Behavior.* Donovan, Robert, et al. 3, s.l. : Journal of Retailing, September 1994, Vol. 70.

49. Stern, Louis and Sturdivant, Frederick. Customer-Driven Distribution Systems. *Harvard Business Review.* July 1987. See also Boonghee Yoo, Naveen Donthu, and Sungho Lee, "An Examination of Selected Marketing Mix Elements and Brand Equity," Journal of the Academy of Marketing Science 28, no. 2 (April 2000): 195–211..

50. Solomon, Michael R. Deep-Seated Materialism: The Case of Levi's 501 Jeans. *Advances in Consumer Research.* 1986. Vol. 13.

51. Karr, Arnold J. Short, Strange Trip: In the Seventies, Jeans Flew Sky High, Then Came Down, Then Grew Up. Far Out. *Women's Wear Daily.* Supplement, May 18, 2000.

52. Ozzard, Janet. Surviving the Basics Slump. *Women's Wear Daily.* August 14, 1997.

53. Better Category Fastest-Growing in Women's. *Women's Wear Daily.* April 3, 2000.

54. Denim Dish. *Women's Wear Daily.* February 25, 1999.

55. Socha, Miles. Status Jeans Gain Momentum. *Women's Wear Daily.* January 15, 1998.

56. D'Innocenzio, Anne. Status Brands: As Consumers Cool, Retailers Reevaluate. *Women's Wear Daily.* March 16, 2000.

57. Agins, Teri. Denim's Lucky 'Seven'—How $100-Plus Jeans Became a Must-Have Fashion Fad; Fixing 'The Gap' Problem. *The Wall Street Journal.* sec. B, April 3, 2002.

58. Williamson, Rusty. Tracking the Teen Shopper: Turf War Heats Up as Retailers Vie for Piece of Growing Junior Market. *Women's Wear Daily* . Supplement, February 25, 1999.

59. Wilson, Eric. After Calvin, Some Wonder If Licensing is a No-Brands Land. *Women's Wear Daily.* August 1, 2000.

60. *Brands without Boundaries: The Internationalization of the Designer Retailer's Brand.* Moore, Christopher M., Fernie, John and Burt, Steve. 8, 2000, European Journal of Marketing, Vol. 34.

61. Larson, Kristin. The Diversification Dynamic. *Women's Wear Daily.* October 10, 2001.

62. Lockwood, Lisa and Curan, Catherine. Karan, Claiborne Set Mega-Licensing Deal for Jeans, Activewear. *Women's Wear Daily* . December 16, 1997.

63. Stewart, Martha. New York : Living Omnimedia Inc., July 29, 1999.

64. Menkes, Suzy. License to Kill: Fashion Houses Tighten Brand Control. *International Herald Tribune.* July 4, 2000.

65. Pogoda, Diane M. The Year of the Merger. *Women's Wear Daily.* December 14, 1998.

66. Greenberg, Julee. Vera Wang Steps on the Gas. *Women's Wear Daily.* December 7, 2001.

67. Calvin Klein Executive Biography. *Hoovers Online,.* [Online] [Cited: 17 09 2001.] www.hoovers.com.

68. Calvin's Designs on Cyberspace. *Women's Wear Daily.* CEO Summit Supplement, June 14, 2000.

69. Calvin Klein, Inc. *Hoovers Online.* [Online] 17 09 2001. http://www.hoovers.com.

70. Sellers, Patricia. Seventh Avenue Smackdown: Fashion Moguls Calvin Klein and Linda Wachner are Going Toe-to-Toe in a Bitter Suit. *Fortune.* September 4, 2000.

71. Agins, Teri and Trachtenberg, Jeffrey A. Designer Troubles: Calvin Klein is Facing a Bind as Magic Touch Appears to be Slipping. *The Wall Street Journal.* sec. A, November 22, 1991.

72. Ingrassia, Michele. Calvin's World. *Newsweek.* September 11, 1995.

73. Phyland, Jan. Go Ahead, Make My Shorts. *The Age.* March 6, 1993.

74. Belcove, Julie L. Master Charge. *Women's Wear Daily.* January 28, 1994.

75. Seo, Diane. A New Obsession: Calvin Klein Ads with a Wholesome Bent. *Los Angeles Times.* sec. D, February 5, 1998.

76. Lockwood, Lisa. Calvin's Credo. *Women's Wear Daily.* July 22, 1997.

77. *Qualitative Research on Calvin Klein Image Recognition.* s.l. : DYG, Inc., February 1997.

78. Schroeder, Jonathan. Gender, Imagery, and Meaning in the cK One Campaign. *Advances in Consumer Research.* 1998. 25.

79. Barrett, Wayne. Calvin Klein's Dirty Laundry. *Talk Magazine.* March 2001.

80. Plaskin, Glenn. Calvin Klein Playboy Interview. *Playboy.* May 1984.

81. Schroeder, Jonathan. *Edouard Manet, Calvin Klein and the Strategic Use of Scandal.* London : Routledge, 2000. Imagining Marketing: Art, Aesthetics, and the Avant-Garde, eds. Stephen Brown and Anthony Patterson.

82. Agins, Teri. Shaken by a Series of Business Setbacks, CKI is Redesigning Itself. *The Wall Street Journal.* sec. B, March 21, 1994.

83. Lockwood, Lisa. Wachner Swings, Simon Gets the Ax—and $4.5 million. *Women's Wear Daily.* December 11, 1997.

84. *Calvin Klein Trademark Trust and Calvin Klein, Inc. v. Linda Wachner, Warnaco Group, Inc.* 00 CIV 4052, s.l. : U.S. District Court, S.D.N.Y, May 30, 2000. Warnaco, Inc., Designer Holdings, Ltd., Inc., Calvin Klein Jeanswear Co., and Outlet Holdings, Inc.,.

85. *Licensing U.S. Midyear Review.* submitted with regard to 00 CIV 4052 S.D.N.Y., CKI-0298181, s.l. : filed in the U.S. District Court, August 1999. CKI.

86. *Defendants' Amended Answer and Counterclaims, Calvin Klein Trademark Trust and Calvin Klein, Inc. v. Linda Wachner, Warnaco Group, Inc., Warnaco, Inc., Designer Holdings, Ltd., Inc., Calvin Klein Jeanswear Co., and Outlet Holdings, Inc.* 00 CIV 4052, s.l. : U.S. District Court S.D.N.Y., June 26, 2000. Exhibit B.

87. Kaufman, Leslie. Calvin Klein Battles Maker of Its Jeans. *The New York Times.* sec. C, June 1, 2000.

88. No Deal: Calvin Pulls His Company Off the Market. *Women's Wear Daily.* April 19, 2000.

89. Calvin Puts Himself in Play. *Women's Wear Daily.* October 6, 1999.

90. *Expert Report of David T. Scheffman, submitted to Williams & Connolly .* with regard to 00 CIV 4052, s.l. : filed in the U.S. District Court, S.D.N.Y.

91. *Qualitative Research on Calvin Klein Image Recognition.* submitted with regard to 00 CIV 4052, P3WAC0006689. filed in the U.S. District Court, S.D.N.Y. : s.n., February 1997. DYG, Inc.

92. *Expert Report of David T. Scheffman, submitted to Williams & Connolly.* with regard to 00 CIV 4052, filed in the U.S. District Court, S.D.N.Y. : s.n. Exhibit 7.

93. *Calvin Klein Information Memorandum.* with regard to 00 CIV 4052, TH 000474.. s.l. : filed in the U.S. District Court, S.D.N.Y., October 1999.

94. *Calvin Klein Brand Audit.* s.l. : CKI, April 26, 2000.

95. *1998 Public Relations and Promotions Plan cK Calvin Klein Jeans.* submitted with regard to 00 CIV 4052, s.l. : filed in the U.S. District Court, S.D.N.Y., CKI-0136192. See also "Calvin Klein Management Presentation December 1999," submitted with regard to 00 CIV 4052 filed in the U.S. District Court S.D.N.Y., TH 002355.

96. CKI. *Marketing Research Overview: cK Jeans Brand Logo Testing.* submitted with regard to 00 CIV 4052, P3WAC0007100-7104. s.l. : filed in the U.S. District Court, S.D.N.Y., September 1997.

97. *Expert Report of Joel H. Steckel, submitted to Williams & Connolly.* with regard to 00 CIV 4052 , s.l. : filed in the U.S. District Court, S.D.N.Y.

98. Smith, Bernard. Fig Leaves and Fortunes: A Fashion Company Named Warnaco. *Business History Review.* 1992, Vol. 66.

99. *Warnaco Inc. Reports the Most Profitable First Quarter in the History of the Company.* s.l. : PR Newswire, April 8, 1986.

100. Strom, Stephanie. Double Trouble at Linda Wachner's Twin Companies. *The New York Times.* sec. 3, August 4, 1996.

101. Caminiti, Susan. American's Most Successful Businesswoman. *Fortune.* June 15, 1992.

102. Domaine, Brian. America's Toughest Bosses. *Fortune.* October 18, 1993.

103. Caminiti, All data in this paragraph is taken from Susan. America's Most Successful Businesswoman. *Fortune.* June 15, 1992.

104. Pappas, Charles. The Top 20 Best-Paid Women in Corporate America. *Working Woman.* February 1998.

105. Agins, Teri and Quick, Rebecca. Illegal Briefs? Behind a Bitter Suit Filed by Calvin Klein Lies Grit of Licensing. *Wall Street Journal.* sec. A, June 1, 2000.

106. Lockwood, Lisa. Calvin: The Control Question. *Women's Wear Daily.* October 6, 1997.

107. White, Constance C. R. Reviving the Halston Legacy. *The New York Times.* sec. B, April 1, 1997.

108. Monget, Karyn and Moin, David. Is Penney's Coming Between Big Stores and Their Calvins? *Women's Wear Daily.* December 6, 1999.

109. Monget, Karyn, Ryan, Thomas J. and Lockwood, Lisa. Wachner's Challenge: Win Back the Street. *Women's Wear Daily.* April 3, 2000.

110. Brown, Christie. The Body Bending Business. *Forbes.* September 11, 1995.

111. Bates, James. W Acquisition and Warnaco Agree on $488-million Deal. *Los Angeles Times.* Home sec., April 26, 1986.

112. Harkavy, Jerry. Stitcher Dons Eyepatch to Battle for Shirt Factory's Survival. *Associated Press Newswires.* May 25, 1996.

113. Monget, Karyn and Rutberg, Sidney. Wachner's World. *Women's Wear Daily.* August 29, 1994.

114. Zagorin, Adam. Short-Shirted in Maine: Hathaway Employees Meet Tough Demand to Double Productivity. They May Face the Ax Anyway. *Time Magazine.* June 3, 1996.

115. Curan, Catherine. No Windfall Expected by Hathaway's Competitors. *Daily News Record.* May 10, 1996.

116. Abend, Jules. Hathaway Recovers Ground. *Bobbin.* April 1, 1999.

117. Singhania, Lisa. New Hathaway Shirt Unveiled. *Associated Press Newswires.* November 19, 1997.

118. Venerable Shirt Maker to Close June 30, with Loss of 300 Jobs. *Associated Press Newswires.* March 19, 2002.

119. Gellers, Stan. Christian Dior Upgrades Men's Apparel Licensees. *Daily News Record.* May 1, 1995.

120. Curan, Catherine. Wachner Needs a Second Act. *Crain's New York Business.* May 22, 2000.

121. Colvin, Goeffrey. America's Worst Boards. *Fortune.* April 17, 2000.

122. Lockwood, Lisa. Calvin Declares War on Linda. *Women's Wear Daily.* May 31, 2000.

123. —. Wachner Swings, Simon Gets the Ax—and $4.5 million. *Women's Wear Daily.* December 11, 1997.

124. *cK Calvin Klein Jeans 1998 Year End Summary.* submitted with regard to 00 CIV 4052, P3WAC0007304. s.l. : filed in the U.S. District Court, S.D.N.Y.

125. Ryan, Thomas J. Warnaco's Billion-Dollar Star: Calvin Klein Jeans, Underwear. *Women's Wear Daily.* August 4, 1999.

126. *Defendant's Motion for Partial Summary Judgment, Calvin Klein Trademark Trust and Calvin Klein, Inc. v. Linda Wachner et al.* 00 CIV 4052, s.l. : U.S. District Court, S.D.N.Y.,. p. 5.

127. *Calvin Klein Trademark Trust and Calvin Klein, Inc. v. Linda Wachner, Warnaco Group, Inc., Warnaco, Inc., Designer Holdings Ltd., Inc., Calvin Klein Jeanswear Co., and Outlet Holdings, Inc.* 00 CIV 4052, s.l. : U.S. District Court, S.D.N.Y., May 30, 2000. Exhibit E.

128. Ryan, Thomas. In Line with Forecast, Warnaco Profits Decline 44.4% in Quarter. *Women's Wear Daily.* March 6, 2000.

129. *District, Expert Report of David T. Scheffman submitted to Williams & Connolly.* with regard to 00 CIV 4052, filed in the U.S. Court, S.D.N.Y. : s.n. Exhibit 19.

130. *Deposition of Linda Wachner.* in conjunction with 00 CIV 4052, December 19, 2000 : filed in the U.S. District Court.

131. *Deposition of Gabriella Forte.* in conjunction with 00 CIV 4052 , November 10, 2000 : filed in the U.S. District Court S.D.N.Y.

132. Transcript. Calvin Klein Discusses His Fashion Empire. *Larry King Live.* s.l. : CNN, June 5, 2002. Web site: http://www.cnn.com, accessed July 9, 2001.

133. Expert report of David T. Scheffman.

134. McGraw-Hill . [Online] McGraw-Hill . [Cited: 12 01 2008.] http://highered.mcgraw-hill.com/sites/0072973714/student_view0/glossary.html.

135. Sen, Kabir C. The Use of Initial Fees and Royalties in Business-format Franchising. *Managerial and Decision Economics.* 1993.

136. Stern, L. W. and El-Ansary, A. I. *Marketing Channels.* Englewood Cliffs, NJ : Prentice-Hall, 1988.

137. Gompers, Paul A. *A Note on Franchsing.* 9-297-108, Boston, MA : s.n., 2001.

138. Purvin, Robert L. *The Franchise Fraud: How to Protect Yourself Before and After You Invest.* New York : John Wiley, 1994.

139. Bond, Robert E. *The Source Book of Franchise Opportunities.* Homewood, IL : Dow Jones-Irwin, 1993.

140. Lafontaine, Francine. Agency Theory and Franchising: Some Empirical Results. *Rand Journal of Economics.* Summer 1992.

141. McDonald's. [Online] taken from:
http://www.mcdonalds.com/corp/franchise/franchisinghome.html.

142. Pepsi Co. . [Online] [Cited: 13 12 2007.] taken from:
http://www.pepsi.com/corporate/company_info/index.php.

143. Walker, Seb. *The Age.* [Online] 14 01 2004. [Cited: 22 12 2007.]
http://www.theage.com.au.

144. Virgin Media. [Online] [Cited: 23 11 2007.] http://pressoffice.virginmedia.com.

145. BT Group. Company Profil. *BT Group.* [Online] [Cited: 11 12 2007.]
http://www.btplc.com/Thegroup/Companyprofile/Companyprofile.htm.

146. Savvas, Antony. *ComputerWeekly.* [Online] 10 12 2007. [Cited: 15 12 2007.]
taken from: http://www.computerweekly.com.

147. HOCHTIEF AirPort (HTA). High-flyer: Athens International Airport Eleftherios
Venizelos. [Online] HOCHTIEF AirPort (HTA). [Cited: 02 01 2008.] taken from:
http://www.hochtief-airport.com/airport_en/16.jhtml.

148. Keay, John. *The Honourable Company - A History of the English East India Company.* London : HarperCollins, 1991. 0-00-217515-0 .

149. Robinson, James Harvey. *Readings in European History: From the opening of the Protestant Revolt to the Present Day.* Boston : Ginn and Co., 1904-1906. Vol. Second Edition.

150. *Saltpeter - the secret salt.* [Online] MRBloch Archive. [Cited: 15 01 2008.]
http://salt.org.il.

151. Draper, William, Sir and Cornish, Samuel, Sir. *A plain narrative of the reduction of Manila and the Philippine Islands.* 1763.

152. East India Company Factory Records. *Adam Matthew Publications .* [Online]
Adam Matthew Publications . [Cited: 10 01 2008.] Sources from the British Library,
London . http://www.ampltd.co.uk/collections_az/EIC-Factory-1/description.aspx.

153. Anthony, Frank. Britain's Betrayal in India: The Story of the Anglo Indian
Community. London : The Simon Wallenberg Press, 2007, Vol. Second Edition.

154. *Mannesmann-Archiv.* Mühlheim an der Ruhr, Germany : s.n., 2006.

155. Mannesmann AG. *Mannesmann AG Anual Report.* s.l. : Mannesmann AG, 1999.

156. *Vodafone Investor Relations .* [Online] [Cited: 30 09 2006.]
http://www.vodafone.com/section_article/0,3035,CATEGORY_ID%253D40101%25
26LANGUAGE_ID%253D0%2526CONTENT_ID%253D230802,00.html.

157. *CNN Money.* [Online] 21 10 1999.
http://money.cnn.com/1999/10/21/europe/orange/.

158. *BBC.* [Online] BBC, 11 02 2000.
http://news.bbc.co.uk/1/hi/business/630293.stm.

159. *Manager Magazin.* [Online] Manager Magazin, 14 12 2006.
http://www.manager-magazin.de/unternehmen/artikel/0,2828,242161-6,00.html.

160. *Tecchannel.de.* [Online] dpa, 11 06 2002.
http://www.tecchannel.de/news/themen/business/411576/.

161. Dreier, N. *Squeeze Out.* s.l. : EWir, 2003.

162. Lessmann, Peter. *Heisse.de.* [Online] Heisse Online, 31 01 2005.
http://www.heise.de/newsticker/meldung/55732.

163. *WDR.de.* [Online] WDR, 14 11 2004.
http://www.wdr.de/themen/wirtschaft/wirtschaftsbranche/mannesmann_abfindu
ngen/fuenf_jahre_seit_uebernahme.jhtml.

164. Vodafone. *Vodafone.* [Online] www.vodafone.com.

165. *teleclick.ca.* [Online] Telecommunications Industry News, 12 06 2005.
http://www.teleclick.ca/2005/12/nokia-predicts-significant-mobile-phone-
industry-growth/.

166. Worldwide Telecom Industry Growth Expected In 2006. *3G.co.uk.* [Online] 19
12 2005. [Cited: 15 11 2006.] http://www.3g.co.uk/PR/Dec2005/2388.htm..

167. *Investorwords.* [Online] Investorwords. [Cited: 17 12 2007.]
http://www.investorwords.com.

168. The World Bank. *Pakistan and the World Bank: Partners in Progress .*
Washington D.C. : The World Bank, 1986.

169. Burki, Shahid Javed. *A Nation in the Making.* Boulder : Westview Press, 1986.

170. *Pakistan's Dairy Industry: Issues and Policy Alternatives.* Islamabad : The Directorate of Agricultural Policy and Chemonics International Consulting Division, 1989.

171. Nestle, S.A. *Nestle, The Story of an International Company.* Vevey : Nestle, S.A., 1991.

172. Dictionary. *BNet.com.* [Online] BNet. [Cited: 02 01 2008.] Adapted from: http://dictionary.bnet.com/definition/Strategic+Alliance.html.

173. *Star Alliance.* [Online] Star Alliance, 2007. [Cited: 03 01 2008.] All data from: http://www.staralliance.com.

174. *IBS - Case Development Centre .* [Online] IBS. [Cited: 03 01 2008.] http://www.ibscdc.org/.

175. China Life, GE in financial alliance deal –report. [Online] Reuters, 24 09 2007. [Cited: 05 01 2008.] http://www.reuters.com/article/companyNewsAndPR/idUSPEK1100320070925.

176. Alliances. *IBM - Alliances.* [Online] IBM. [Cited: 17 09 2007.] http://www-935.ibm.com/services/us/index.wss/offerfamily/gbs/a1002843.

177. Ford Motor Company. *Company History .* [Online] Ford Moto Company. [Cited: 03 01 2008.] http://www.fordmotorcompany.co.za/corporate/history/mazda.asp.

178. Telefónica Móviles. *Press release.* 07 04 2003.

179. *Telefónica Móviles case interview.* 23 07 2004.

180. Europeans to threaten Vodafone's dominance. *The Herald.* 08 04 2003.

181. [Online] 03 2003. http://www.vodafone.com.

182. Mobile operators unveil FreeMove alliance. s.l. : Total Telecom, 29 03 2004.

183. [Online] http://www.gsmworld.com.

184. Molodovanu and Jehiel. *The European UMTS - IMT-2000 License Auctions.* 2001.

185. Xfera y el Ministerio revisan los compromisos de la licencia de UMTS. [Online] 26 01 2004. http://www.vnunet.es.

186. *FT unchanged by Orange buyout.* [Online] 01 09 2003.
http://www.boardwatch.com.

187. [Online] http://www.freemovealliance.net.

188. Mobiles: FreeMove plans 'roam like home'. 30 03 2004.

189. FreeMove. [Online] 29 03 2004. FreeMove press release.
http://www.freemovealliance.net.

190. —. Alliance Members Align Under FreeMove Brand. 29 03 2004. press release.

191. Western European mobile subscribers. [Online] 02 2004.
http://www.cellular.co.za.

192. Deutsche Telekom presents possibility of dividend to shareholders for 2005. 18 04 2004. TMO press release.

193. Yankee Group. 2003.

194. T-Mobile and BT Wíreles agree on UMTS cooperation. 12 06 2001. TMO press release.

195. T-Mobile and Sony Music announce broad, global, strategic partnership to distribute a wide range of mobile music content. 26 02 2004. TMO press release.

196. Sony Ericsson and T-Mobile in exclusive partnership for the T630 camera phone. 07 01 2005. TMO press release.

197. [Online] 05 07 2004. http://www.onvista.com.

198. Telefónica Moviles Espana to Launch i-mode Service in Spain. 25 06 2003. NTTDoCoMo press release.

199. TIM: The shareholders' meeting approves the financial statements for the 2003 fiscal year. 04 05 2004. TIM press release.

200. [Online] 05 07 2004. http://www.onvista.com.

201. TIM. Investor Relations. [Online] TIM, 05 06 2004. http://www.tim.it.

202. "FreeMove to challenge Vodafone. *Financial Times.* 30 03 2004.

203. consolidated revenues 2003 and 2002. *France Telecom website* . [Online]
http://www.agence.francetelecom.com/.

204. Orange Set to Join Pan-European Mobile Alliance. 23 06 2003. WMRC.

205. [Online] 06 07 2004. www.onvista.com.

206. Total Telecom. European operator alliance plans m-payment system. 23 06
2003.

207. Telecom groups link up to push for combined mobile and fixed services.
Financial Times. 08 06 2004.

208. Microsoft and Vodafone plan mobile venture. *Financial Times.* 14 10 3003.

209. [Online] http://www.symbian.com.

210. [Online] 03 2003. http://www.vodafone.com.

211. "Vodafone-Verizon Ties to Be Tested - US Firm May Have to Buy Part of
Wireless Venture For as Much as $ 10 Billion. *The Wall Street Journal Europe.* 10 06
2004.

212. figures for mobile business only. 26 04 2004. Wind press release .

213. Sources: www.cellular.co.za; www.budde.com; www.itfacts.biz.

214. Pandraud, R. *Lecture in International Business Management.* [Lecture Notes].
Paris : Management Labortory, 2006.

215. Wojnicki, A. Lecture in Managing Customer Value. s.l. : University of Toronto,
2006.

216. Couturier, J. Lecture in International Business Management. [Lecture Notes].
Paris : ESCP-EAP Paris, 2006.

217. Rowley, T. Lecture in Strategic Management. [Lecture Notes]. Toronto, Canada :
University of Toronto, 2006.

218. Porter, Michael. *The McKinsey Quarterly.* 1980.

219. Japan-guide (2006). *japan-guide.com.* [Online] [Cited: 15 11 2006.]
http://www.japan-guide.com/e/e644.html.

220. *BUYUSA.GOV.* [Online] BUYUSA.GOV. [Cited: 19 11 2006.]
http://www.buyusa.gov/japan/en/mom.html.

221. Dunning, J John H. *Explaining foreign direct investment in Japan: some theoretical in-sights, Foreign Direct Investment.* Cheltenham, UK : s.n., 1996. ed. Masaru Yoshitomi and Edward M. Graham.

222. Attridge, William. *Commentary on: 'What are the actual experiences of foreign mul-tinationals in Japan? The European point of view', Reinhard Neumann, Foreign Direct Investment.* Cheltenham, UK : s.n., 1996. ed. Masaru Yoshitomi and Edward M. Graham.

223. Jordan, Thomas F. *The future of foreign direct investment in Japan.* Cheltenham, UK : s.n., 1996. pp. 195-201. ed. Masaru Yoshitomi, Edward M. Graham.

224. *Economist.com.* [Online] Economist , 2006. [Cited: 19 11 2006.]
http://www.economist.com/research/backgrounders/displayBackgrounder.cfm?bg=53.

225. Japan. *Answer.com.* [Online] [Cited: 03 11 2006.]
http://www.answers.com/topic/japan.

226. Institut für Japanstudien (Hrsg.). *Die Wirtschaft Japans: Strukturen zwischen Kontinuität und Wandel.* Berlin : Springer Verlag, 1998.

227. Kirin. *Annual Report 2005.* s.l. : Kirin, 2006. http://www.kirin.com .

228. Asahi Breweries. *Annual report 2005.* s.l. : Asahi Breweries, 2005. Annual report. http://www.asahibeer.co.jp/english/.

229. *Findarticles.com.* [Online] Findarticles. [Cited: 07 11 2006.]
http://www.findarticles.com/p/articles/mi_m3469/is_50_53/ai_95912802.

230. Jetro Marketing Guidebook for Major Imported Products – Alcoholic beverages . [Online] 2003. [Cited: 12 12 2006.]
http://www.books.jetro.go.jp/bookshop/sample/mgb2004e.pdf.

231. Alcoholic Drinks in Japan. [Online] 2006. [Cited: 10 11 2006.]
http://www.euromonitor.com/Alcoholic_Drinks_in_Japan.

232. Wilcox, G. J. Hey Kirin, this Bud's for you vannuys plant brewing Ice beer for Japan. *Los Angeles Daily News.* April, 9. 1994.

233. Anheuser-Busch, Kirin brewery expand business, trade partnership; Kirin beer introduced. *PR Newswire.* March, 10. 1994.

234. *Springerlink.com.* [Online] Springerlink . [Cited: 25 11 2006.] http://www.springerlink.com/content/jq183584vx60811j/.

235. Homepage of ports. [Online] Yokohama. [Cited: 25 11 2006.] http://www.city.yokohama.jp/me/port/en/index.html.

236. Messow, F. [Online] 1998. [Cited: 11 11 2006.]

237. Masuko, Makiko. 27 11 2006.

238. Morgan, J. C., Morgan, J. J. *Cracking the Japanese Market.* New York : s.n., 1991.

239. Fujita, J. For the Japanese, Budweiser ads fall flat. *The Record.* 12 12 1999.

240. *American Companies in Japan: Food and agricultural products.* February, 1. 1995. Japan-U.S. Business Report. Vol. 199, No. 305.

241. Japan Venture for Budweiser. *NYTimes.com.* [Online] New York Times Archives, 2006. [Cited: 12 12 2006.] http://query.nytimes.com/gst/fullpage.html?res=9F0CE1DB163CF933A1575AC0A 965958260.

242. *Wabash Collage Homepge.* [Online] Wabash Collage. [Cited: 17 11 2006.] www.wabash.edu/dept/economics.

243. Yumiko Ono. *The Wall Street Journal.* 28 10 1993.

244. Look, no lizards! *Advertising Age International.* May, 2000.

245. Japan's Kirin, Anheuser-Busch in sales licensing deal for US market. *Global Factiva.* [Online] 20 11 2006. [Cited: 25 11 2006.] http://www.global.factiva.com.

246. World news. *Nation's Restaurant News.* Vol. 29, 37.

247. Official FIFA Partners Extend Their Global Soccer Commitment Through Marketing Programs on Official Site. *Yahoo News.* [Online] Yahoo! Inc., 28 11 2001. [Cited: 20 11 2006.] http://www.news.yahoo.com.

248. Definition. *Merriam-Webster.* [Online] Merriam-Webster. [Cited: 20 01 2008.] http://www.m-w.com/dictionary/behavior.

249. Johns, Gary and Saks, Alan M. *Organizational Behaviour.* 6th. Toronto : Pearson Prentice Hall, 2005. 0-13-127049-4.

250. Ameline, N., et al. *Publicité: Nouvelle Culture?* s.l. : AACC Culture Pub, 2003.

251. Culture Definition. *The Columbia Electronic Encyclopaedia.* [Online] The Columbia Electronic Encyclopaedia. [Cited: 21 11 2007.] http://www.reference.com/browse/columbia/culture.

252. Hall, Edward T. and Hall, Mildred Reed. *Understanding Cultural Differences.* London : Intercultural Press, Inc. , 1990. 1-877864-07-2.

253. *The Free Dictionary.* [Online] Farlex. [Cited: 15 12 2007.] http://www.thefreedictionary.com.

254. Mulder, Mauk. *Macht verkracht .* s.l. : Gopher Publishers , 2003. 978-9051790153 .

255. Hofsteede, Geert. *Culture's Consequences.* London : Sage Publications Inc., 2001. 0-8039-7324-1.

256. *University Van Tilburg.* [Online] University Van Tilburg. [Cited: 17 12 2007.] http://feweb.uvt.nl/center/hofstede/page3.htm.

257. Trompenaars, Fons. *Riding the wave of cultures.* London : Nicholas Brealey Publishing , 2007. 978-1-85788-176-9.

258. Bendix. 1956/1974.

259. D'Iribarne. 1989.

260. Edwards. 1978.

261. Gertson and Sonderberg. *Cultural Dimensions of International Mergers and Acquisitions .* s.l. : Walter de Gruyter , 1998. 978-3110157994 .

262. *Washington State University.* [Online] Washington State University. [Cited: 23 11 2007.] http://www.wsu.edu/gened/learn-modules/top_culture/culture-definition.html.

263. *Kwintessential.* [Online] Kwintessential. [Cited: 18 11 2007.] http://www.kwintessential.co.uk.

264. Finance Glossary. [Online] London South East. [Cited: 22 12 2007.] http://lse.co.uk/financeglossary.asp.

265. Stark, Andrew. What's the Matter with Business Ethics? . *Harvard Business Press.* May-June 1993, 6.

266. Carter McNamara, MBA, PhD. Complete Guide to Ethics Management: An Ethics Toolkit for Managers. *Free Management Library* . [Online] [Cited: 28 12 2007.] http://www.managementhelp.org/ethics/ethxgde.htm.

Market Entry Strategies

Made in the USA
Lexington, KY
29 September 2012